D1366955

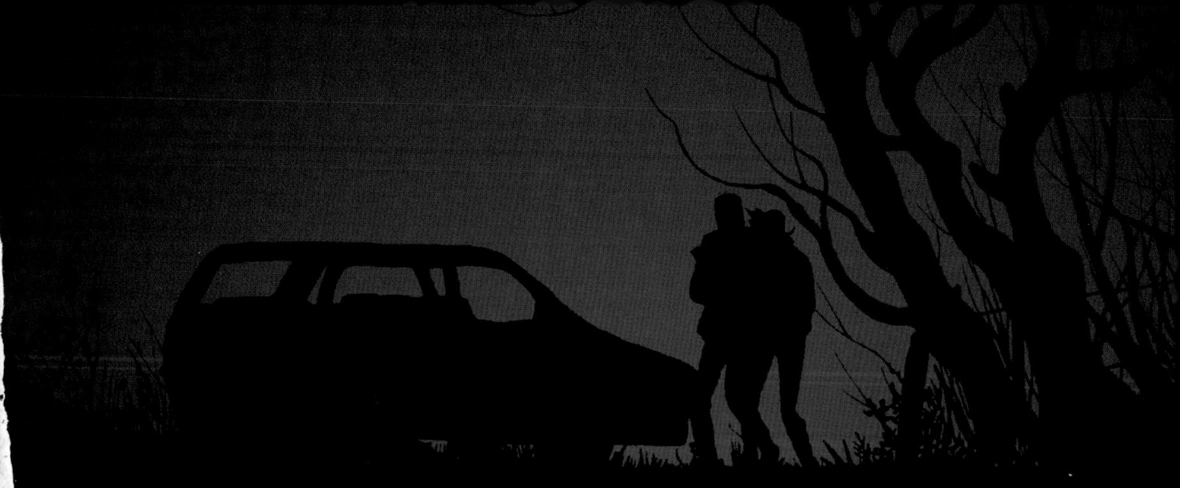

DYNAMITE PROUDLY PRESENTS

CHARLAINE HARRIS

GRAVE SURPRISE™

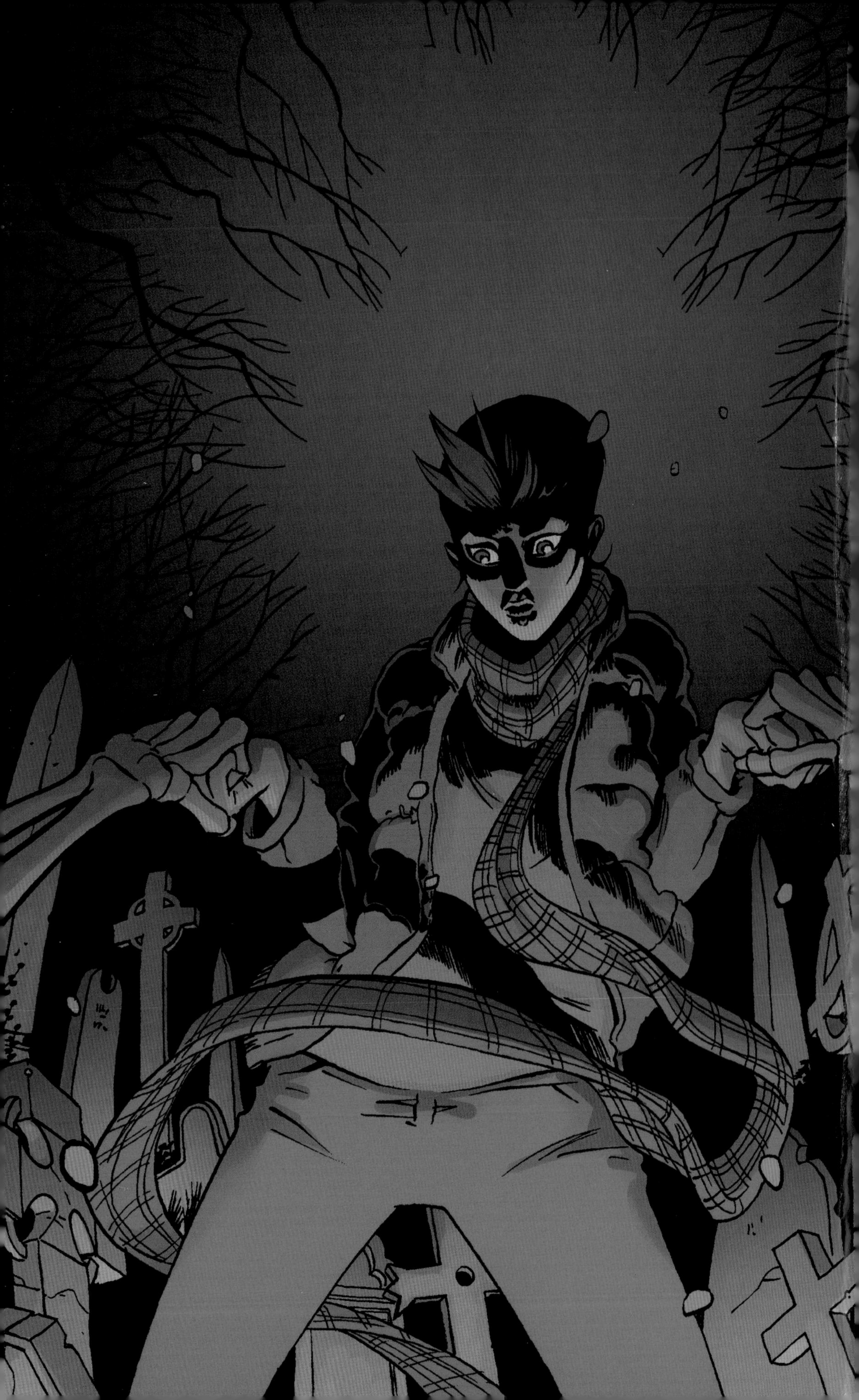

written by
CHARLAINE HARRIS & ROYAL McGRAW

art by
ILIAS KYRIAZIS

colors by
TAMRA BONVILLAIN

letters by
BILL TORTOLINI

collection cover by
ILIAS KYRIAZIS

editor RICH YOUNG
special thanks to JOSHUA BILMES

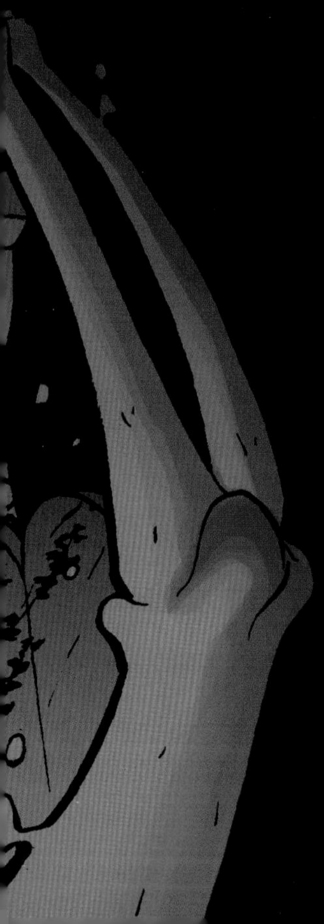

Online at www.DYNAMITE.com
On Facebook /Dynamitecomics
On Instagram /Dynamitecomics
On Tumblr dynamitecomics.tumblr.com
On Twitter @Dynamitecomics
On YouTube /Dynamitecomics

standard edition ISBN: 978-1-5241-0228-9
signed edition ISBN: 978-1-5241-0229-6

First Printing
10 9 8 7 6 5 4 3 2 1
Printed in China

Nick Barrucci, CEO / Publisher
Juan Collado, President / COO

Joe Rybandt, Executive Editor
Matt Idelson, Senior Editor
Anthony Marques, Assistant Editor
Kevin Ketner, Editorial Assistant

Jason Ullmeyer, Art Director
Geoff Harkins, Senior Graphic Designer
Cathleen Heard, Graphic Designer
Alexis Persson, Production Artist
Chris Caniano, Digital Associate
Rachel Kilbury, Digital Assistant

Brandon Dante Primavera, Director of IT/Operations
Rich Young, Director of Business Development

Alan Payne, V.P. of Sales and Marketing
Keith Davidsen, Marketing Director
Pat O'Connell, Sales Manager

For media rights, foreign rights, promotions, licensing, and advertising: marketing@dynamite.com

Harper Connelly has what you might call a strange job: she finds dead people. She can sense the final location of a person who's passed, and share their very last moment. The way Harper sees it, she's providing a service to the dead while bringing some closure to the living.

Not everyone sees it that way...

CHAPTER ONE

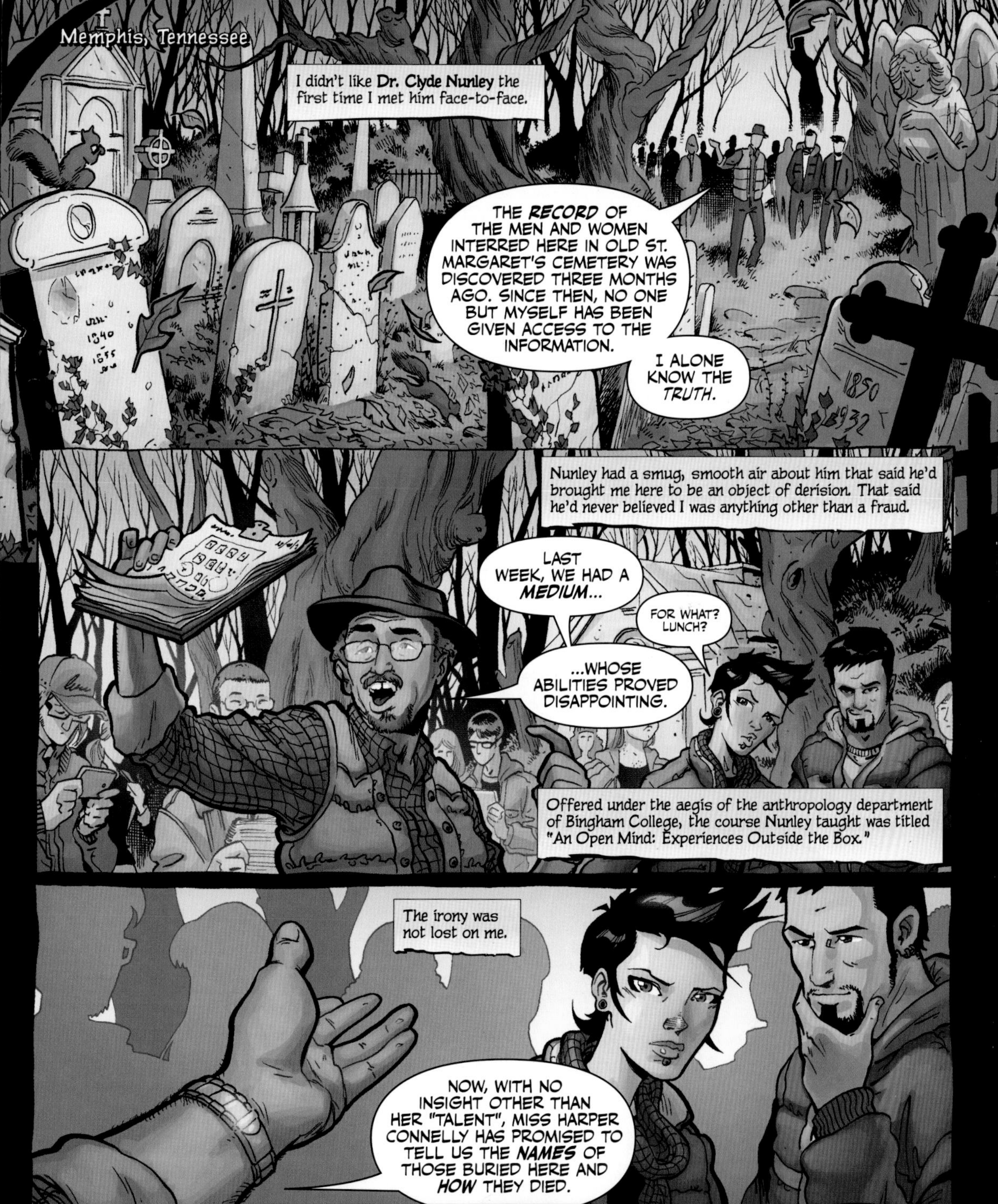
Memphis, Tennessee
I didn't like Dr. Clyde Nunley the first time I met him face-to-face.
THE RECORD OF THE MEN AND WOMEN INTERRED HERE IN OLD ST. MARGARET'S CEMETERY WAS DISCOVERED THREE MONTHS AGO. SINCE THEN, NO ONE BUT MYSELF HAS BEEN GIVEN ACCESS TO THE INFORMATION.
I ALONE KNOW THE TRUTH.
1850
1932
Nunley had a smug, smooth air about him that said he'd brought me here to be an object of derision. That said he'd never believed I was anything other than a fraud.
LAST WEEK, WE HAD A MEDIUM...
FOR WHAT? LUNCH?
...WHOSE ABILITIES PROVED DISAPPOINTING.
Offered under the aegis of the anthropology department of Bingham College, the course Nunley taught was titled "An Open Mind: Experiences Outside the Box."
The irony was not lost on me.
NOW, WITH NO INSIGHT OTHER THAN HER "TALENT", MISS HARPER CONNELLY HAS PROMISED TO TELL US THE NAMES OF THOSE BURIED HERE AND HOW THEY DIED.

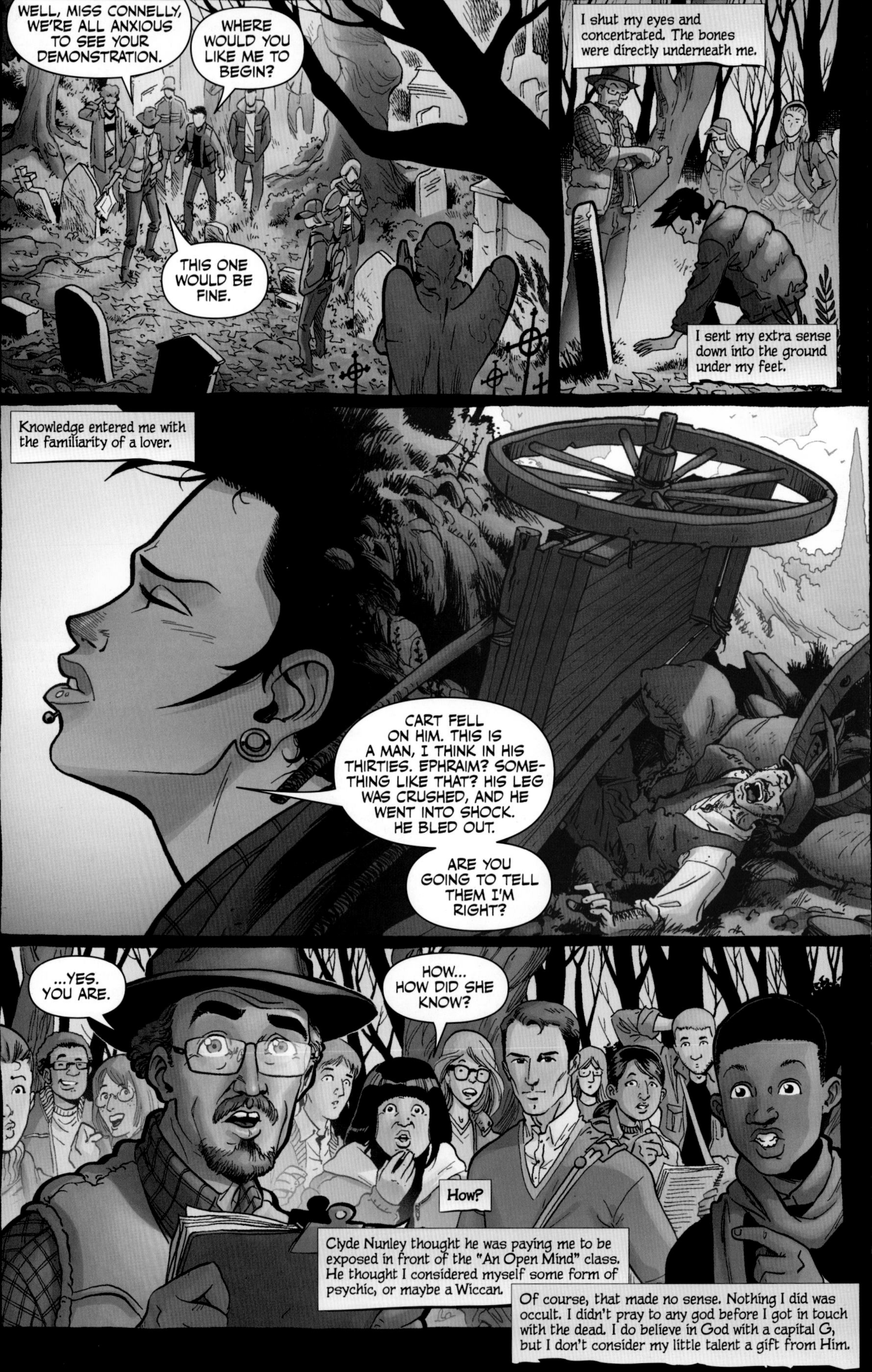
WELL, MISS CONNELLY, WE'RE ALL ANXIOUS TO SEE YOUR DEMONSTRATION.
WHERE WOULD YOU LIKE ME TO BEGIN?
THIS ONE WOULD BE FINE.
I shut my eyes and concentrated. The bones were directly underneath me.
I sent my extra sense down into the ground under my feet.
Knowledge entered me with the familiarity of a lover.
CART FELL ON HIM. THIS IS A MAN, I THINK IN HIS THIRTIES. EPHRAIM? SOMETHING LIKE THAT? HIS LEG WAS CRUSHED, AND HE WENT INTO SHOCK. HE BLED OUT.
ARE YOU GOING TO TELL THEM I'M RIGHT?
...YES. YOU ARE.
HOW... HOW DID SHE KNOW?
How?
Clyde Nunley thought he was paying me to be exposed in front of the "An Open Mind" class. He thought I considered myself some form of psychic, or maybe a Wiccan.
Of course, that made no sense. Nothing I did was occult. I didn't pray to any god before I got in touch with the dead. I do believe in God with a capital G, but I don't consider my little talent a gift from Him.

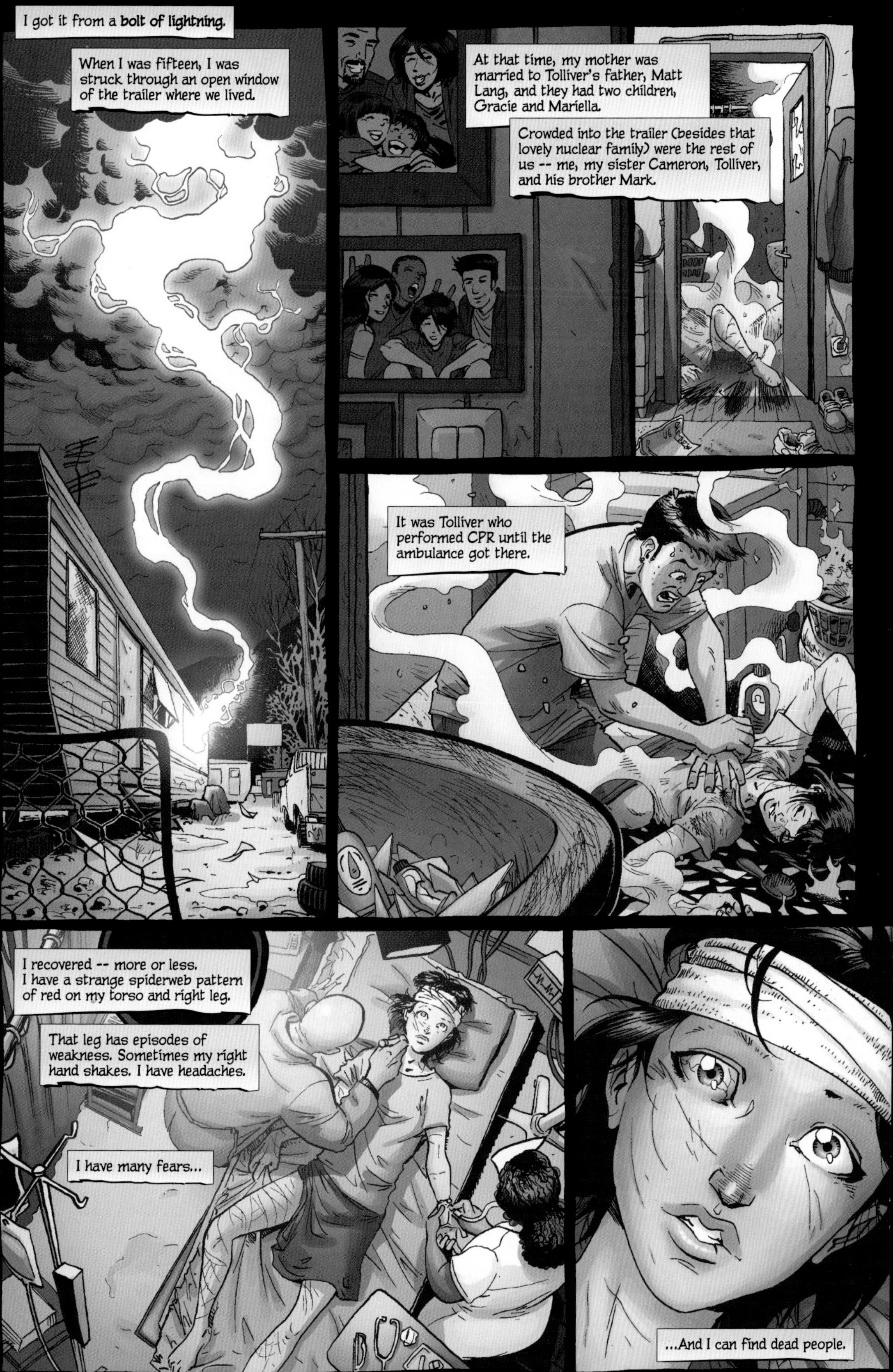
I got it from a **bolt of lightning.**
When I was fifteen, I was struck through an open window of the trailer where we lived.
At that time, my mother was married to Tolliver's father, Matt Lang, and they had two children, Gracie and Mariella.
Crowded into the trailer (besides that lovely nuclear family) were the rest of us -- me, my sister Cameron, Tolliver, and his brother Mark.
It was Tolliver who performed CPR until the ambulance got there.
I recovered -- more or less. I have a strange spiderweb pattern of red on my torso and right leg.
That leg has episodes of weakness. Sometimes my right hand shakes. I have headaches.
I have many fears...
...And I can find dead people.

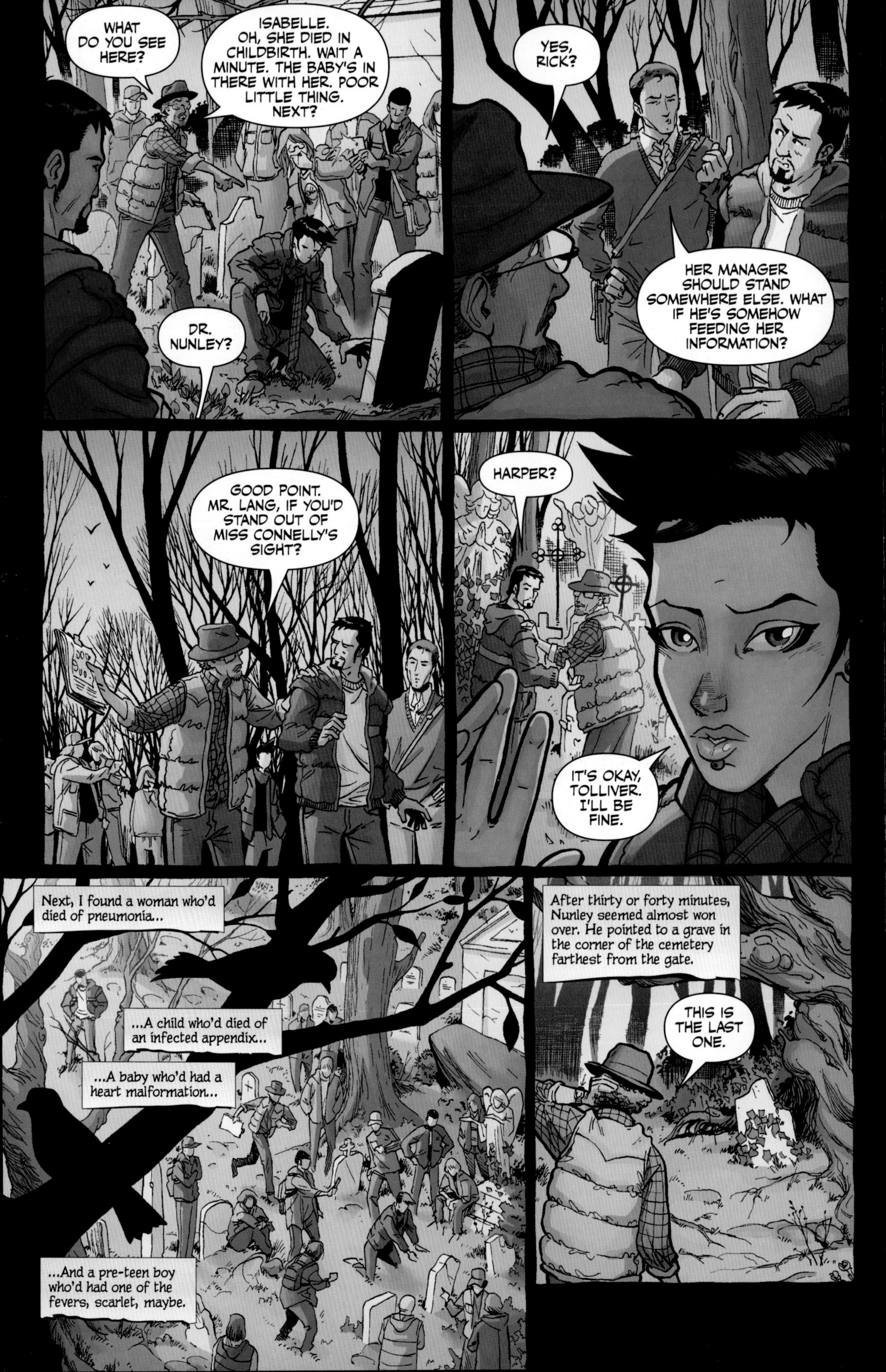
WHAT DO YOU SEE HERE?
ISABELLE. OH, SHE DIED IN CHILDBIRTH. WAIT A MINUTE. THE BABY'S IN THERE WITH HER. POOR LITTLE THING. NEXT?
DR. NUNLEY?
YES, RICK?
HER MANAGER SHOULD STAND SOMEWHERE ELSE. WHAT IF HE'S SOMEHOW FEEDING HER INFORMATION?
GOOD POINT. MR. LANG, IF YOU'D STAND OUT OF MISS CONNELLY'S SIGHT?
HARPER?
IT'S OKAY, TOLLIVER. I'LL BE FINE.
Next, I found a woman who'd died of pneumonia...
...A child who'd died of an infected appendix...
...A baby who'd had a heart malformation...
...And a pre-teen boy who'd had one of the fevers, scarlet, maybe.
After thirty or forty minutes, Nunley seemed almost won over. He pointed to a grave in the corner of the cemetery farthest from the gate.
THIS IS THE LAST ONE.

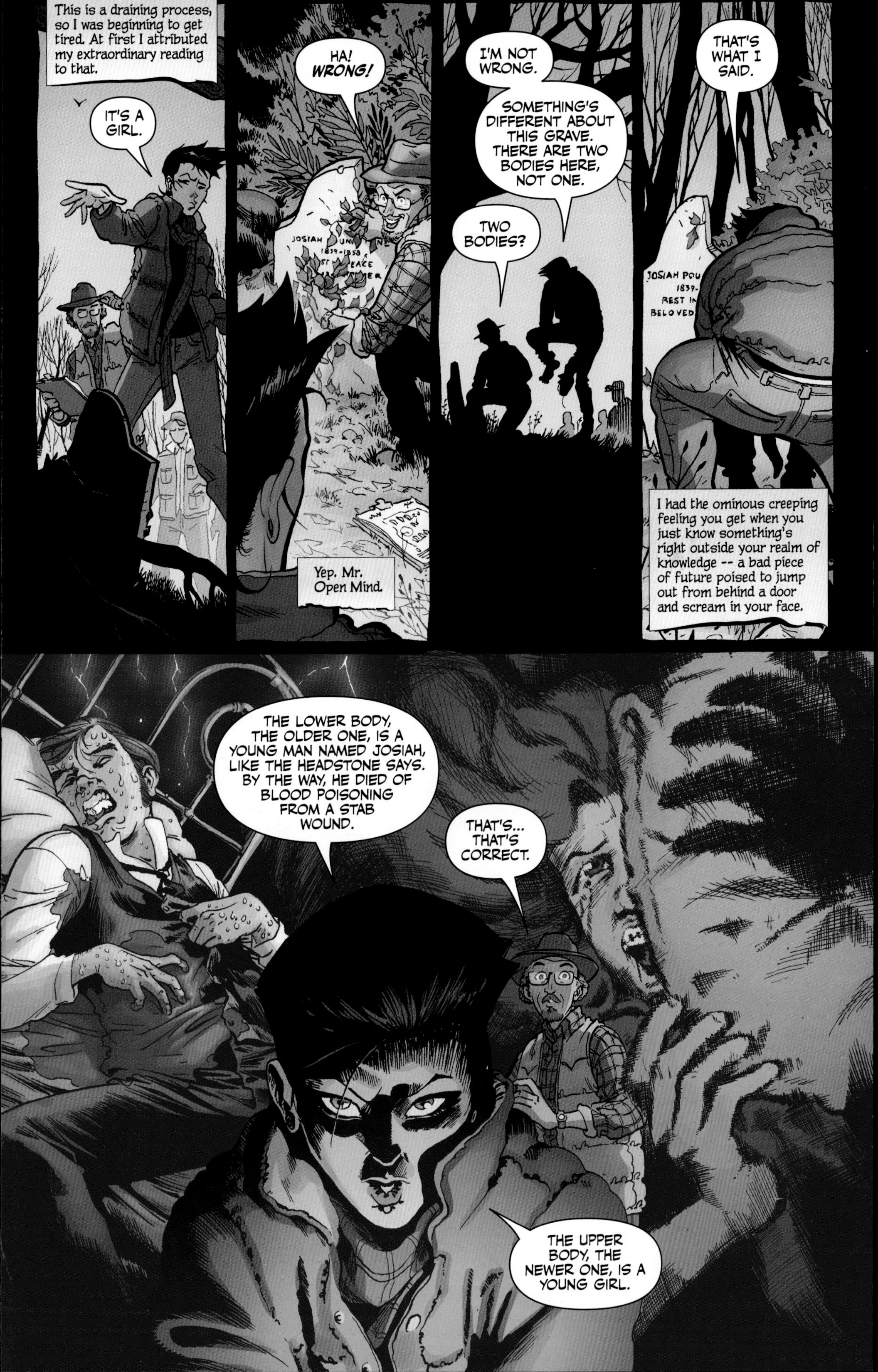
This is a draining process, so I was beginning to get tired. At first I attributed my extraordinary reading to that.
IT'S A GIRL.
HA! WRONG!
JOSIAH
1839-1858
Yep. Mr. Open Mind.
I'M NOT WRONG.
SOMETHING'S DIFFERENT ABOUT THIS GRAVE. THERE ARE TWO BODIES HERE, NOT ONE.
TWO BODIES?
THAT'S WHAT I SAID.
JOSIAH POU
1839-
REST IN
BELOVED
I had the ominous creeping feeling you get when you just know something's right outside your realm of knowledge -- a bad piece of future poised to jump out from behind a door and scream in your face.
THE LOWER BODY, THE OLDER ONE, IS A YOUNG MAN NAMED JOSIAH, LIKE THE HEADSTONE SAYS. BY THE WAY, HE DIED OF BLOOD POISONING FROM A STAB WOUND.
THAT'S... THAT'S CORRECT.
THE UPPER BODY, THE NEWER ONE, IS A YOUNG GIRL.

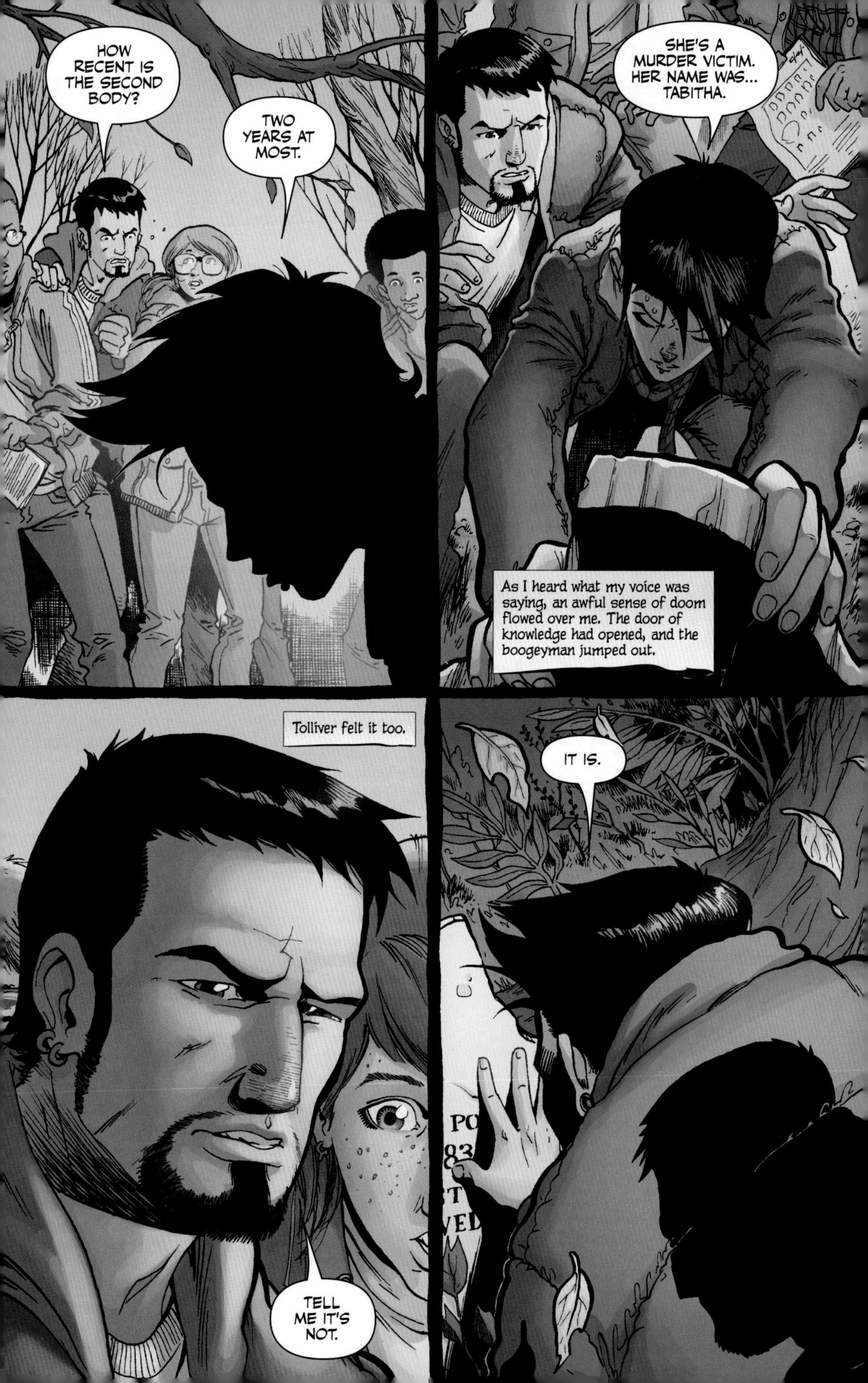
HOW RECENT IS THE SECOND BODY?
TWO YEARS AT MOST.
SHE'S A MURDER VICTIM. HER NAME WAS... TABITHA.
As I heard what my voice was saying, an awful sense of doom flowed over me. The door of knowledge had opened, and the boogeyman jumped out.
Tolliver felt it too.
TELL ME IT'S NOT.
IT IS.

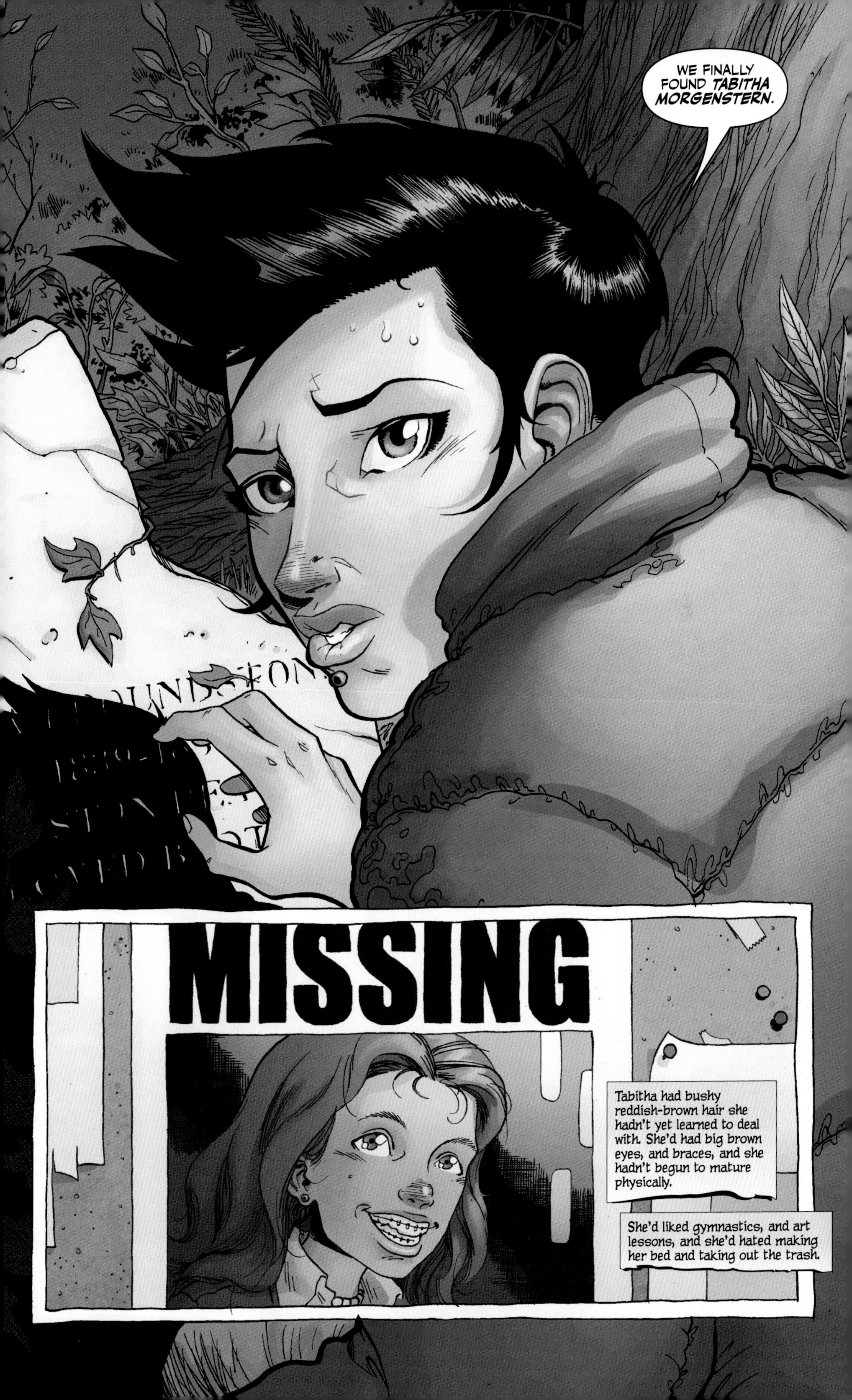
WE FINALLY FOUND TABITHA MORGENSTERN.
MISSING
Tabitha had bushy reddish-brown hair she hadn't yet learned to deal with. She'd had big brown eyes, and braces, and she hadn't begun to mature physically.
She'd liked gymnastics, and art lessons, and she'd hated making her bed and taking out the trash.

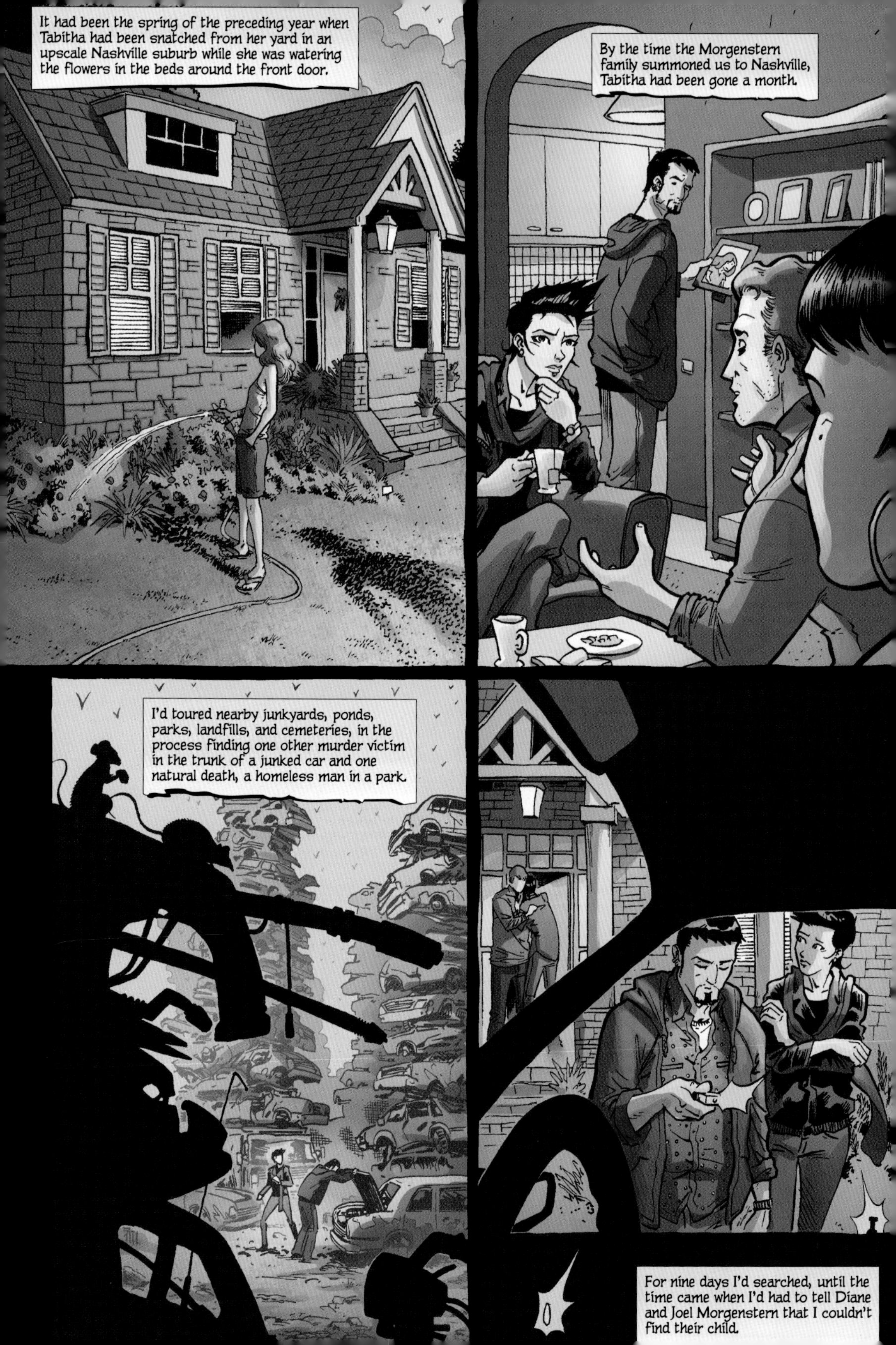
It had been the spring of the preceding year when Tabitha had been snatched from her yard in an upscale Nashville suburb while she was watering the flowers in the beds around the front door.
By the time the Morgenstern family summoned us to Nashville, Tabitha had been gone a month.
I'd toured nearby junkyards, ponds, parks, landfills, and cemeteries, in the process finding one other murder victim in the trunk of a junked car and one natural death, a homeless man in a park.
For nine days I'd searched, until the time came when I'd had to tell Diane and Joel Morgenstern that I couldn't find their child.

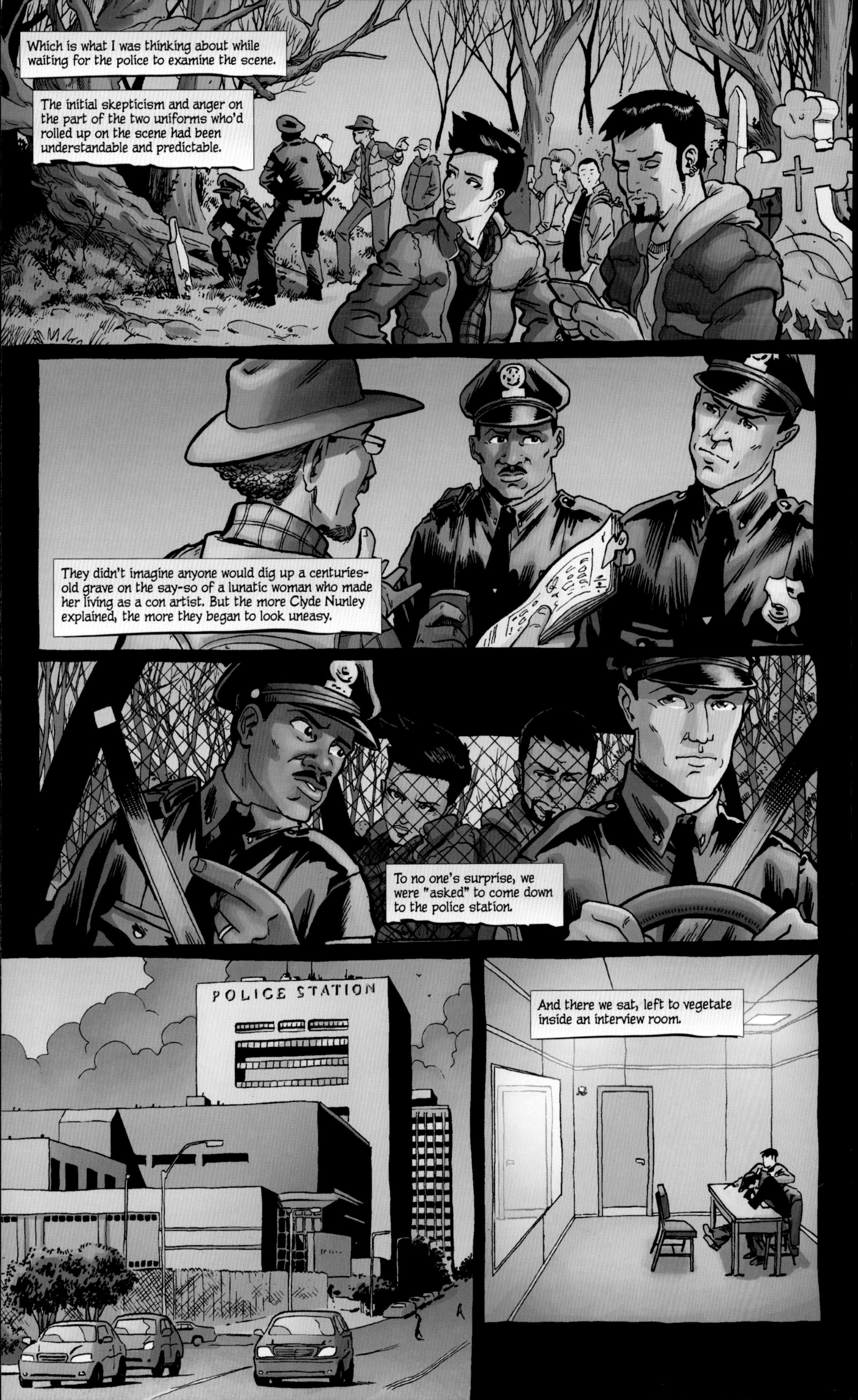
Which is what I was thinking about while waiting for the police to examine the scene.
The initial skepticism and anger on the part of the two uniforms who'd rolled up on the scene had been understandable and predictable.
They didn't imagine anyone would dig up a centuries-old grave on the say-so of a lunatic woman who made her living as a con artist. But the more Clyde Nunley explained, the more they began to look uneasy.
To no one's surprise, we were "asked" to come down to the police station.
POLICE STATION
And there we sat, left to vegetate inside an interview room.

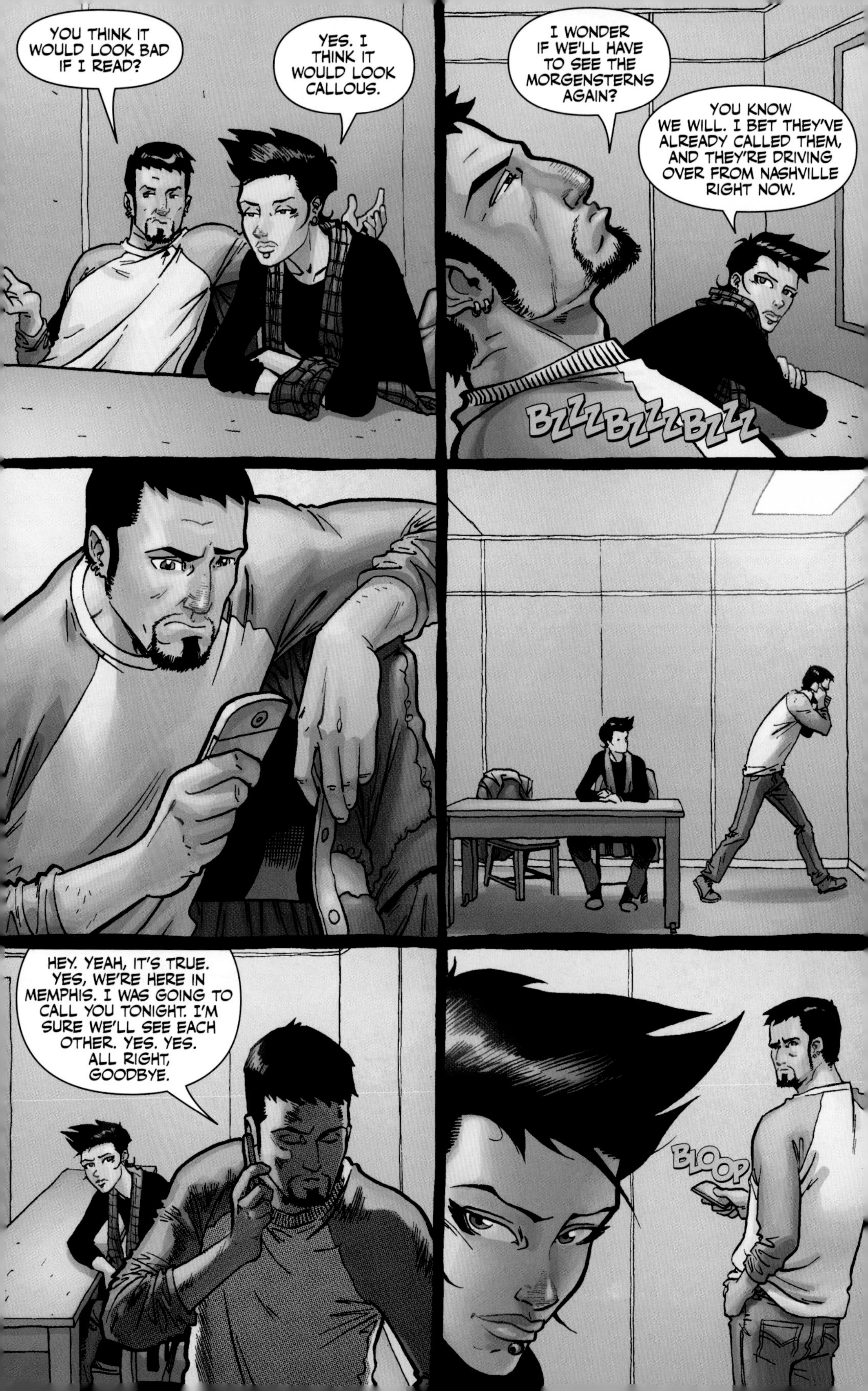
YOU THINK IT WOULD LOOK BAD IF I READ?
YES. I THINK IT WOULD LOOK CALLOUS.
I WONDER IF WE'LL HAVE TO SEE THE MORGENSTERNS AGAIN?
YOU KNOW WE WILL. I BET THEY'VE ALREADY CALLED THEM, AND THEY'RE DRIVING OVER FROM NASHVILLE RIGHT NOW.
BZZZBZZZBZZZ
HEY. YEAH, IT'S TRUE. YES, WE'RE HERE IN MEMPHIS. I WAS GOING TO CALL YOU TONIGHT. I'M SURE WE'LL SEE EACH OTHER. YES. YES. ALL RIGHT, GOODBYE.
BLOOP

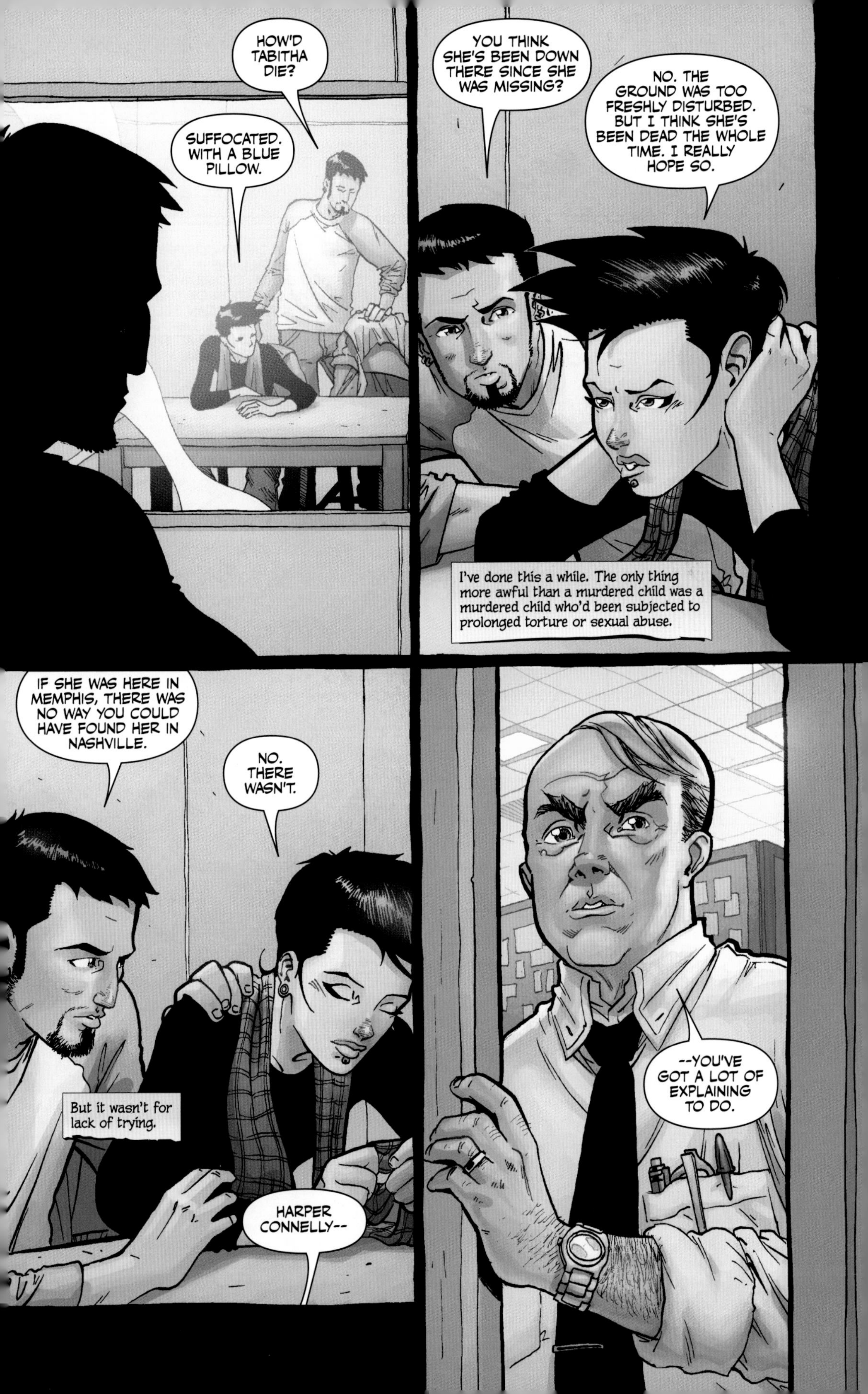
HOW'D TABITHA DIE?
SUFFOCATED. WITH A BLUE PILLOW.
YOU THINK SHE'S BEEN DOWN THERE SINCE SHE WAS MISSING?
NO. THE GROUND WAS TOO FRESHLY DISTURBED. BUT I THINK SHE'S BEEN DEAD THE WHOLE TIME. I REALLY HOPE SO.
I've done this a while. The only thing more awful than a murdered child was a murdered child who'd been subjected to prolonged torture or sexual abuse.
IF SHE WAS HERE IN MEMPHIS, THERE WAS NO WAY YOU COULD HAVE FOUND HER IN NASHVILLE.
NO. THERE WASN'T.
But it wasn't for lack of trying.
HARPER CONNELLY--
--YOU'VE GOT A LOT OF EXPLAINING TO DO.

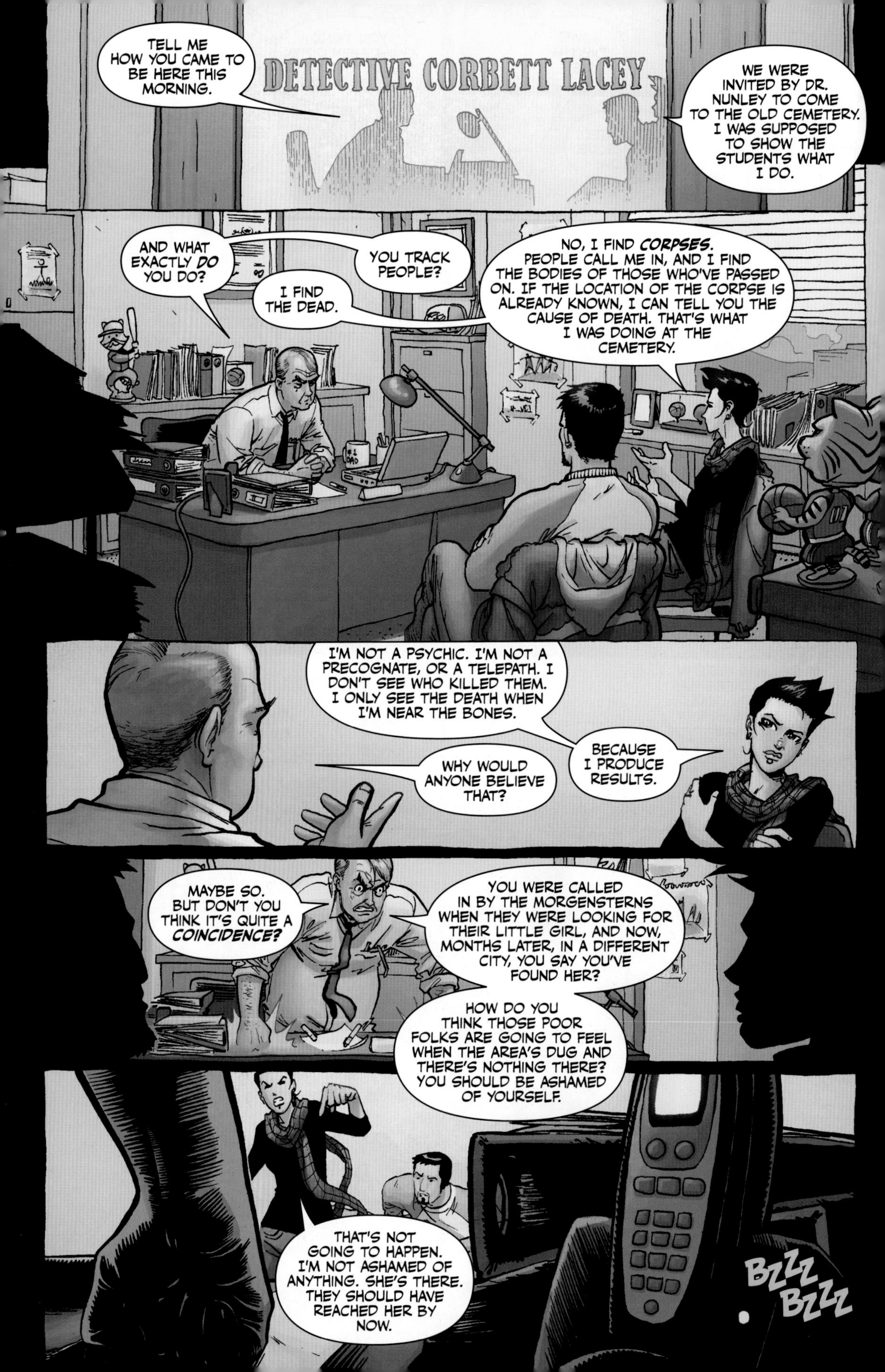
DETECTIVE CORBETT LACEY
TELL ME HOW YOU CAME TO BE HERE THIS MORNING.
WE WERE INVITED BY DR. NUNLEY TO COME TO THE OLD CEMETERY. I WAS SUPPOSED TO SHOW THE STUDENTS WHAT I DO.
AND WHAT EXACTLY *DO* YOU DO?
I FIND THE DEAD.
YOU TRACK PEOPLE?
NO, I FIND ***CORPSES.*** PEOPLE CALL ME IN, AND I FIND THE BODIES OF THOSE WHO'VE PASSED ON. IF THE LOCATION OF THE CORPSE IS ALREADY KNOWN, I CAN TELL YOU THE CAUSE OF DEATH. THAT'S WHAT I WAS DOING AT THE CEMETERY.
I'M NOT A PSYCHIC. I'M NOT A PRECOGNATE, OR A TELEPATH. I DON'T SEE WHO KILLED THEM. I ONLY SEE THE DEATH WHEN I'M NEAR THE BONES.
WHY WOULD ANYONE BELIEVE THAT?
BECAUSE I PRODUCE RESULTS.
MAYBE SO. BUT DON'T YOU THINK IT'S QUITE A ***COINCIDENCE?***
YOU WERE CALLED IN BY THE MORGENSTERNS WHEN THEY WERE LOOKING FOR THEIR LITTLE GIRL, AND NOW, MONTHS LATER, IN A DIFFERENT CITY, YOU SAY YOU'VE FOUND HER?
HOW DO YOU THINK THOSE POOR FOLKS ARE GOING TO FEEL WHEN THE AREA'S DUG AND THERE'S NOTHING THERE? YOU SHOULD BE ASHAMED OF YOURSELF.
THAT'S NOT GOING TO HAPPEN. I'M NOT ASHAMED OF ANYTHING. SHE'S THERE. THEY SHOULD HAVE REACHED HER BY NOW.
BZZZ BZZZ

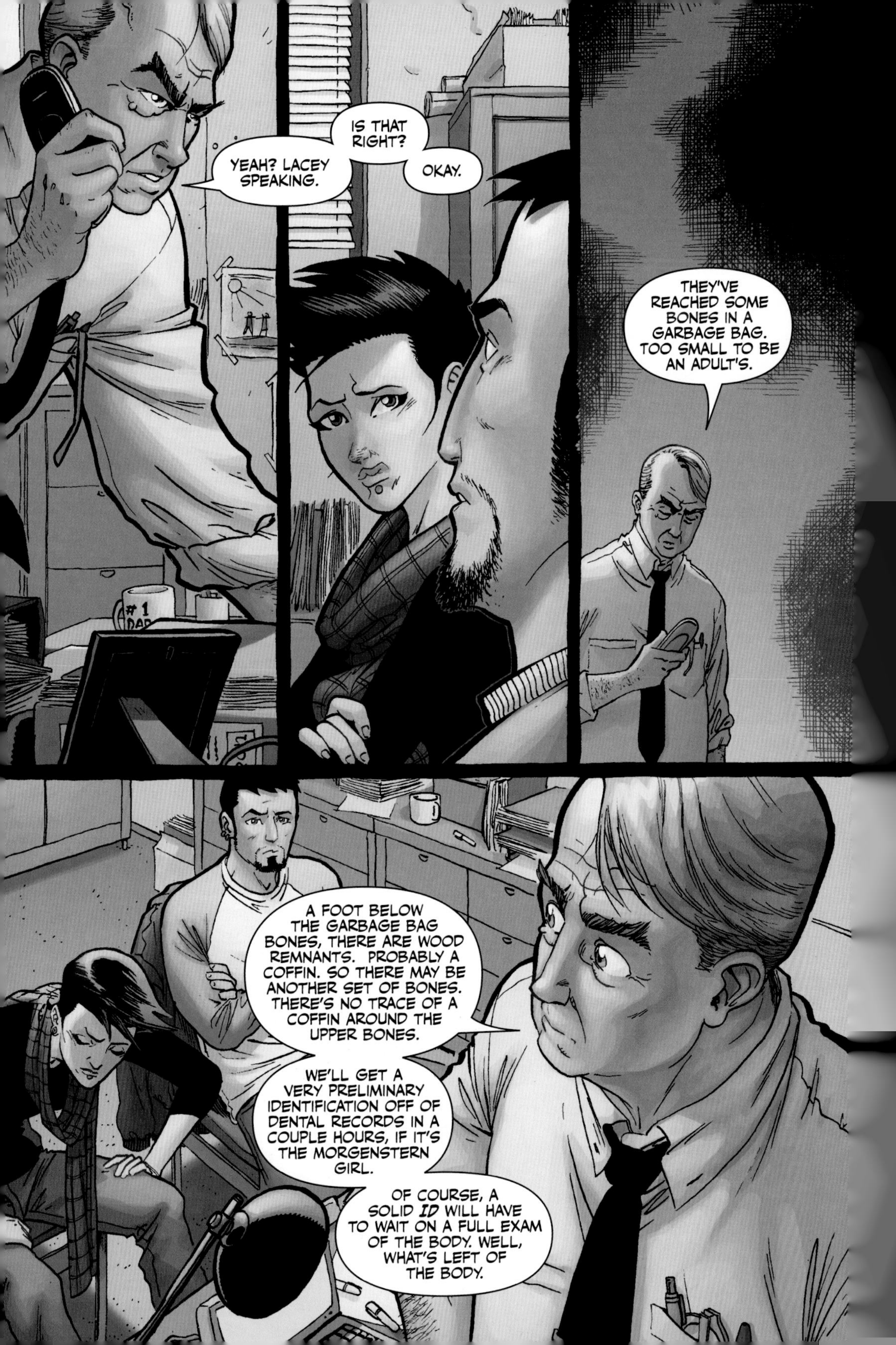
YEAH? LACEY SPEAKING.
IS THAT RIGHT?
OKAY.
#1 DAD
THEY'VE REACHED SOME BONES IN A GARBAGE BAG. TOO SMALL TO BE AN ADULT'S.
A FOOT BELOW THE GARBAGE BAG BONES, THERE ARE WOOD REMNANTS. PROBABLY A COFFIN. SO THERE MAY BE ANOTHER SET OF BONES. THERE'S NO TRACE OF A COFFIN AROUND THE UPPER BONES.
WE'LL GET A VERY PRELIMINARY IDENTIFICATION OFF OF DENTAL RECORDS IN A COUPLE HOURS, IF IT'S THE MORGENSTERN GIRL.
OF COURSE, A SOLID *ID* WILL HAVE TO WAIT ON A FULL EXAM OF THE BODY. WELL, WHAT'S LEFT OF THE BODY.

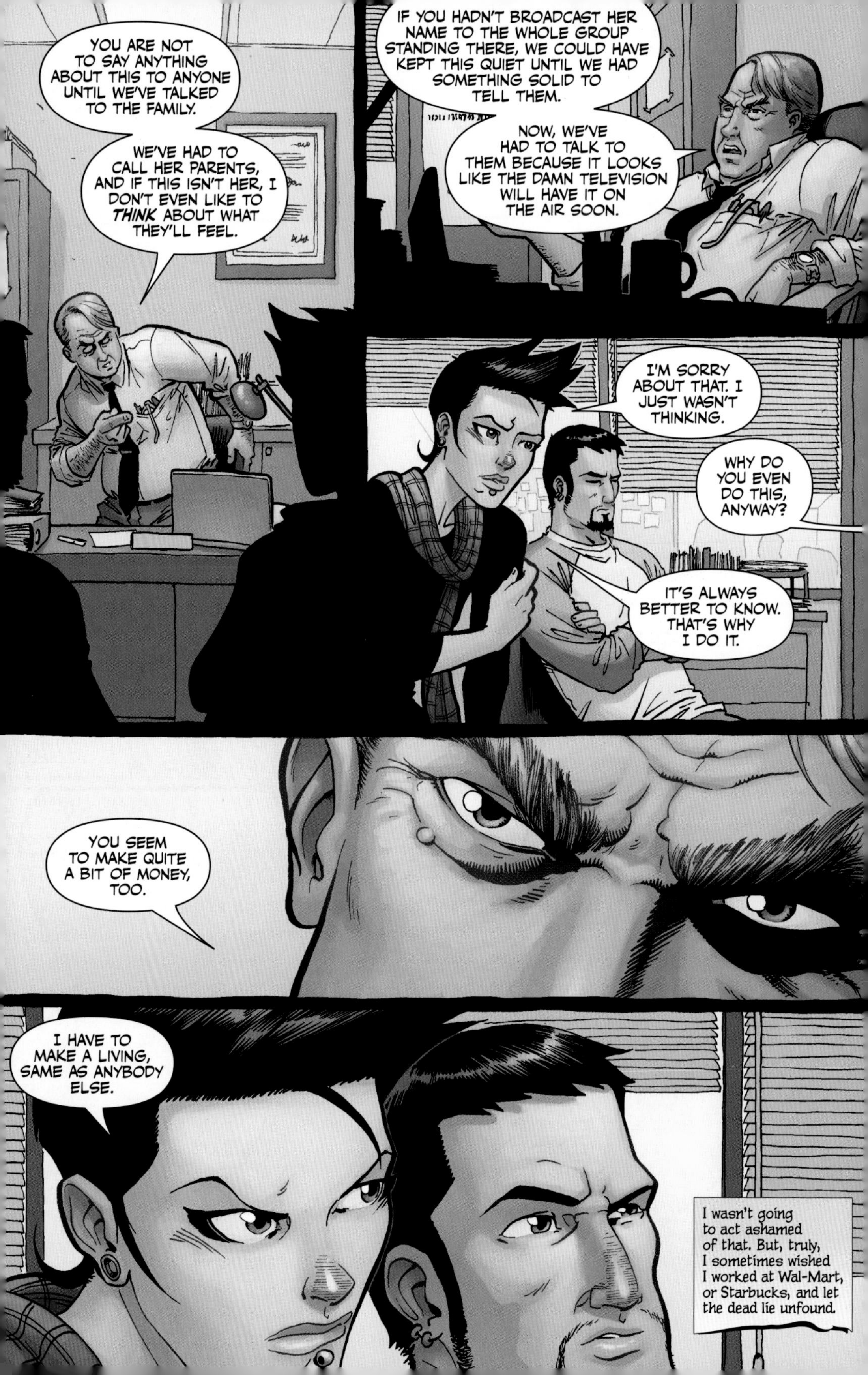
YOU ARE NOT TO SAY ANYTHING ABOUT THIS TO ANYONE UNTIL WE'VE TALKED TO THE FAMILY.
WE'VE HAD TO CALL HER PARENTS, AND IF THIS ISN'T HER, I DON'T EVEN LIKE TO THINK ABOUT WHAT THEY'LL FEEL.
IF YOU HADN'T BROADCAST HER NAME TO THE WHOLE GROUP STANDING THERE, WE COULD HAVE KEPT THIS QUIET UNTIL WE HAD SOMETHING SOLID TO TELL THEM.
NOW, WE'VE HAD TO TALK TO THEM BECAUSE IT LOOKS LIKE THE DAMN TELEVISION WILL HAVE IT ON THE AIR SOON.
I'M SORRY ABOUT THAT. I JUST WASN'T THINKING.
WHY DO YOU EVEN DO THIS, ANYWAY?
IT'S ALWAYS BETTER TO KNOW. THAT'S WHY I DO IT.
YOU SEEM TO MAKE QUITE A BIT OF MONEY, TOO.
I HAVE TO MAKE A LIVING, SAME AS ANYBODY ELSE.
I wasn't going to act ashamed of that. But, truly, I sometimes wished I worked at Wal-Mart, or Starbucks, and let the dead lie unfound.

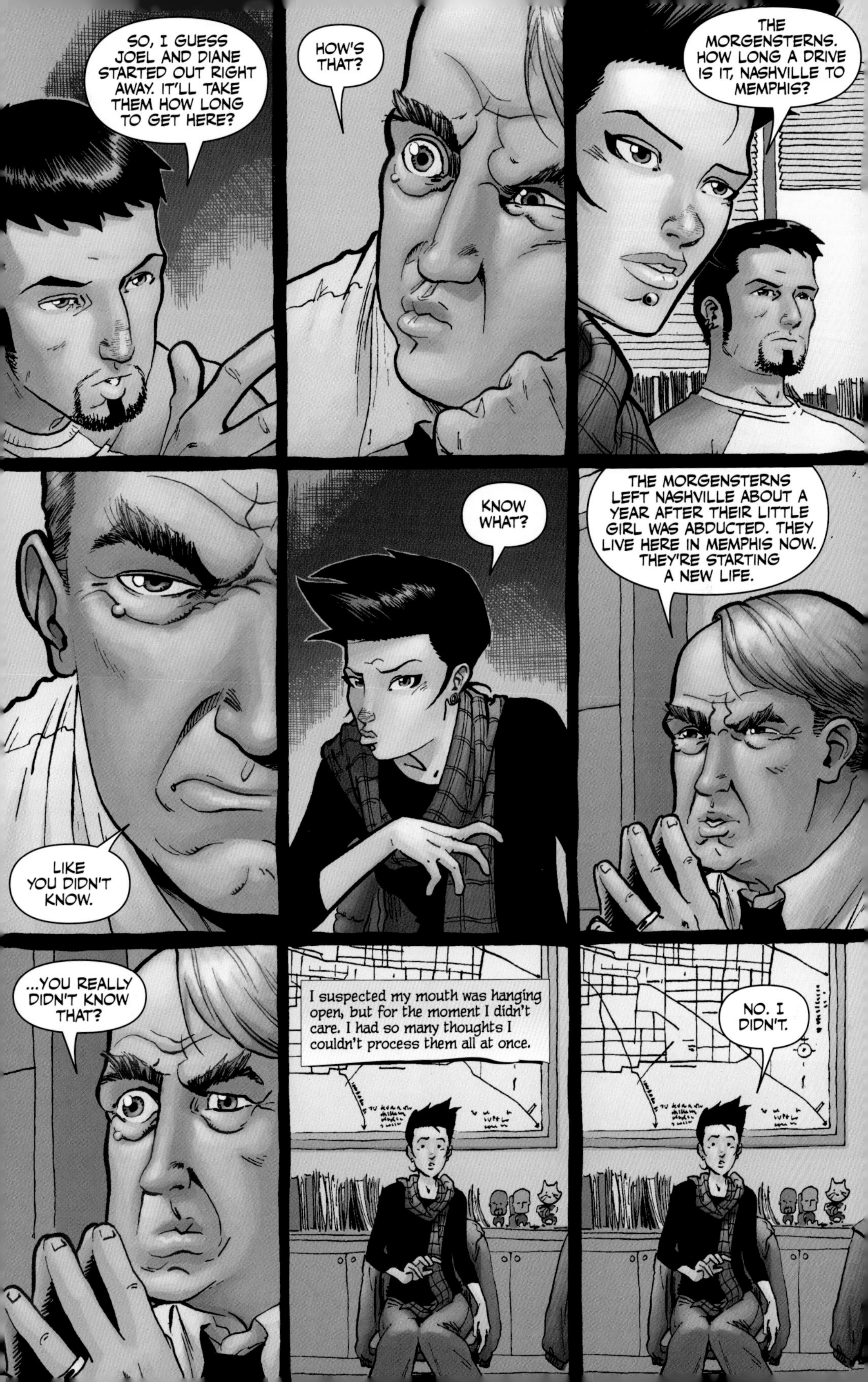
SO, I GUESS JOEL AND DIANE STARTED OUT RIGHT AWAY. IT'LL TAKE THEM HOW LONG TO GET HERE?
HOW'S THAT?
THE MORGENSTERNS. HOW LONG A DRIVE IS IT, NASHVILLE TO MEMPHIS?
LIKE YOU DIDN'T KNOW.
KNOW WHAT?
THE MORGENSTERNS LEFT NASHVILLE ABOUT A YEAR AFTER THEIR LITTLE GIRL WAS ABDUCTED. THEY LIVE HERE IN MEMPHIS NOW. THEY'RE STARTING A NEW LIFE.
...YOU REALLY DIDN'T KNOW THAT?
I suspected my mouth was hanging open, but for the moment I didn't care. I had so many thoughts I couldn't process them all at once.
NO. I DIDN'T.

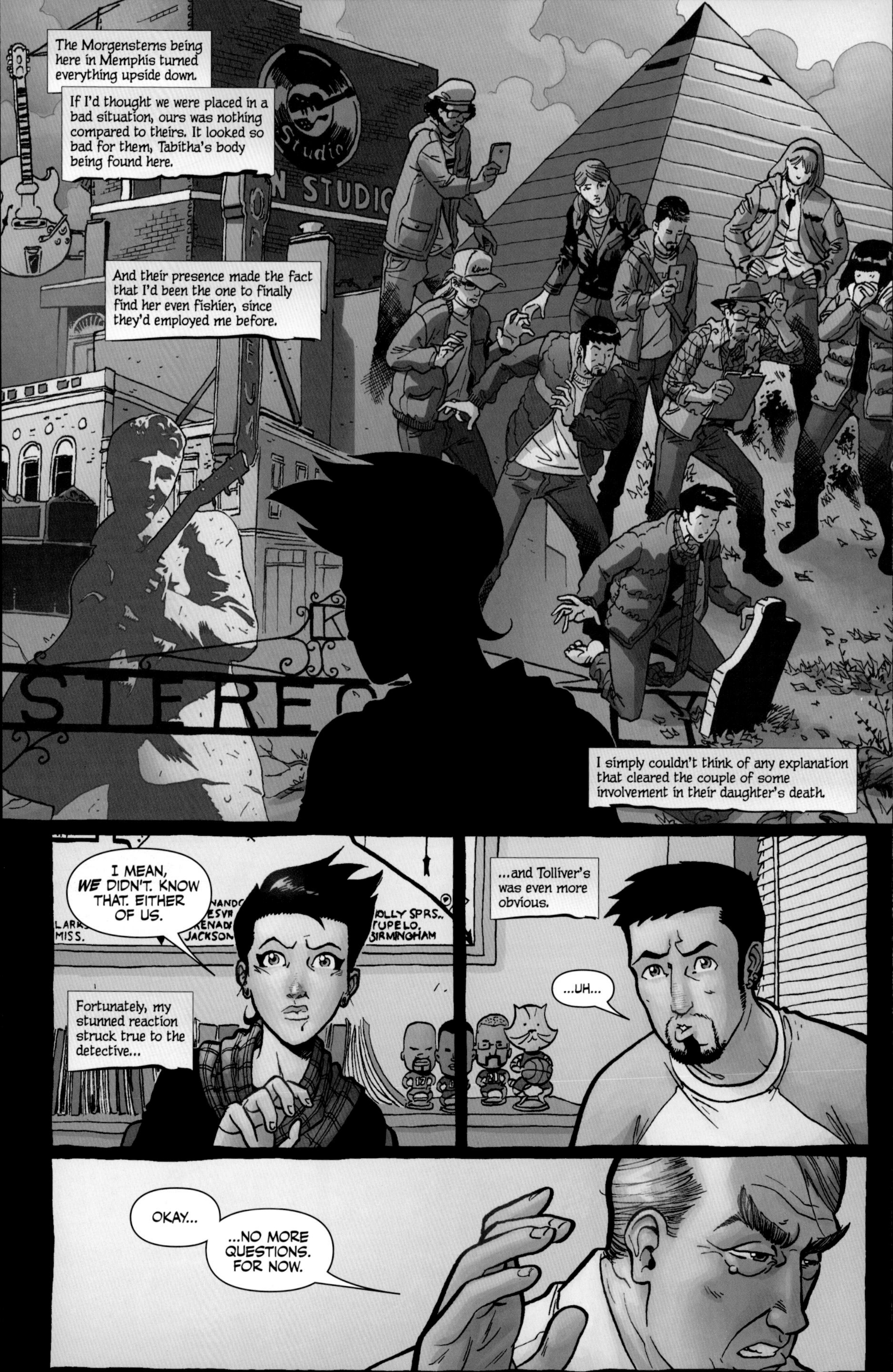

The Morgensterns being here in Memphis turned everything upside down.
If I'd thought we were placed in a bad situation, ours was nothing compared to theirs. It looked so bad for them, Tabitha's body being found here.
Studio
N STUDIO
And their presence made the fact that I'd been the one to finally find her even fishier, since they'd employed me before.
STEREO
I simply couldn't think of any explanation that cleared the couple of some involvement in their daughter's death.
I MEAN, WE DIDN'T. KNOW THAT. EITHER OF US.
Fortunately, my stunned reaction struck true to the detective...
...and Tolliver's was even more obvious.
...UH...
OKAY...
...NO MORE QUESTIONS. FOR NOW.

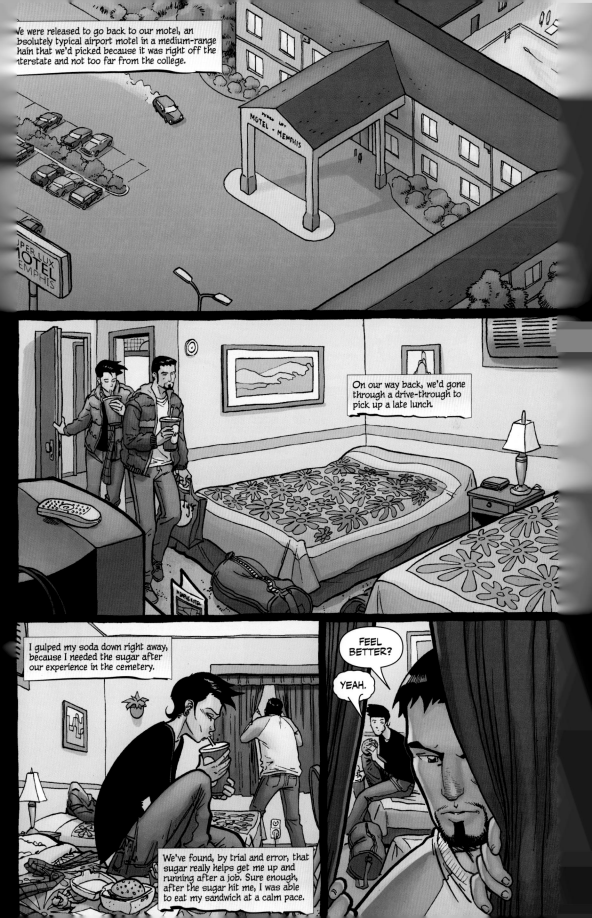

We were released to go back to our motel, an absolutely typical airport motel in a medium-range chain that we'd picked because it was right off the interstate and not too far from the college.

MOTEL · MEMPHIS

SUPER LUX MOTEL MEMPHIS

On our way back, we'd gone through a drive-through to pick up a late lunch.

I gulped my soda down right away, because I needed the sugar after our experience in the cemetery.

FEEL BETTER?

YEAH.

We've found, by trial and error, that sugar really helps get me up and running after a job. Sure enough, after the sugar hit me, I was able to eat my sandwich at a calm pace.

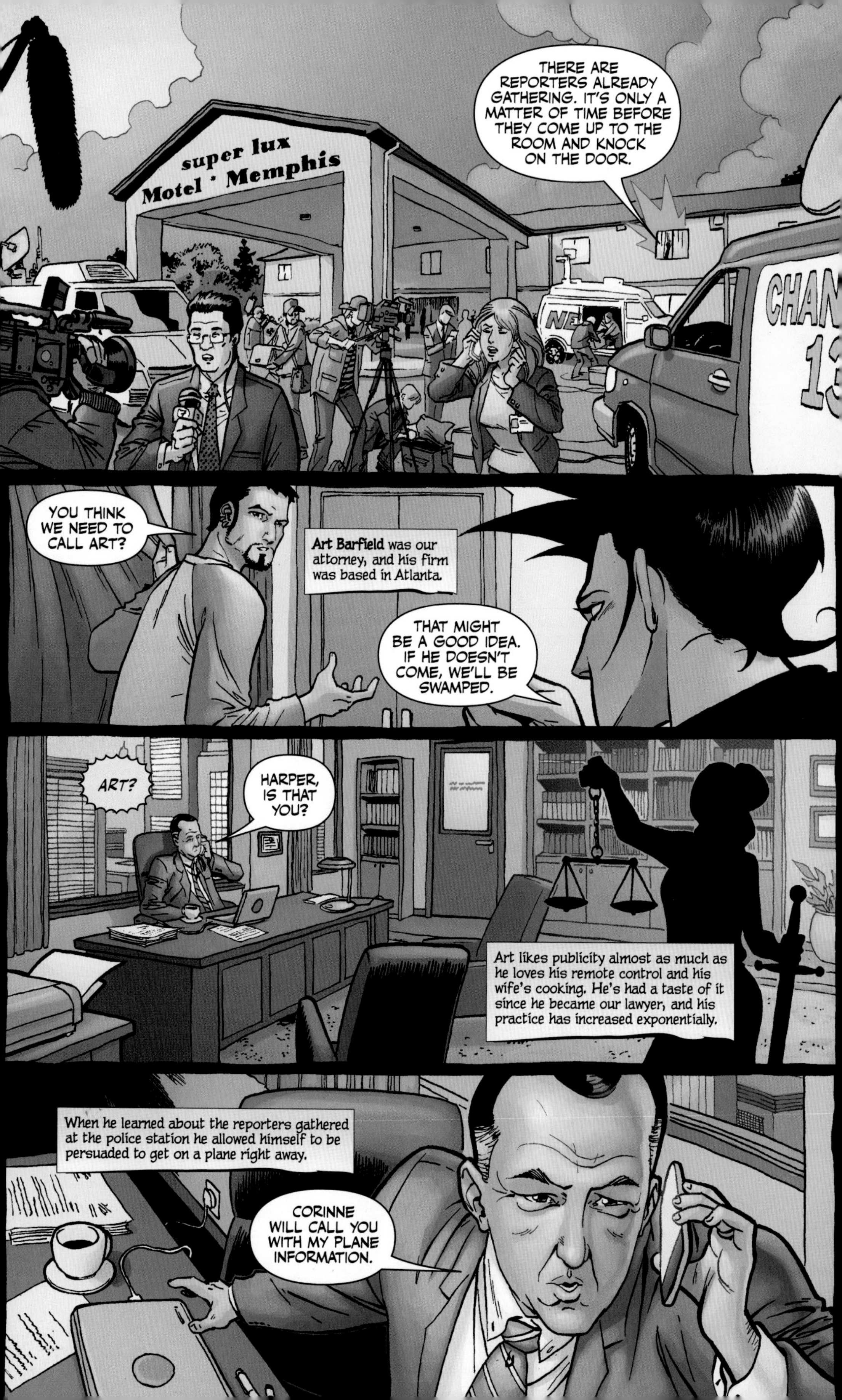
super lux Motel * Memphis
THERE ARE REPORTERS ALREADY GATHERING. IT'S ONLY A MATTER OF TIME BEFORE THEY COME UP TO THE ROOM AND KNOCK ON THE DOOR.
YOU THINK WE NEED TO CALL ART?
Art Barfield was our attorney, and his firm was based in Atlanta.
THAT MIGHT BE A GOOD IDEA. IF HE DOESN'T COME, WE'LL BE SWAMPED.
ART?
HARPER, IS THAT YOU?
Art likes publicity almost as much as he loves his remote control and his wife's cooking. He's had a taste of it since he became our lawyer, and his practice has increased exponentially.
When he learned about the reporters gathered at the police station he allowed himself to be persuaded to get on a plane right away.
CORINNE WILL CALL YOU WITH MY PLANE INFORMATION.

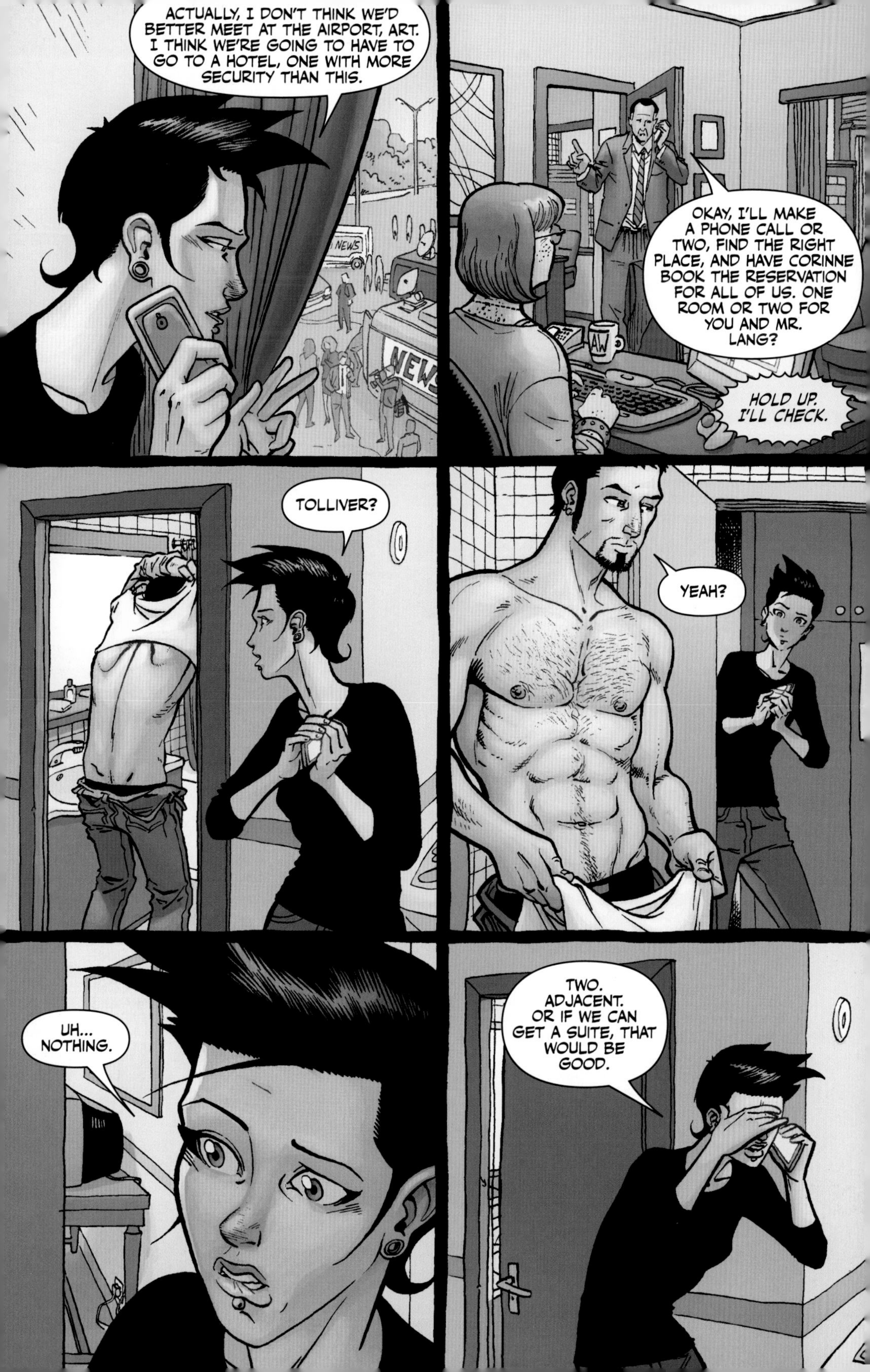
ACTUALLY, I DON'T THINK WE'D BETTER MEET AT THE AIRPORT, ART. I THINK WE'RE GOING TO HAVE TO GO TO A HOTEL, ONE WITH MORE SECURITY THAN THIS.
NEWS
NEWS
OKAY, I'LL MAKE A PHONE CALL OR TWO, FIND THE RIGHT PLACE, AND HAVE CORINNE BOOK THE RESERVATION FOR ALL OF US. ONE ROOM OR TWO FOR YOU AND MR. LANG?
AW
HOLD UP. I'LL CHECK.
TOLLIVER?
YEAH?
UH... NOTHING.
TWO. ADJACENT. OR IF WE CAN GET A SUITE, THAT WOULD BE GOOD.

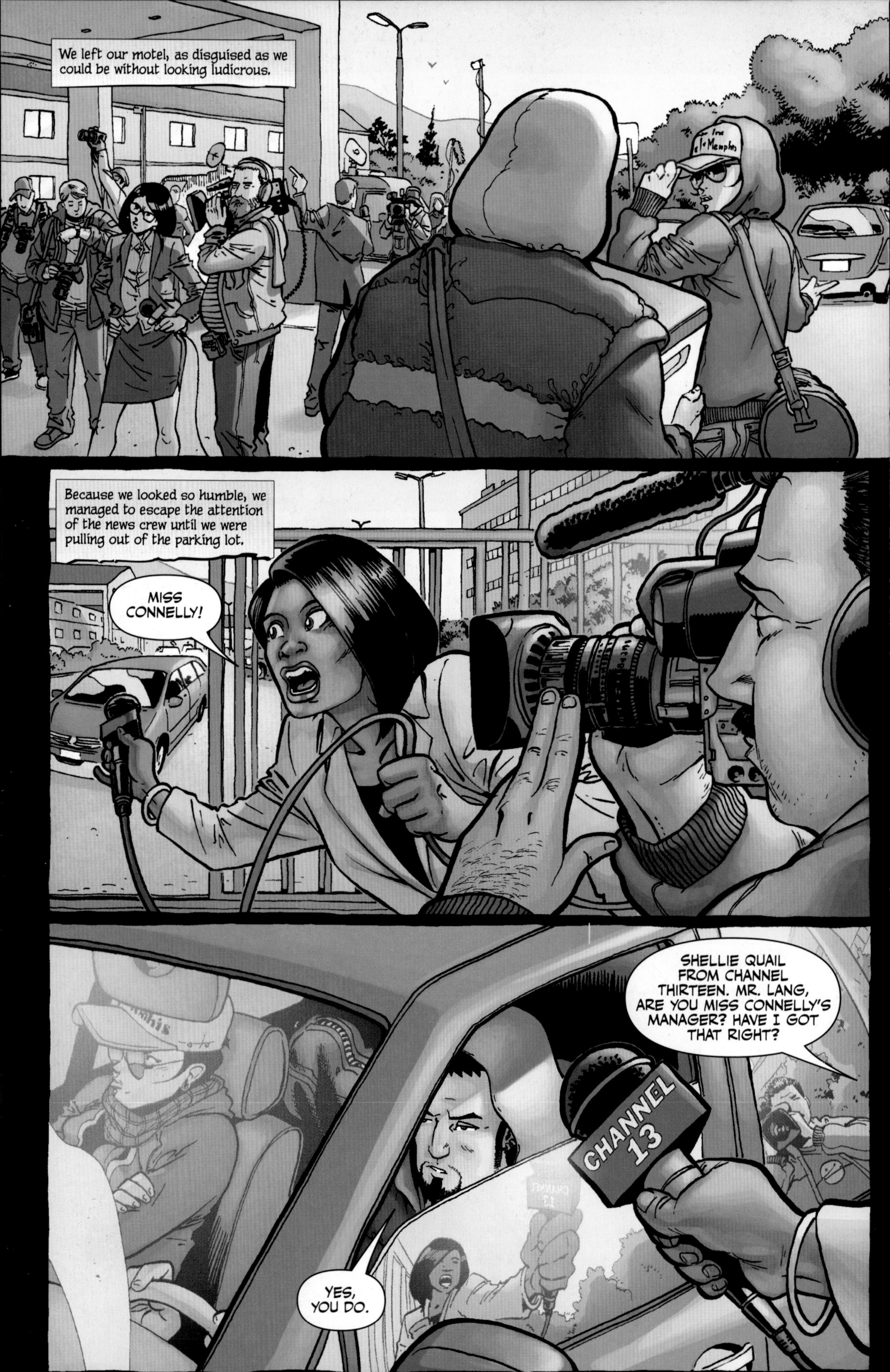
We left our motel, as disguised as we could be without looking ludicrous.
Because we looked so humble, we managed to escape the attention of the news crew until we were pulling out of the parking lot.
MISS CONNELLY!
SHELLIE QUAIL FROM CHANNEL THIRTEEN. MR. LANG, ARE YOU MISS CONNELLY'S MANAGER? HAVE I GOT THAT RIGHT?
CHANNEL 13
YES, YOU DO.

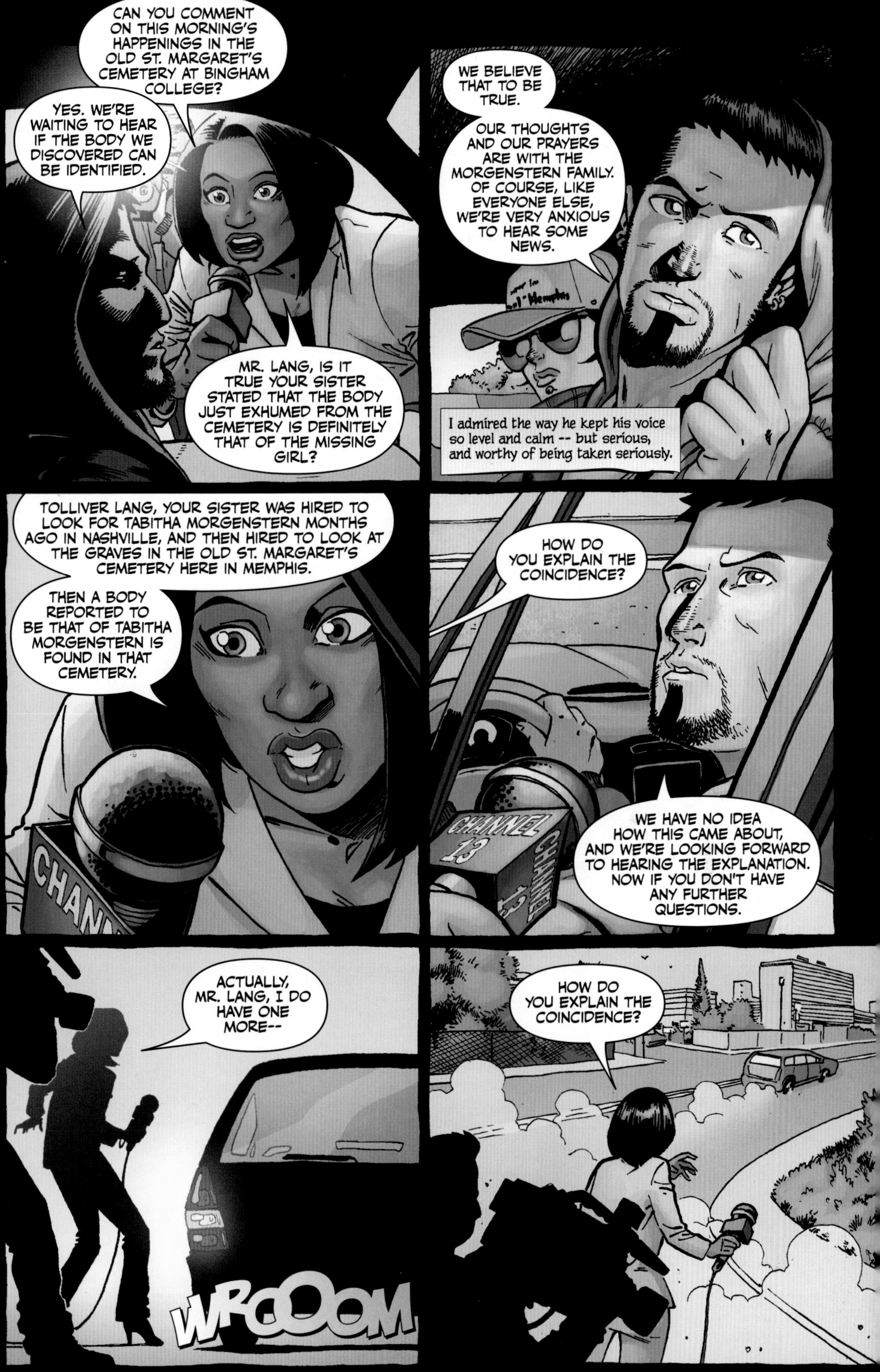
CAN YOU COMMENT ON THIS MORNING'S HAPPENINGS IN THE OLD ST. MARGARET'S CEMETERY AT BINGHAM COLLEGE?
YES. WE'RE WAITING TO HEAR IF THE BODY WE DISCOVERED CAN BE IDENTIFIED.
MR. LANG, IS IT TRUE YOUR SISTER STATED THAT THE BODY JUST EXHUMED FROM THE CEMETERY IS DEFINITELY THAT OF THE MISSING GIRL?
WE BELIEVE THAT TO BE TRUE.
OUR THOUGHTS AND OUR PRAYERS ARE WITH THE MORGENSTERN FAMILY. OF COURSE, LIKE EVERYONE ELSE, WE'RE VERY ANXIOUS TO HEAR SOME NEWS.
I admired the way he kept his voice so level and calm -- but serious, and worthy of being taken seriously.
TOLLIVER LANG, YOUR SISTER WAS HIRED TO LOOK FOR TABITHA MORGENSTERN MONTHS AGO IN NASHVILLE, AND THEN HIRED TO LOOK AT THE GRAVES IN THE OLD ST. MARGARET'S CEMETERY HERE IN MEMPHIS.
THEN A BODY REPORTED TO BE THAT OF TABITHA MORGENSTERN IS FOUND IN THAT CEMETERY.
HOW DO YOU EXPLAIN THE COINCIDENCE?
CHANNEL 13
WE HAVE NO IDEA HOW THIS CAME ABOUT, AND WE'RE LOOKING FORWARD TO HEARING THE EXPLANATION. NOW IF YOU DON'T HAVE ANY FURTHER QUESTIONS.
ACTUALLY, MR. LANG, I DO HAVE ONE MORE--
WROOOM
HOW DO YOU EXPLAIN THE COINCIDENCE?

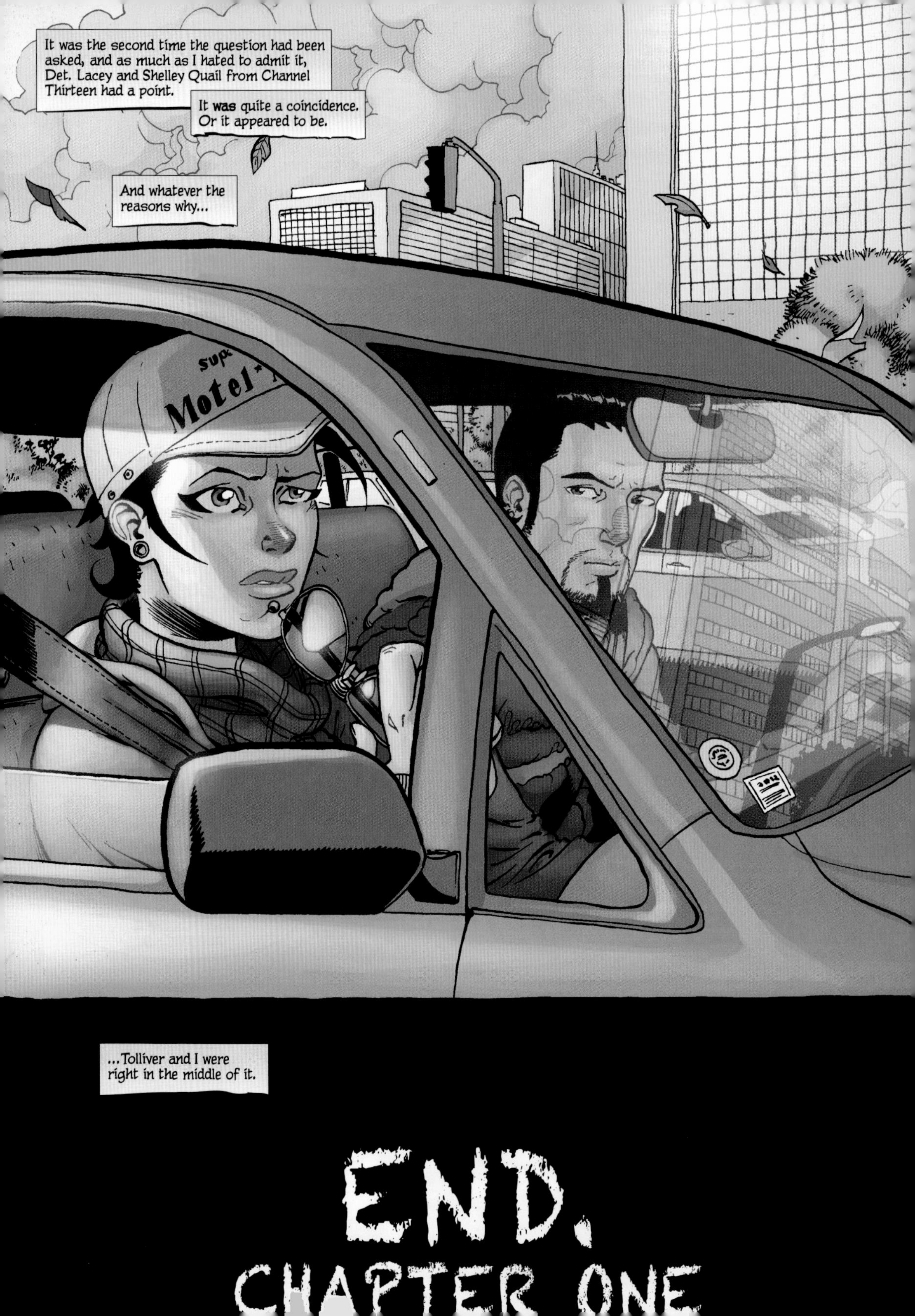
It was the second time the question had been asked, and as much as I hated to admit it, Det. Lacey and Shelley Quail from Channel Thirteen had a point.
It **was** quite a coincidence. Or it appeared to be.
And whatever the reasons why...
...Tolliver and I were right in the middle of it.
END.
CHAPTER ONE

CHAPTER TWO

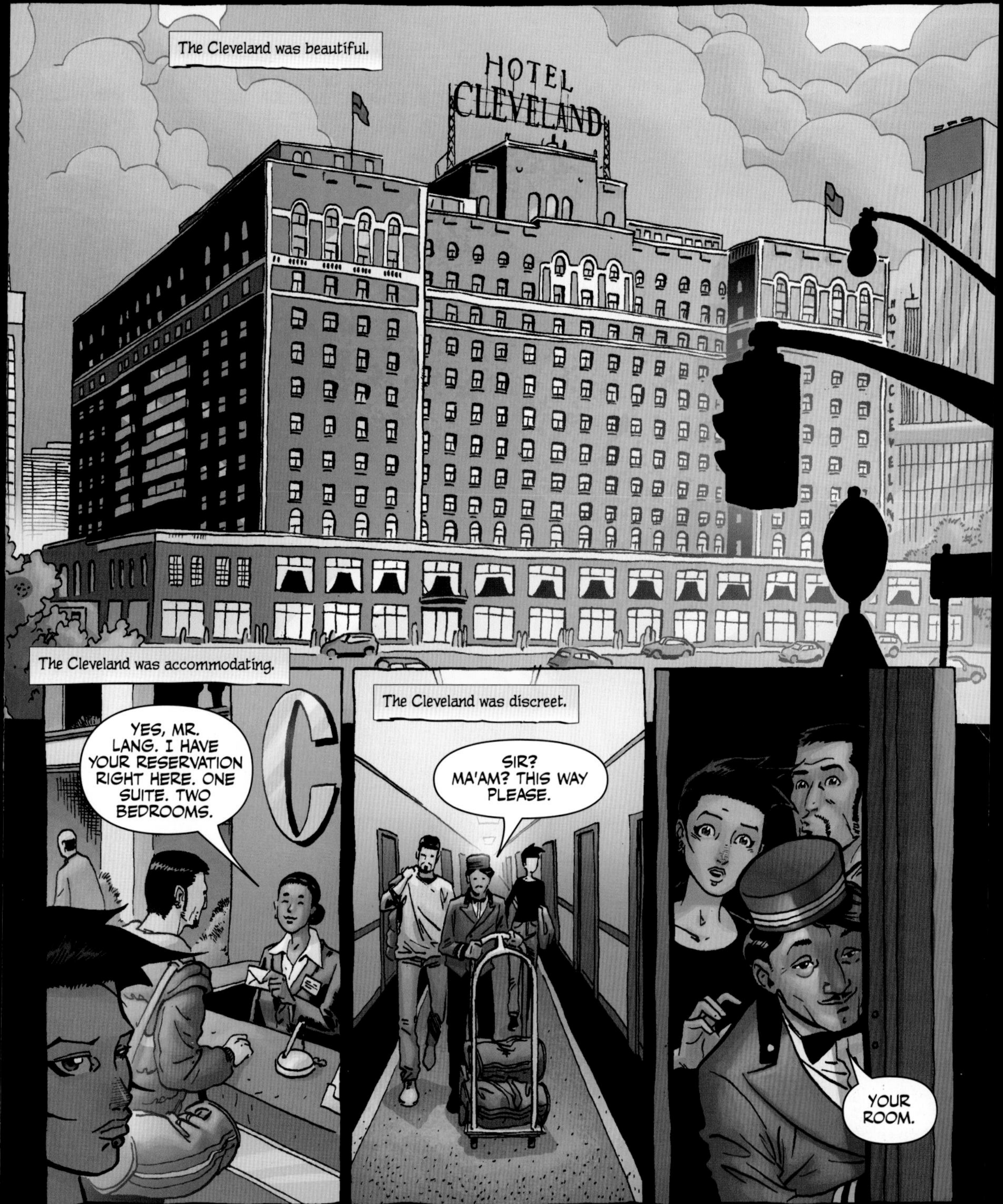
The Cleveland was beautiful.
HOTEL CLEVELAND
The Cleveland was accommodating.
YES, MR. LANG. I HAVE YOUR RESERVATION RIGHT HERE. ONE SUITE. TWO BEDROOMS.
The Cleveland was discreet.
SIR? MA'AM? THIS WAY PLEASE.
YOUR ROOM.

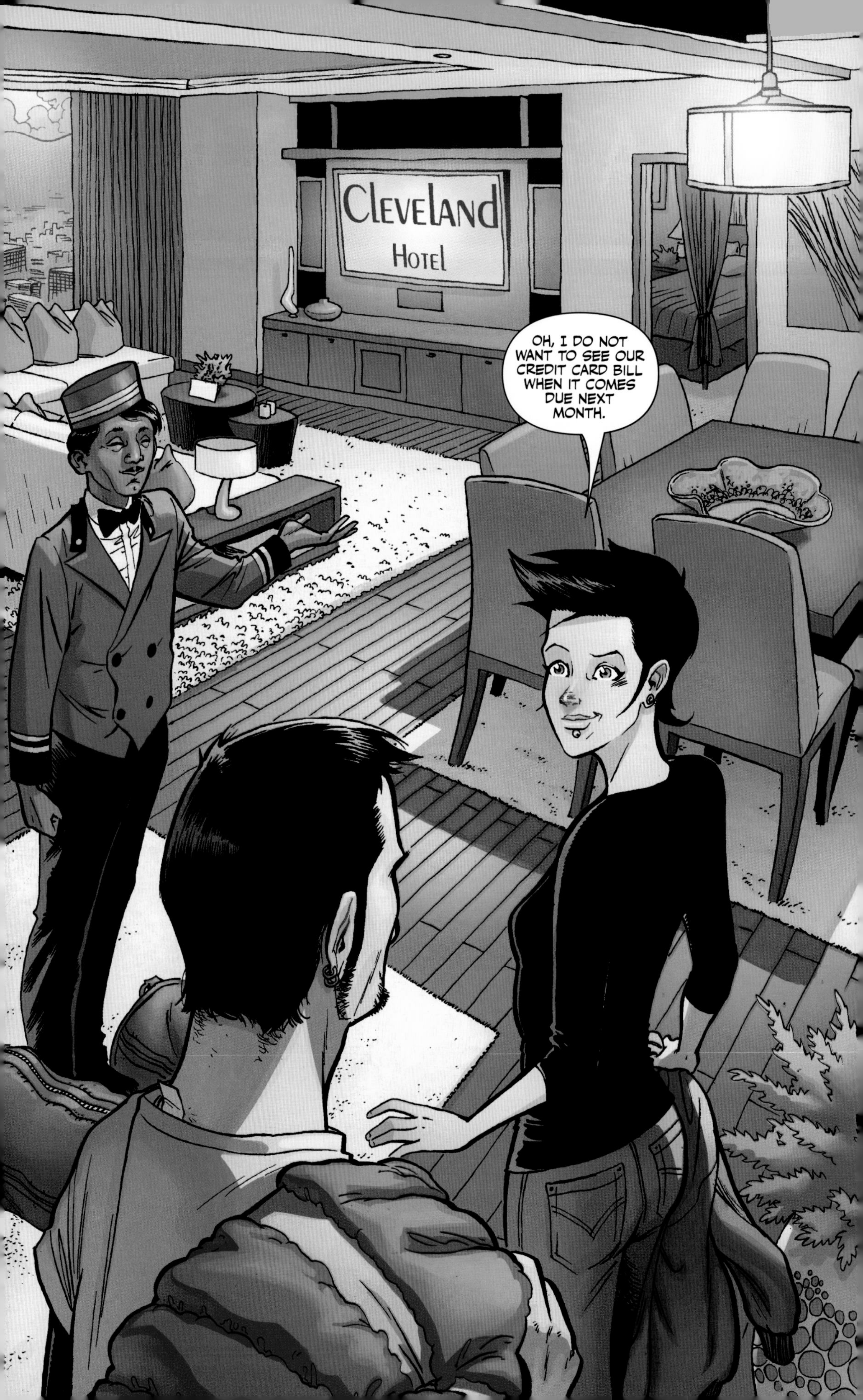
Cleveland
Hotel
OH, I DO NOT WANT TO SEE OUR CREDIT CARD BILL WHEN IT COMES DUE NEXT MONTH.

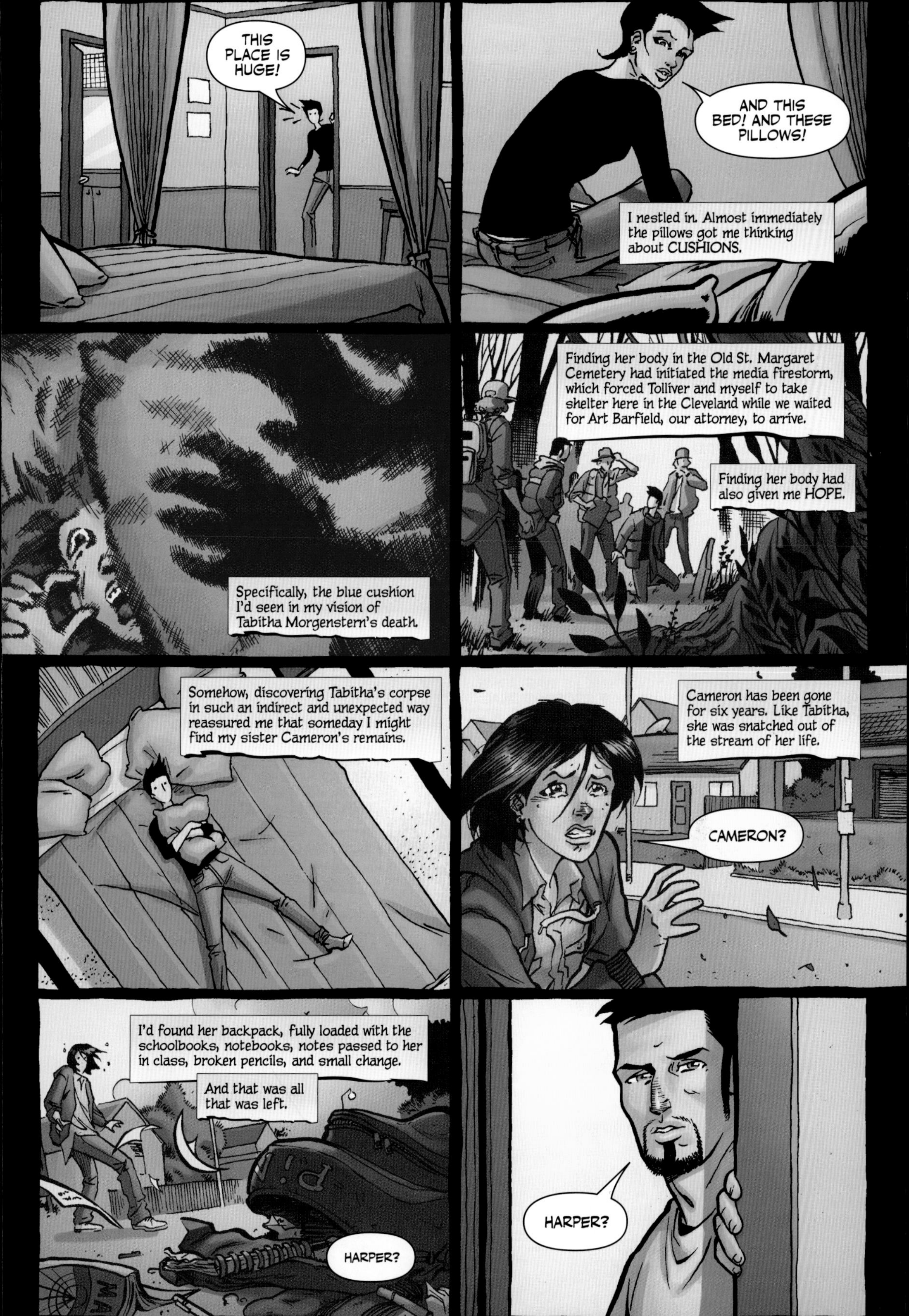
THIS PLACE IS HUGE!
AND THIS BED! AND THESE PILLOWS!
I nestled in. Almost immediately the pillows got me thinking about CUSHIONS.
Specifically, the blue cushion I'd seen in my vision of Tabitha Morgenstern's death.
Finding her body in the Old St. Margaret Cemetery had initiated the media firestorm, which forced Tolliver and myself to take shelter here in the Cleveland while we waited for Art Barfield, our attorney, to arrive.
Finding her body had also given me HOPE.
Somehow, discovering Tabitha's corpse in such an indirect and unexpected way reassured me that someday I might find my sister Cameron's remains.
Cameron has been gone for six years. Like Tabitha, she was snatched out of the stream of her life.
CAMERON?
I'd found her backpack, fully loaded with the schoolbooks, notebooks, notes passed to her in class, broken pencils, and small change.
And that was all that was left.
HARPER?
HARPER?

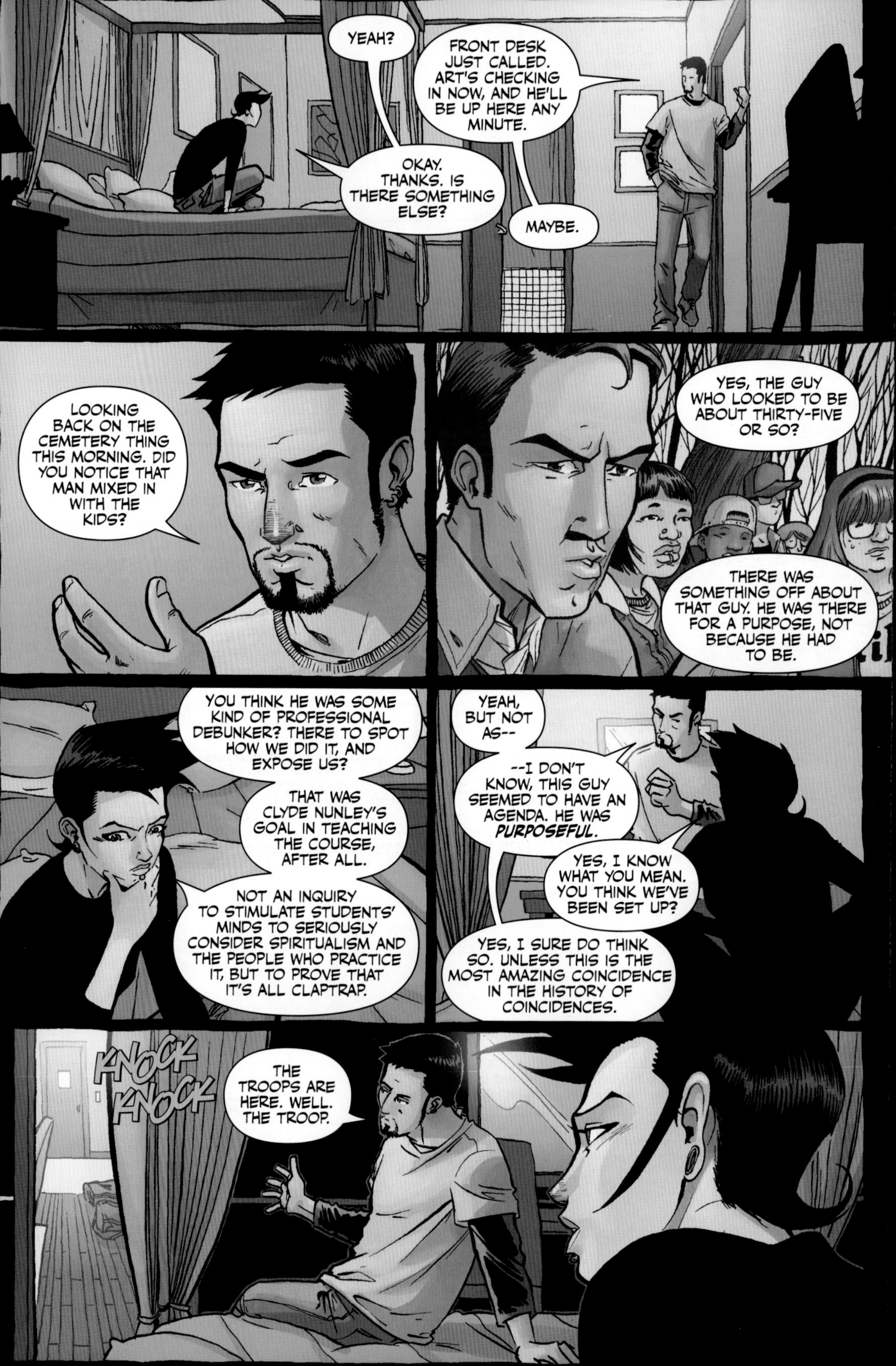
YEAH?
FRONT DESK JUST CALLED. ART'S CHECKING IN NOW, AND HE'LL BE UP HERE ANY MINUTE.
OKAY. THANKS. IS THERE SOMETHING ELSE?
MAYBE.
LOOKING BACK ON THE CEMETERY THING THIS MORNING. DID YOU NOTICE THAT MAN MIXED IN WITH THE KIDS?
YES, THE GUY WHO LOOKED TO BE ABOUT THIRTY-FIVE OR SO?
THERE WAS SOMETHING OFF ABOUT THAT GUY. HE WAS THERE FOR A PURPOSE, NOT BECAUSE HE HAD TO BE.
YOU THINK HE WAS SOME KIND OF PROFESSIONAL DEBUNKER? THERE TO SPOT HOW WE DID IT, AND EXPOSE US?
THAT WAS CLYDE NUNLEY'S GOAL IN TEACHING THE COURSE, AFTER ALL.
NOT AN INQUIRY TO STIMULATE STUDENTS' MINDS TO SERIOUSLY CONSIDER SPIRITUALISM AND THE PEOPLE WHO PRACTICE IT, BUT TO PROVE THAT IT'S ALL CLAPTRAP.
YEAH, BUT NOT AS--
--I DON'T KNOW, THIS GUY SEEMED TO HAVE AN AGENDA. HE WAS *PURPOSEFUL*.
YES, I KNOW WHAT YOU MEAN. YOU THINK WE'VE BEEN SET UP?
YES, I SURE DO THINK SO. UNLESS THIS IS THE MOST AMAZING COINCIDENCE IN THE HISTORY OF COINCIDENCES.
KNOCK KNOCK
THE TROOPS ARE HERE. WELL. THE TROOP.

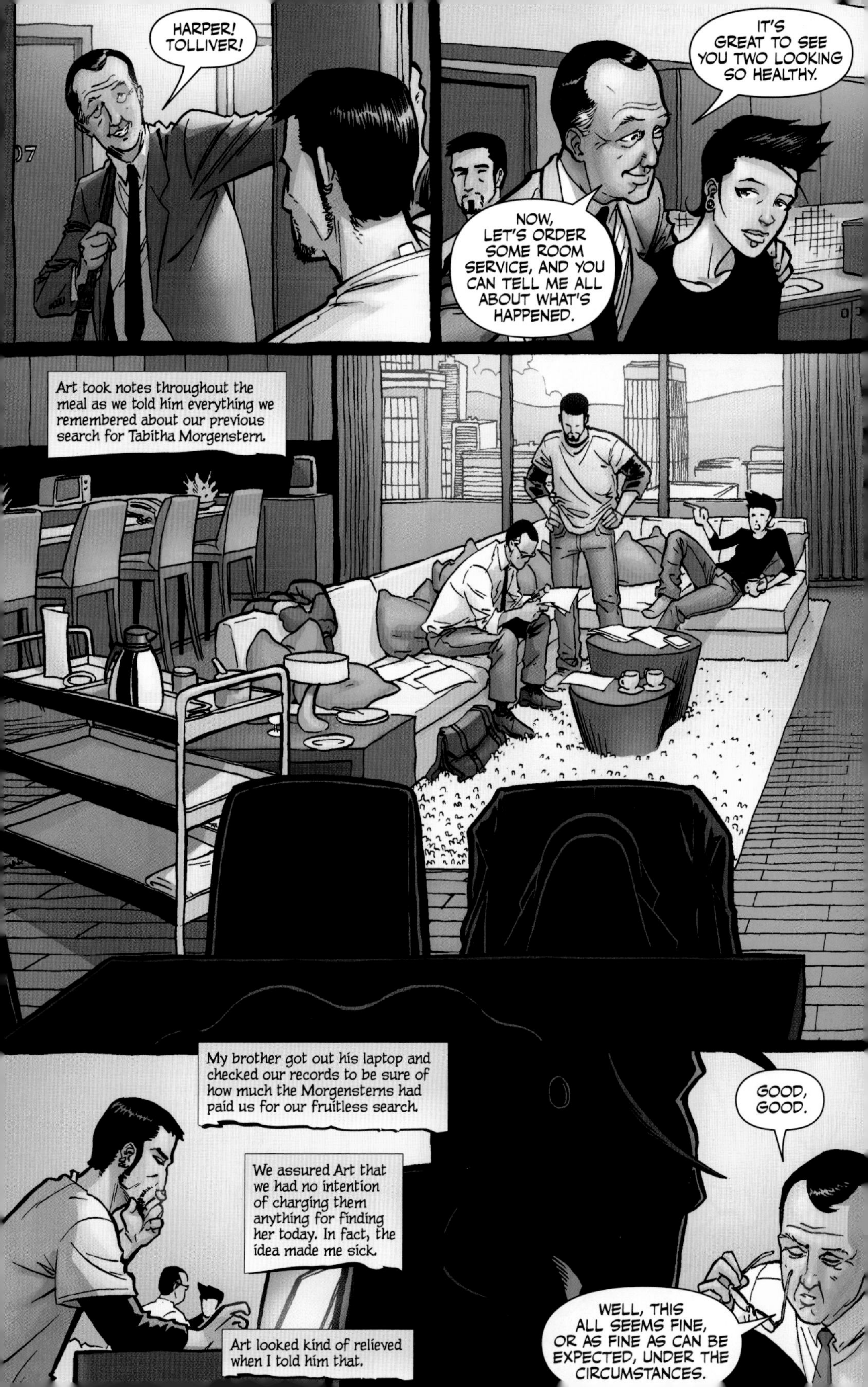
HARPER! TOLLIVER!
IT'S GREAT TO SEE YOU TWO LOOKING SO HEALTHY.
NOW, LET'S ORDER SOME ROOM SERVICE, AND YOU CAN TELL ME ALL ABOUT WHAT'S HAPPENED.
Art took notes throughout the meal as we told him everything we remembered about our previous search for Tabitha Morgenstern.
My brother got out his laptop and checked our records to be sure of how much the Morgensterns had paid us for our fruitless search.
We assured Art that we had no intention of charging them anything for finding her today. In fact, the idea made me sick.
Art looked kind of relieved when I told him that.
GOOD, GOOD.
WELL, THIS ALL SEEMS FINE, OR AS FINE AS CAN BE EXPECTED, UNDER THE CIRCUMSTANCES.

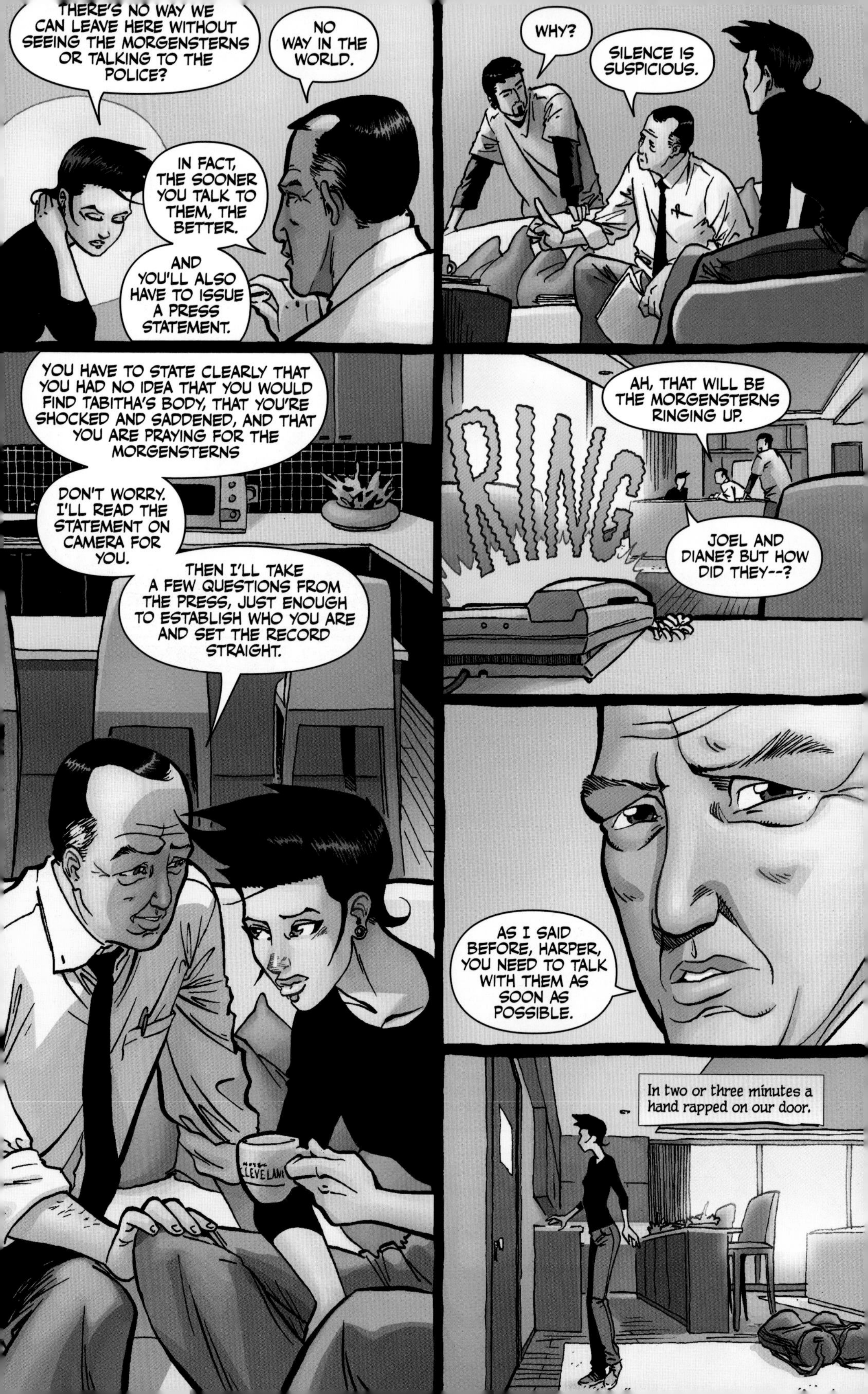
THERE'S NO WAY WE CAN LEAVE HERE WITHOUT SEEING THE MORGENSTERNS OR TALKING TO THE POLICE?
NO WAY IN THE WORLD.
IN FACT, THE SOONER YOU TALK TO THEM, THE BETTER.
AND YOU'LL ALSO HAVE TO ISSUE A PRESS STATEMENT.
WHY?
SILENCE IS SUSPICIOUS.
YOU HAVE TO STATE CLEARLY THAT YOU HAD NO IDEA THAT YOU WOULD FIND TABITHA'S BODY, THAT YOU'RE SHOCKED AND SADDENED, AND THAT YOU ARE PRAYING FOR THE MORGENSTERNS
DON'T WORRY. I'LL READ THE STATEMENT ON CAMERA FOR YOU.
THEN I'LL TAKE A FEW QUESTIONS FROM THE PRESS, JUST ENOUGH TO ESTABLISH WHO YOU ARE AND SET THE RECORD STRAIGHT.
RING
AH, THAT WILL BE THE MORGENSTERNS RINGING UP.
JOEL AND DIANE? BUT HOW DID THEY--?
AS I SAID BEFORE, HARPER, YOU NEED TO TALK WITH THEM AS SOON AS POSSIBLE.
In two or three minutes a hand rapped on our door.

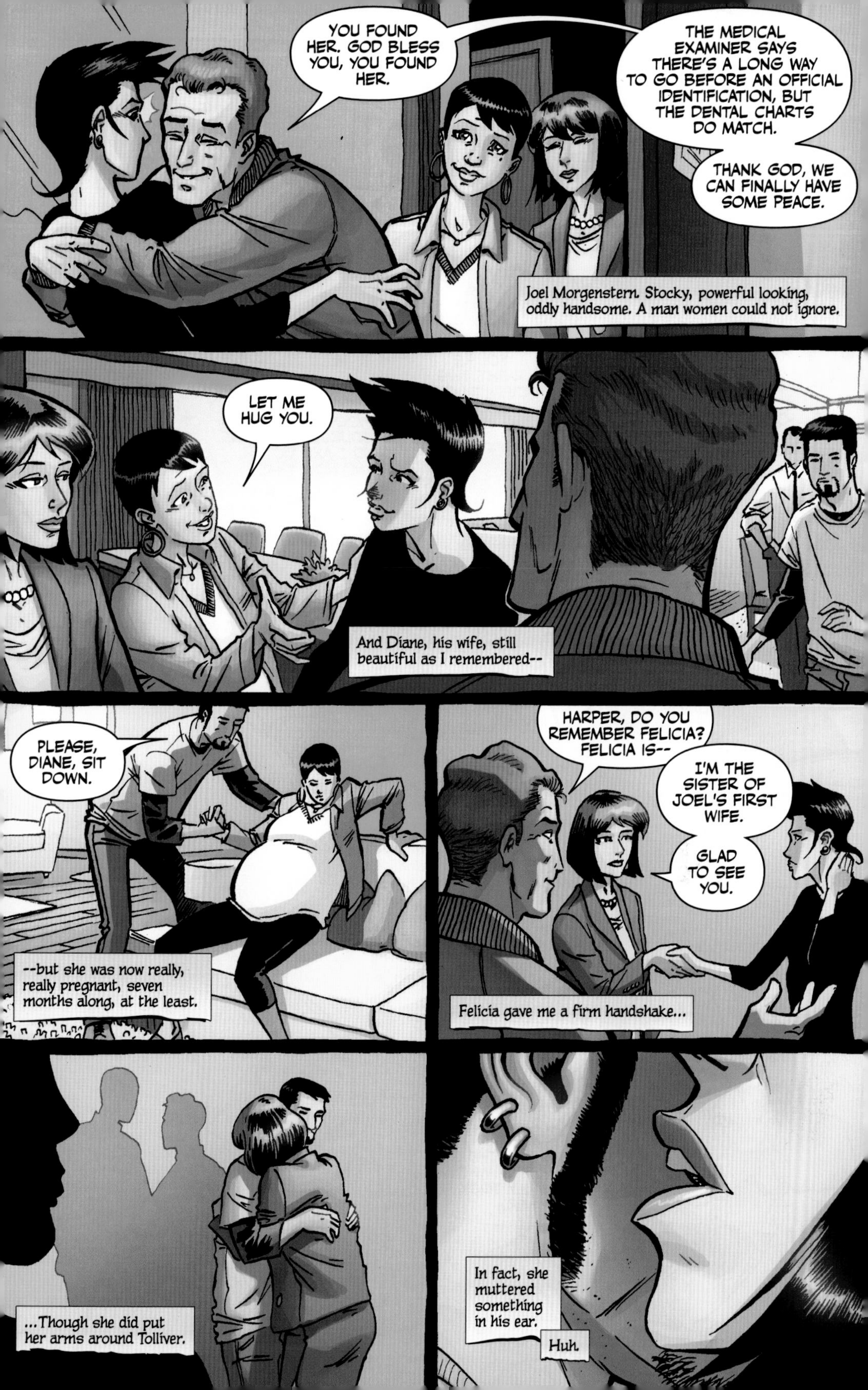
YOU FOUND HER. GOD BLESS YOU, YOU FOUND HER.
THE MEDICAL EXAMINER SAYS THERE'S A LONG WAY TO GO BEFORE AN OFFICIAL IDENTIFICATION, BUT THE DENTAL CHARTS DO MATCH.
THANK GOD, WE CAN FINALLY HAVE SOME PEACE.
Joel Morgenstern. Stocky, powerful looking, oddly handsome. A man women could not ignore.
LET ME HUG YOU.
And Diane, his wife, still beautiful as I remembered--
PLEASE, DIANE, SIT DOWN.
--but she was now really, really pregnant, seven months along, at the least.
HARPER, DO YOU REMEMBER FELICIA? FELICIA IS--
I'M THE SISTER OF JOEL'S FIRST WIFE.
GLAD TO SEE YOU.
Felicia gave me a firm handshake...
...Though she did put her arms around Tolliver.
In fact, she muttered something in his ear.
Huh.

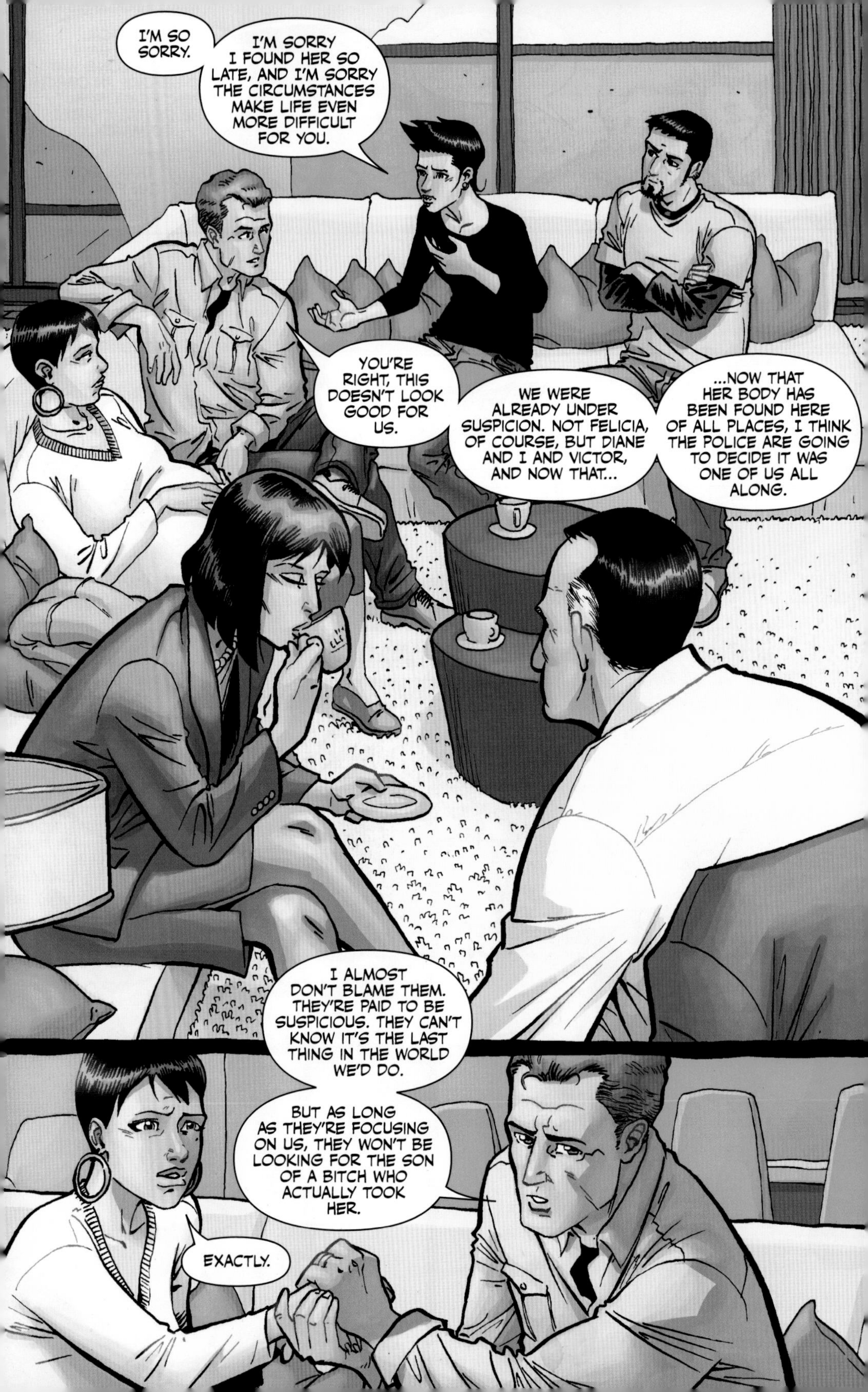
I'M SO SORRY.
I'M SORRY I FOUND HER SO LATE, AND I'M SORRY THE CIRCUMSTANCES MAKE LIFE EVEN MORE DIFFICULT FOR YOU.
YOU'RE RIGHT, THIS DOESN'T LOOK GOOD FOR US.
WE WERE ALREADY UNDER SUSPICION. NOT FELICIA, OF COURSE, BUT DIANE AND I AND VICTOR, AND NOW THAT...
...NOW THAT HER BODY HAS BEEN FOUND HERE OF ALL PLACES, I THINK THE POLICE ARE GOING TO DECIDE IT WAS ONE OF US ALL ALONG.
I ALMOST DON'T BLAME THEM. THEY'RE PAID TO BE SUSPICIOUS. THEY CAN'T KNOW IT'S THE LAST THING IN THE WORLD WE'D DO.
BUT AS LONG AS THEY'RE FOCUSING ON US, THEY WON'T BE LOOKING FOR THE SON OF A BITCH WHO ACTUALLY TOOK HER.
EXACTLY.

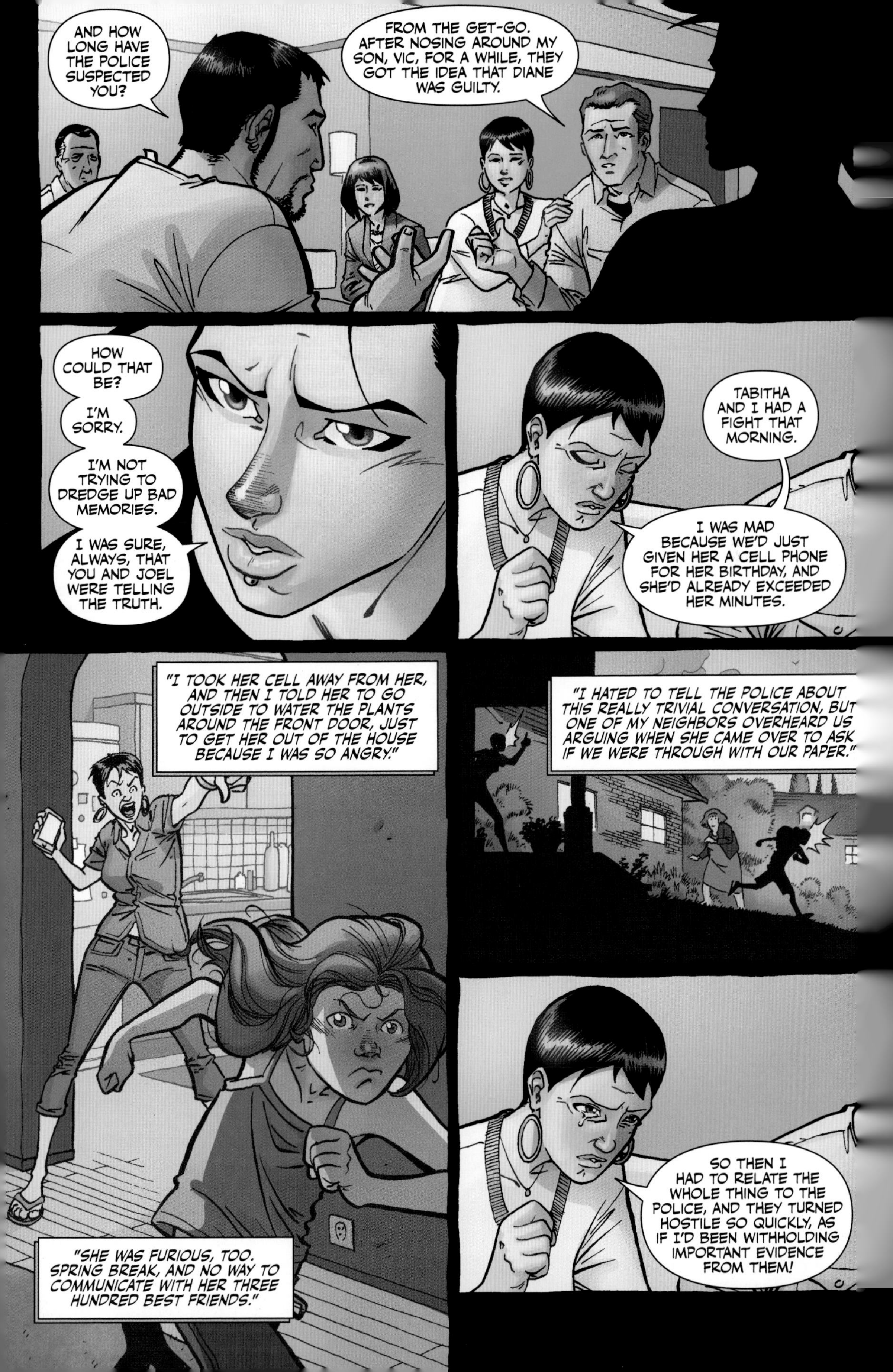
AND HOW LONG HAVE THE POLICE SUSPECTED YOU?
FROM THE GET-GO. AFTER NOSING AROUND MY SON, VIC, FOR A WHILE, THEY GOT THE IDEA THAT DIANE WAS GUILTY.
HOW COULD THAT BE?
I'M SORRY.
I'M NOT TRYING TO DREDGE UP BAD MEMORIES.
I WAS SURE, ALWAYS, THAT YOU AND JOEL WERE TELLING THE TRUTH.
TABITHA AND I HAD A FIGHT THAT MORNING.
I WAS MAD BECAUSE WE'D JUST GIVEN HER A CELL PHONE FOR HER BIRTHDAY, AND SHE'D ALREADY EXCEEDED HER MINUTES.
"I TOOK HER CELL AWAY FROM HER, AND THEN I TOLD HER TO GO OUTSIDE TO WATER THE PLANTS AROUND THE FRONT DOOR, JUST TO GET HER OUT OF THE HOUSE BECAUSE I WAS SO ANGRY."
"SHE WAS FURIOUS, TOO. SPRING BREAK, AND NO WAY TO COMMUNICATE WITH HER THREE HUNDRED BEST FRIENDS."
"I HATED TO TELL THE POLICE ABOUT THIS REALLY TRIVIAL CONVERSATION, BUT ONE OF MY NEIGHBORS OVERHEARD US ARGUING WHEN SHE CAME OVER TO ASK IF WE WERE THROUGH WITH OUR PAPER."
SO THEN I HAD TO RELATE THE WHOLE THING TO THE POLICE, AND THEY TURNED HOSTILE SO QUICKLY, AS IF I'D BEEN WITHHOLDING IMPORTANT EVIDENCE FROM THEM!

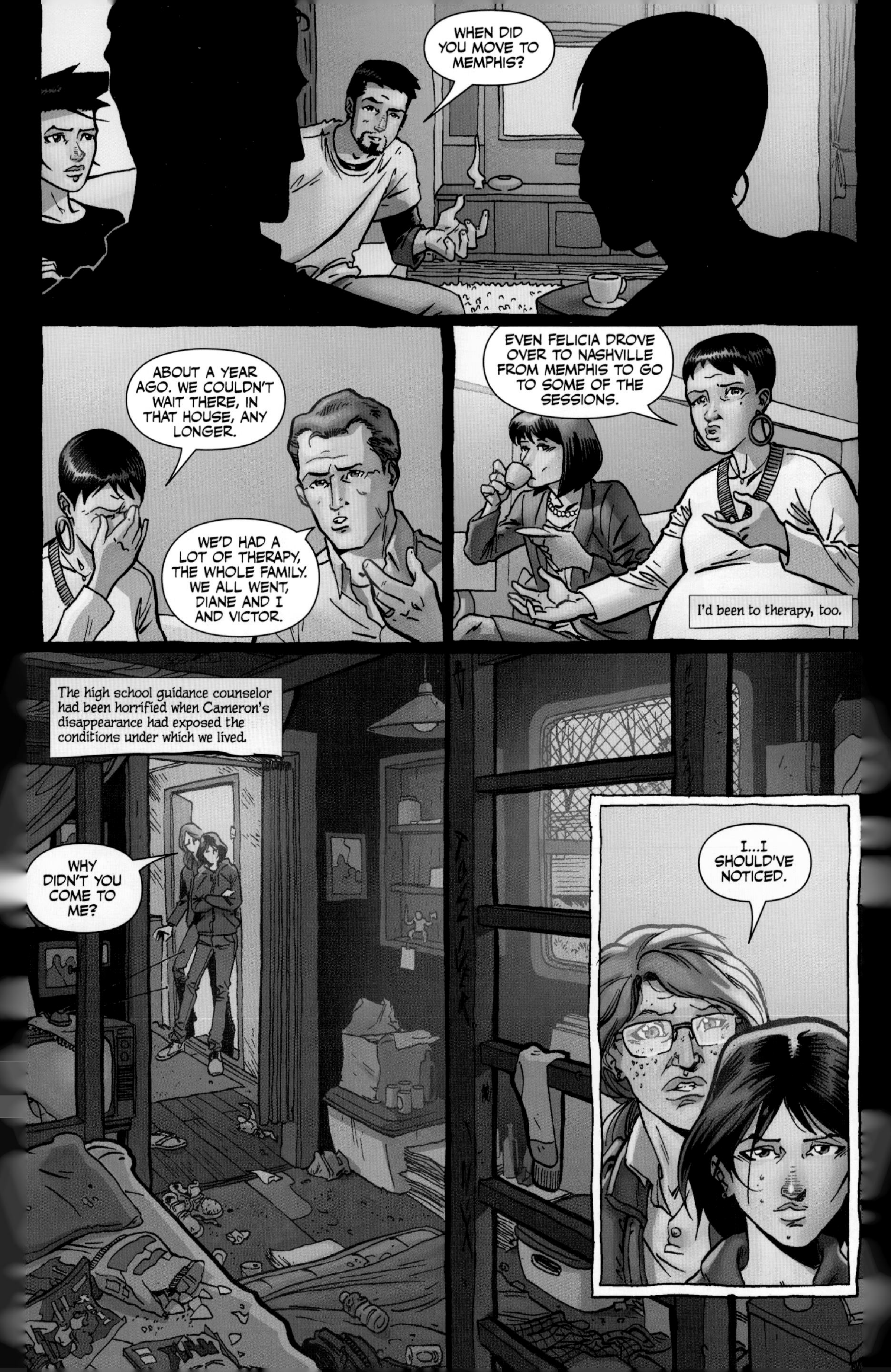
WHEN DID YOU MOVE TO MEMPHIS?
ABOUT A YEAR AGO. WE COULDN'T WAIT THERE, IN THAT HOUSE, ANY LONGER.
WE'D HAD A LOT OF THERAPY, THE WHOLE FAMILY. WE ALL WENT, DIANE AND I AND VICTOR.
EVEN FELICIA DROVE OVER TO NASHVILLE FROM MEMPHIS TO GO TO SOME OF THE SESSIONS.
I'd been to therapy, too.
The high school guidance counselor had been horrified when Cameron's disappearance had exposed the conditions under which we lived.
WHY DIDN'T YOU COME TO ME?
I...I SHOULD'VE NOTICED.

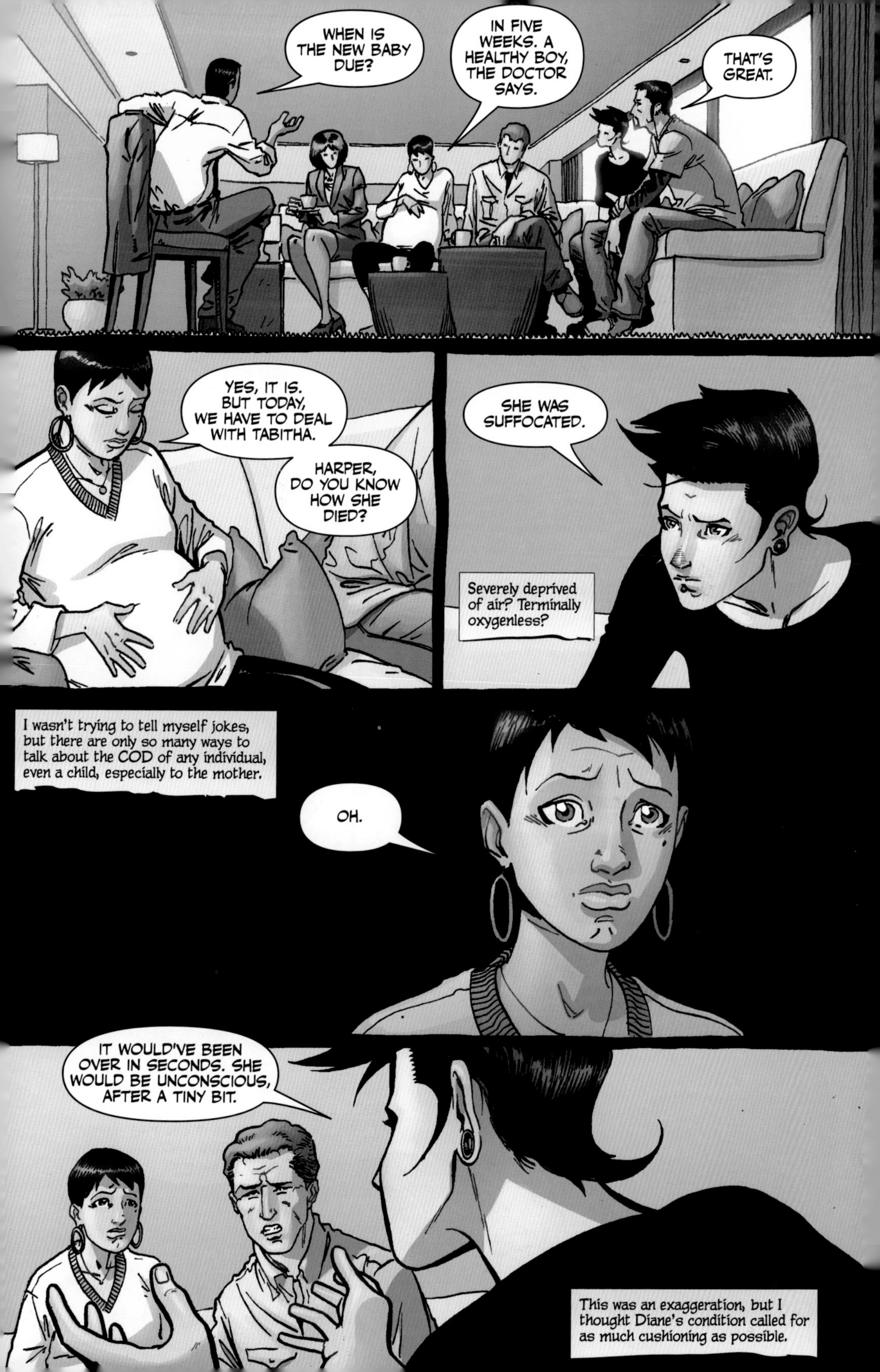
WHEN IS THE NEW BABY DUE?
IN FIVE WEEKS. A HEALTHY BOY, THE DOCTOR SAYS.
THAT'S GREAT.
YES, IT IS. BUT TODAY, WE HAVE TO DEAL WITH TABITHA.
HARPER, DO YOU KNOW HOW SHE DIED?
SHE WAS SUFFOCATED.
Severely deprived of air? Terminally oxygenless?
I wasn't trying to tell myself jokes, but there are only so many ways to talk about the COD of any individual, even a child, especially to the mother.
OH.
IT WOULD'VE BEEN OVER IN SECONDS. SHE WOULD BE UNCONSCIOUS, AFTER A TINY BIT.
This was an exaggeration, but I thought Diane's condition called for as much cushioning as possible.

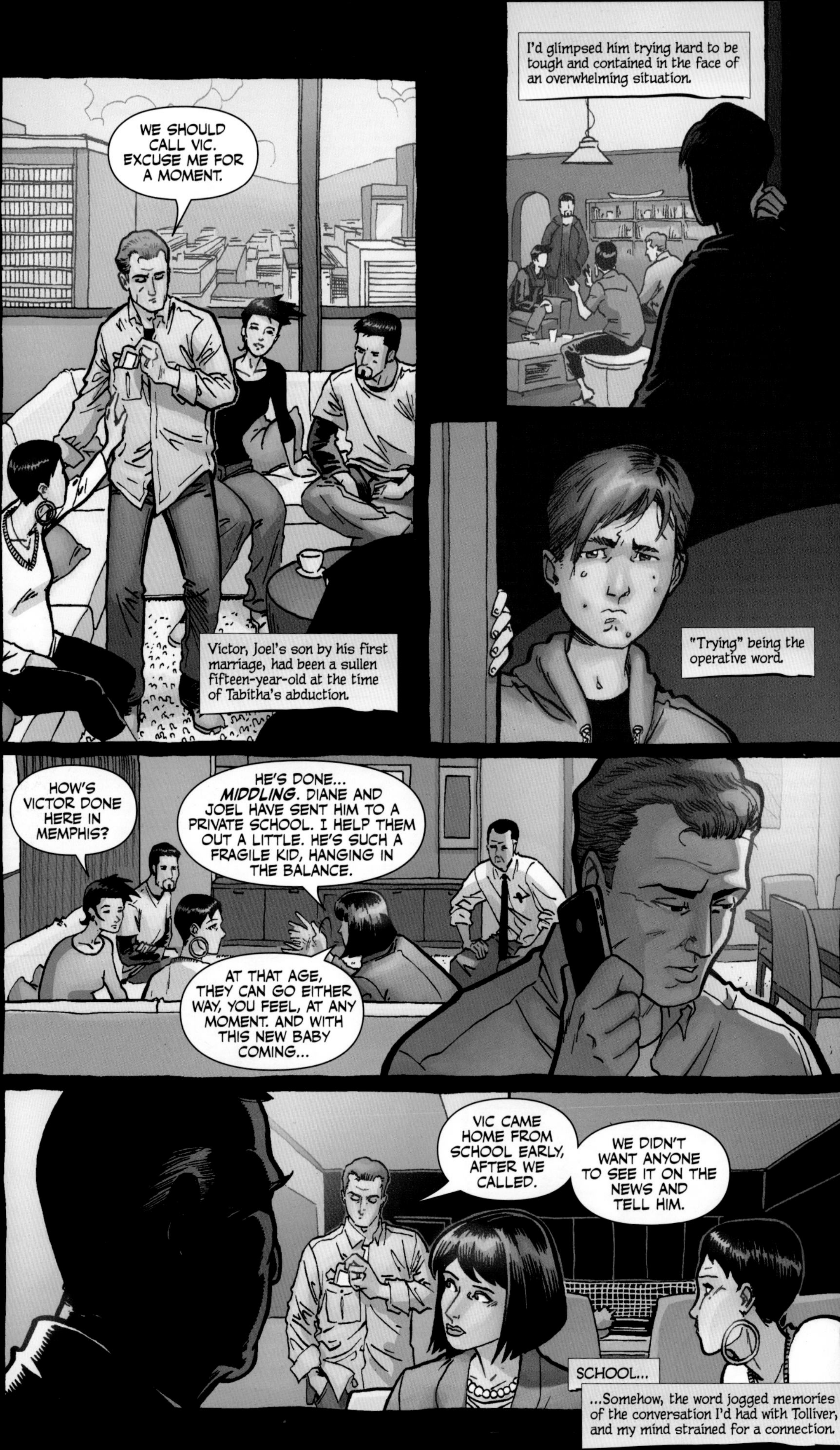
WE SHOULD CALL VIC. EXCUSE ME FOR A MOMENT.
Victor, Joel's son by his first marriage, had been a sullen fifteen-year-old at the time of Tabitha's abduction.
I'd glimpsed him trying hard to be tough and contained in the face of an overwhelming situation.
"Trying" being the operative word.
HOW'S VICTOR DONE HERE IN MEMPHIS?
HE'S DONE... MIDDLING. DIANE AND JOEL HAVE SENT HIM TO A PRIVATE SCHOOL. I HELP THEM OUT A LITTLE. HE'S SUCH A FRAGILE KID, HANGING IN THE BALANCE.
AT THAT AGE, THEY CAN GO EITHER WAY, YOU FEEL, AT ANY MOMENT. AND WITH THIS NEW BABY COMING...
VIC CAME HOME FROM SCHOOL EARLY, AFTER WE CALLED.
WE DIDN'T WANT ANYONE TO SEE IT ON THE NEWS AND TELL HIM.
SCHOOL...
...Somehow, the word jogged memories of the conversation I'd had with Tolliver, and my mind strained for a connection.

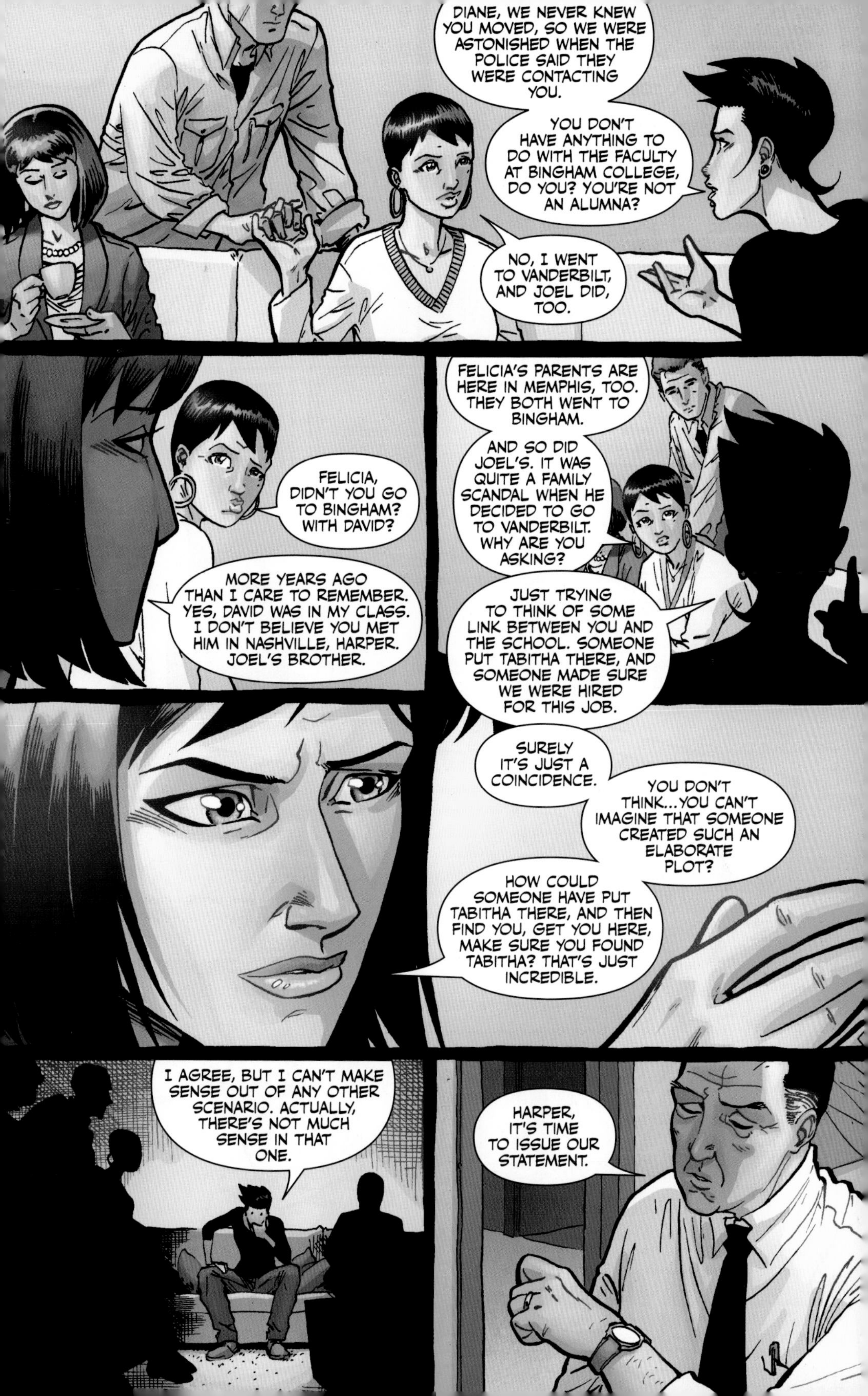
DIANE, WE NEVER KNEW YOU MOVED, SO WE WERE ASTONISHED WHEN THE POLICE SAID THEY WERE CONTACTING YOU.
YOU DON'T HAVE ANYTHING TO DO WITH THE FACULTY AT BINGHAM COLLEGE, DO YOU? YOU'RE NOT AN ALUMNA?
NO, I WENT TO VANDERBILT, AND JOEL DID, TOO.
FELICIA, DIDN'T YOU GO TO BINGHAM? WITH DAVID?
MORE YEARS AGO THAN I CARE TO REMEMBER. YES, DAVID WAS IN MY CLASS. I DON'T BELIEVE YOU MET HIM IN NASHVILLE, HARPER. JOEL'S BROTHER.
FELICIA'S PARENTS ARE HERE IN MEMPHIS, TOO. THEY BOTH WENT TO BINGHAM.
AND SO DID JOEL'S. IT WAS QUITE A FAMILY SCANDAL WHEN HE DECIDED TO GO TO VANDERBILT. WHY ARE YOU ASKING?
JUST TRYING TO THINK OF SOME LINK BETWEEN YOU AND THE SCHOOL. SOMEONE PUT TABITHA THERE, AND SOMEONE MADE SURE WE WERE HIRED FOR THIS JOB.
SURELY IT'S JUST A COINCIDENCE.
YOU DON'T THINK...YOU CAN'T IMAGINE THAT SOMEONE CREATED SUCH AN ELABORATE PLOT?
HOW COULD SOMEONE HAVE PUT TABITHA THERE, AND THEN FIND YOU, GET YOU HERE, MAKE SURE YOU FOUND TABITHA? THAT'S JUST INCREDIBLE.
I AGREE, BUT I CAN'T MAKE SENSE OUT OF ANY OTHER SCENARIO. ACTUALLY, THERE'S NOT MUCH SENSE IN THAT ONE.
HARPER, IT'S TIME TO ISSUE OUR STATEMENT.

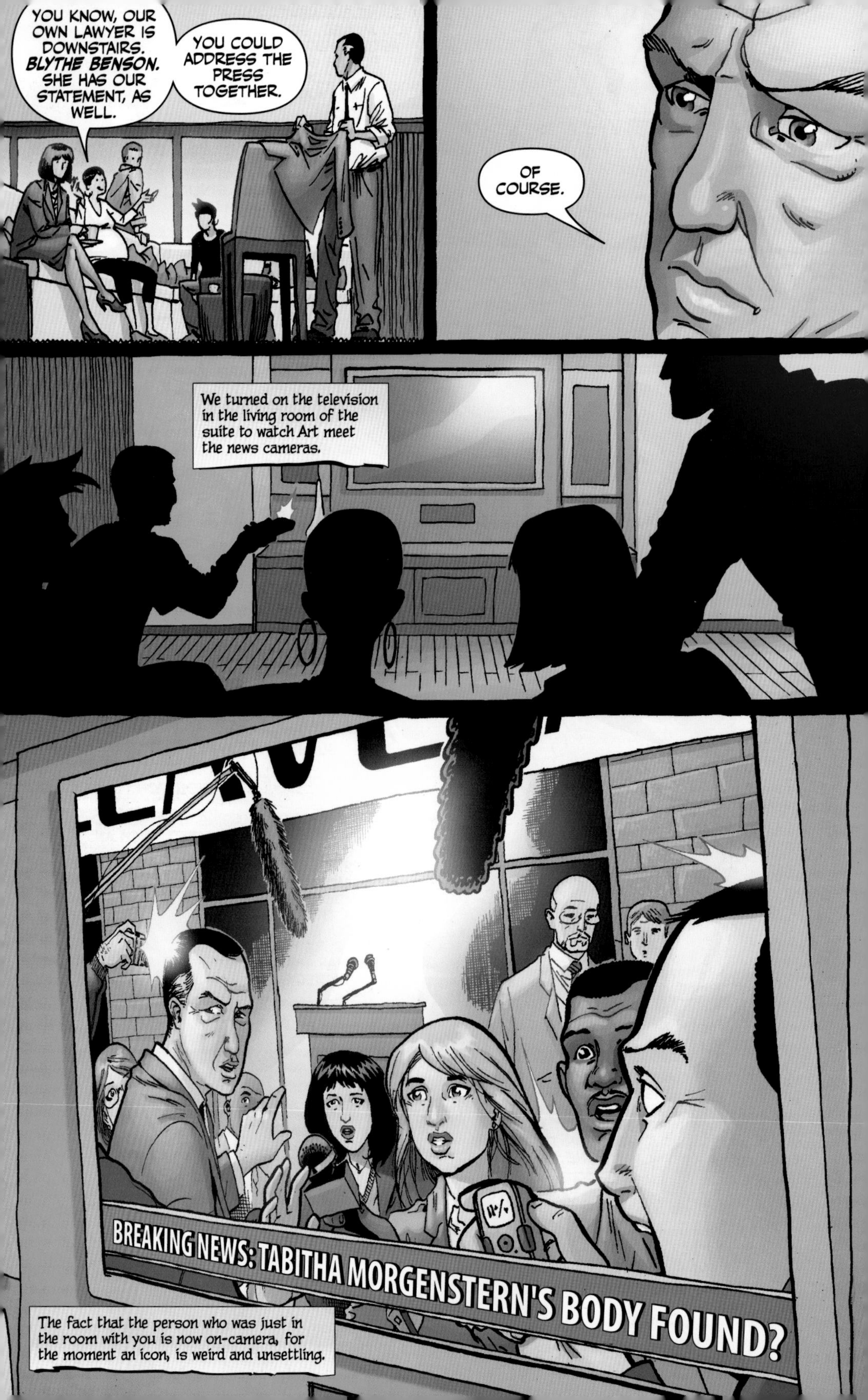
YOU KNOW, OUR OWN LAWYER IS DOWNSTAIRS. BLYTHE BENSON. SHE HAS OUR STATEMENT, AS WELL.
YOU COULD ADDRESS THE PRESS TOGETHER.
OF COURSE.
We turned on the television in the living room of the suite to watch Art meet the news cameras.
BREAKING NEWS: TABITHA MORGENSTERN'S BODY FOUND?
The fact that the person who was just in the room with you is now on-camera, for the moment an icon, is weird and unsettling.

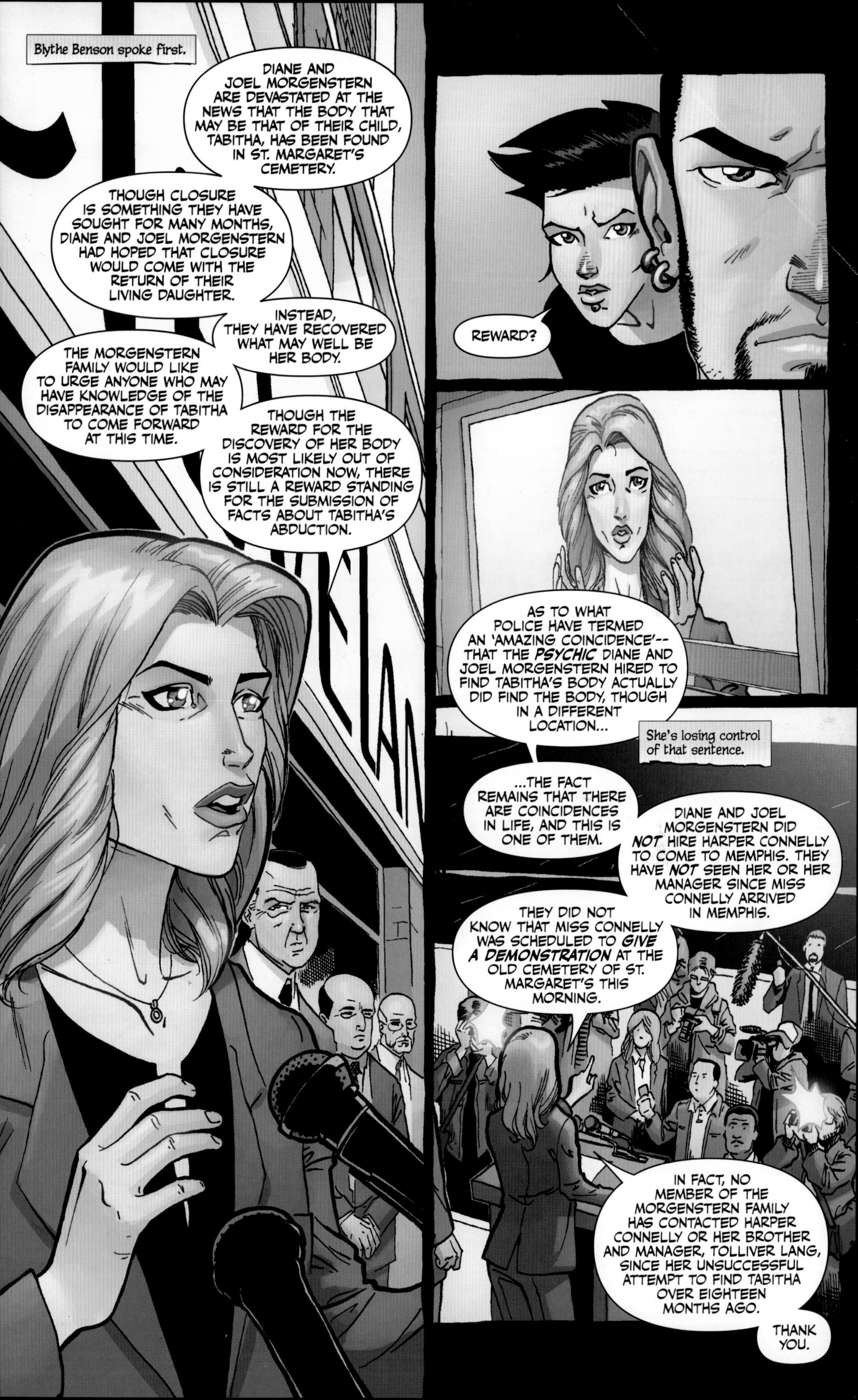
Blythe Benson spoke first.
DIANE AND JOEL MORGENSTERN ARE DEVASTATED AT THE NEWS THAT THE BODY THAT MAY BE THAT OF THEIR CHILD, TABITHA, HAS BEEN FOUND IN ST. MARGARET'S CEMETERY.
THOUGH CLOSURE IS SOMETHING THEY HAVE SOUGHT FOR MANY MONTHS, DIANE AND JOEL MORGENSTERN HAD HOPED THAT CLOSURE WOULD COME WITH THE RETURN OF THEIR LIVING DAUGHTER.
INSTEAD, THEY HAVE RECOVERED WHAT MAY WELL BE HER BODY.
THE MORGENSTERN FAMILY WOULD LIKE TO URGE ANYONE WHO MAY HAVE KNOWLEDGE OF THE DISAPPEARANCE OF TABITHA TO COME FORWARD AT THIS TIME.
THOUGH THE REWARD FOR THE DISCOVERY OF HER BODY IS MOST LIKELY OUT OF CONSIDERATION NOW, THERE IS STILL A REWARD STANDING FOR THE SUBMISSION OF FACTS ABOUT TABITHA'S ABDUCTION.
REWARD?
AS TO WHAT POLICE HAVE TERMED AN 'AMAZING COINCIDENCE'-- THAT THE *PSYCHIC* DIANE AND JOEL MORGENSTERN HIRED TO FIND TABITHA'S BODY ACTUALLY DID FIND THE BODY, THOUGH IN A DIFFERENT LOCATION...
She's losing control of that sentence.
...THE FACT REMAINS THAT THERE ARE COINCIDENCES IN LIFE, AND THIS IS ONE OF THEM.
DIANE AND JOEL MORGENSTERN DID *NOT* HIRE HARPER CONNELLY TO COME TO MEMPHIS. THEY HAVE *NOT* SEEN HER OR HER MANAGER SINCE MISS CONNELLY ARRIVED IN MEMPHIS.
THEY DID NOT KNOW THAT MISS CONNELLY WAS SCHEDULED TO *GIVE A DEMONSTRATION* AT THE OLD CEMETERY OF ST. MARGARET'S THIS MORNING.
IN FACT, NO MEMBER OF THE MORGENSTERN FAMILY HAS CONTACTED HARPER CONNELLY OR HER BROTHER AND MANAGER, TOLLIVER LANG, SINCE HER UNSUCCESSFUL ATTEMPT TO FIND TABITHA OVER EIGHTEEN MONTHS AGO.
THANK YOU.

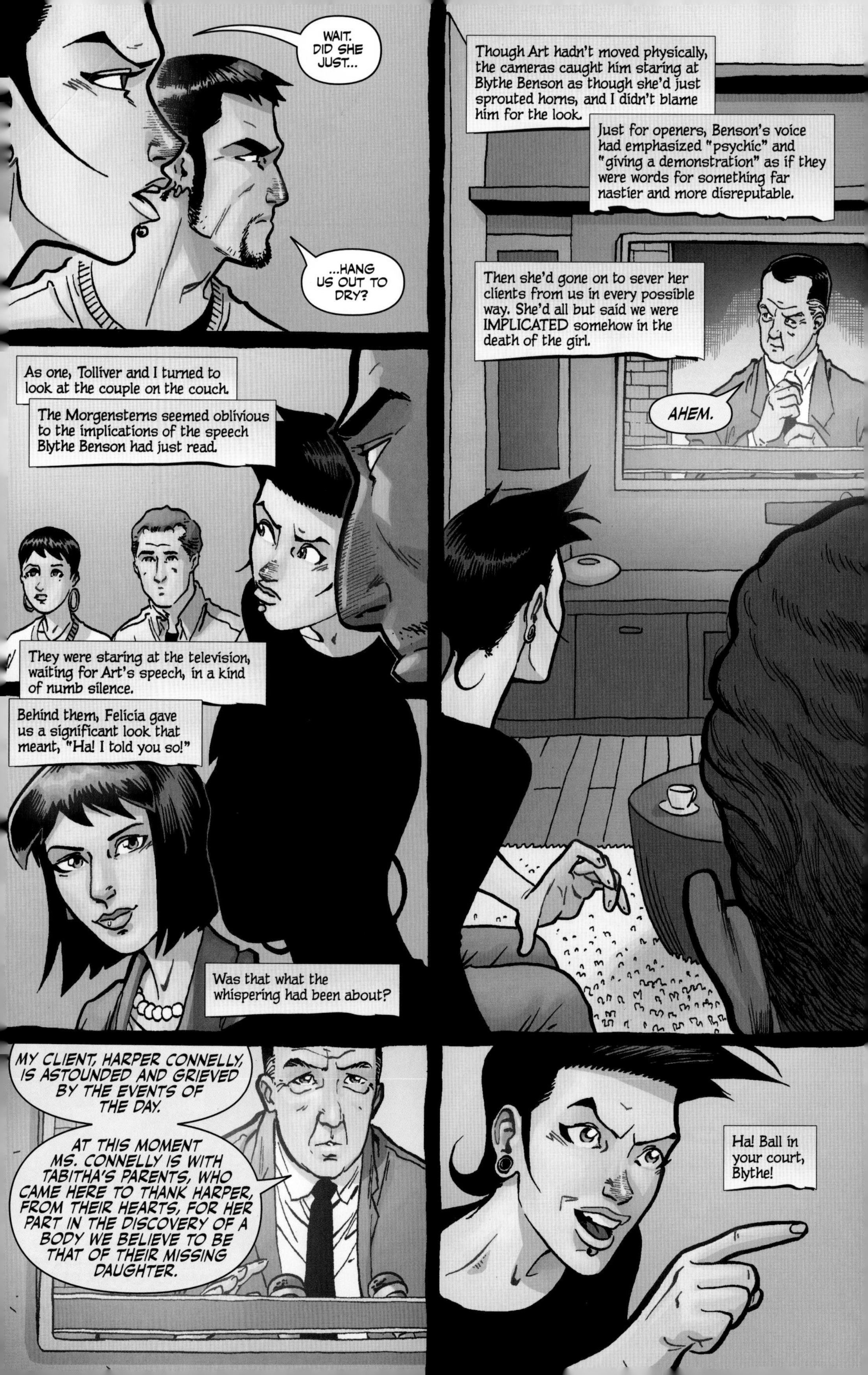
WAIT. DID SHE JUST...
...HANG US OUT TO DRY?
Though Art hadn't moved physically, the cameras caught him staring at Blythe Benson as though she'd just sprouted horns, and I didn't blame him for the look.
Just for openers, Benson's voice had emphasized "psychic" and "giving a demonstration" as if they were words for something far nastier and more disreputable.
Then she'd gone on to sever her clients from us in every possible way. She'd all but said we were IMPLICATED somehow in the death of the girl.
AHEM.
As one, Tolliver and I turned to look at the couple on the couch.
The Morgensterns seemed oblivious to the implications of the speech Blythe Benson had just read.
They were staring at the television, waiting for Art's speech, in a kind of numb silence.
Behind them, Felicia gave us a significant look that meant, "Ha! I told you so!"
Was that what the whispering had been about?
MY CLIENT, HARPER CONNELLY, IS ASTOUNDED AND GRIEVED BY THE EVENTS OF THE DAY.
AT THIS MOMENT MS. CONNELLY IS WITH TABITHA'S PARENTS, WHO CAME HERE TO THANK HARPER, FROM THEIR HEARTS, FOR HER PART IN THE DISCOVERY OF A BODY WE BELIEVE TO BE THAT OF THEIR MISSING DAUGHTER.
Ha! Ball in your court, Blythe!

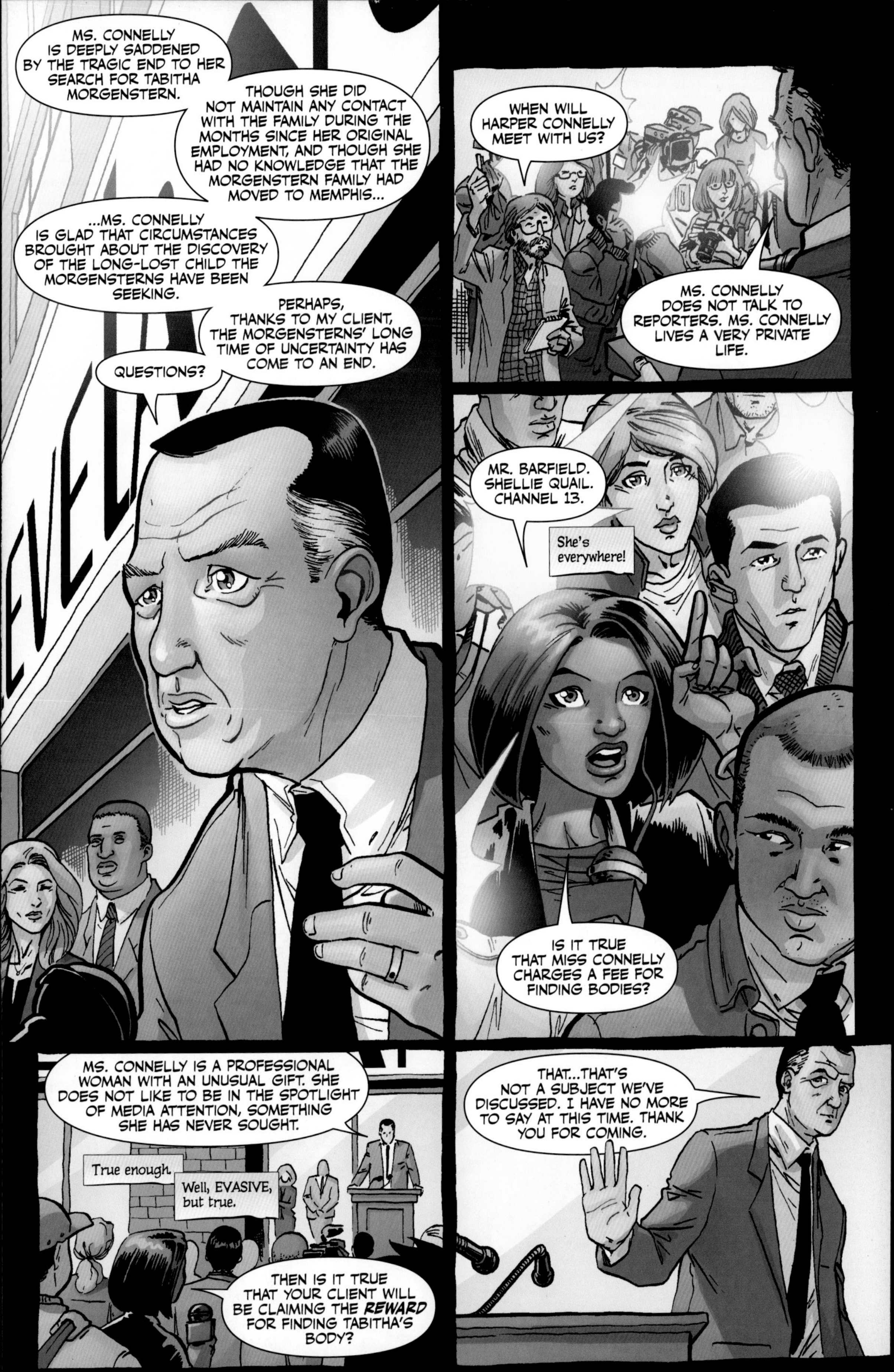
MS. CONNELLY IS DEEPLY SADDENED BY THE TRAGIC END TO HER SEARCH FOR TABITHA MORGENSTERN.
THOUGH SHE DID NOT MAINTAIN ANY CONTACT WITH THE FAMILY DURING THE MONTHS SINCE HER ORIGINAL EMPLOYMENT, AND THOUGH SHE HAD NO KNOWLEDGE THAT THE MORGENSTERN FAMILY HAD MOVED TO MEMPHIS...
...MS. CONNELLY IS GLAD THAT CIRCUMSTANCES BROUGHT ABOUT THE DISCOVERY OF THE LONG-LOST CHILD THE MORGENSTERNS HAVE BEEN SEEKING.
PERHAPS, THANKS TO MY CLIENT, THE MORGENSTERNS' LONG TIME OF UNCERTAINTY HAS COME TO AN END.
QUESTIONS?
WHEN WILL HARPER CONNELLY MEET WITH US?
MS. CONNELLY DOES NOT TALK TO REPORTERS. MS. CONNELLY LIVES A VERY PRIVATE LIFE.
MR. BARFIELD. SHELLIE QUAIL. CHANNEL 13.
She's everywhere!
IS IT TRUE THAT MISS CONNELLY CHARGES A FEE FOR FINDING BODIES?
MS. CONNELLY IS A PROFESSIONAL WOMAN WITH AN UNUSUAL GIFT. SHE DOES NOT LIKE TO BE IN THE SPOTLIGHT OF MEDIA ATTENTION, SOMETHING SHE HAS NEVER SOUGHT.
True enough.
Well, EVASIVE, but true.
THEN IS IT TRUE THAT YOUR CLIENT WILL BE CLAIMING THE REWARD FOR FINDING TABITHA'S BODY?
THAT...THAT'S NOT A SUBJECT WE'VE DISCUSSED. I HAVE NO MORE TO SAY AT THIS TIME. THANK YOU FOR COMING.

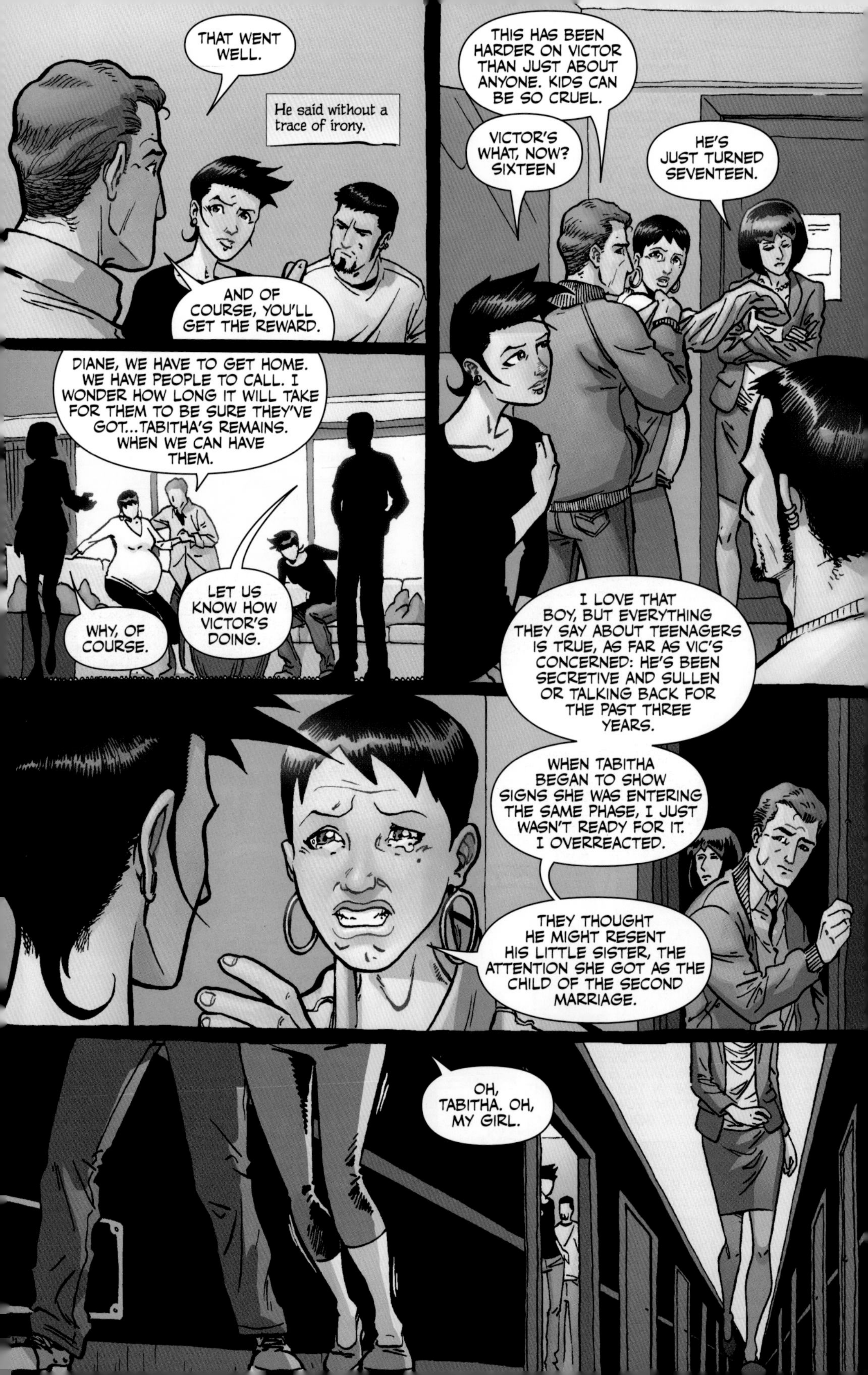
THAT WENT WELL.
He said without a trace of irony.
AND OF COURSE, YOU'LL GET THE REWARD.
DIANE, WE HAVE TO GET HOME. WE HAVE PEOPLE TO CALL. I WONDER HOW LONG IT WILL TAKE FOR THEM TO BE SURE THEY'VE GOT...TABITHA'S REMAINS. WHEN WE CAN HAVE THEM.
LET US KNOW HOW VICTOR'S DOING.
WHY, OF COURSE.
THIS HAS BEEN HARDER ON VICTOR THAN JUST ABOUT ANYONE. KIDS CAN BE SO CRUEL.
VICTOR'S WHAT, NOW? SIXTEEN
HE'S JUST TURNED SEVENTEEN.
I LOVE THAT BOY, BUT EVERYTHING THEY SAY ABOUT TEENAGERS IS TRUE, AS FAR AS VIC'S CONCERNED: HE'S BEEN SECRETIVE AND SULLEN OR TALKING BACK FOR THE PAST THREE YEARS.
WHEN TABITHA BEGAN TO SHOW SIGNS SHE WAS ENTERING THE SAME PHASE, I JUST WASN'T READY FOR IT. I OVERREACTED.
THEY THOUGHT HE MIGHT RESENT HIS LITTLE SISTER, THE ATTENTION SHE GOT AS THE CHILD OF THE SECOND MARRIAGE.
OH, TABITHA. OH, MY GIRL.

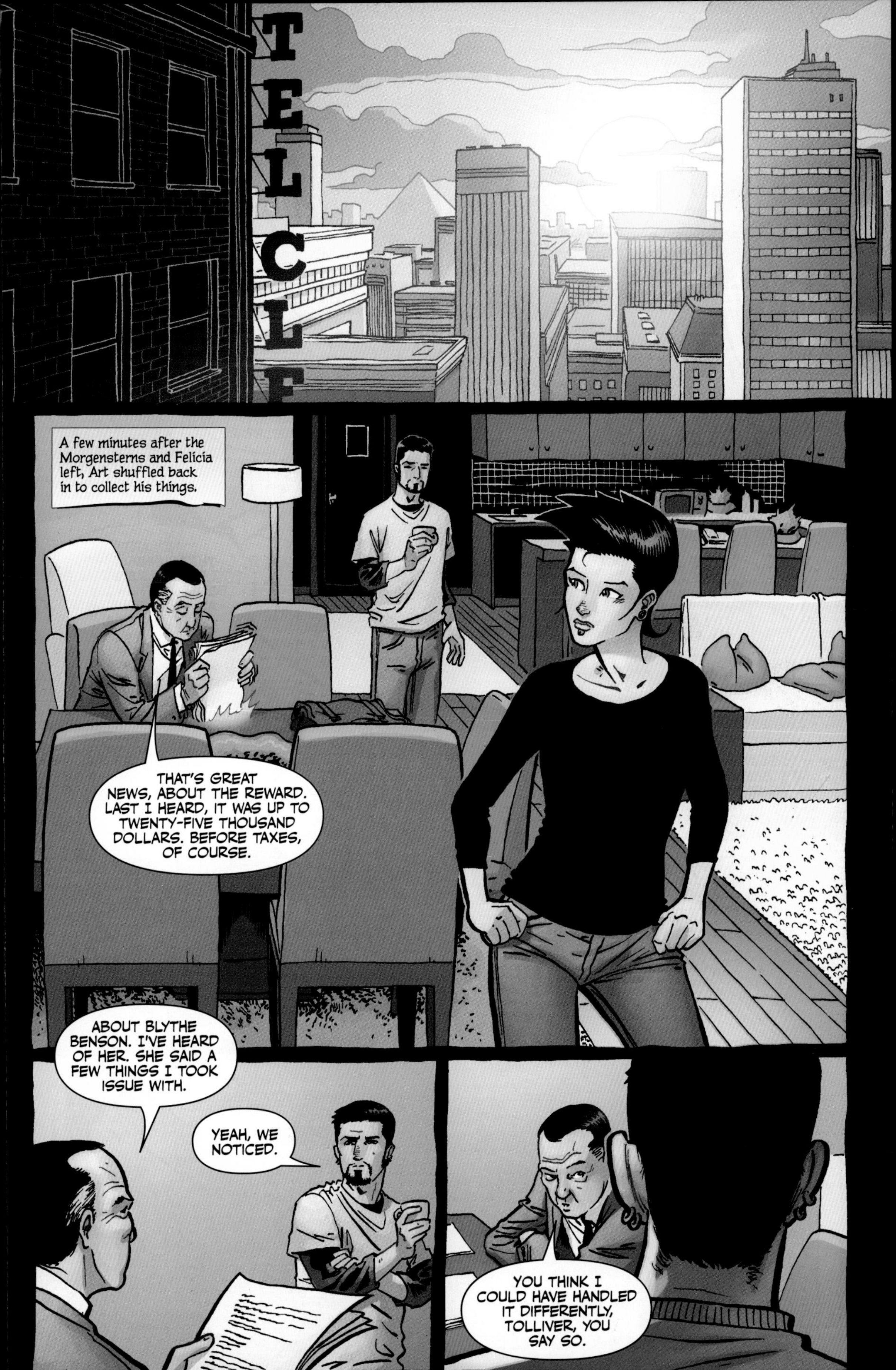

TELCLE
A few minutes after the Morgensterns and Felicia left, Art shuffled back in to collect his things.
THAT'S GREAT NEWS, ABOUT THE REWARD. LAST I HEARD, IT WAS UP TO TWENTY-FIVE THOUSAND DOLLARS. BEFORE TAXES, OF COURSE.
ABOUT BLYTHE BENSON. I'VE HEARD OF HER. SHE SAID A FEW THINGS I TOOK ISSUE WITH.
YEAH, WE NOTICED.
YOU THINK I COULD HAVE HANDLED IT DIFFERENTLY, TOLLIVER, YOU SAY SO.

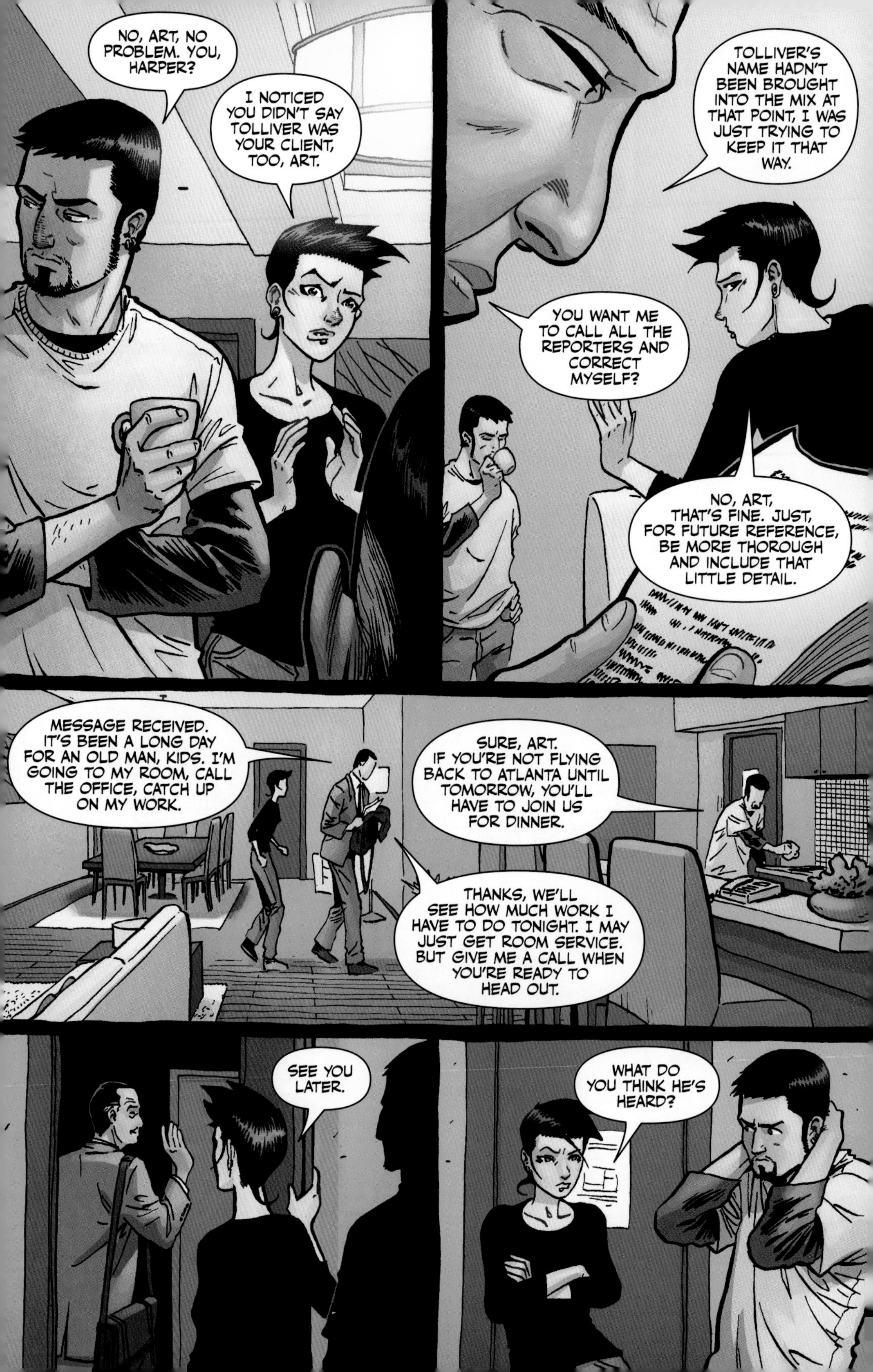
NO, ART, NO PROBLEM. YOU, HARPER?
I NOTICED YOU DIDN'T SAY TOLLIVER WAS YOUR CLIENT, TOO, ART.
TOLLIVER'S NAME HADN'T BEEN BROUGHT INTO THE MIX AT THAT POINT, I WAS JUST TRYING TO KEEP IT THAT WAY.
YOU WANT ME TO CALL ALL THE REPORTERS AND CORRECT MYSELF?
NO, ART, THAT'S FINE. JUST, FOR FUTURE REFERENCE, BE MORE THOROUGH AND INCLUDE THAT LITTLE DETAIL.
MESSAGE RECEIVED. IT'S BEEN A LONG DAY FOR AN OLD MAN, KIDS. I'M GOING TO MY ROOM, CALL THE OFFICE, CATCH UP ON MY WORK.
SURE, ART. IF YOU'RE NOT FLYING BACK TO ATLANTA UNTIL TOMORROW, YOU'LL HAVE TO JOIN US FOR DINNER.
THANKS, WE'LL SEE HOW MUCH WORK I HAVE TO DO TONIGHT. I MAY JUST GET ROOM SERVICE. BUT GIVE ME A CALL WHEN YOU'RE READY TO HEAD OUT.
SEE YOU LATER.
WHAT DO YOU THINK HE'S HEARD?

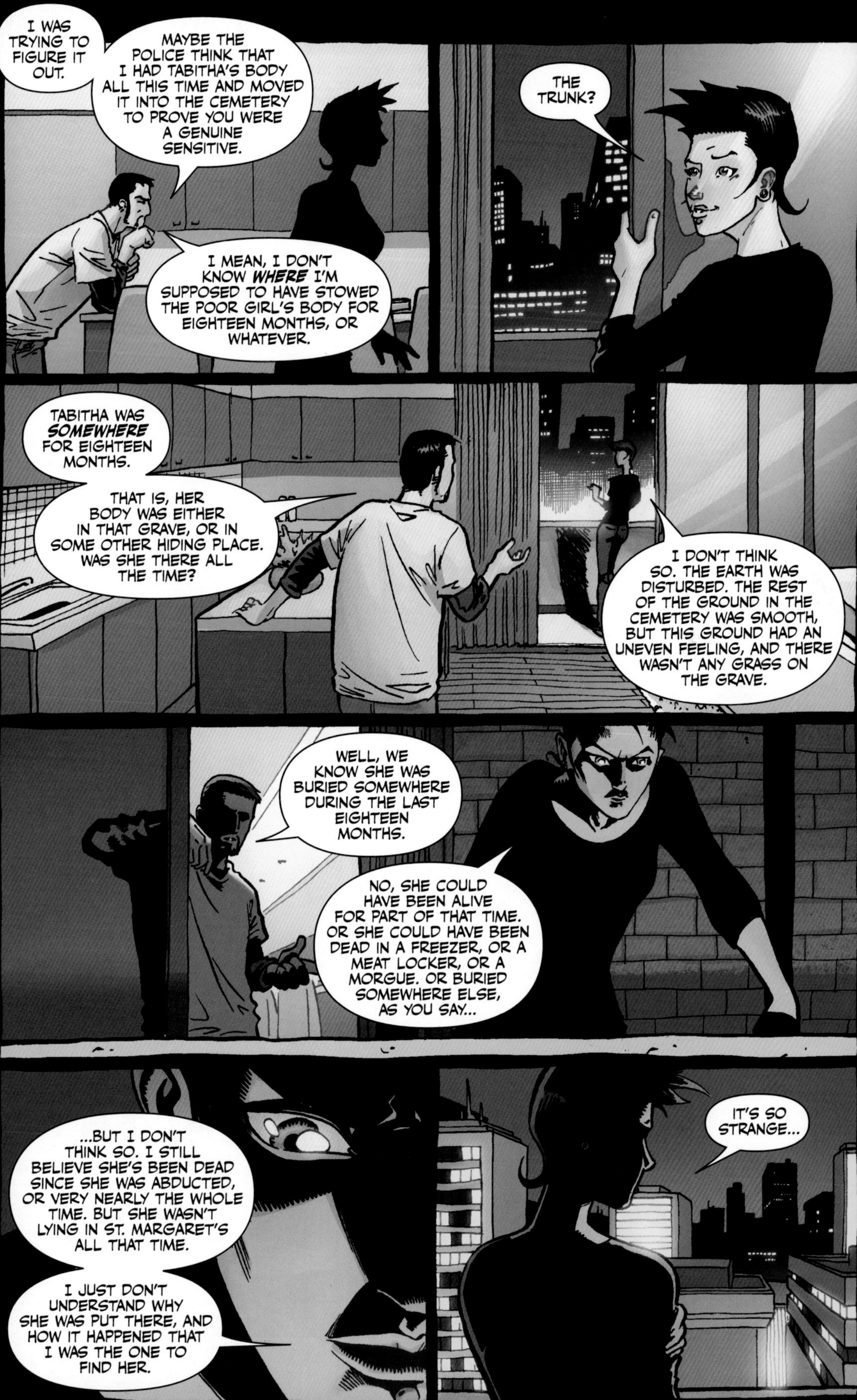

I WAS TRYING TO FIGURE IT OUT.
MAYBE THE POLICE THINK THAT I HAD TABITHA'S BODY ALL THIS TIME AND MOVED IT INTO THE CEMETERY TO PROVE YOU WERE A GENUINE SENSITIVE.
I MEAN, I DON'T KNOW *WHERE* I'M SUPPOSED TO HAVE STOWED THE POOR GIRL'S BODY FOR EIGHTEEN MONTHS, OR WHATEVER.
THE TRUNK?
TABITHA WAS *SOMEWHERE* FOR EIGHTEEN MONTHS.
THAT IS, HER BODY WAS EITHER IN THAT GRAVE, OR IN SOME OTHER HIDING PLACE. WAS SHE THERE ALL THE TIME?
I DON'T THINK SO. THE EARTH WAS DISTURBED. THE REST OF THE GROUND IN THE CEMETERY WAS SMOOTH, BUT THIS GROUND HAD AN UNEVEN FEELING, AND THERE WASN'T ANY GRASS ON THE GRAVE.
WELL, WE KNOW SHE WAS BURIED SOMEWHERE DURING THE LAST EIGHTEEN MONTHS.
NO, SHE COULD HAVE BEEN ALIVE FOR PART OF THAT TIME. OR SHE COULD HAVE BEEN DEAD IN A FREEZER, OR A MEAT LOCKER, OR A MORGUE. OR BURIED SOMEWHERE ELSE, AS YOU SAY...
...BUT I DON'T THINK SO. I STILL BELIEVE SHE'S BEEN DEAD SINCE SHE WAS ABDUCTED, OR VERY NEARLY THE WHOLE TIME. BUT SHE WASN'T LYING IN ST. MARGARET'S ALL THAT TIME.
I JUST DON'T UNDERSTAND WHY SHE WAS PUT THERE, AND HOW IT HAPPENED THAT I WAS THE ONE TO FIND HER.
IT'S SO STRANGE...

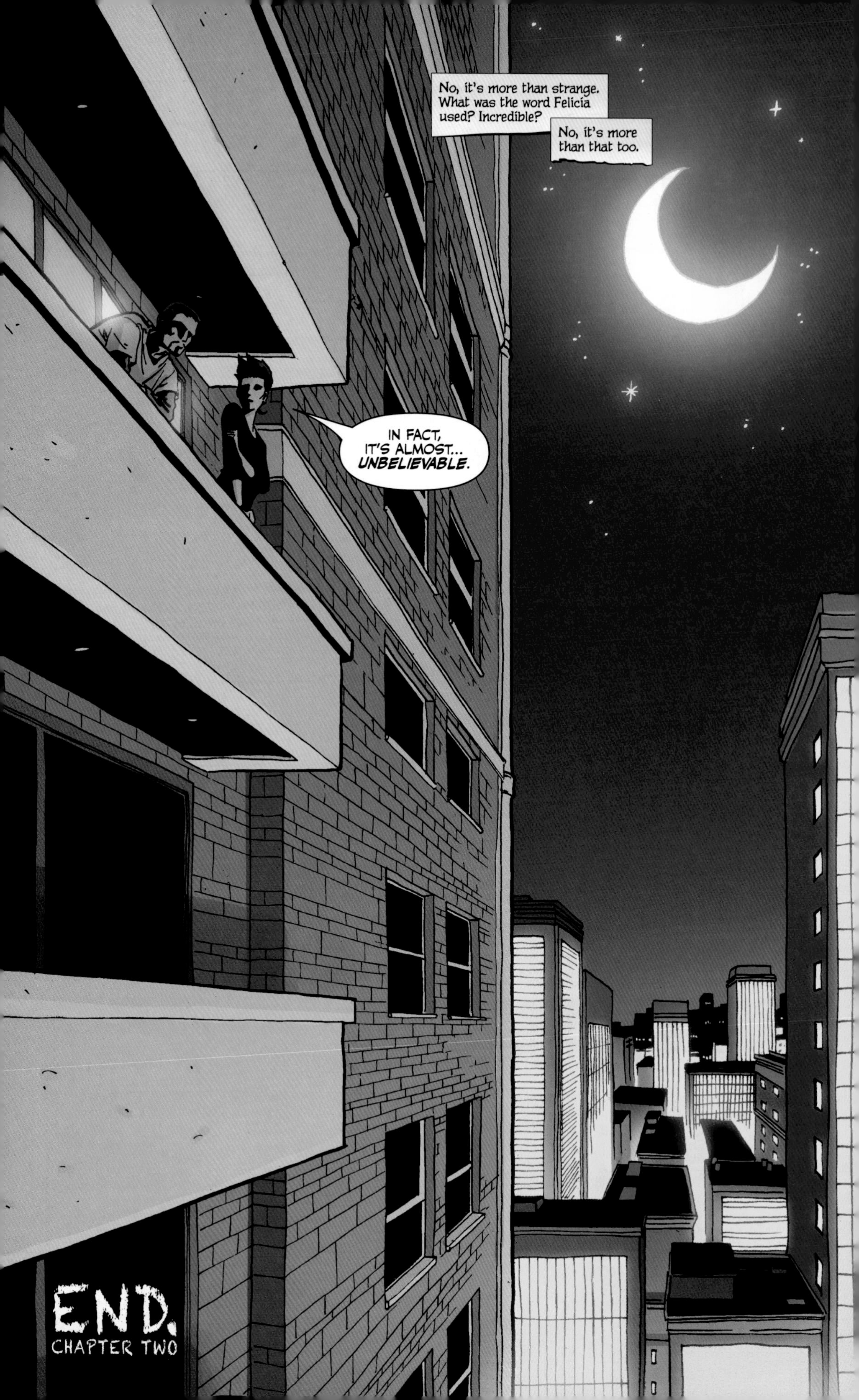
No, it's more than strange. What was the word Felicia used? Incredible?
No, it's more than that too.
IN FACT, IT'S ALMOST... UNBELIEVABLE.
END.
CHAPTER TWO

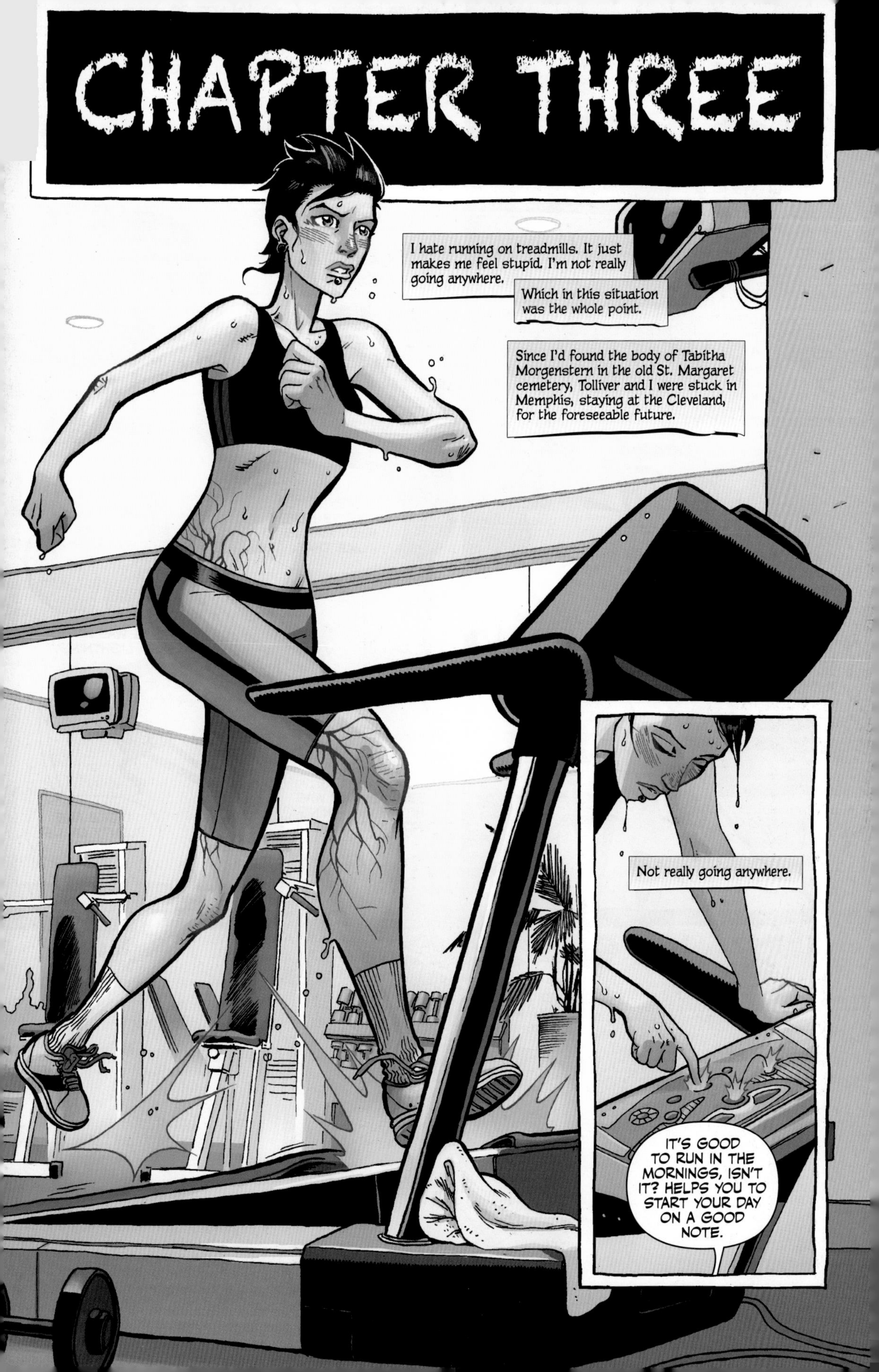
CHAPTER THREE
I hate running on treadmills. It just makes me feel stupid. I'm not really going anywhere.
Which in this situation was the whole point.
Since I'd found the body of Tabitha Morgenstern in the old St. Margaret cemetery, Tolliver and I were stuck in Memphis, staying at the Cleveland, for the foreseeable future.
Not really going anywhere.
IT'S GOOD TO RUN IN THE MORNINGS, ISN'T IT? HELPS YOU TO START YOUR DAY ON A GOOD NOTE.

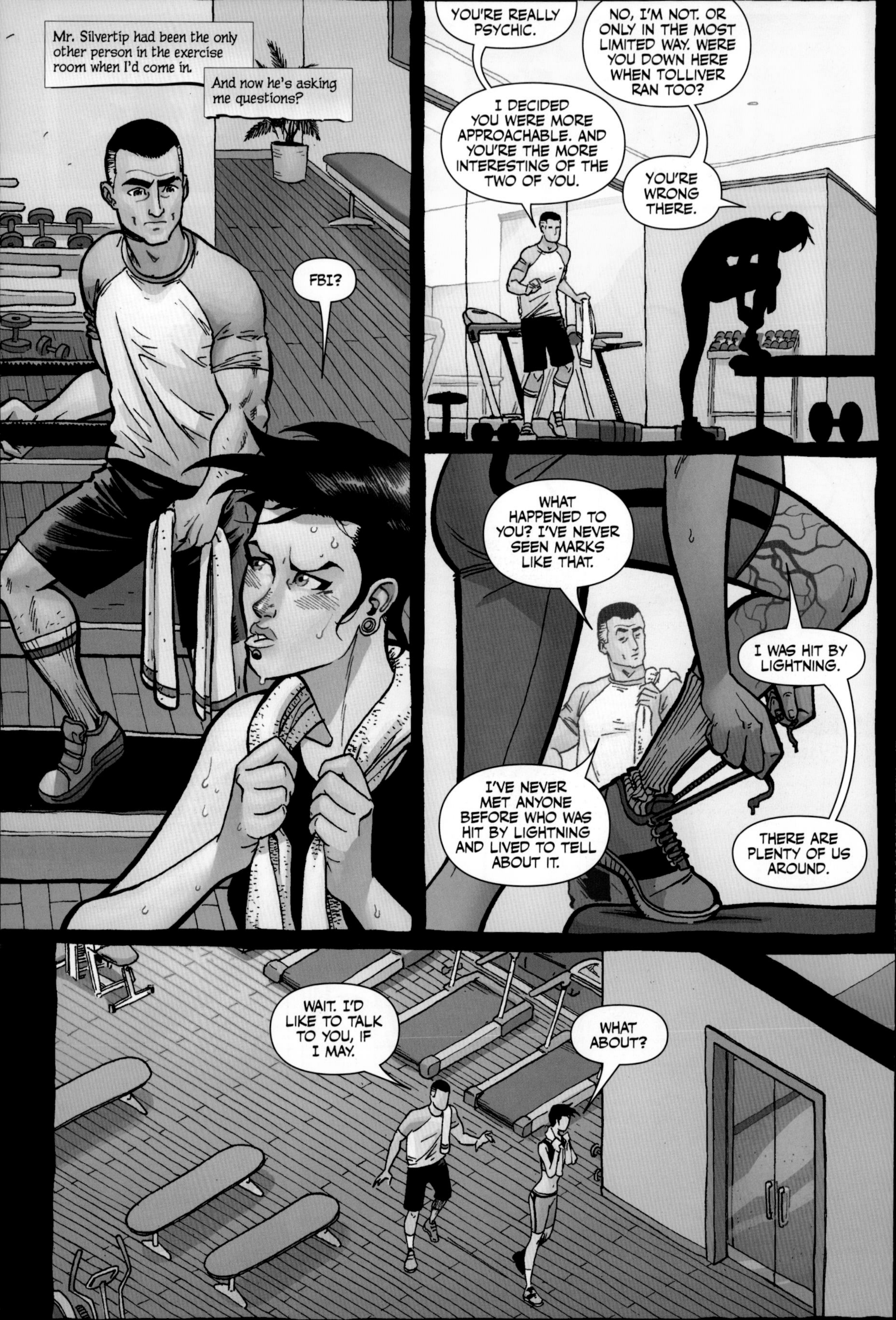
Mr. Silvertip had been the only other person in the exercise room when I'd come in.
And now he's asking me questions?
FBI?
YOU'RE REALLY PSYCHIC.
NO, I'M NOT. OR ONLY IN THE MOST LIMITED WAY. WERE YOU DOWN HERE WHEN TOLLIVER RAN TOO?
I DECIDED YOU WERE MORE APPROACHABLE. AND YOU'RE THE MORE INTERESTING OF THE TWO OF YOU.
YOU'RE WRONG THERE.
WHAT HAPPENED TO YOU? I'VE NEVER SEEN MARKS LIKE THAT.
I WAS HIT BY LIGHTNING.
I'VE NEVER MET ANYONE BEFORE WHO WAS HIT BY LIGHTNING AND LIVED TO TELL ABOUT IT.
THERE ARE PLENTY OF US AROUND.
WAIT. I'D LIKE TO TALK TO YOU, IF I MAY.
WHAT ABOUT?

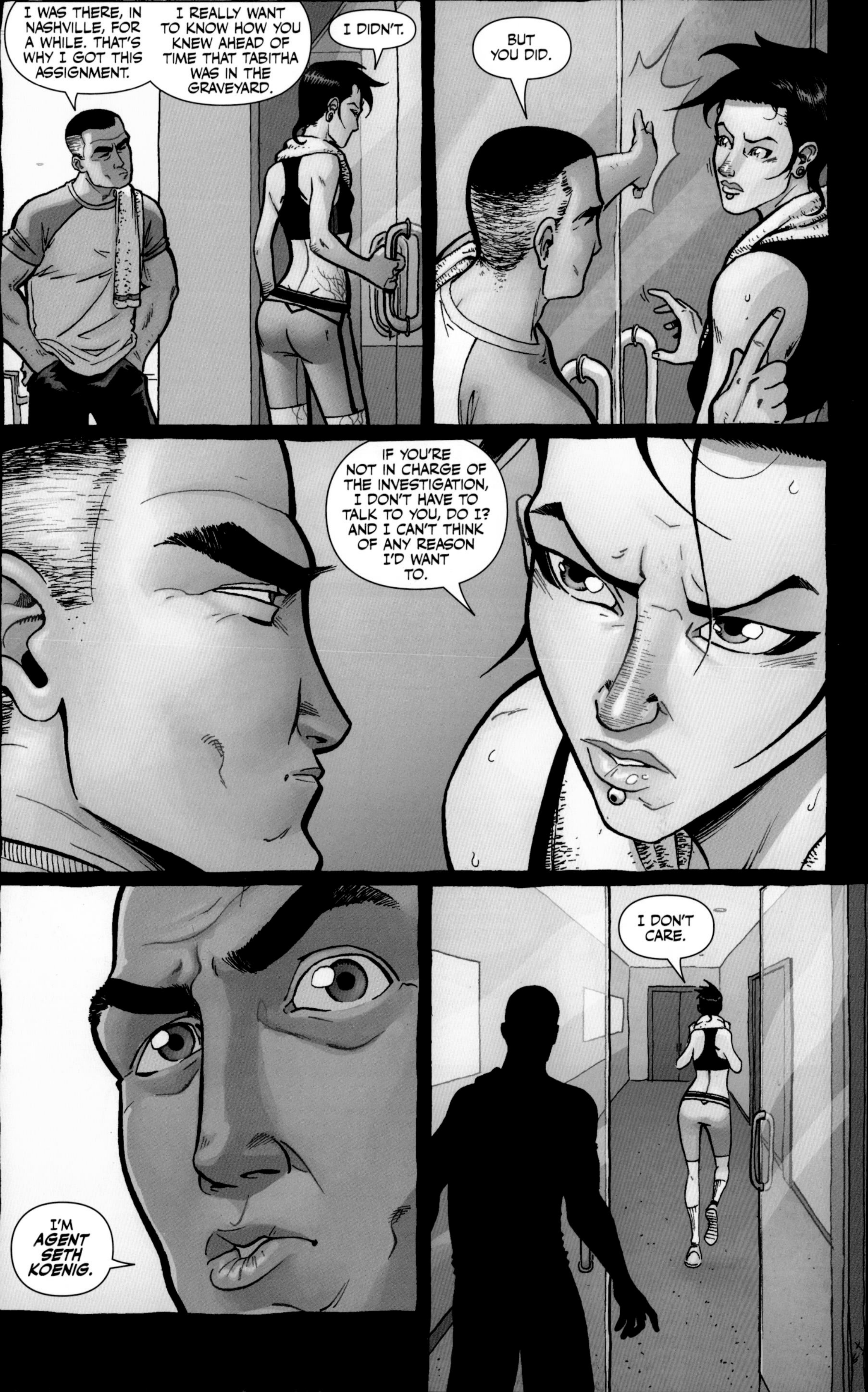
I WAS THERE, IN NASHVILLE, FOR A WHILE. THAT'S WHY I GOT THIS ASSIGNMENT.
I REALLY WANT TO KNOW HOW YOU KNEW AHEAD OF TIME THAT TABITHA WAS IN THE GRAVEYARD.
I DIDN'T.
BUT YOU DID.
IF YOU'RE NOT IN CHARGE OF THE INVESTIGATION, I DON'T HAVE TO TALK TO YOU, DO I? AND I CAN'T THINK OF ANY REASON I'D WANT TO.
I'M AGENT SETH KOENIG.
I DON'T CARE.

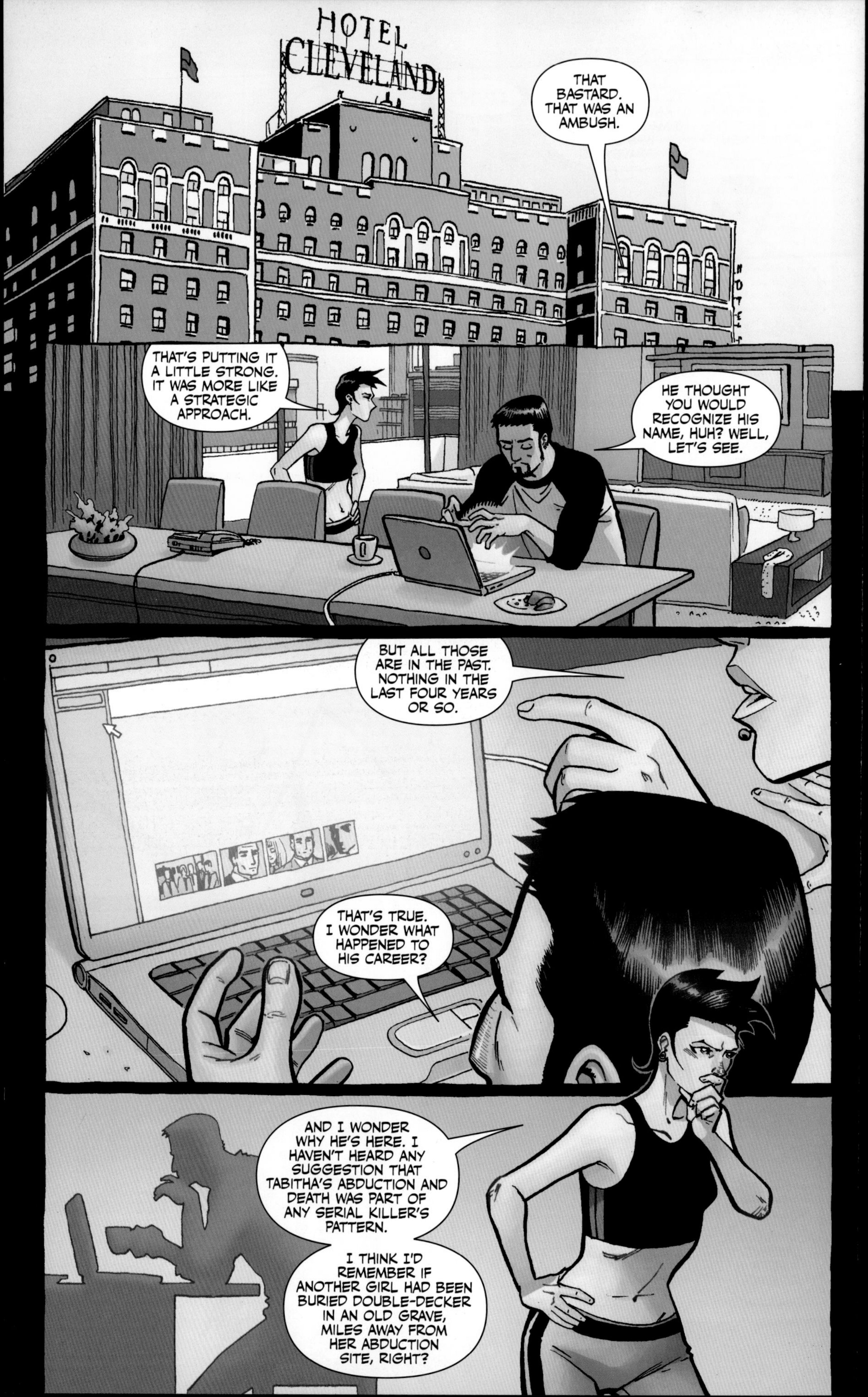
HOTEL CLEVELAND
THAT BASTARD. THAT WAS AN AMBUSH.
THAT'S PUTTING IT A LITTLE STRONG. IT WAS MORE LIKE A STRATEGIC APPROACH.
HE THOUGHT YOU WOULD RECOGNIZE HIS NAME, HUH? WELL, LET'S SEE.
BUT ALL THOSE ARE IN THE PAST. NOTHING IN THE LAST FOUR YEARS OR SO.
THAT'S TRUE. I WONDER WHAT HAPPENED TO HIS CAREER?
AND I WONDER WHY HE'S HERE. I HAVEN'T HEARD ANY SUGGESTION THAT TABITHA'S ABDUCTION AND DEATH WAS PART OF ANY SERIAL KILLER'S PATTERN.
I THINK I'D REMEMBER IF ANOTHER GIRL HAD BEEN BURIED DOUBLE-DECKER IN AN OLD GRAVE, MILES AWAY FROM HER ABDUCTION SITE, RIGHT?

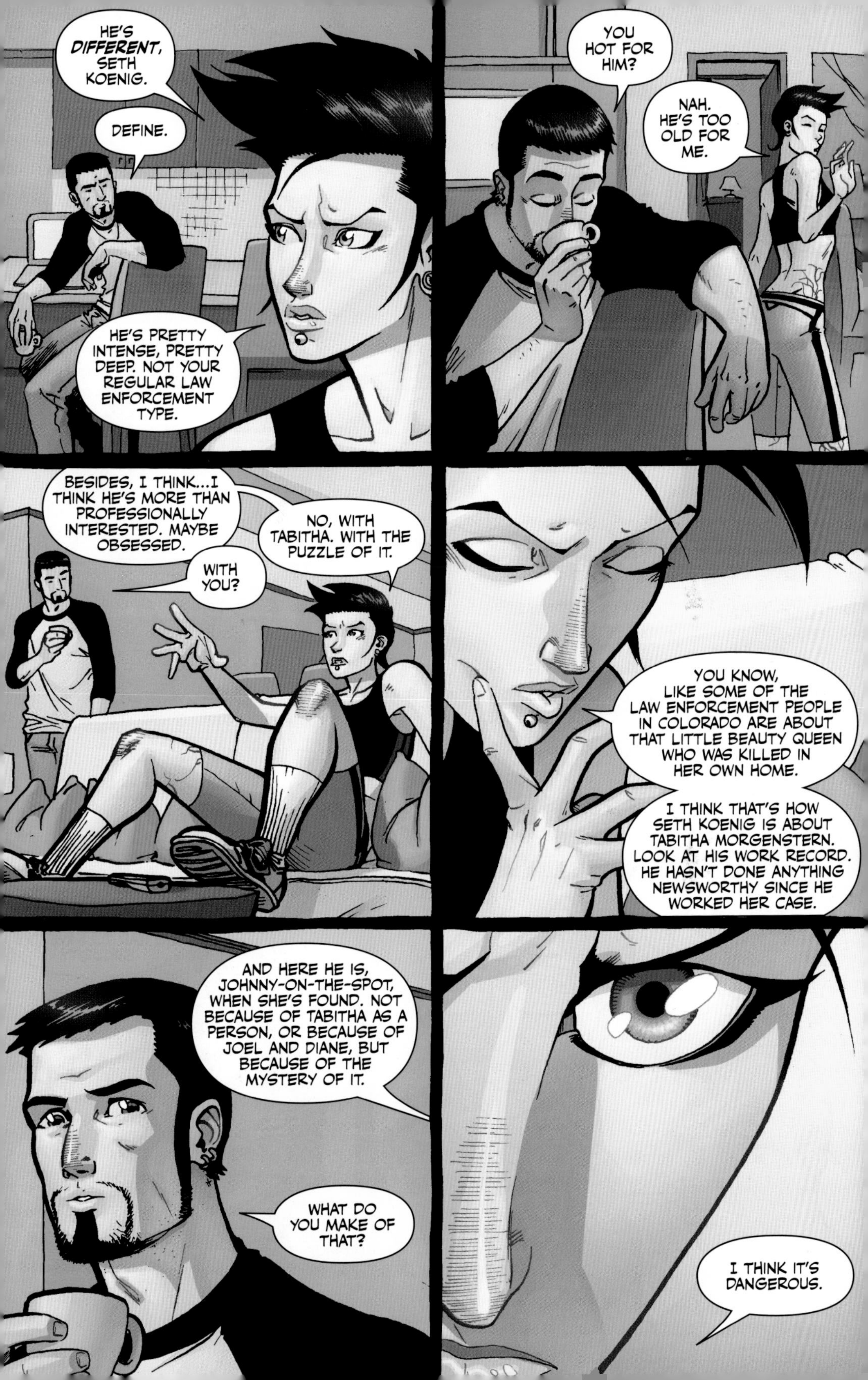

HE'S *DIFFERENT*, SETH KOENIG.
DEFINE.
HE'S PRETTY INTENSE, PRETTY DEEP. NOT YOUR REGULAR LAW ENFORCEMENT TYPE.
YOU HOT FOR HIM?
NAH. HE'S TOO OLD FOR ME.
BESIDES, I THINK...I THINK HE'S MORE THAN PROFESSIONALLY INTERESTED. MAYBE OBSESSED.
WITH YOU?
NO, WITH TABITHA. WITH THE PUZZLE OF IT.
YOU KNOW, LIKE SOME OF THE LAW ENFORCEMENT PEOPLE IN COLORADO ARE ABOUT THAT LITTLE BEAUTY QUEEN WHO WAS KILLED IN HER OWN HOME.
I THINK THAT'S HOW SETH KOENIG IS ABOUT TABITHA MORGENSTERN. LOOK AT HIS WORK RECORD. HE HASN'T DONE ANYTHING NEWSWORTHY SINCE HE WORKED HER CASE.
AND HERE HE IS, JOHNNY-ON-THE-SPOT, WHEN SHE'S FOUND. NOT BECAUSE OF TABITHA AS A PERSON, OR BECAUSE OF JOEL AND DIANE, BUT BECAUSE OF THE MYSTERY OF IT.
WHAT DO YOU MAKE OF THAT?
I THINK IT'S DANGEROUS.

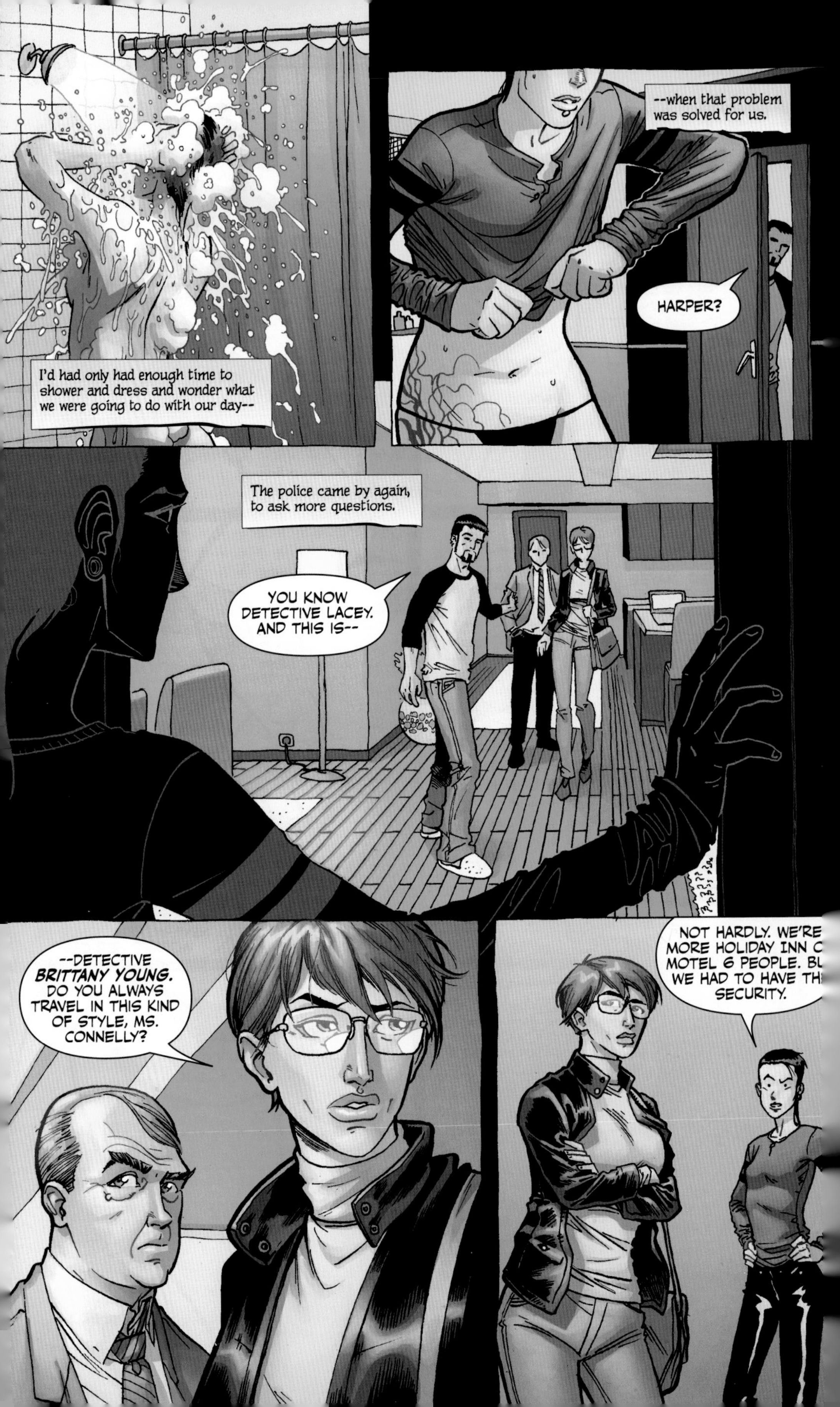
I'd had only had enough time to shower and dress and wonder what we were going to do with our day--
--when that problem was solved for us.
HARPER?
The police came by again, to ask more questions.
YOU KNOW DETECTIVE LACEY. AND THIS IS--
--DETECTIVE BRITTANY YOUNG. DO YOU ALWAYS TRAVEL IN THIS KIND OF STYLE, MS. CONNELLY?
NOT HARDLY. WE'RE MORE HOLIDAY INN OR MOTEL 6 PEOPLE. BUT WE HAD TO HAVE THE SECURITY.

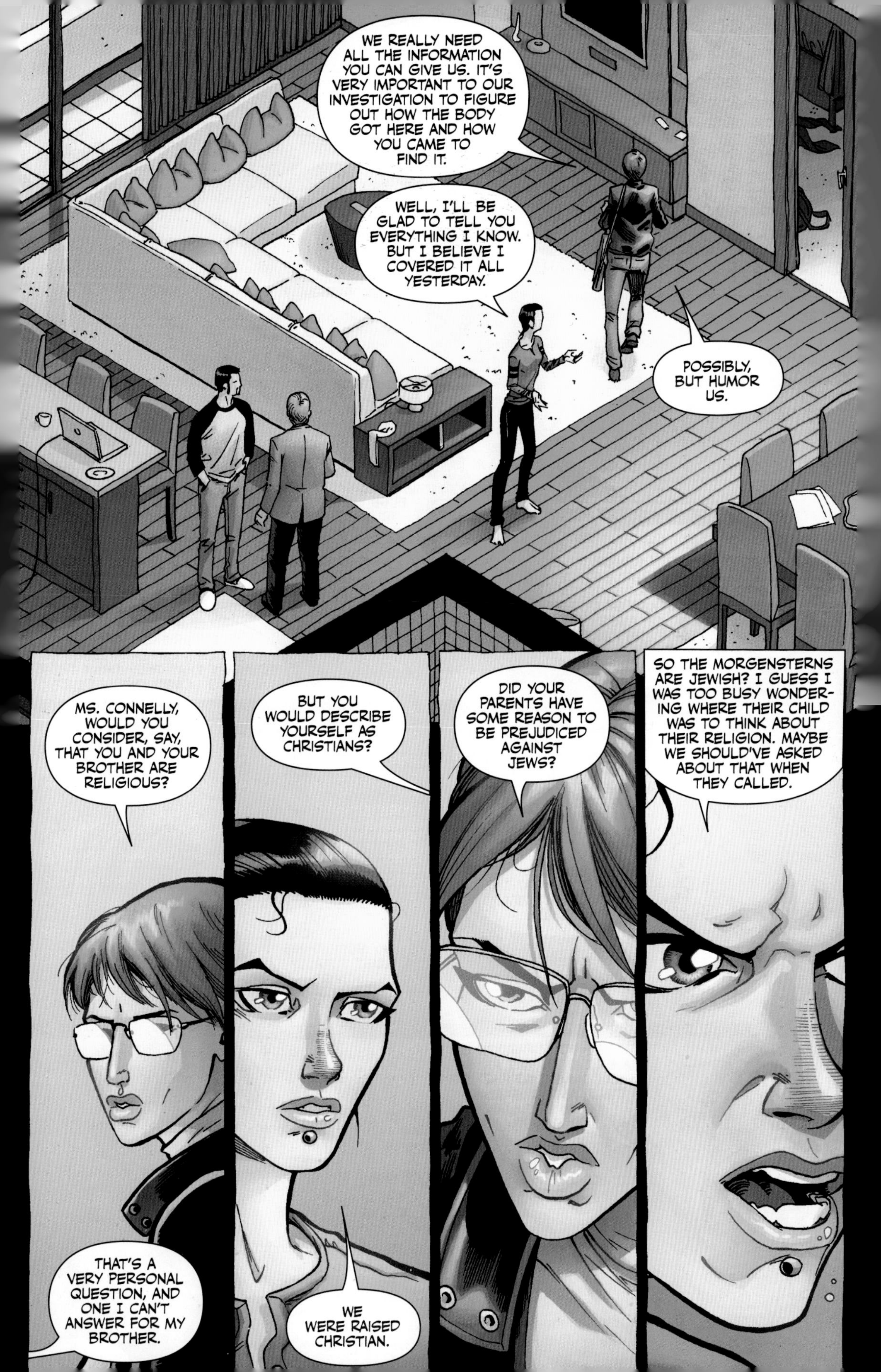
WE REALLY NEED ALL THE INFORMATION YOU CAN GIVE US. IT'S VERY IMPORTANT TO OUR INVESTIGATION TO FIGURE OUT HOW THE BODY GOT HERE AND HOW YOU CAME TO FIND IT.
WELL, I'LL BE GLAD TO TELL YOU EVERYTHING I KNOW. BUT I BELIEVE I COVERED IT ALL YESTERDAY.
POSSIBLY, BUT HUMOR US.
MS. CONNELLY, WOULD YOU CONSIDER, SAY, THAT YOU AND YOUR BROTHER ARE RELIGIOUS?
THAT'S A VERY PERSONAL QUESTION, AND ONE I CAN'T ANSWER FOR MY BROTHER.
BUT YOU WOULD DESCRIBE YOURSELF AS CHRISTIANS?
WE WERE RAISED CHRISTIAN.
DID YOUR PARENTS HAVE SOME REASON TO BE PREJUDICED AGAINST JEWS?
SO THE MORGENSTERNS ARE JEWISH? I GUESS I WAS TOO BUSY WONDERING WHERE THEIR CHILD WAS TO THINK ABOUT THEIR RELIGION. MAYBE WE SHOULD'VE ASKED ABOUT THAT WHEN THEY CALLED.

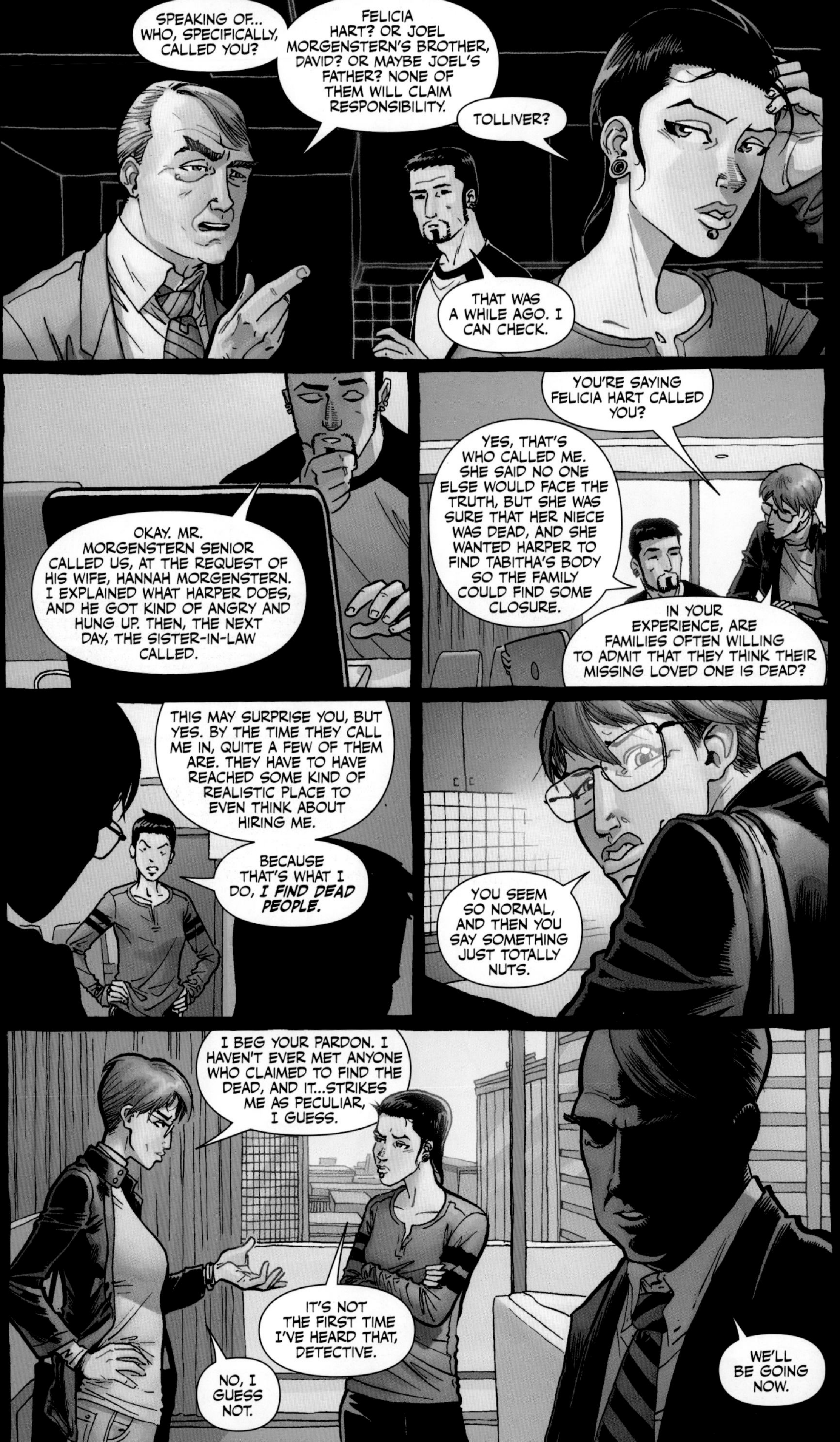

SPEAKING OF... WHO, SPECIFICALLY, CALLED YOU?
FELICIA HART? OR JOEL MORGENSTERN'S BROTHER, DAVID? OR MAYBE JOEL'S FATHER? NONE OF THEM WILL CLAIM RESPONSIBILITY.
TOLLIVER?
THAT WAS A WHILE AGO. I CAN CHECK.
OKAY. MR. MORGENSTERN SENIOR CALLED US, AT THE REQUEST OF HIS WIFE, HANNAH MORGENSTERN. I EXPLAINED WHAT HARPER DOES, AND HE GOT KIND OF ANGRY AND HUNG UP. THEN, THE NEXT DAY, THE SISTER-IN-LAW CALLED.
YOU'RE SAYING FELICIA HART CALLED YOU?
YES, THAT'S WHO CALLED ME. SHE SAID NO ONE ELSE WOULD FACE THE TRUTH, BUT SHE WAS SURE THAT HER NIECE WAS DEAD, AND SHE WANTED HARPER TO FIND TABITHA'S BODY SO THE FAMILY COULD FIND SOME CLOSURE.
IN YOUR EXPERIENCE, ARE FAMILIES OFTEN WILLING TO ADMIT THAT THEY THINK THEIR MISSING LOVED ONE IS DEAD?
THIS MAY SURPRISE YOU, BUT YES. BY THE TIME THEY CALL ME IN, QUITE A FEW OF THEM ARE. THEY HAVE TO HAVE REACHED SOME KIND OF REALISTIC PLACE TO EVEN THINK ABOUT HIRING ME.
BECAUSE THAT'S WHAT I DO, *I FIND DEAD PEOPLE.*
YOU SEEM SO NORMAL, AND THEN YOU SAY SOMETHING JUST TOTALLY NUTS.
I BEG YOUR PARDON. I HAVEN'T EVER MET ANYONE WHO CLAIMED TO FIND THE DEAD, AND IT...STRIKES ME AS PECULIAR, I GUESS.
IT'S NOT THE FIRST TIME I'VE HEARD THAT, DETECTIVE.
NO, I GUESS NOT.
WE'LL BE GOING NOW.

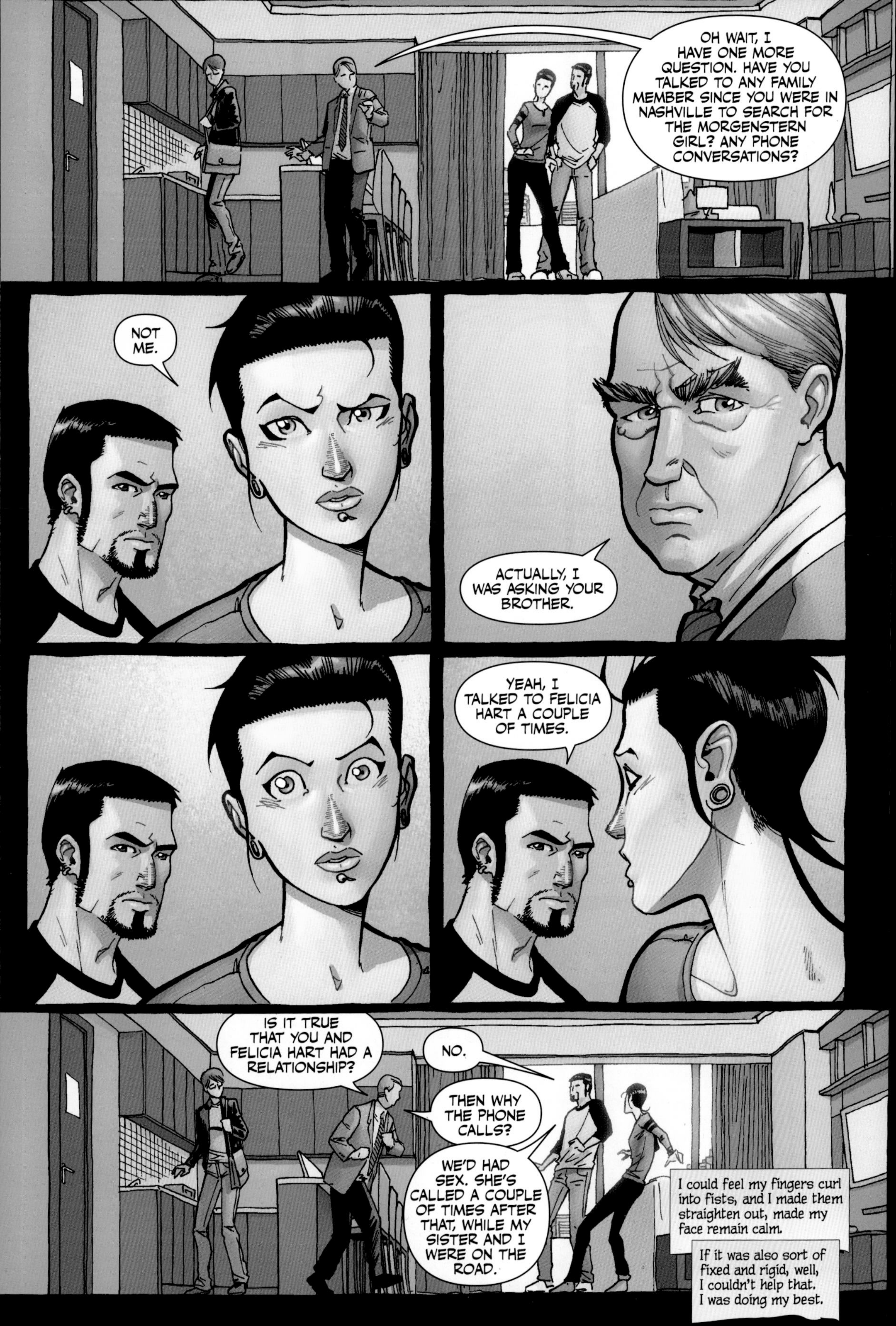
OH WAIT, I HAVE ONE MORE QUESTION. HAVE YOU TALKED TO ANY FAMILY MEMBER SINCE YOU WERE IN NASHVILLE TO SEARCH FOR THE MORGENSTERN GIRL? ANY PHONE CONVERSATIONS?
NOT ME.
ACTUALLY, I WAS ASKING YOUR BROTHER.
YEAH, I TALKED TO FELICIA HART A COUPLE OF TIMES.
IS IT TRUE THAT YOU AND FELICIA HART HAD A RELATIONSHIP?
NO.
THEN WHY THE PHONE CALLS?
WE'D HAD SEX. SHE'S CALLED A COUPLE OF TIMES AFTER THAT, WHILE MY SISTER AND I WERE ON THE ROAD.
I could feel my fingers curl into fists, and I made them straighten out, made my face remain calm.
If it was also sort of fixed and rigid, well, I couldn't help that. I was doing my best.

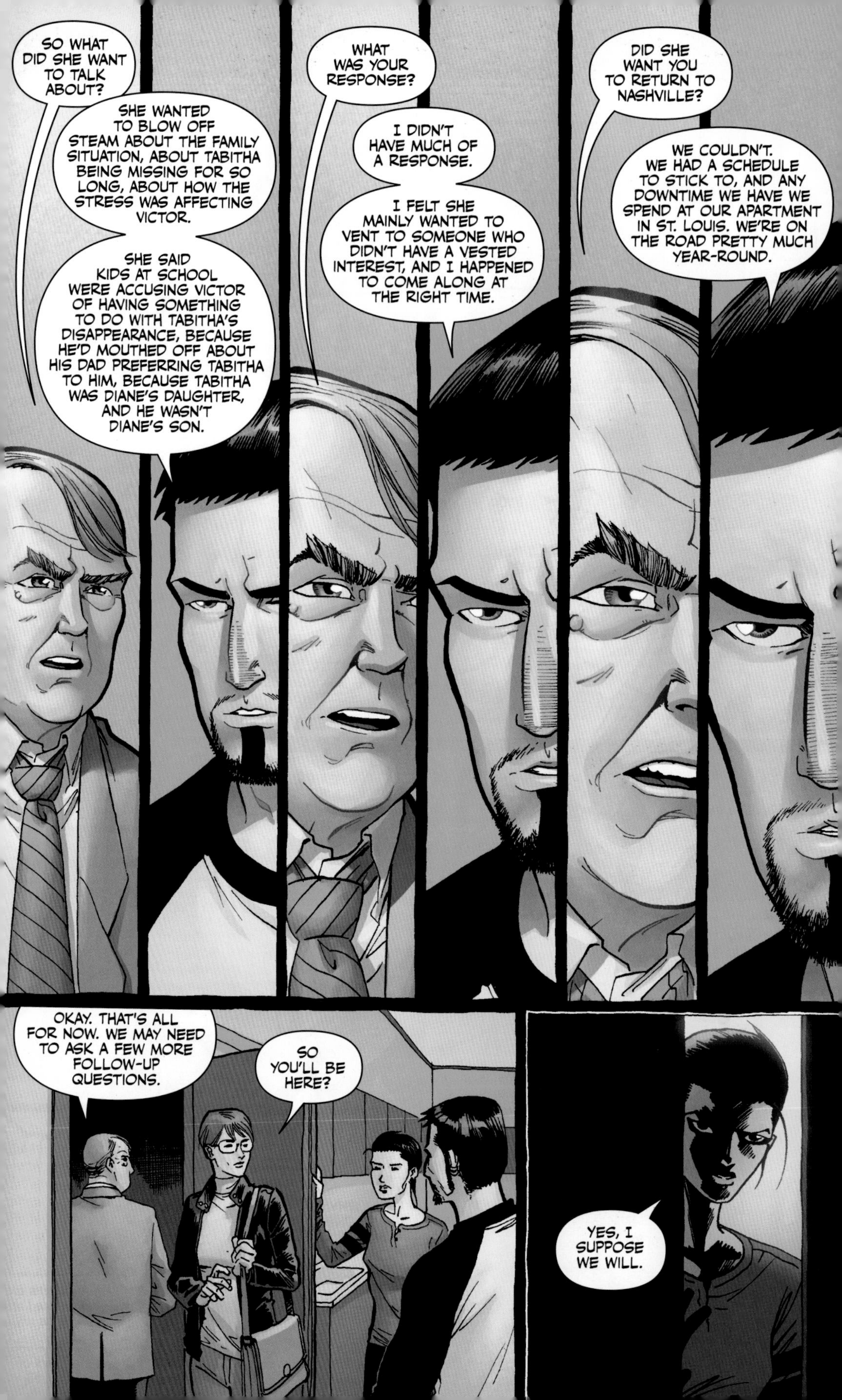
SO WHAT DID SHE WANT TO TALK ABOUT?
SHE WANTED TO BLOW OFF STEAM ABOUT THE FAMILY SITUATION, ABOUT TABITHA BEING MISSING FOR SO LONG, ABOUT HOW THE STRESS WAS AFFECTING VICTOR.
SHE SAID KIDS AT SCHOOL WERE ACCUSING VICTOR OF HAVING SOMETHING TO DO WITH TABITHA'S DISAPPEARANCE, BECAUSE HE'D MOUTHED OFF ABOUT HIS DAD PREFERRING TABITHA TO HIM, BECAUSE TABITHA WAS DIANE'S DAUGHTER, AND HE WASN'T DIANE'S SON.
WHAT WAS YOUR RESPONSE?
I DIDN'T HAVE MUCH OF A RESPONSE.
I FELT SHE MAINLY WANTED TO VENT TO SOMEONE WHO DIDN'T HAVE A VESTED INTEREST, AND I HAPPENED TO COME ALONG AT THE RIGHT TIME.
DID SHE WANT YOU TO RETURN TO NASHVILLE?
WE COULDN'T. WE HAD A SCHEDULE TO STICK TO, AND ANY DOWNTIME WE HAVE WE SPEND AT OUR APARTMENT IN ST. LOUIS. WE'RE ON THE ROAD PRETTY MUCH YEAR-ROUND.
OKAY. THAT'S ALL FOR NOW. WE MAY NEED TO ASK A FEW MORE FOLLOW-UP QUESTIONS.
SO YOU'LL BE HERE?
YES, I SUPPOSE WE WILL.

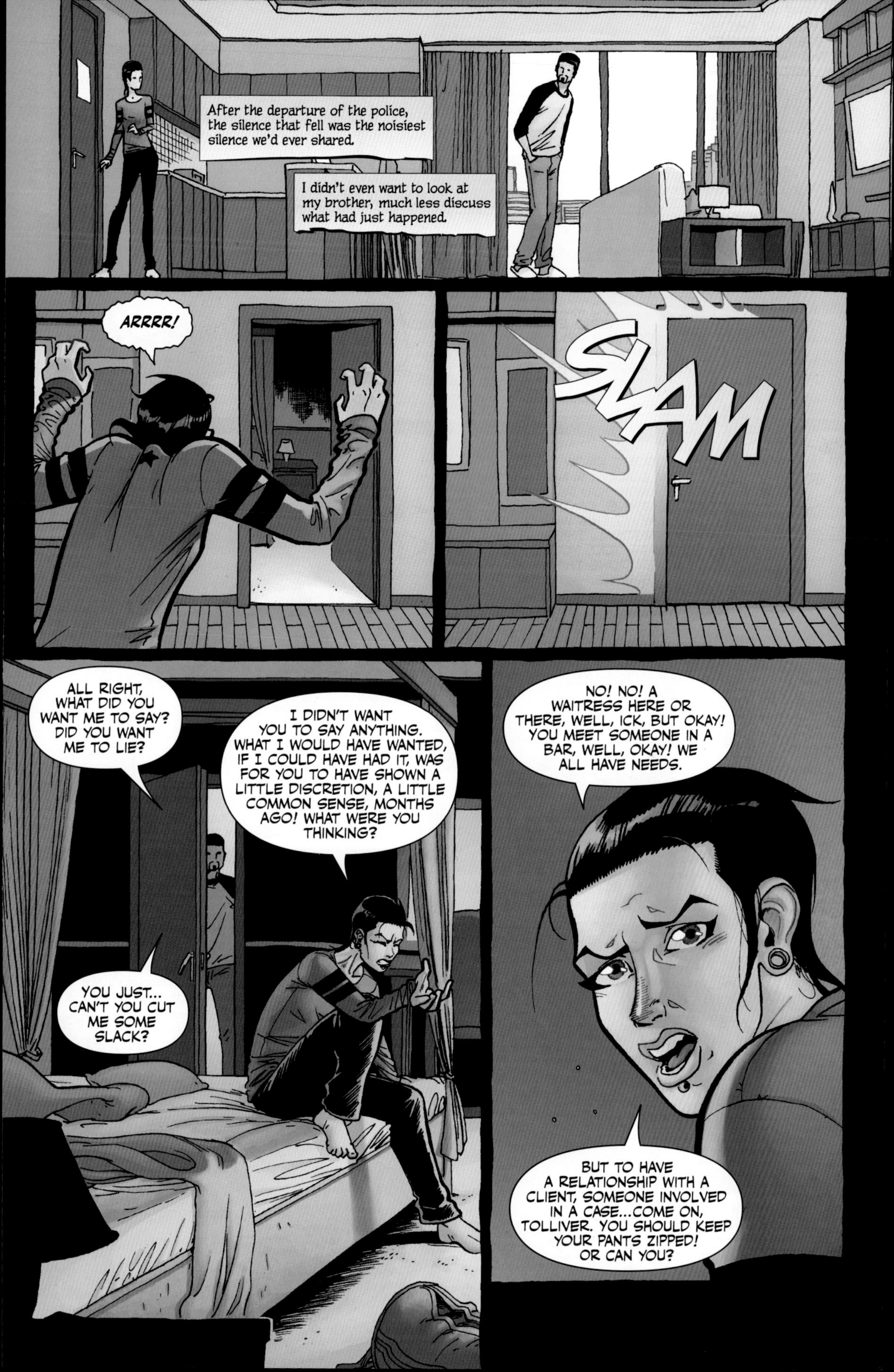
After the departure of the police, the silence that fell was the noisiest silence we'd ever shared.
I didn't even want to look at my brother, much less discuss what had just happened.
ARRRR!
SLAM
ALL RIGHT, WHAT DID YOU WANT ME TO SAY? DID YOU WANT ME TO LIE?
I DIDN'T WANT YOU TO SAY ANYTHING. WHAT I WOULD HAVE WANTED, IF I COULD HAVE HAD IT, WAS FOR YOU TO HAVE SHOWN A LITTLE DISCRETION, A LITTLE COMMON SENSE, MONTHS AGO! WHAT WERE YOU THINKING?
YOU JUST... CAN'T YOU CUT ME SOME SLACK?
NO! NO! A WAITRESS HERE OR THERE, WELL, ICK, BUT OKAY! YOU MEET SOMEONE IN A BAR, WELL, OKAY! WE ALL HAVE NEEDS.
BUT TO HAVE A RELATIONSHIP WITH A CLIENT, SOMEONE INVOLVED IN A CASE...COME ON, TOLLIVER. YOU SHOULD KEEP YOUR PANTS ZIPPED! OR CAN YOU?

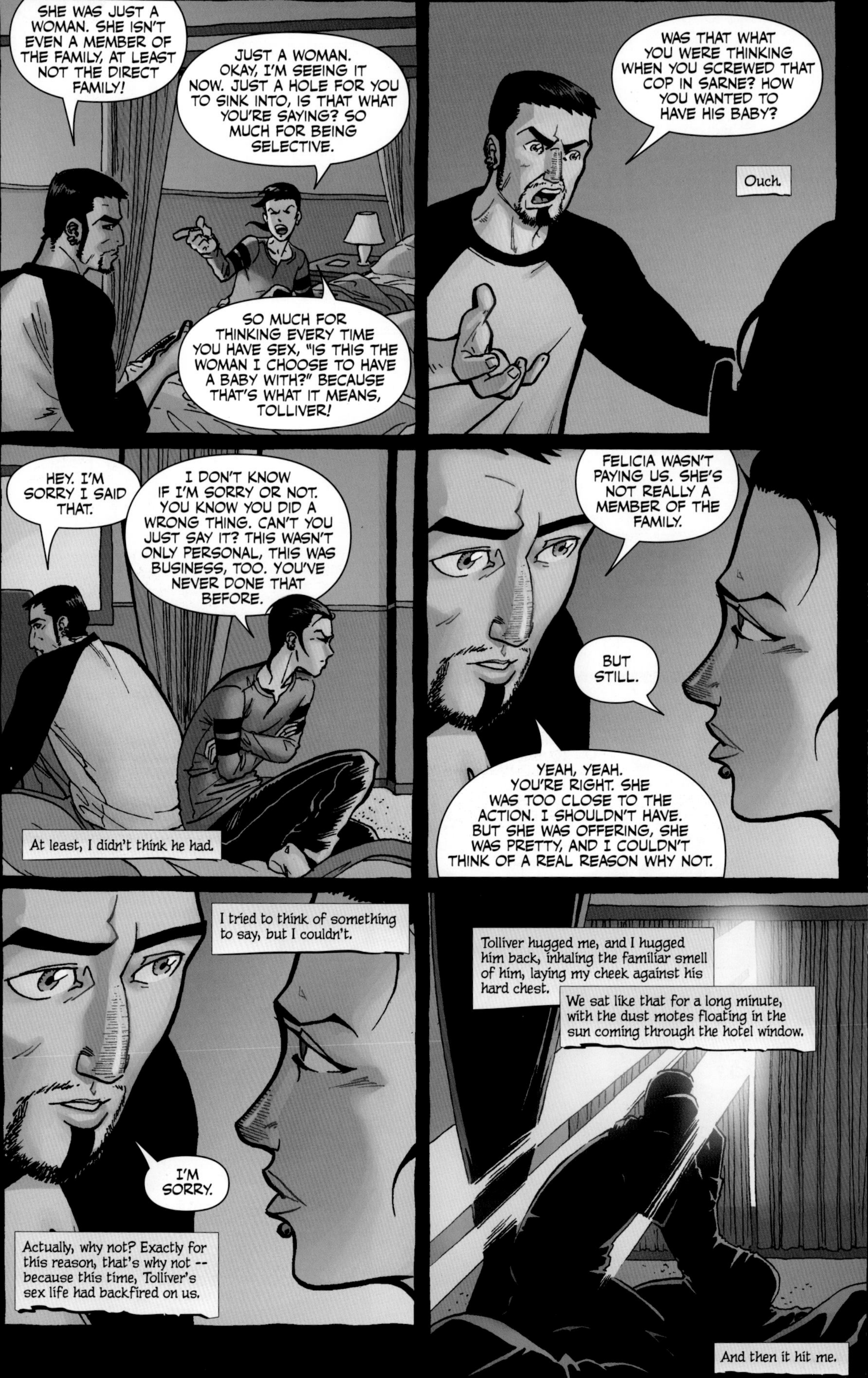
SHE WAS JUST A WOMAN. SHE ISN'T EVEN A MEMBER OF THE FAMILY, AT LEAST NOT THE DIRECT FAMILY!
JUST A WOMAN. OKAY, I'M SEEING IT NOW. JUST A HOLE FOR YOU TO SINK INTO, IS THAT WHAT YOU'RE SAYING? SO MUCH FOR BEING SELECTIVE.
SO MUCH FOR THINKING EVERY TIME YOU HAVE SEX, "IS THIS THE WOMAN I CHOOSE TO HAVE A BABY WITH?" BECAUSE THAT'S WHAT IT MEANS, TOLLIVER!
WAS THAT WHAT YOU WERE THINKING WHEN YOU SCREWED THAT COP IN SARNE? HOW YOU WANTED TO HAVE HIS BABY?
Ouch.
HEY. I'M SORRY I SAID THAT.
I DON'T KNOW IF I'M SORRY OR NOT. YOU KNOW YOU DID A WRONG THING. CAN'T YOU JUST SAY IT? THIS WASN'T ONLY PERSONAL, THIS WAS BUSINESS, TOO. YOU'VE NEVER DONE THAT BEFORE.
At least, I didn't think he had.
FELICIA WASN'T PAYING US. SHE'S NOT REALLY A MEMBER OF THE FAMILY.
BUT STILL.
YEAH, YEAH. YOU'RE RIGHT. SHE WAS TOO CLOSE TO THE ACTION. I SHOULDN'T HAVE. BUT SHE WAS OFFERING, SHE WAS PRETTY, AND I COULDN'T THINK OF A REAL REASON WHY NOT.
I tried to think of something to say, but I couldn't.
I'M SORRY.
Actually, why not? Exactly for this reason, that's why not -- because this time, Tolliver's sex life had backfired on us.
Tolliver hugged me, and I hugged him back, inhaling the familiar smell of him, laying my cheek against his hard chest.
We sat like that for a long minute, with the dust motes floating in the sun coming through the hotel window.
And then it hit me.

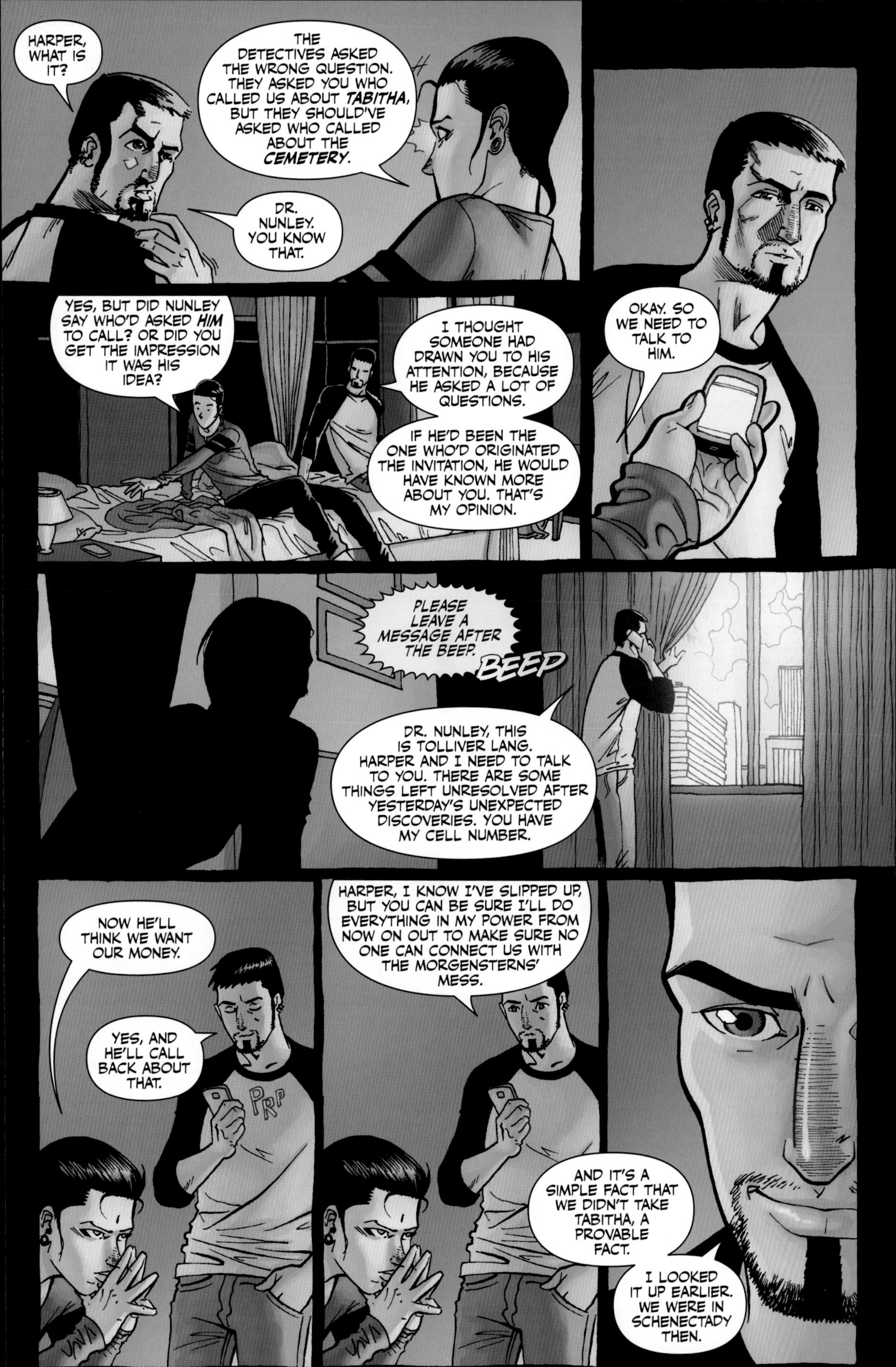
HARPER, WHAT IS IT?
THE DETECTIVES ASKED THE WRONG QUESTION. THEY ASKED YOU WHO CALLED US ABOUT *TABITHA*, BUT THEY SHOULD'VE ASKED WHO CALLED ABOUT THE *CEMETERY*.
DR. NUNLEY. YOU KNOW THAT.
YES, BUT DID NUNLEY SAY WHO'D ASKED *HIM* TO CALL? OR DID YOU GET THE IMPRESSION IT WAS HIS IDEA?
I THOUGHT SOMEONE HAD DRAWN YOU TO HIS ATTENTION, BECAUSE HE ASKED A LOT OF QUESTIONS.
IF HE'D BEEN THE ONE WHO'D ORIGINATED THE INVITATION, HE WOULD HAVE KNOWN MORE ABOUT YOU. THAT'S MY OPINION.
OKAY. SO WE NEED TO TALK TO HIM.
PLEASE LEAVE A MESSAGE AFTER THE BEEP.
BEEP
DR. NUNLEY, THIS IS TOLLIVER LANG. HARPER AND I NEED TO TALK TO YOU. THERE ARE SOME THINGS LEFT UNRESOLVED AFTER YESTERDAY'S UNEXPECTED DISCOVERIES. YOU HAVE MY CELL NUMBER.
NOW HE'LL THINK WE WANT OUR MONEY.
YES, AND HE'LL CALL BACK ABOUT THAT.
HARPER, I KNOW I'VE SLIPPED UP, BUT YOU CAN BE SURE I'LL DO EVERYTHING IN MY POWER FROM NOW ON OUT TO MAKE SURE NO ONE CAN CONNECT US WITH THE MORGENSTERNS' MESS.
AND IT'S A SIMPLE FACT THAT WE DIDN'T TAKE TABITHA, A PROVABLE FACT.
I LOOKED IT UP EARLIER. WE WERE IN SCHENECTADY THEN.

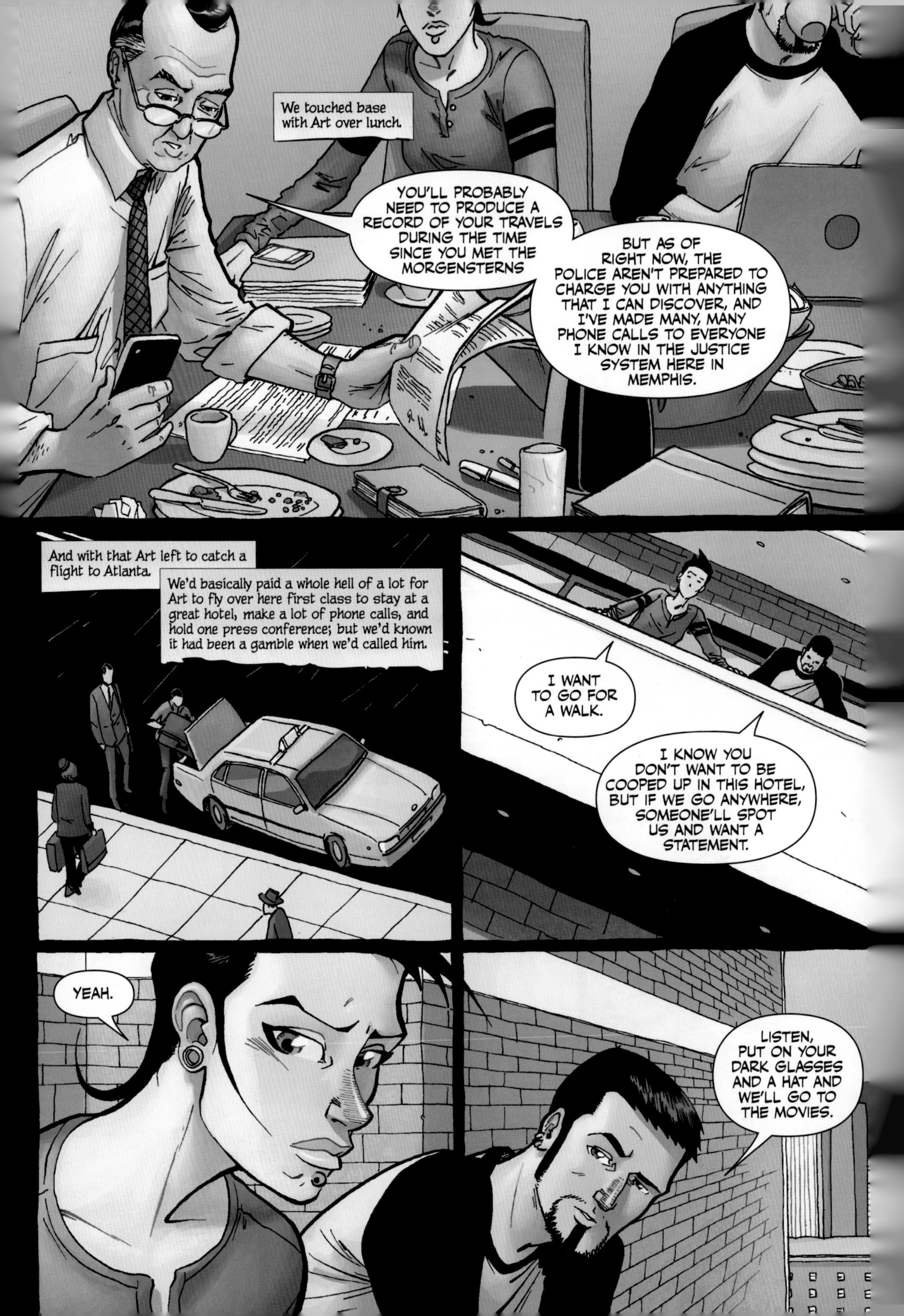

We touched base with Art over lunch.
YOU'LL PROBABLY NEED TO PRODUCE A RECORD OF YOUR TRAVELS DURING THE TIME SINCE YOU MET THE MORGENSTERNS
BUT AS OF RIGHT NOW, THE POLICE AREN'T PREPARED TO CHARGE YOU WITH ANYTHING THAT I CAN DISCOVER, AND I'VE MADE MANY, MANY PHONE CALLS TO EVERYONE I KNOW IN THE JUSTICE SYSTEM HERE IN MEMPHIS.
And with that Art left to catch a flight to Atlanta.
We'd basically paid a whole hell of a lot for Art to fly over here first class to stay at a great hotel, make a lot of phone calls, and hold one press conference; but we'd known it had been a gamble when we'd called him.
I WANT TO GO FOR A WALK.
I KNOW YOU DON'T WANT TO BE COOPED UP IN THIS HOTEL, BUT IF WE GO ANYWHERE, SOMEONE'LL SPOT US AND WANT A STATEMENT.
YEAH.
LISTEN, PUT ON YOUR DARK GLASSES AND A HAT AND WE'LL GO TO THE MOVIES.

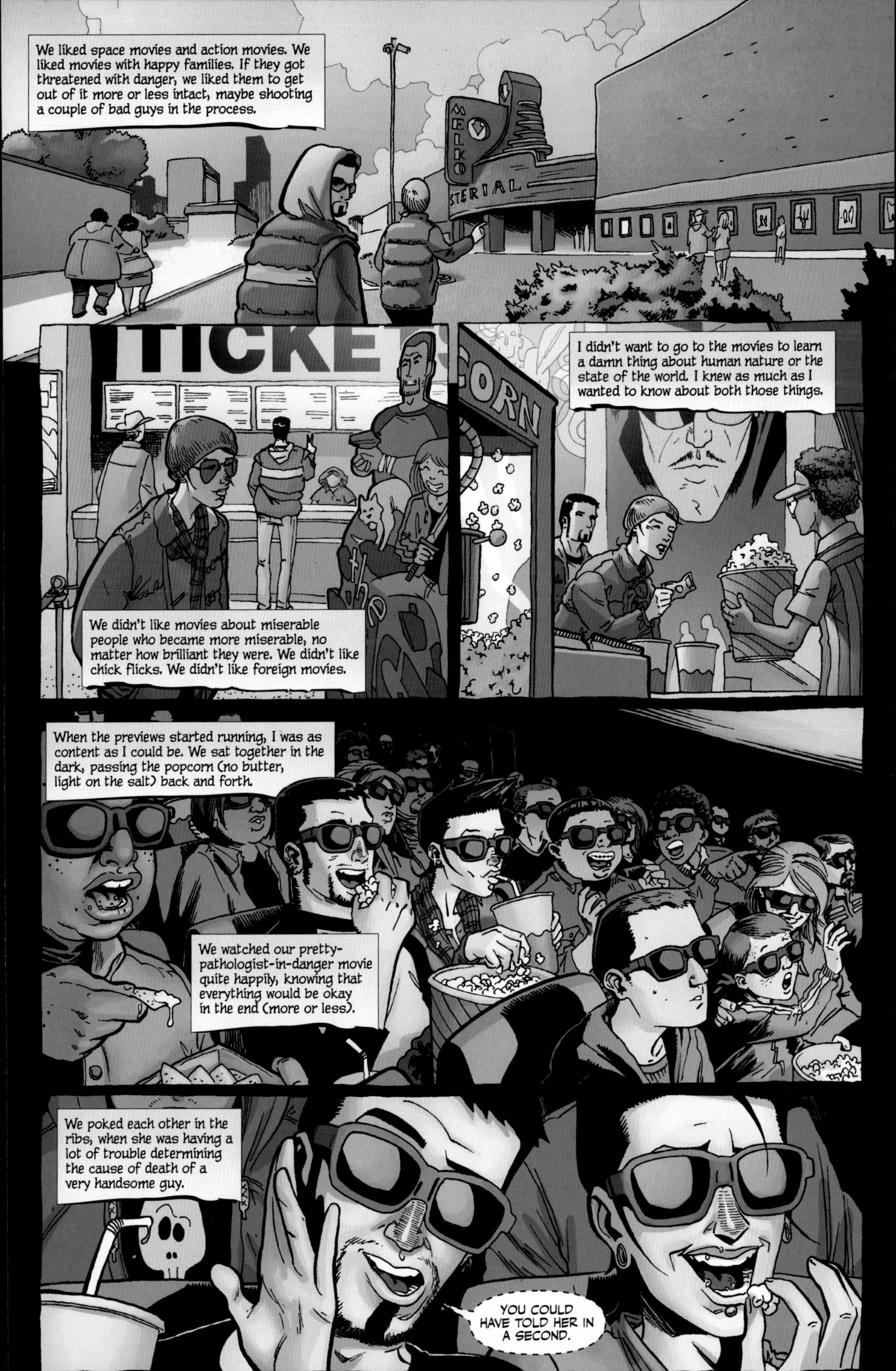
We liked space movies and action movies. We liked movies with happy families. If they got threatened with danger, we liked them to get out of it more or less intact, maybe shooting a couple of bad guys in the process.
MELKO
STERIAL
TICKE
CORN
I didn't want to go to the movies to learn a damn thing about human nature or the state of the world. I knew as much as I wanted to know about both those things.
We didn't like movies about miserable people who became more miserable, no matter how brilliant they were. We didn't like chick flicks. We didn't like foreign movies.
When the previews started running, I was as content as I could be. We sat together in the dark, passing the popcorn (no butter, light on the salt) back and forth.
We watched our pretty-pathologist-in-danger movie quite happily, knowing that everything would be okay in the end (more or less).
We poked each other in the ribs, when she was having a lot of trouble determining the cause of death of a very handsome guy.
YOU COULD HAVE TOLD HER IN A SECOND.

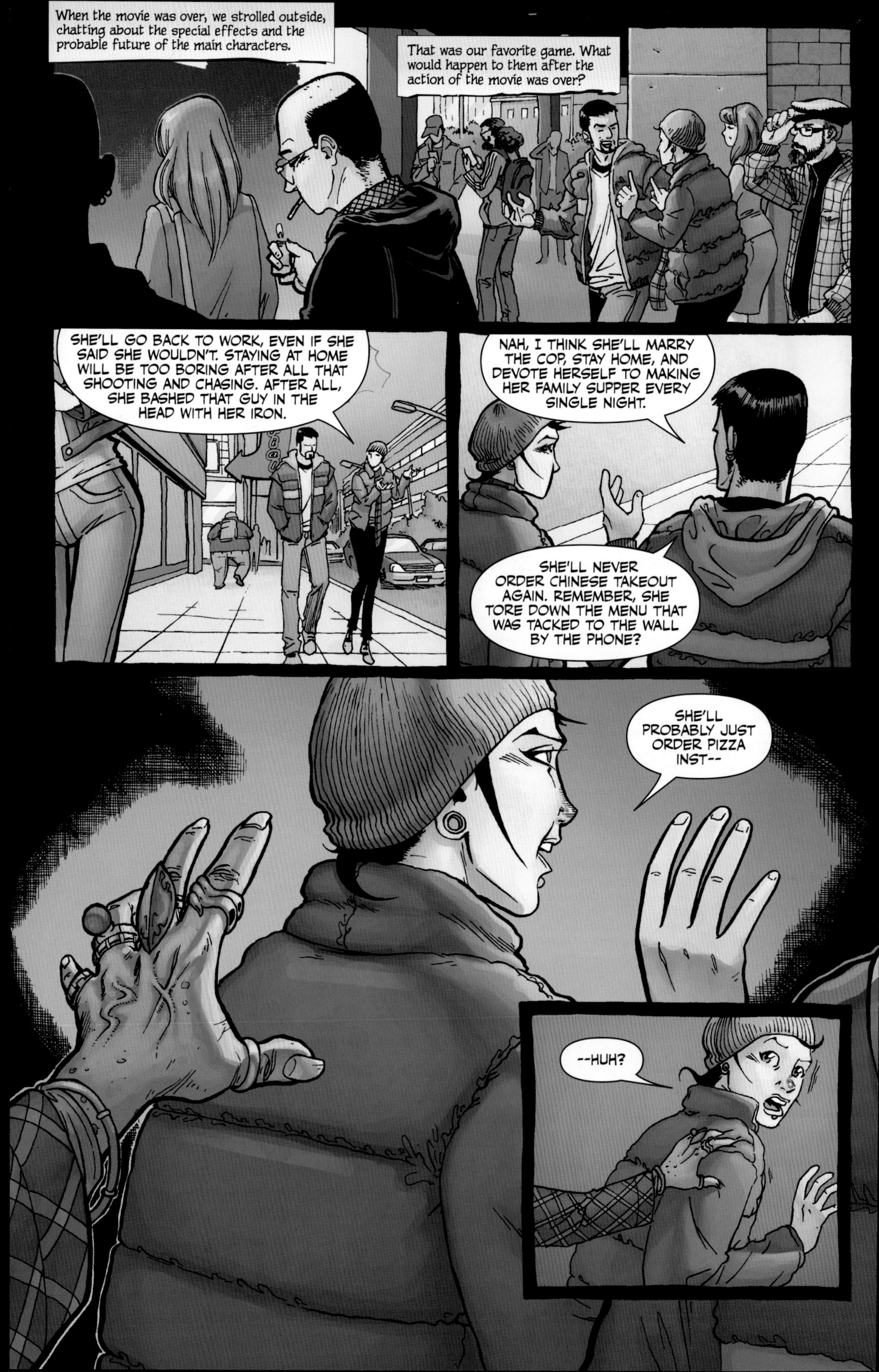
When the movie was over, we strolled outside, chatting about the special effects and the probable future of the main characters.
That was our favorite game. What would happen to them after the action of the movie was over?
SHE'LL GO BACK TO WORK, EVEN IF SHE SAID SHE WOULDN'T. STAYING AT HOME WILL BE TOO BORING AFTER ALL THAT SHOOTING AND CHASING. AFTER ALL, SHE BASHED THAT GUY IN THE HEAD WITH HER IRON.
NAH, I THINK SHE'LL MARRY THE COP, STAY HOME, AND DEVOTE HERSELF TO MAKING HER FAMILY SUPPER EVERY SINGLE NIGHT.
SHE'LL NEVER ORDER CHINESE TAKEOUT AGAIN. REMEMBER, SHE TORE DOWN THE MENU THAT WAS TACKED TO THE WALL BY THE PHONE?
SHE'LL PROBABLY JUST ORDER PIZZA INST--
--HUH?

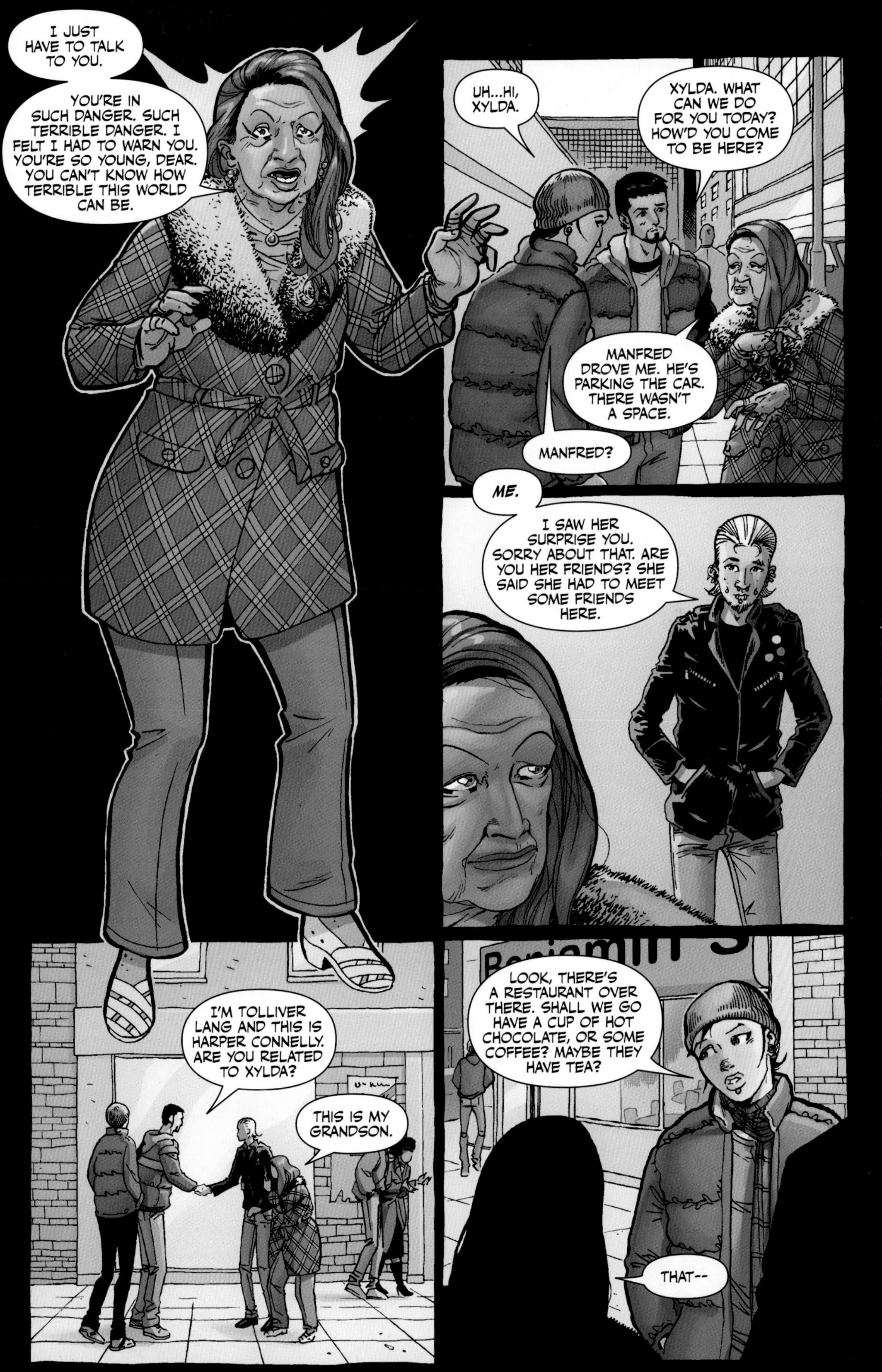
I JUST HAVE TO TALK TO YOU.
YOU'RE IN SUCH DANGER. SUCH TERRIBLE DANGER. I FELT I HAD TO WARN YOU. YOU'RE SO YOUNG, DEAR. YOU CAN'T KNOW HOW TERRIBLE THIS WORLD CAN BE.
UH...HI, XYLDA.
XYLDA. WHAT CAN WE DO FOR YOU TODAY? HOW'D YOU COME TO BE HERE?
MANFRED DROVE ME. HE'S PARKING THE CAR. THERE WASN'T A SPACE.
MANFRED?
ME.
I SAW HER SURPRISE YOU. SORRY ABOUT THAT. ARE YOU HER FRIENDS? SHE SAID SHE HAD TO MEET SOME FRIENDS HERE.
I'M TOLLIVER LANG AND THIS IS HARPER CONNELLY. ARE YOU RELATED TO XYLDA?
THIS IS MY GRANDSON.
LOOK, THERE'S A RESTAURANT OVER THERE. SHALL WE GO HAVE A CUP OF HOT CHOCOLATE, OR SOME COFFEE? MAYBE THEY HAVE TEA?
THAT--

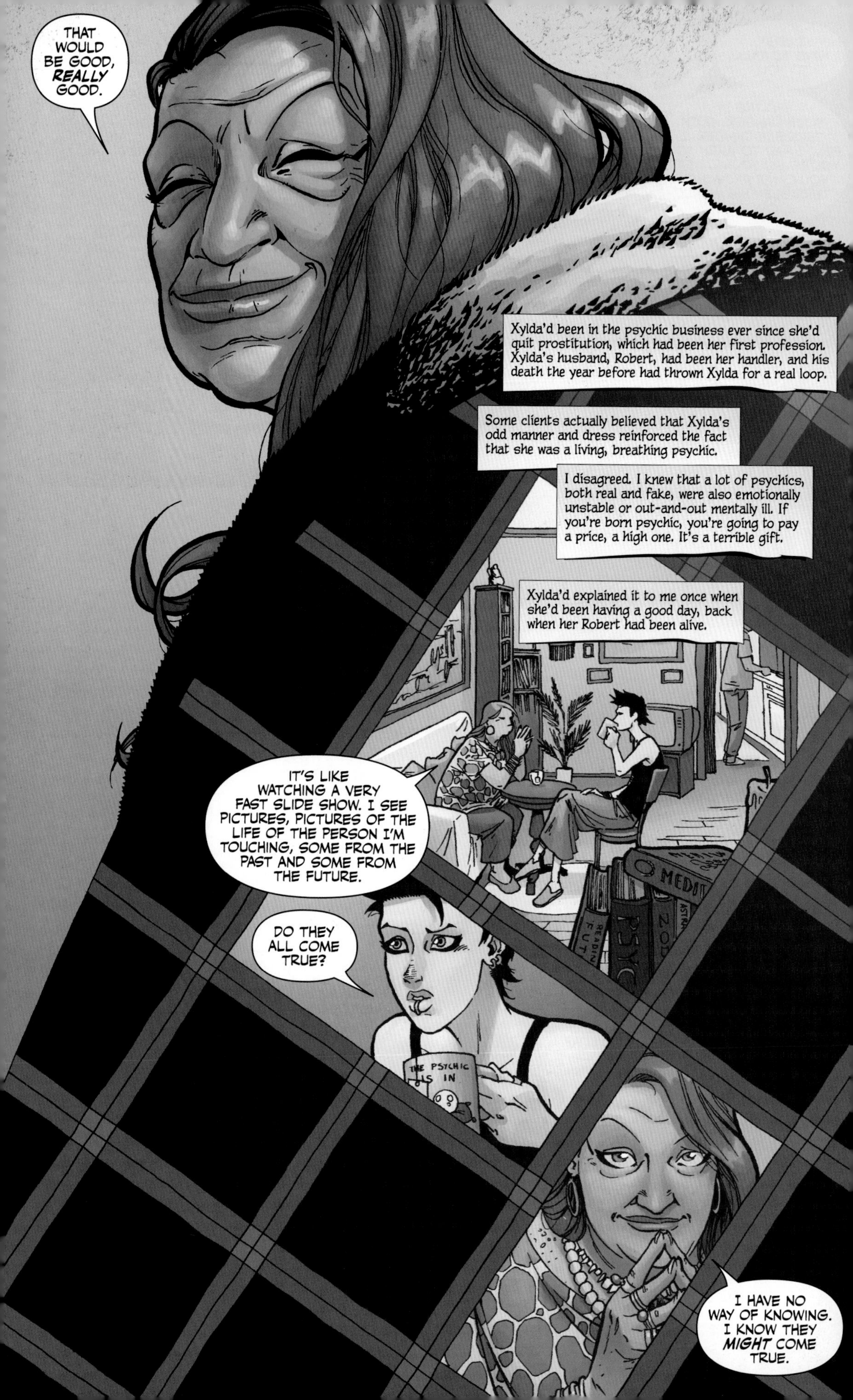
THAT WOULD BE GOOD, *REALLY* GOOD.
Xylda'd been in the psychic business ever since she'd quit prostitution, which had been her first profession. Xylda's husband, Robert, had been her handler, and his death the year before had thrown Xylda for a real loop.
Some clients actually believed that Xylda's odd manner and dress reinforced the fact that she was a living, breathing psychic.
I disagreed. I knew that a lot of psychics, both real and fake, were also emotionally unstable or out-and-out mentally ill. If you're born psychic, you're going to pay a price, a high one. It's a terrible gift.
Xylda'd explained it to me once when she'd been having a good day, back when her Robert had been alive.
IT'S LIKE WATCHING A VERY FAST SLIDE SHOW. I SEE PICTURES, PICTURES OF THE LIFE OF THE PERSON I'M TOUCHING, SOME FROM THE PAST AND SOME FROM THE FUTURE.
DO THEY ALL COME TRUE?
THE PSYCHIC IS IN
I HAVE NO WAY OF KNOWING. I KNOW THEY *MIGHT* COME TRUE.

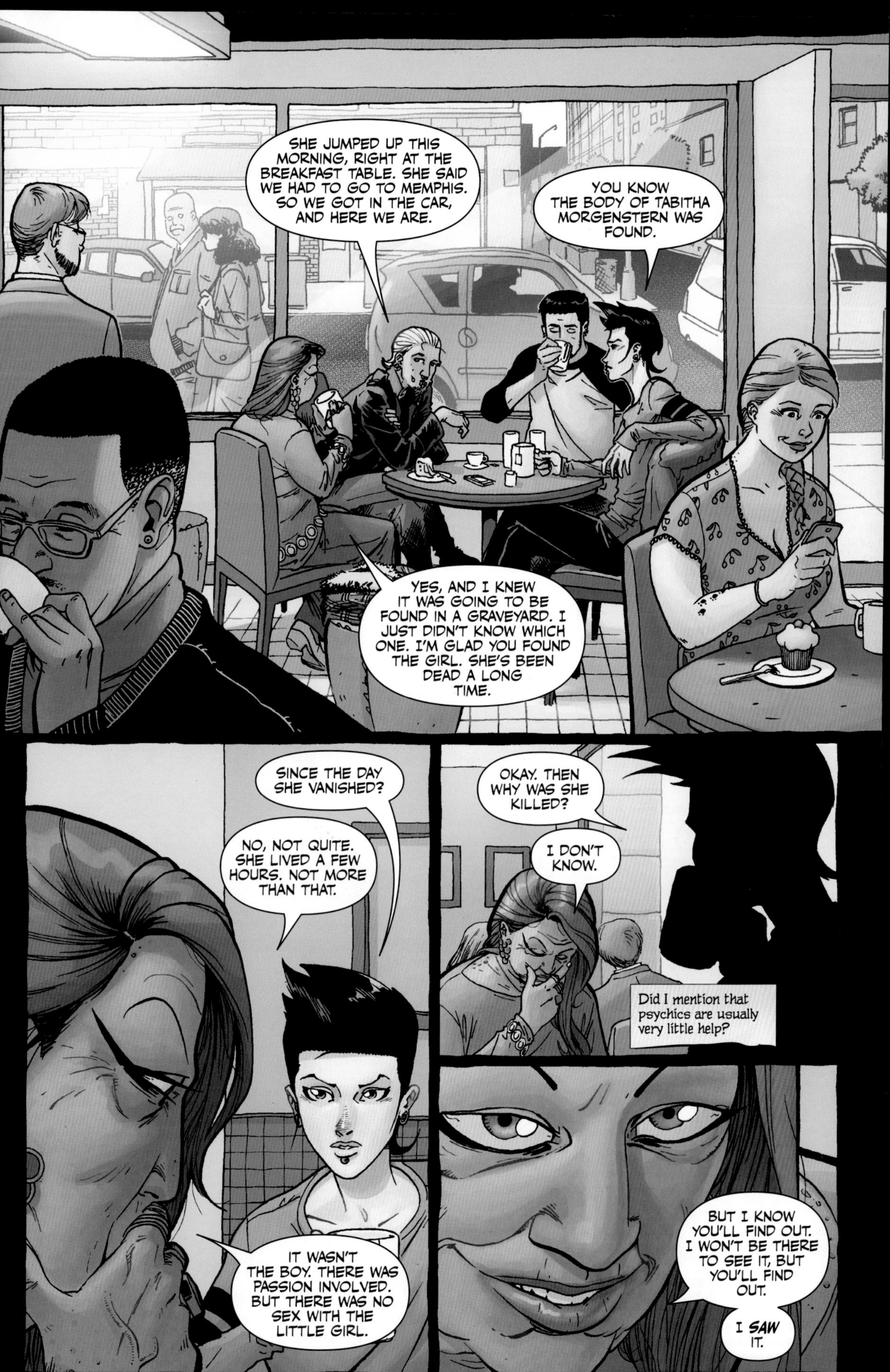

SHE JUMPED UP THIS MORNING, RIGHT AT THE BREAKFAST TABLE. SHE SAID WE HAD TO GO TO MEMPHIS. SO WE GOT IN THE CAR, AND HERE WE ARE.
YOU KNOW THE BODY OF TABITHA MORGENSTERN WAS FOUND.
YES, AND I KNEW IT WAS GOING TO BE FOUND IN A GRAVEYARD. I JUST DIDN'T KNOW WHICH ONE. I'M GLAD YOU FOUND THE GIRL. SHE'S BEEN DEAD A LONG TIME.
SINCE THE DAY SHE VANISHED?
NO, NOT QUITE. SHE LIVED A FEW HOURS. NOT MORE THAN THAT.
IT WASN'T THE BOY. THERE WAS PASSION INVOLVED. BUT THERE WAS NO SEX WITH THE LITTLE GIRL.
OKAY. THEN WHY WAS SHE KILLED?
I DON'T KNOW.
Did I mention that psychics are usually very little help?
BUT I KNOW YOU'LL FIND OUT. I WON'T BE THERE TO SEE IT, BUT YOU'LL FIND OUT.
I *SAW* IT.

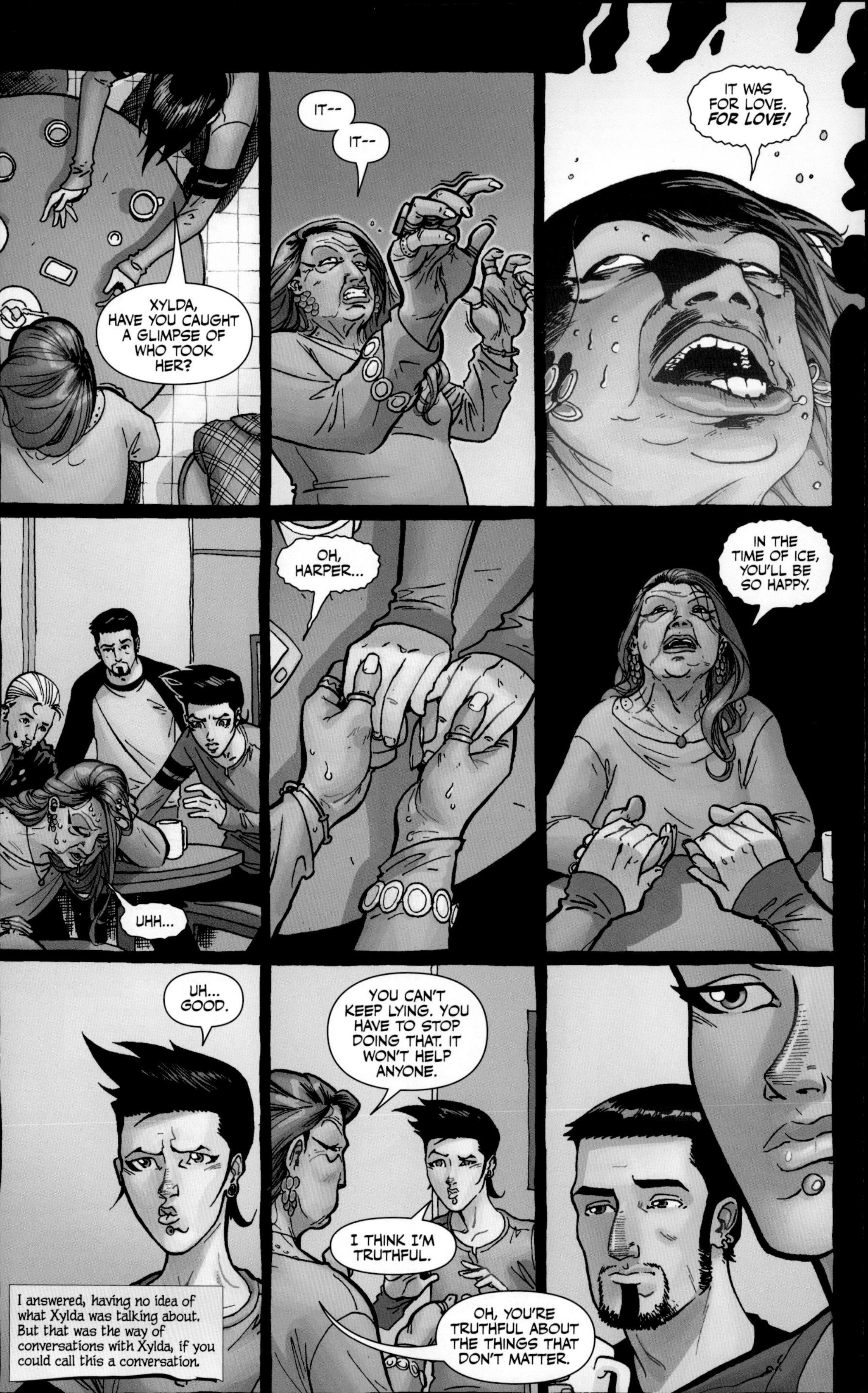
XYLDA, HAVE YOU CAUGHT A GLIMPSE OF WHO TOOK HER?
IT--
IT--
IT WAS FOR LOVE. FOR LOVE!
UHH...
OH, HARPER...
IN THE TIME OF ICE, YOU'LL BE SO HAPPY.
UH... GOOD.
I answered, having no idea of what Xylda was talking about. But that was the way of conversations with Xylda, if you could call this a conversation.
YOU CAN'T KEEP LYING. YOU HAVE TO STOP DOING THAT. IT WON'T HELP ANYONE.
I THINK I'M TRUTHFUL.
OH, YOU'RE TRUTHFUL ABOUT THE THINGS THAT DON'T MATTER.

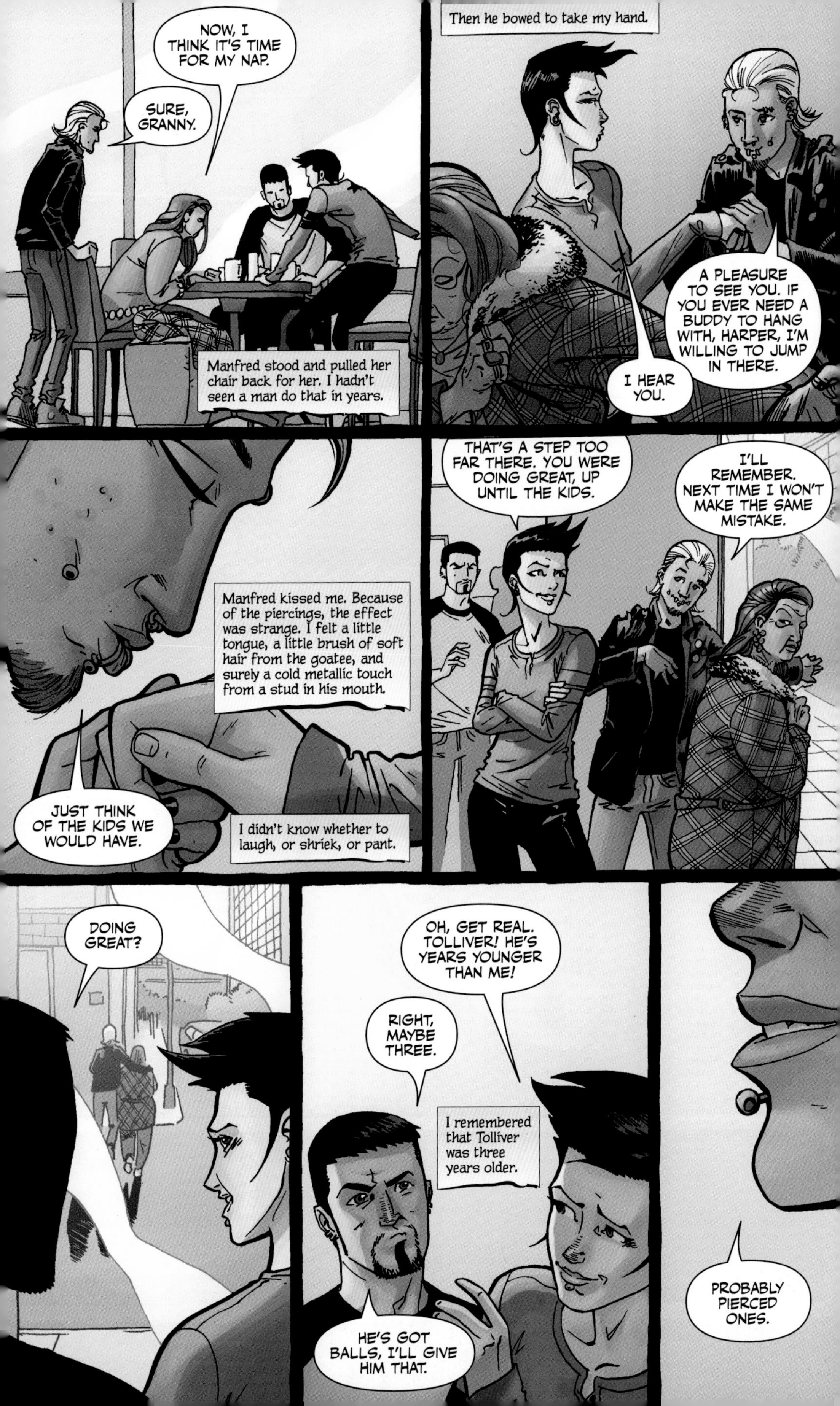
NOW, I THINK IT'S TIME FOR MY NAP.
SURE, GRANNY.
Manfred stood and pulled her chair back for her. I hadn't seen a man do that in years.
Then he bowed to take my hand.
A PLEASURE TO SEE YOU. IF YOU EVER NEED A BUDDY TO HANG WITH, HARPER, I'M WILLING TO JUMP IN THERE.
I HEAR YOU.
Manfred kissed me. Because of the piercings, the effect was strange. I felt a little tongue, a little brush of soft hair from the goatee, and surely a cold metallic touch from a stud in his mouth.
JUST THINK OF THE KIDS WE WOULD HAVE.
I didn't know whether to laugh, or shriek, or pant.
THAT'S A STEP TOO FAR THERE. YOU WERE DOING GREAT, UP UNTIL THE KIDS.
I'LL REMEMBER. NEXT TIME I WON'T MAKE THE SAME MISTAKE.
DOING GREAT?
OH, GET REAL. TOLLIVER! HE'S YEARS YOUNGER THAN ME!
RIGHT, MAYBE THREE.
I remembered that Tolliver was three years older.
HE'S GOT BALLS, I'LL GIVE HIM THAT.
PROBABLY PIERCED ONES.

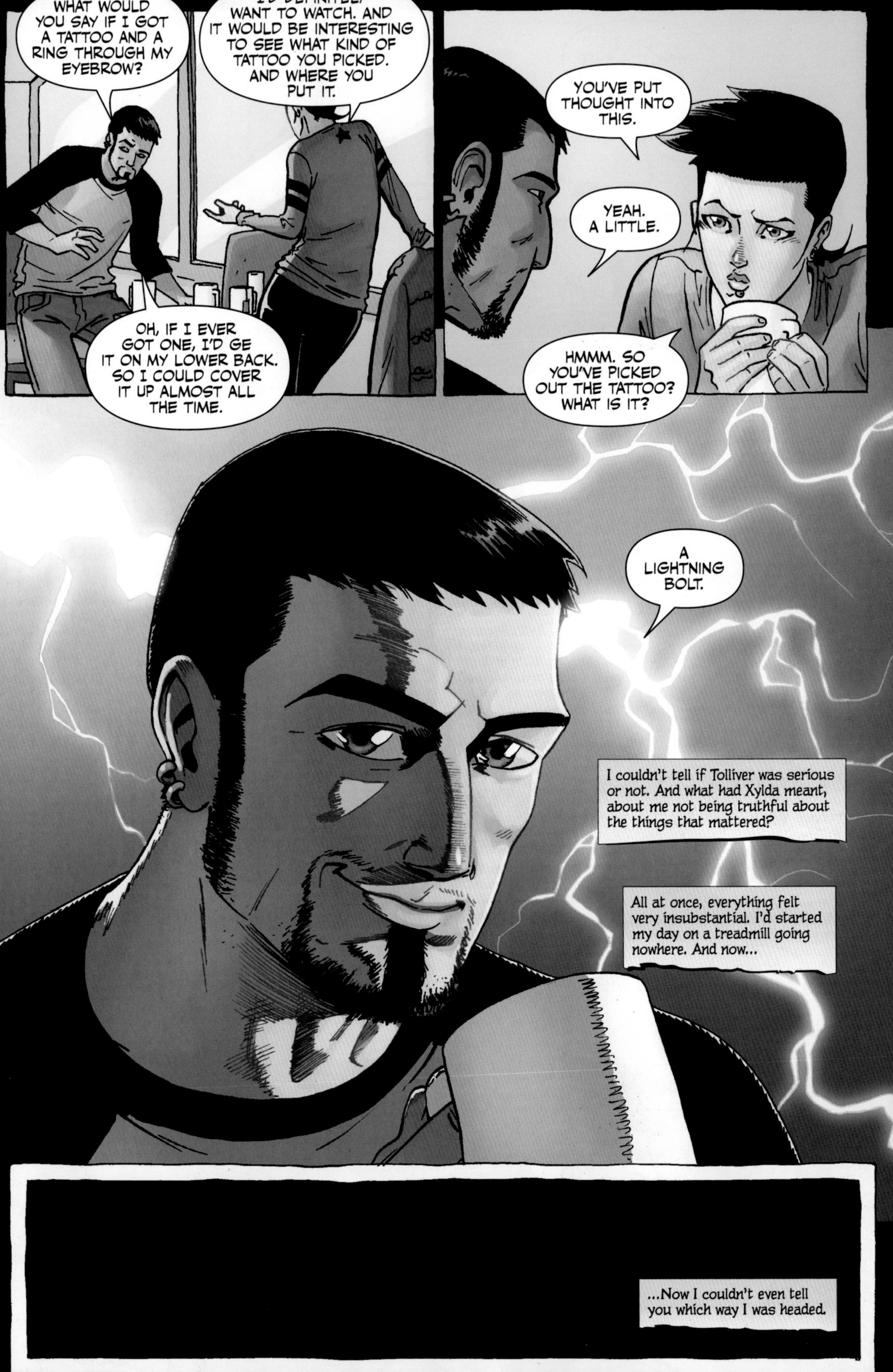
WHAT WOULD YOU SAY IF I GOT A TATTOO AND A RING THROUGH MY EYEBROW?
I'D DEFINITELY WANT TO WATCH. AND IT WOULD BE INTERESTING TO SEE WHAT KIND OF TATTOO YOU PICKED. AND WHERE YOU PUT IT.
OH, IF I EVER GOT ONE, I'D GE IT ON MY LOWER BACK. SO I COULD COVER IT UP ALMOST ALL THE TIME.
YOU'VE PUT THOUGHT INTO THIS.
YEAH. A LITTLE.
HMMM. SO YOU'VE PICKED OUT THE TATTOO? WHAT IS IT?
A LIGHTNING BOLT.
I couldn't tell if Tolliver was serious or not. And what had Xylda meant, about me not being truthful about the things that mattered?
All at once, everything felt very insubstantial. I'd started my day on a treadmill going nowhere. And now...
...Now I couldn't even tell you which way I was headed.

CHAPTER FOUR

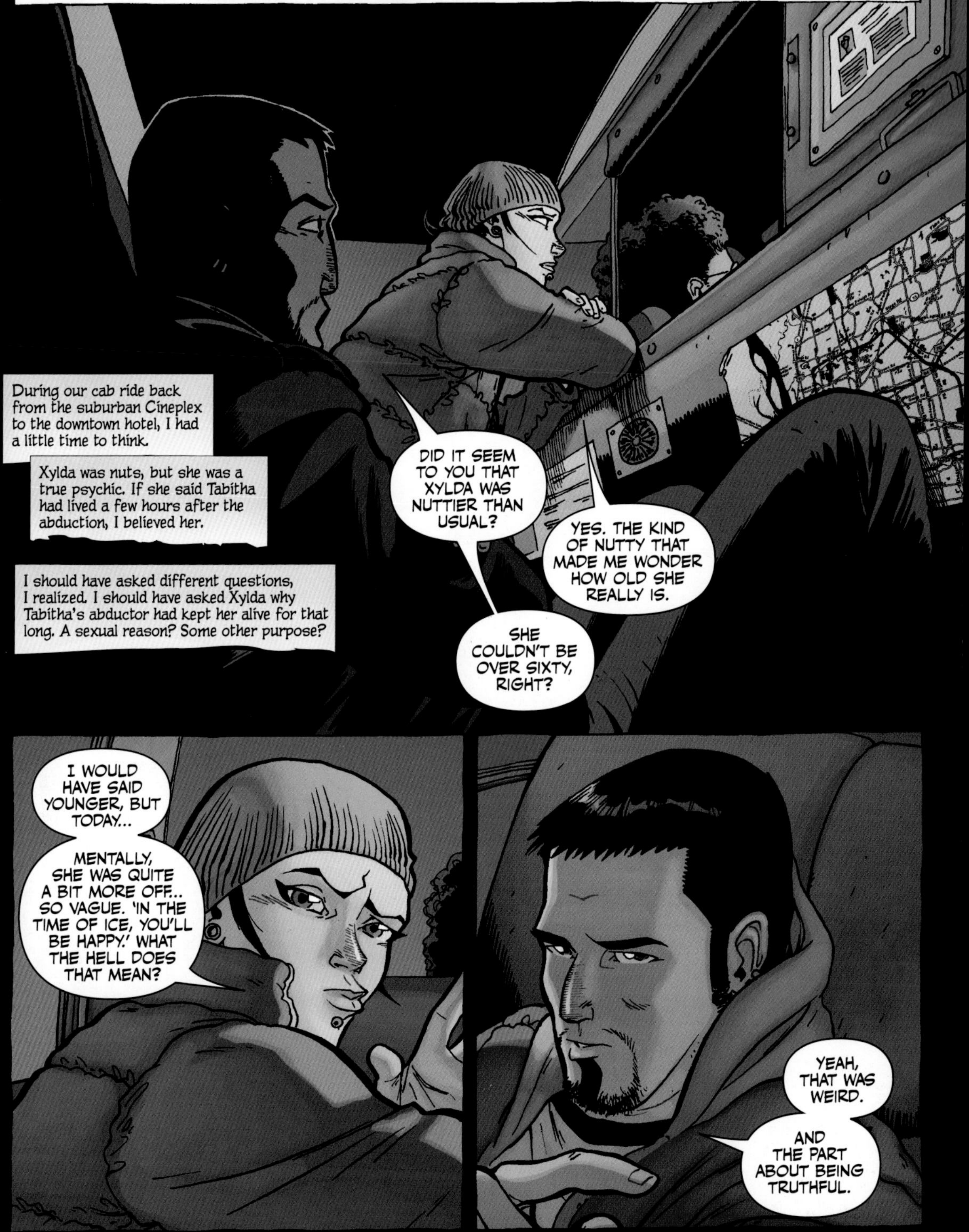
During our cab ride back from the suburban Cineplex to the downtown hotel, I had a little time to think.
Xylda was nuts, but she was a true psychic. If she said Tabitha had lived a few hours after the abduction, I believed her.
I should have asked different questions, I realized. I should have asked Xylda why Tabitha's abductor had kept her alive for that long. A sexual reason? Some other purpose?
DID IT SEEM TO YOU THAT XYLDA WAS NUTTIER THAN USUAL?
YES. THE KIND OF NUTTY THAT MADE ME WONDER HOW OLD SHE REALLY IS.
SHE COULDN'T BE OVER SIXTY, RIGHT?
I WOULD HAVE SAID YOUNGER, BUT TODAY...
MENTALLY, SHE WAS QUITE A BIT MORE OFF... SO VAGUE. 'IN THE TIME OF ICE, YOU'LL BE HAPPY.' WHAT THE HELL DOES THAT MEAN?
YEAH, THAT WAS WEIRD.
AND THE PART ABOUT BEING TRUTHFUL.

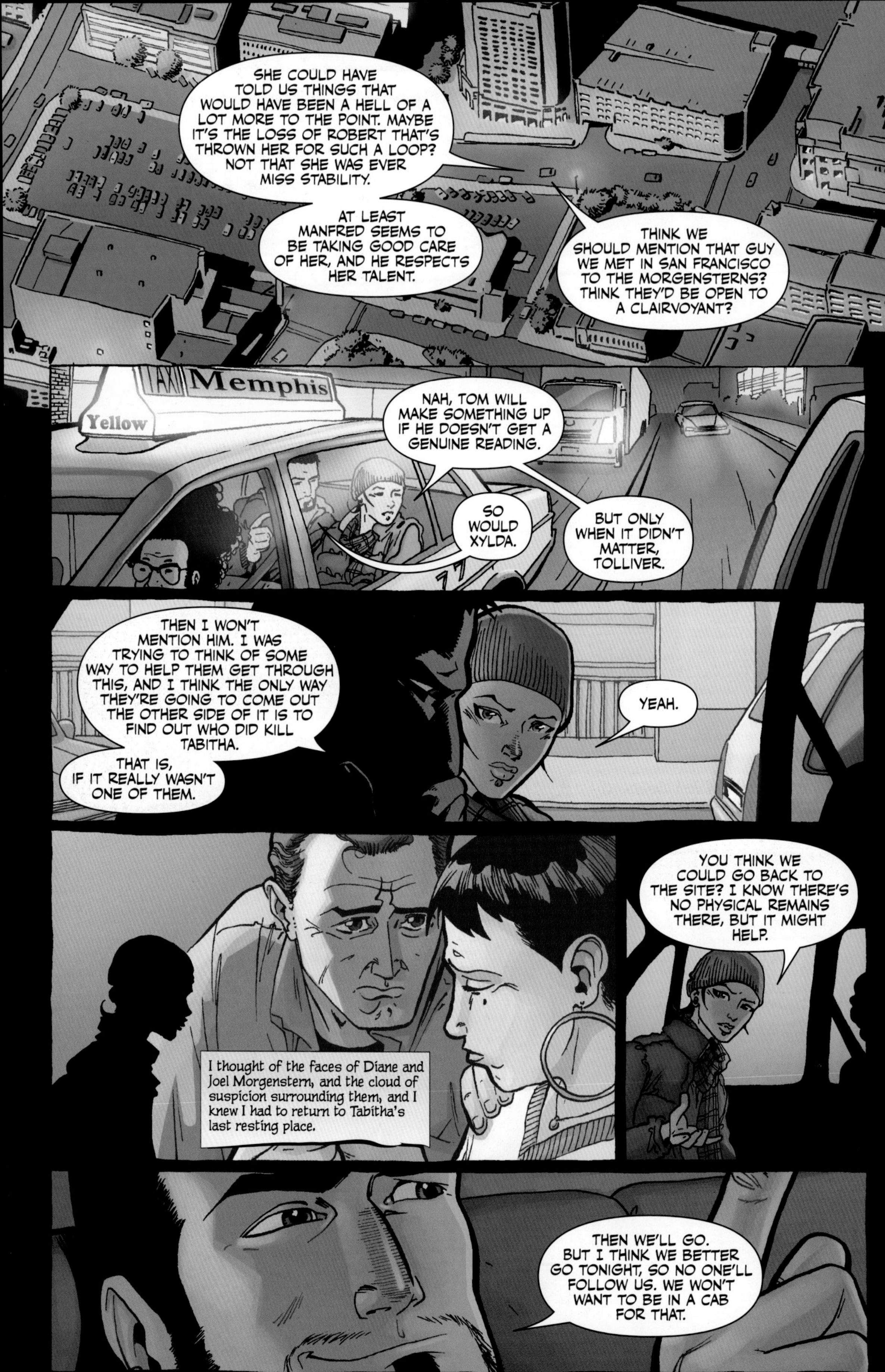
SHE COULD HAVE TOLD US THINGS THAT WOULD HAVE BEEN A HELL OF A LOT MORE TO THE POINT. MAYBE IT'S THE LOSS OF ROBERT THAT'S THROWN HER FOR SUCH A LOOP? NOT THAT SHE WAS EVER MISS STABILITY.
AT LEAST MANFRED SEEMS TO BE TAKING GOOD CARE OF HER, AND HE RESPECTS HER TALENT.
THINK WE SHOULD MENTION THAT GUY WE MET IN SAN FRANCISCO TO THE MORGENSTERNS? THINK THEY'D BE OPEN TO A CLAIRVOYANT?
TAXI Memphis
Yellow
NAH, TOM WILL MAKE SOMETHING UP IF HE DOESN'T GET A GENUINE READING.
SO WOULD XYLDA.
BUT ONLY WHEN IT DIDN'T MATTER, TOLLIVER.
THEN I WON'T MENTION HIM. I WAS TRYING TO THINK OF SOME WAY TO HELP THEM GET THROUGH THIS, AND I THINK THE ONLY WAY THEY'RE GOING TO COME OUT THE OTHER SIDE OF IT IS TO FIND OUT WHO DID KILL TABITHA.
THAT IS, IF IT REALLY WASN'T ONE OF THEM.
YEAH.
I thought of the faces of Diane and Joel Morgenstern, and the cloud of suspicion surrounding them, and I knew I had to return to Tabitha's last resting place.
YOU THINK WE COULD GO BACK TO THE SITE? I KNOW THERE'S NO PHYSICAL REMAINS THERE, BUT IT MIGHT HELP.
THEN WE'LL GO. BUT I THINK WE BETTER GO TONIGHT, SO NO ONE'LL FOLLOW US. WE WON'T WANT TO BE IN A CAB FOR THAT.

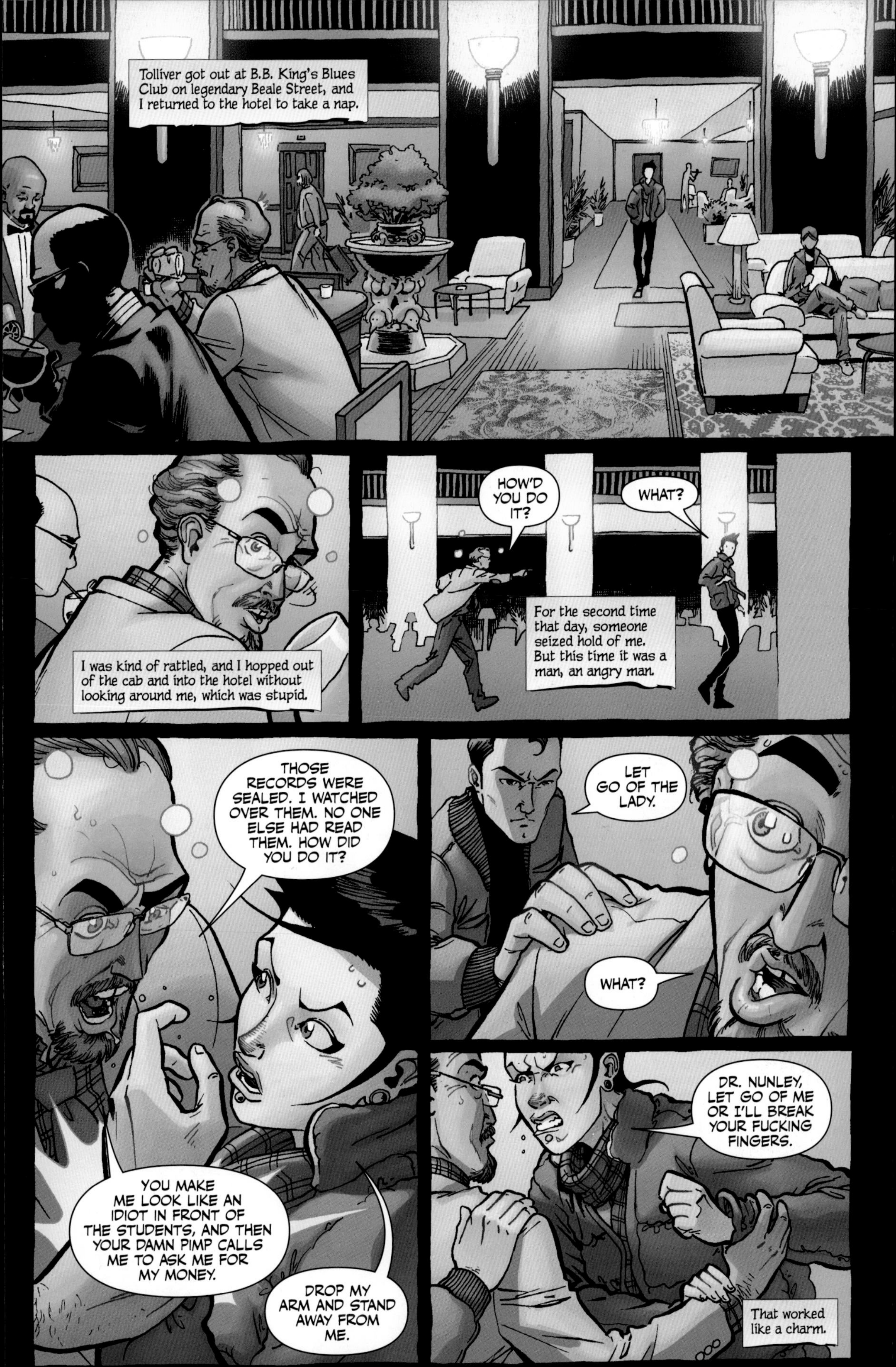
Tolliver got out at B.B. King's Blues Club on legendary Beale Street, and I returned to the hotel to take a nap.
I was kind of rattled, and I hopped out of the cab and into the hotel without looking around me, which was stupid.
HOW'D YOU DO IT?
WHAT?
For the second time that day, someone seized hold of me. But this time it was a man, an angry man.
THOSE RECORDS WERE SEALED. I WATCHED OVER THEM. NO ONE ELSE HAD READ THEM. HOW DID YOU DO IT?
YOU MAKE ME LOOK LIKE AN IDIOT IN FRONT OF THE STUDENTS, AND THEN YOUR DAMN PIMP CALLS ME TO ASK ME FOR MY MONEY.
DROP MY ARM AND STAND AWAY FROM ME.
LET GO OF THE LADY.
WHAT?
DR. NUNLEY, LET GO OF ME OR I'LL BREAK YOUR FUCKING FINGERS.
That worked like a charm.

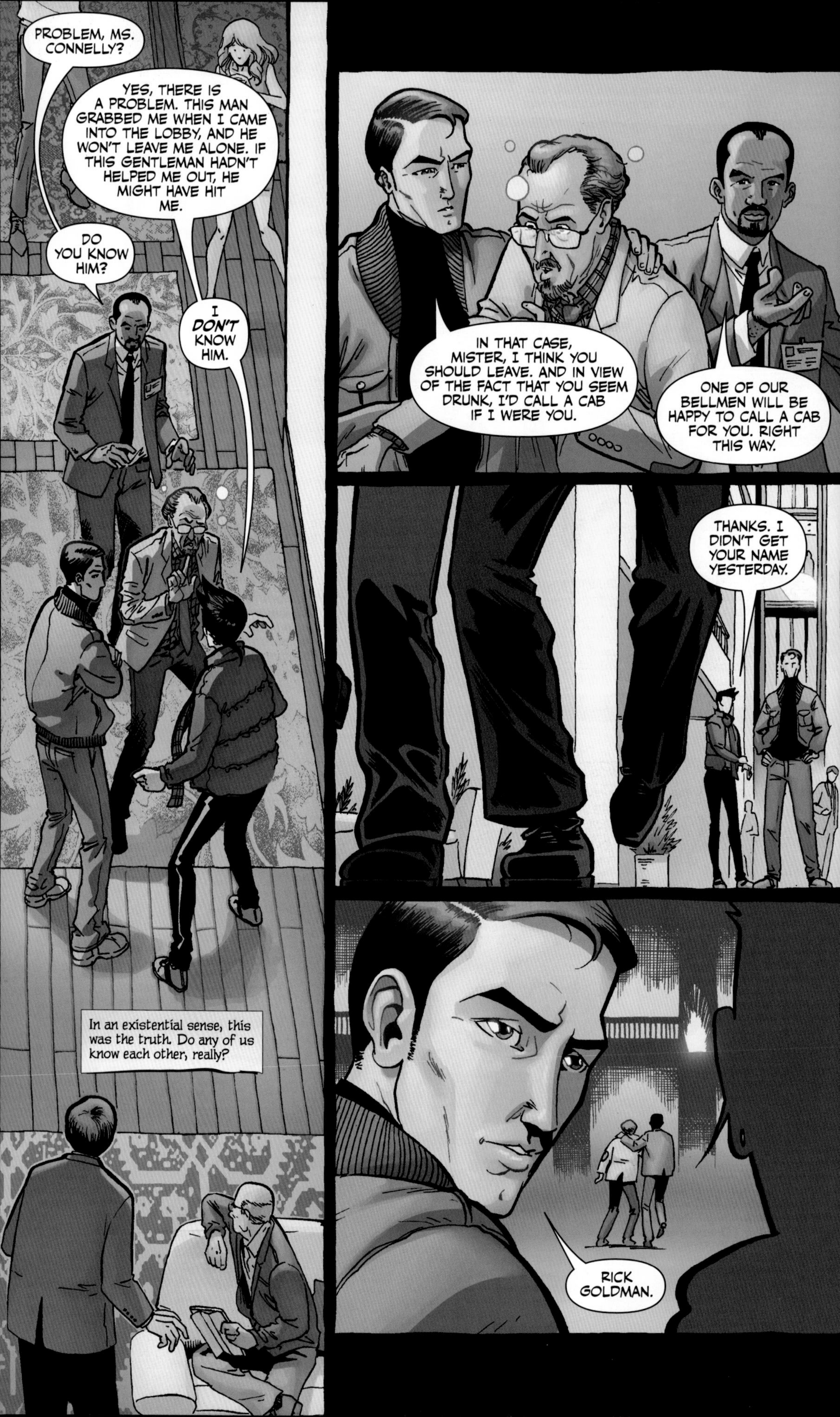
PROBLEM, MS. CONNELLY?
YES, THERE IS A PROBLEM. THIS MAN GRABBED ME WHEN I CAME INTO THE LOBBY, AND HE WON'T LEAVE ME ALONE. IF THIS GENTLEMAN HADN'T HELPED ME OUT, HE MIGHT HAVE HIT ME.
DO YOU KNOW HIM?
I *DON'T* KNOW HIM.
In an existential sense, this was the truth. Do any of us know each other, really?
IN THAT CASE, MISTER, I THINK YOU SHOULD LEAVE. AND IN VIEW OF THE FACT THAT YOU SEEM DRUNK, I'D CALL A CAB IF I WERE YOU.
ONE OF OUR BELLMEN WILL BE HAPPY TO CALL A CAB FOR YOU. RIGHT THIS WAY.
THANKS. I DIDN'T GET YOUR NAME YESTERDAY.
RICK GOLDMAN.

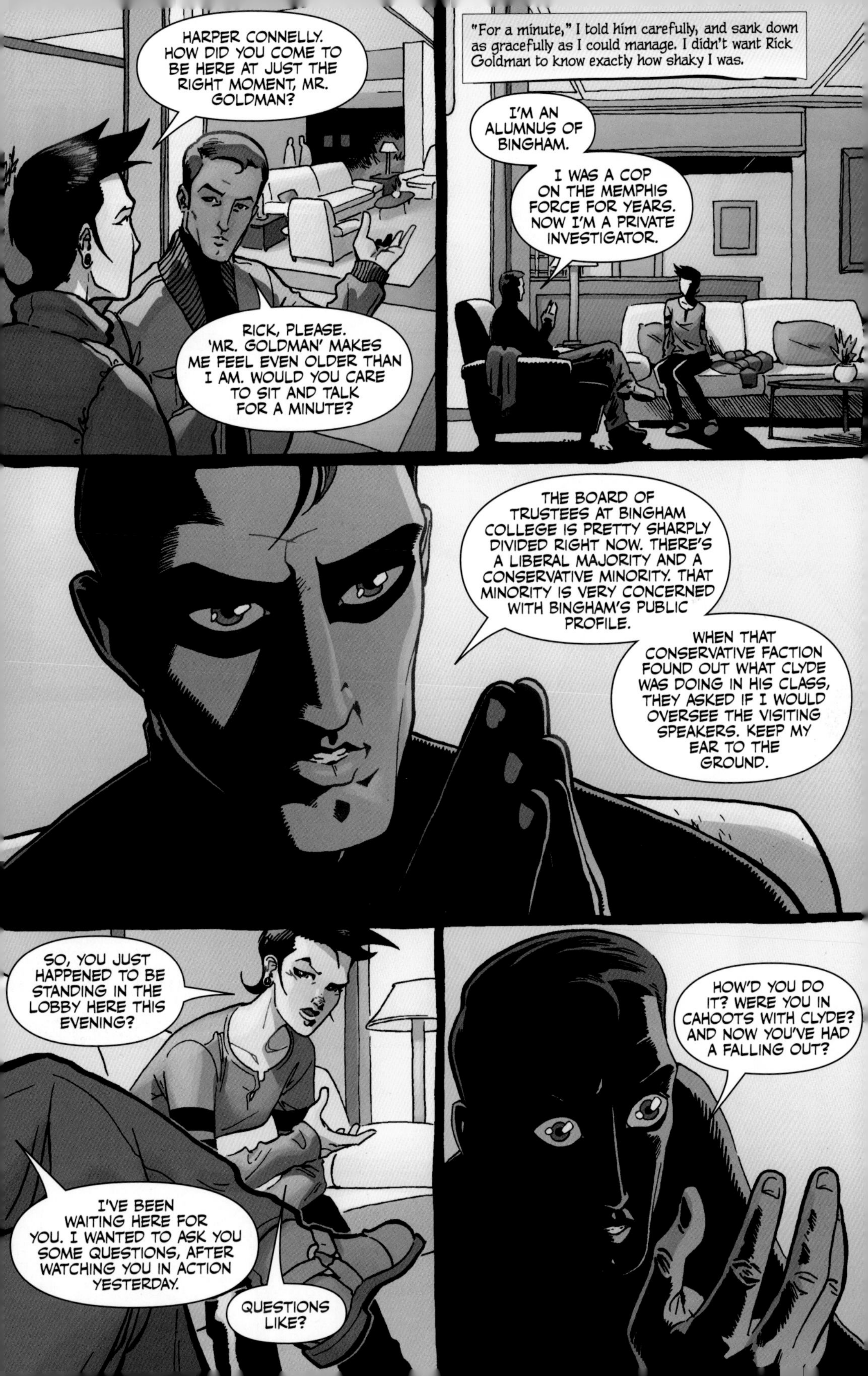
HARPER CONNELLY. HOW DID YOU COME TO BE HERE AT JUST THE RIGHT MOMENT, MR. GOLDMAN?
RICK, PLEASE. 'MR. GOLDMAN' MAKES ME FEEL EVEN OLDER THAN I AM. WOULD YOU CARE TO SIT AND TALK FOR A MINUTE?
"For a minute," I told him carefully, and sank down as gracefully as I could manage. I didn't want Rick Goldman to know exactly how shaky I was.
I'M AN ALUMNUS OF BINGHAM.
I WAS A COP ON THE MEMPHIS FORCE FOR YEARS. NOW I'M A PRIVATE INVESTIGATOR.
THE BOARD OF TRUSTEES AT BINGHAM COLLEGE IS PRETTY SHARPLY DIVIDED RIGHT NOW. THERE'S A LIBERAL MAJORITY AND A CONSERVATIVE MINORITY. THAT MINORITY IS VERY CONCERNED WITH BINGHAM'S PUBLIC PROFILE.
WHEN THAT CONSERVATIVE FACTION FOUND OUT WHAT CLYDE WAS DOING IN HIS CLASS, THEY ASKED IF I WOULD OVERSEE THE VISITING SPEAKERS. KEEP MY EAR TO THE GROUND.
SO, YOU JUST HAPPENED TO BE STANDING IN THE LOBBY HERE THIS EVENING?
I'VE BEEN WAITING HERE FOR YOU. I WANTED TO ASK YOU SOME QUESTIONS, AFTER WATCHING YOU IN ACTION YESTERDAY.
QUESTIONS LIKE?
HOW'D YOU DO IT? WERE YOU IN CAHOOTS WITH CLYDE? AND NOW YOU'VE HAD A FALLING OUT?

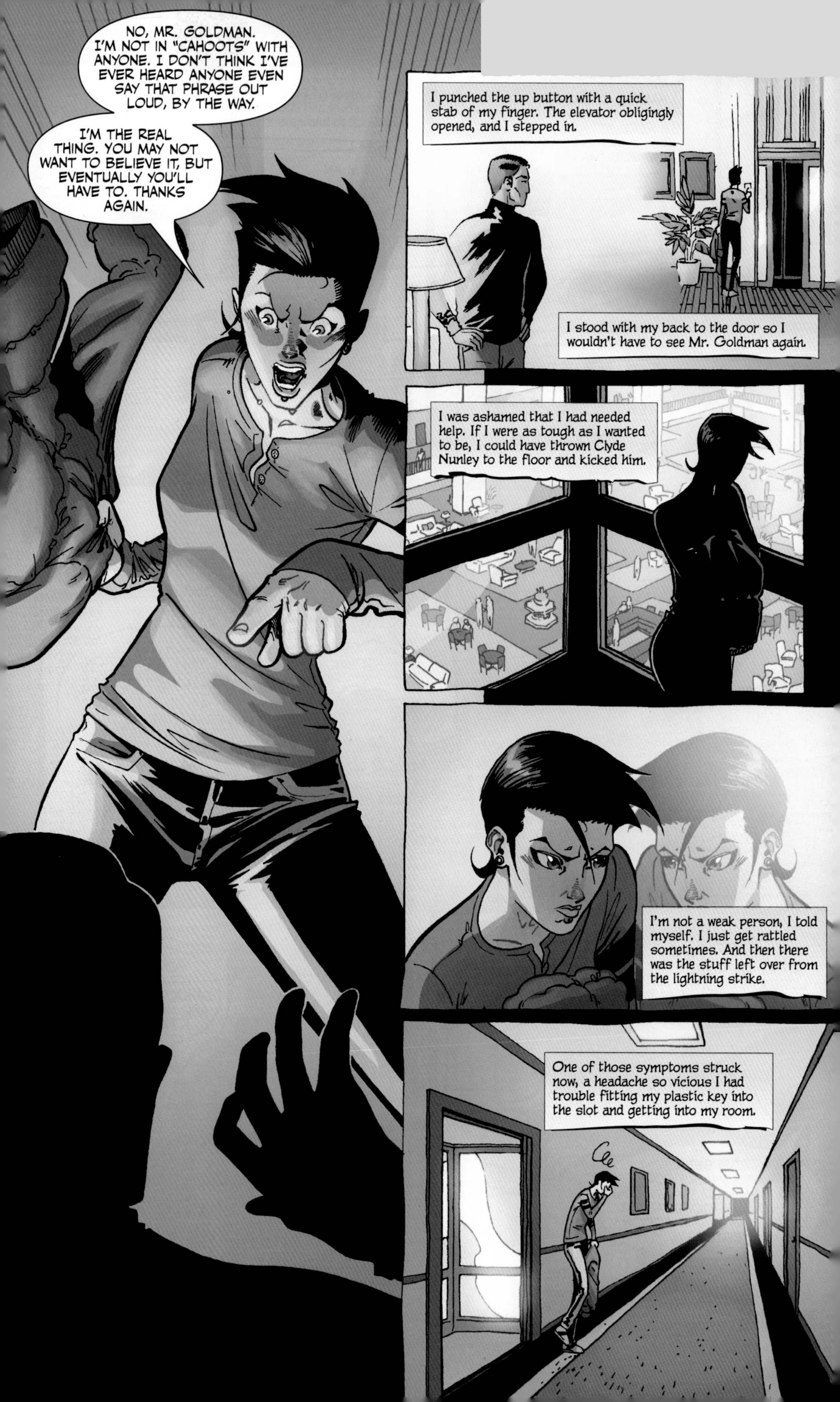
NO, MR. GOLDMAN. I'M NOT IN "CAHOOTS" WITH ANYONE. I DON'T THINK I'VE EVER HEARD ANYONE EVEN SAY THAT PHRASE OUT LOUD, BY THE WAY.
I'M THE REAL THING. YOU MAY NOT WANT TO BELIEVE IT, BUT EVENTUALLY YOU'LL HAVE TO. THANKS AGAIN.
I punched the up button with a quick stab of my finger. The elevator obligingly opened, and I stepped in.
I stood with my back to the door so I wouldn't have to see Mr. Goldman again.
I was ashamed that I had needed help. If I were as tough as I wanted to be, I could have thrown Clyde Nunley to the floor and kicked him.
I'm not a weak person, I told myself. I just get rattled sometimes. And then there was the stuff left over from the lightning strike.
One of those symptoms struck now, a headache so vicious I had trouble fitting my plastic key into the slot and getting into my room.

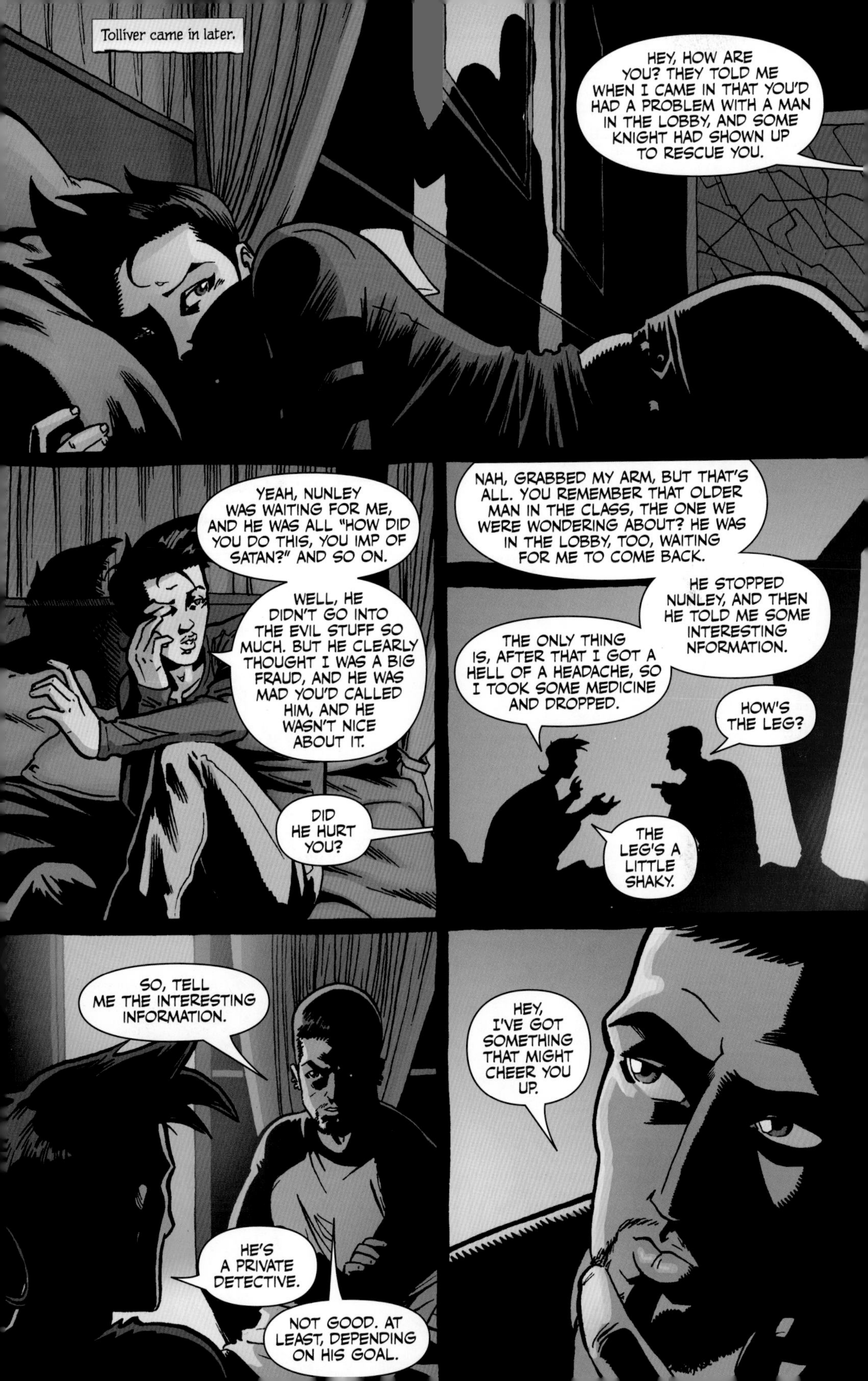
Tolliver came in later.
HEY, HOW ARE YOU? THEY TOLD ME WHEN I CAME IN THAT YOU'D HAD A PROBLEM WITH A MAN IN THE LOBBY, AND SOME KNIGHT HAD SHOWN UP TO RESCUE YOU.
YEAH, NUNLEY WAS WAITING FOR ME, AND HE WAS ALL "HOW DID YOU DO THIS, YOU IMP OF SATAN?" AND SO ON.
WELL, HE DIDN'T GO INTO THE EVIL STUFF SO MUCH. BUT HE CLEARLY THOUGHT I WAS A BIG FRAUD, AND HE WAS MAD YOU'D CALLED HIM, AND HE WASN'T NICE ABOUT IT.
DID HE HURT YOU?
NAH, GRABBED MY ARM, BUT THAT'S ALL. YOU REMEMBER THAT OLDER MAN IN THE CLASS, THE ONE WE WERE WONDERING ABOUT? HE WAS IN THE LOBBY, TOO, WAITING FOR ME TO COME BACK.
HE STOPPED NUNLEY, AND THEN HE TOLD ME SOME INTERESTING NFORMATION.
THE ONLY THING IS, AFTER THAT I GOT A HELL OF A HEADACHE, SO I TOOK SOME MEDICINE AND DROPPED.
HOW'S THE LEG?
THE LEG'S A LITTLE SHAKY.
SO, TELL ME THE INTERESTING INFORMATION.
HE'S A PRIVATE DETECTIVE.
NOT GOOD. AT LEAST, DEPENDING ON HIS GOAL.
HEY, I'VE GOT SOMETHING THAT MIGHT CHEER YOU UP.

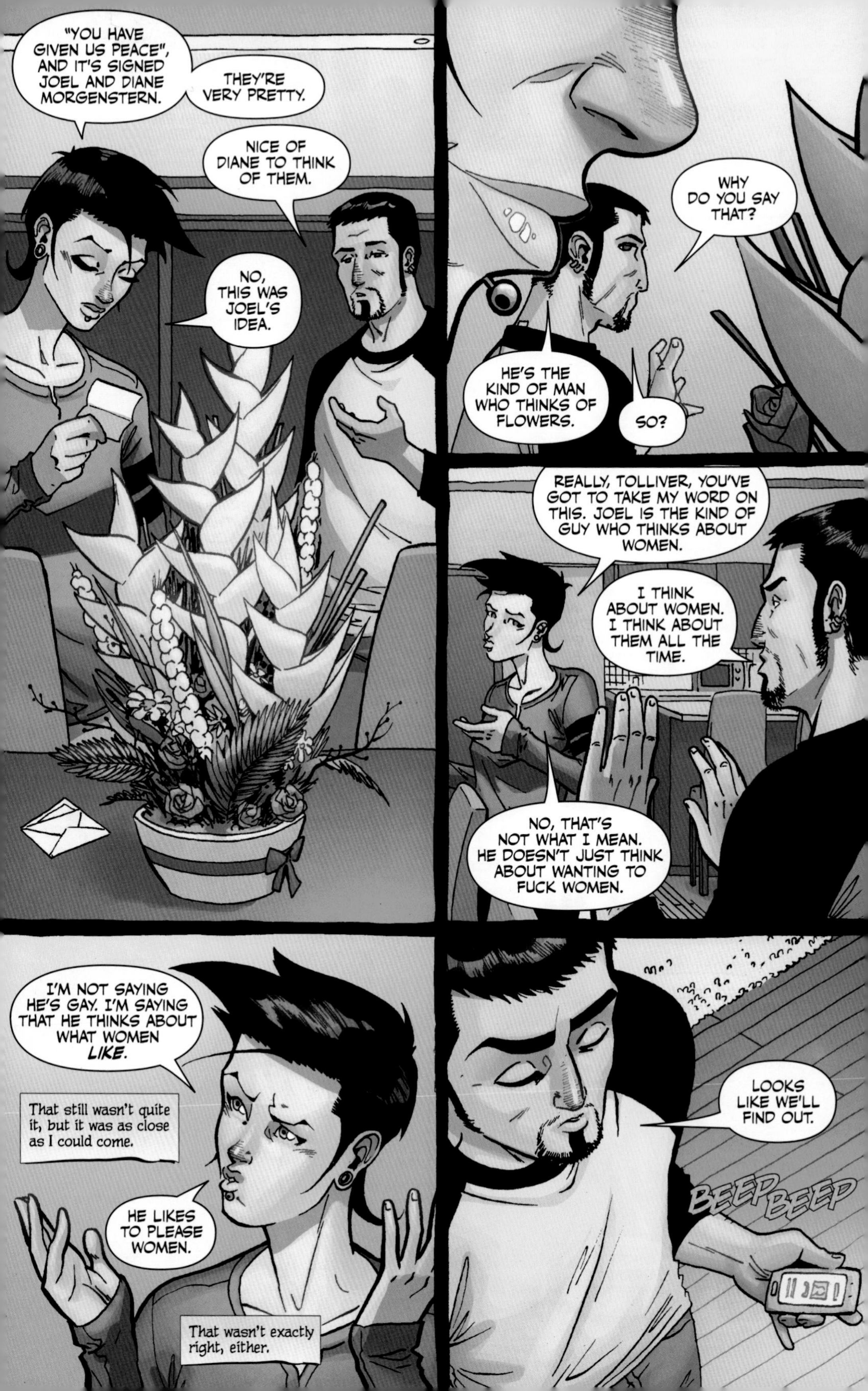
"YOU HAVE GIVEN US PEACE", AND IT'S SIGNED JOEL AND DIANE MORGENSTERN.
THEY'RE VERY PRETTY.
NICE OF DIANE TO THINK OF THEM.
NO, THIS WAS JOEL'S IDEA.
WHY DO YOU SAY THAT?
HE'S THE KIND OF MAN WHO THINKS OF FLOWERS.
SO?
REALLY, TOLLIVER, YOU'VE GOT TO TAKE MY WORD ON THIS. JOEL IS THE KIND OF GUY WHO THINKS ABOUT WOMEN.
I THINK ABOUT WOMEN. I THINK ABOUT THEM ALL THE TIME.
NO, THAT'S NOT WHAT I MEAN. HE DOESN'T JUST THINK ABOUT WANTING TO FUCK WOMEN.
I'M NOT SAYING HE'S GAY. I'M SAYING THAT HE THINKS ABOUT WHAT WOMEN LIKE.
That still wasn't quite it, but it was as close as I could come.
HE LIKES TO PLEASE WOMEN.
That wasn't exactly right, either.
LOOKS LIKE WE'LL FIND OUT.
BEEP BEEP

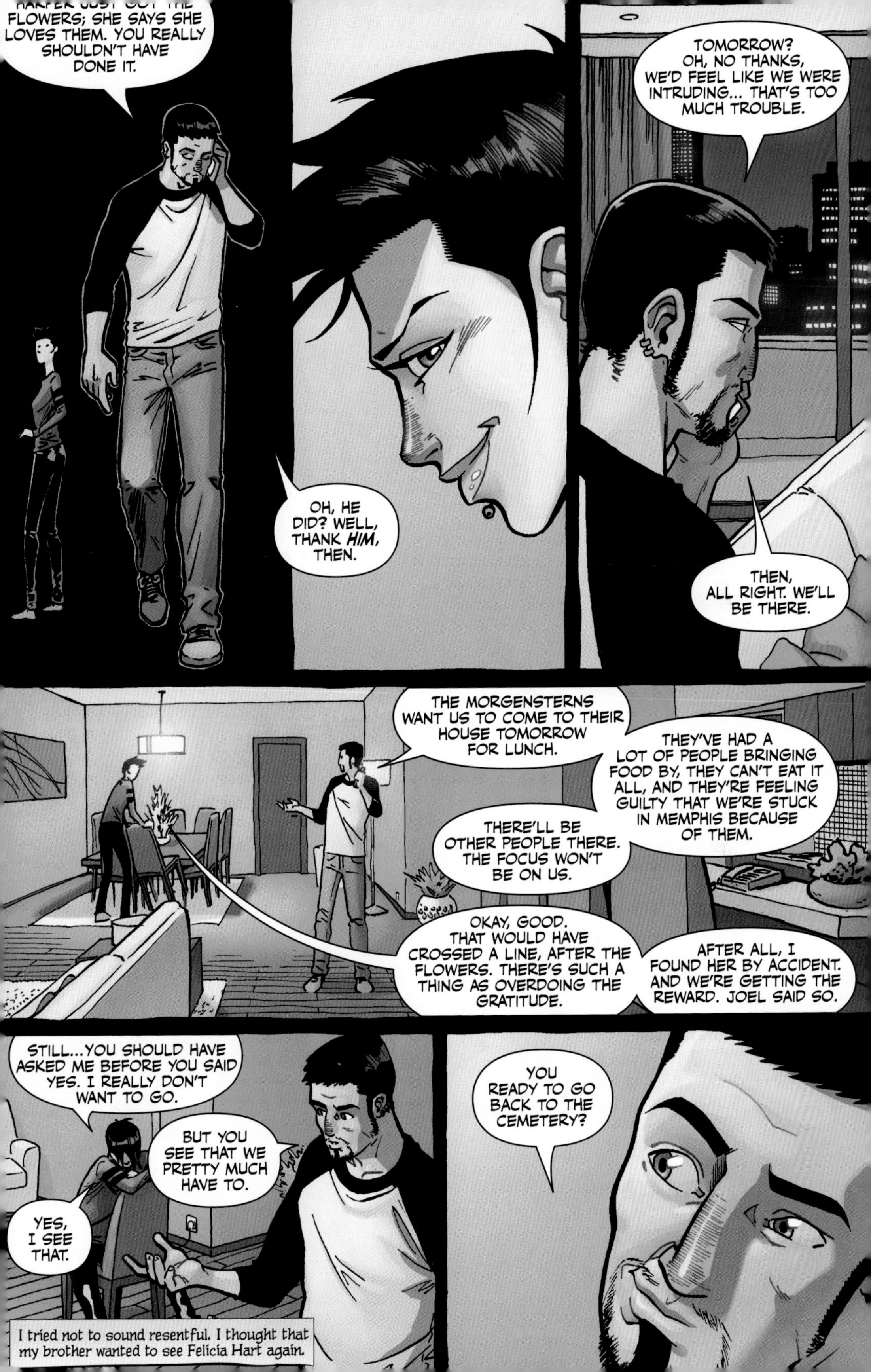

FLOWERS; SHE SAYS SHE LOVES THEM. YOU REALLY SHOULDN'T HAVE DONE IT.
OH, HE DID? WELL, THANK *HIM*, THEN.
TOMORROW? OH, NO THANKS, WE'D FEEL LIKE WE WERE INTRUDING... THAT'S TOO MUCH TROUBLE.
THEN, ALL RIGHT. WE'LL BE THERE.
THE MORGENSTERNS WANT US TO COME TO THEIR HOUSE TOMORROW FOR LUNCH.
THEY'VE HAD A LOT OF PEOPLE BRINGING FOOD BY, THEY CAN'T EAT IT ALL, AND THEY'RE FEELING GUILTY THAT WE'RE STUCK IN MEMPHIS BECAUSE OF THEM.
THERE'LL BE OTHER PEOPLE THERE. THE FOCUS WON'T BE ON US.
OKAY, GOOD. THAT WOULD HAVE CROSSED A LINE, AFTER THE FLOWERS. THERE'S SUCH A THING AS OVERDOING THE GRATITUDE.
AFTER ALL, I FOUND HER BY ACCIDENT. AND WE'RE GETTING THE REWARD. JOEL SAID SO.
STILL...YOU SHOULD HAVE ASKED ME BEFORE YOU SAID YES. I REALLY DON'T WANT TO GO.
BUT YOU SEE THAT WE PRETTY MUCH HAVE TO.
YES, I SEE THAT.
I tried not to sound resentful. I thought that my brother wanted to see Felicia Hart again.
YOU READY TO GO BACK TO THE CEMETERY?

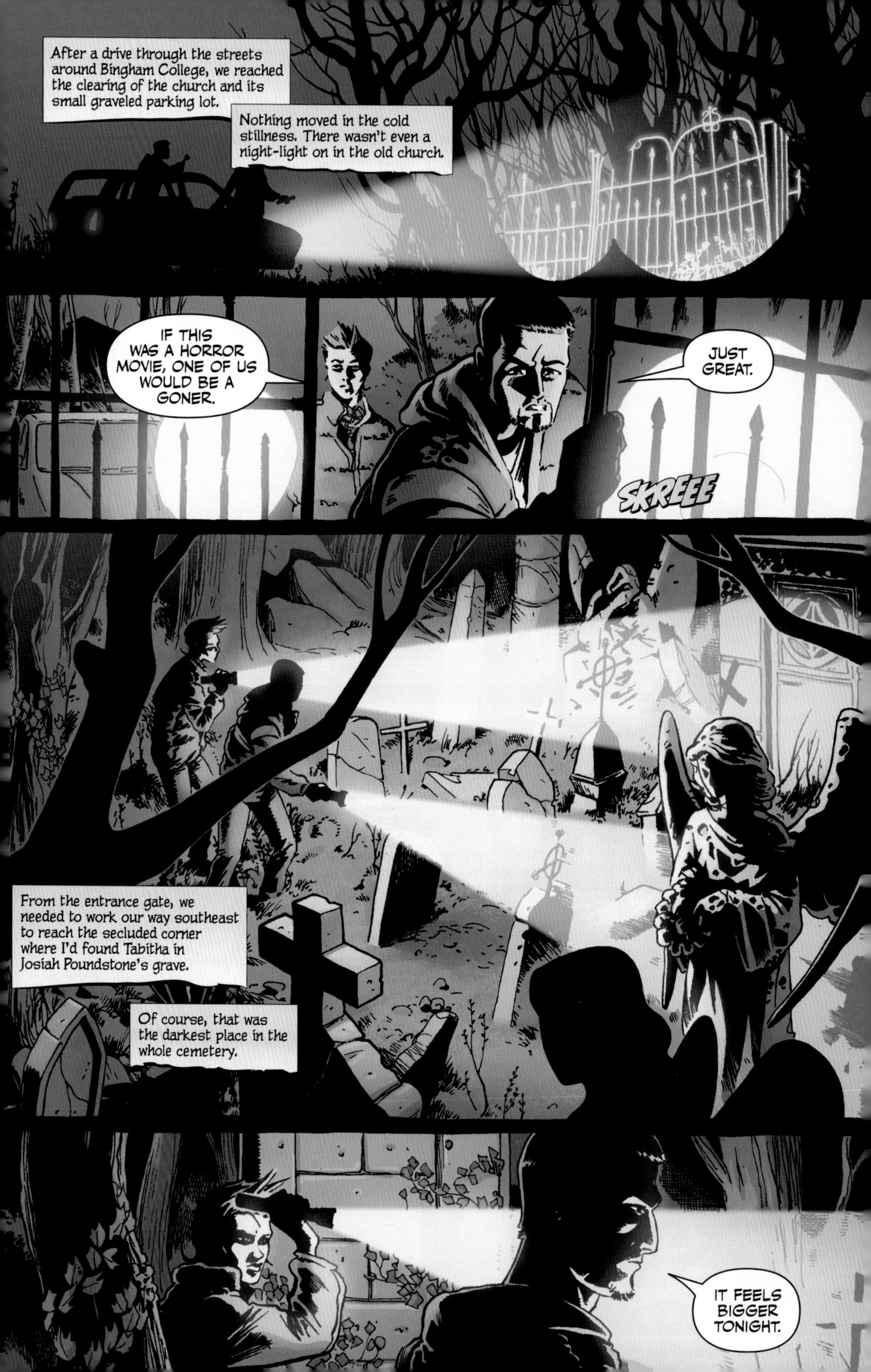
After a drive through the streets around Bingham College, we reached the clearing of the church and its small graveled parking lot.
Nothing moved in the cold stillness. There wasn't even a night-light on in the old church.
IF THIS WAS A HORROR MOVIE, ONE OF US WOULD BE A GONER.
JUST GREAT.
SKREEEE
From the entrance gate, we needed to work our way southeast to reach the secluded corner where I'd found Tabitha in Josiah Poundstone's grave.
Of course, that was the darkest place in the whole cemetery.
IT FEELS BIGGER TONIGHT.

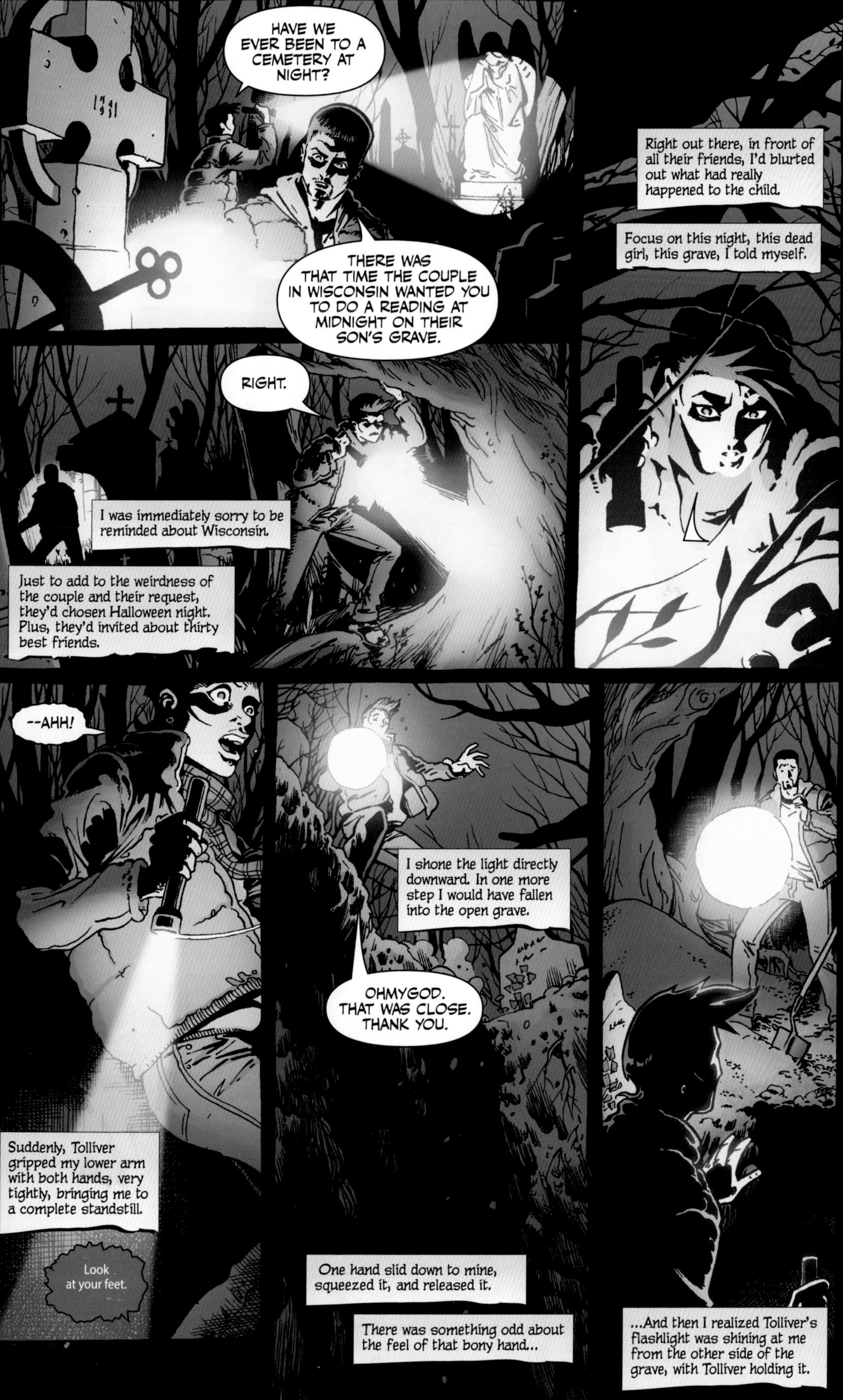
HAVE WE EVER BEEN TO A CEMETERY AT NIGHT?
THERE WAS THAT TIME THE COUPLE IN WISCONSIN WANTED YOU TO DO A READING AT MIDNIGHT ON THEIR SON'S GRAVE.
Right out there, in front of all their friends, I'd blurted out what had really happened to the child.
Focus on this night, this dead girl, this grave, I told myself.
RIGHT.
I was immediately sorry to be reminded about Wisconsin.
Just to add to the weirdness of the couple and their request, they'd chosen Halloween night. Plus, they'd invited about thirty best friends.
--AHH!
Suddenly, Tolliver gripped my lower arm with both hands, very tightly, bringing me to a complete standstill.
Look at your feet.
I shone the light directly downward. In one more step I would have fallen into the open grave.
OHMYGOD. THAT WAS CLOSE. THANK YOU.
One hand slid down to mine, squeezed it, and released it.
There was something odd about the feel of that bony hand...
...And then I realized Tolliver's flashlight was shining at me from the other side of the grave, with Tolliver holding it.

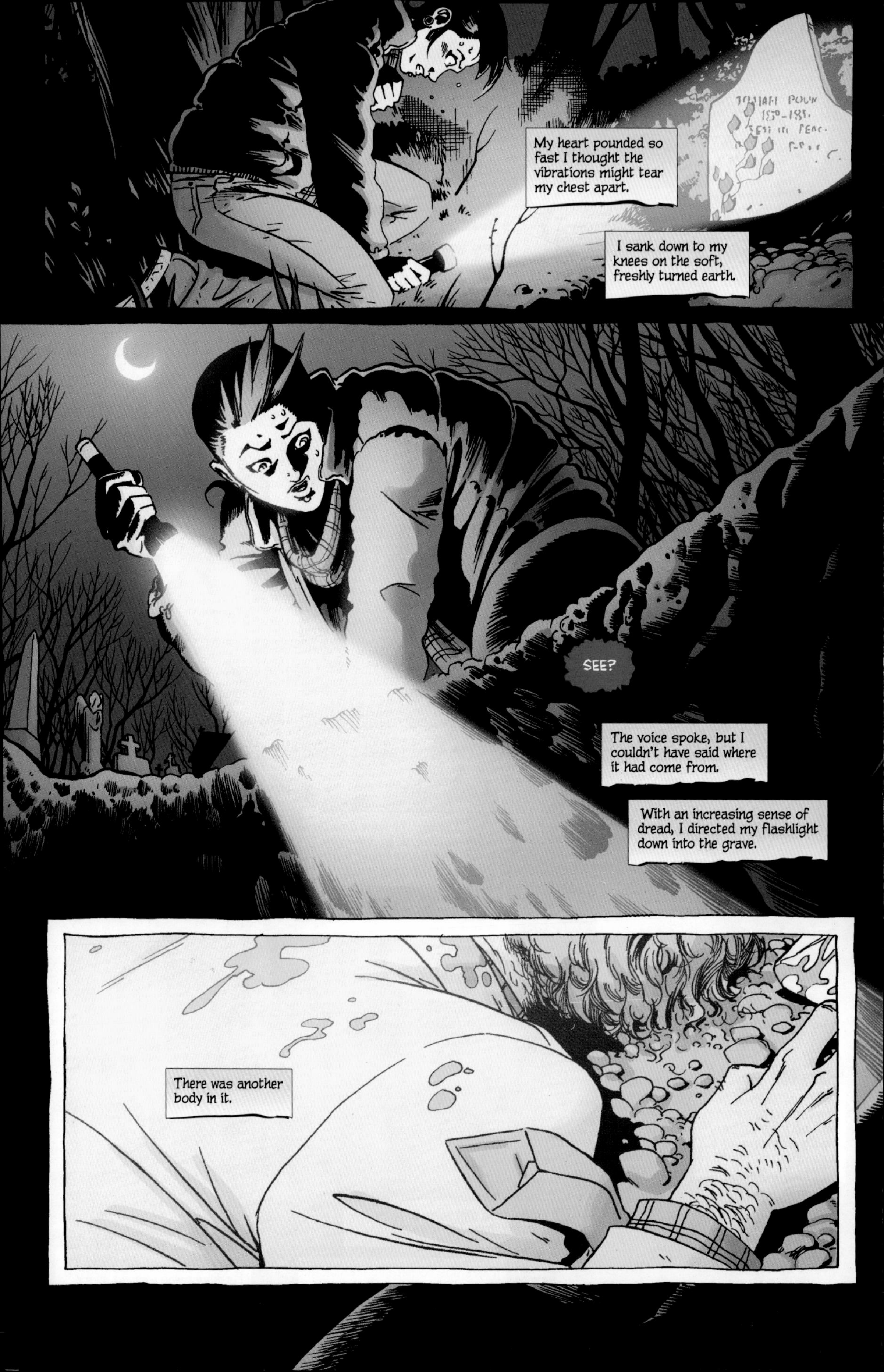
My heart pounded so fast I thought the vibrations might tear my chest apart.
I sank down to my knees on the soft, freshly turned earth.
SEE?
The voice spoke, but I couldn't have said where it had come from.
With an increasing sense of dread, I directed my flashlight down into the grave.
There was another body in it.

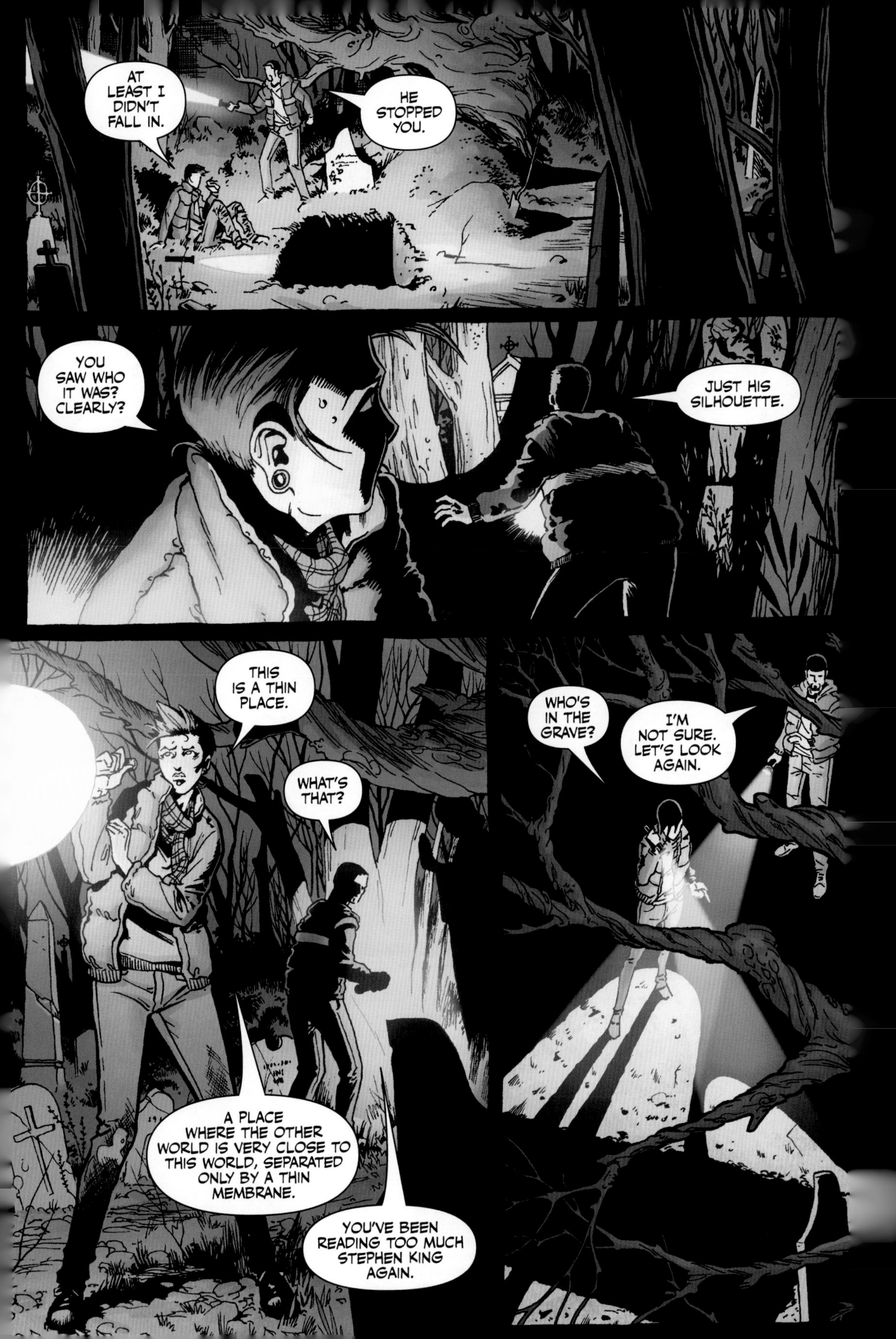
AT LEAST I DIDN'T FALL IN.
HE STOPPED YOU.
YOU SAW WHO IT WAS? CLEARLY?
JUST HIS SILHOUETTE.
THIS IS A THIN PLACE.
WHAT'S THAT?
A PLACE WHERE THE OTHER WORLD IS VERY CLOSE TO THIS WORLD, SEPARATED ONLY BY A THIN MEMBRANE.
YOU'VE BEEN READING TOO MUCH STEPHEN KING AGAIN.
WHO'S IN THE GRAVE?
I'M NOT SURE. LET'S LOOK AGAIN.

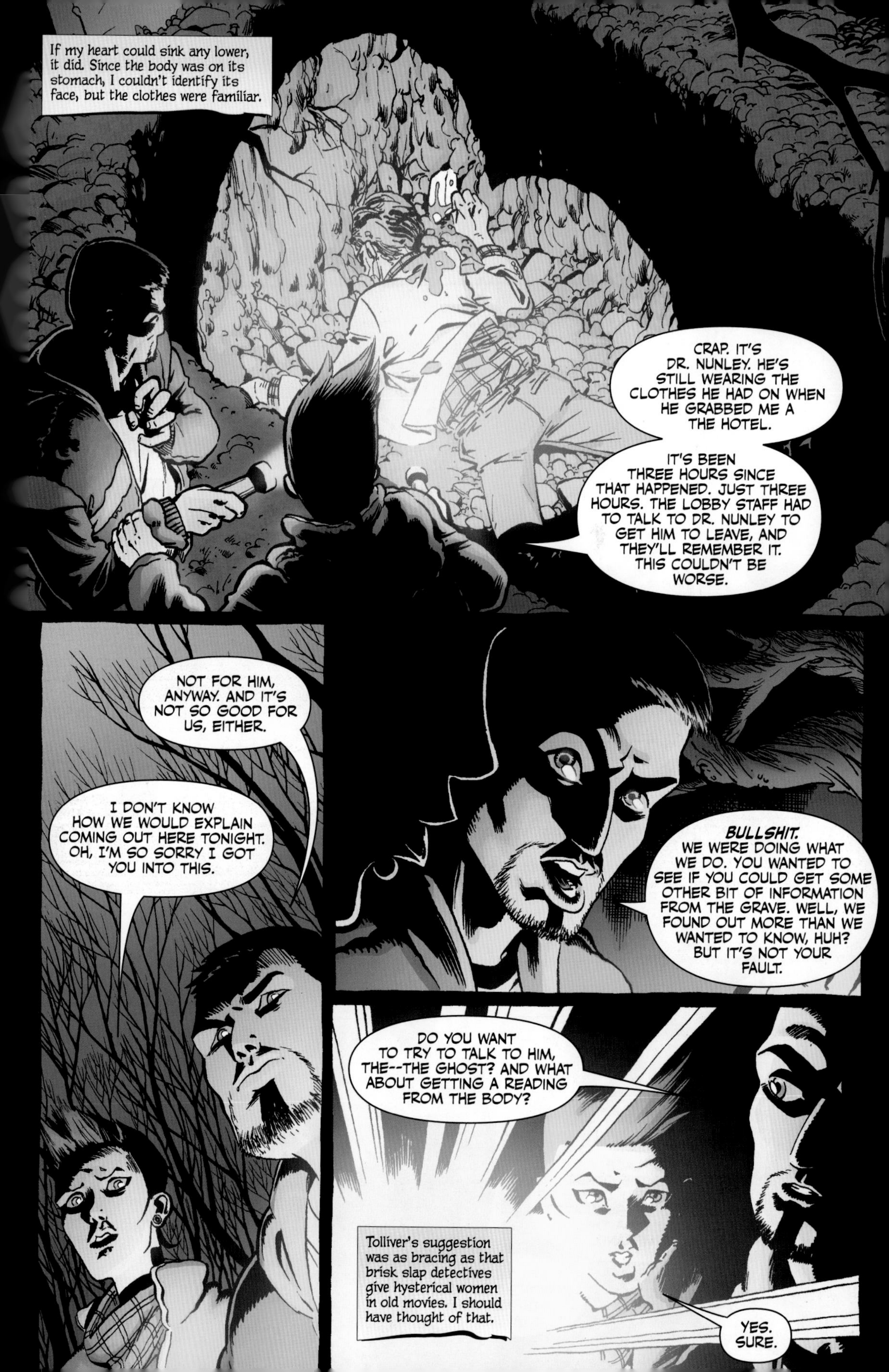
If my heart could sink any lower, it did. Since the body was on its stomach, I couldn't identify its face, but the clothes were familiar.
CRAP. IT'S DR. NUNLEY. HE'S STILL WEARING THE CLOTHES HE HAD ON WHEN HE GRABBED ME A THE HOTEL.
IT'S BEEN THREE HOURS SINCE THAT HAPPENED. JUST THREE HOURS. THE LOBBY STAFF HAD TO TALK TO DR. NUNLEY TO GET HIM TO LEAVE, AND THEY'LL REMEMBER IT. THIS COULDN'T BE WORSE.
NOT FOR HIM, ANYWAY. AND IT'S NOT SO GOOD FOR US, EITHER.
I DON'T KNOW HOW WE WOULD EXPLAIN COMING OUT HERE TONIGHT. OH, I'M SO SORRY I GOT YOU INTO THIS.
BULLSHIT. WE WERE DOING WHAT WE DO. YOU WANTED TO SEE IF YOU COULD GET SOME OTHER BIT OF INFORMATION FROM THE GRAVE. WELL, WE FOUND OUT MORE THAN WE WANTED TO KNOW, HUH? BUT IT'S NOT YOUR FAULT.
DO YOU WANT TO TRY TO TALK TO HIM, THE--THE GHOST? AND WHAT ABOUT GETTING A READING FROM THE BODY?
Tolliver's suggestion was as bracing as that brisk slap detectives give hysterical women in old movies. I should have thought of that.
YES. SURE.

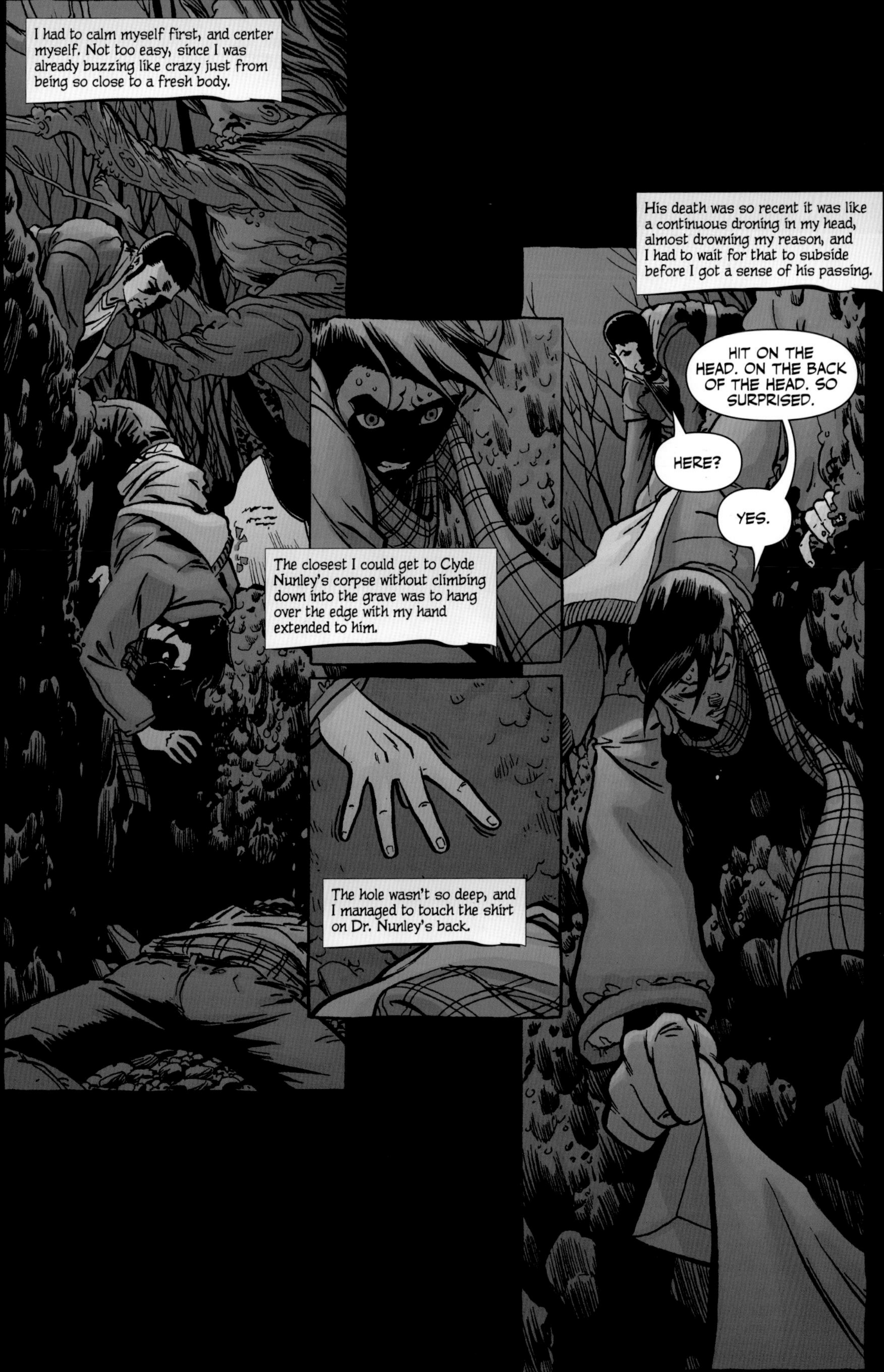
I had to calm myself first, and center myself. Not too easy, since I was already buzzing like crazy just from being so close to a fresh body.
The closest I could get to Clyde Nunley's corpse without climbing down into the grave was to hang over the edge with my hand extended to him.
The hole wasn't so deep, and I managed to touch the shirt on Dr. Nunley's back.
His death was so recent it was like a continuous droning in my head, almost drowning my reason, and I had to wait for that to subside before I got a sense of his passing.
HIT ON THE HEAD. ON THE BACK OF THE HEAD. SO SURPRISED.
HERE?
YES.

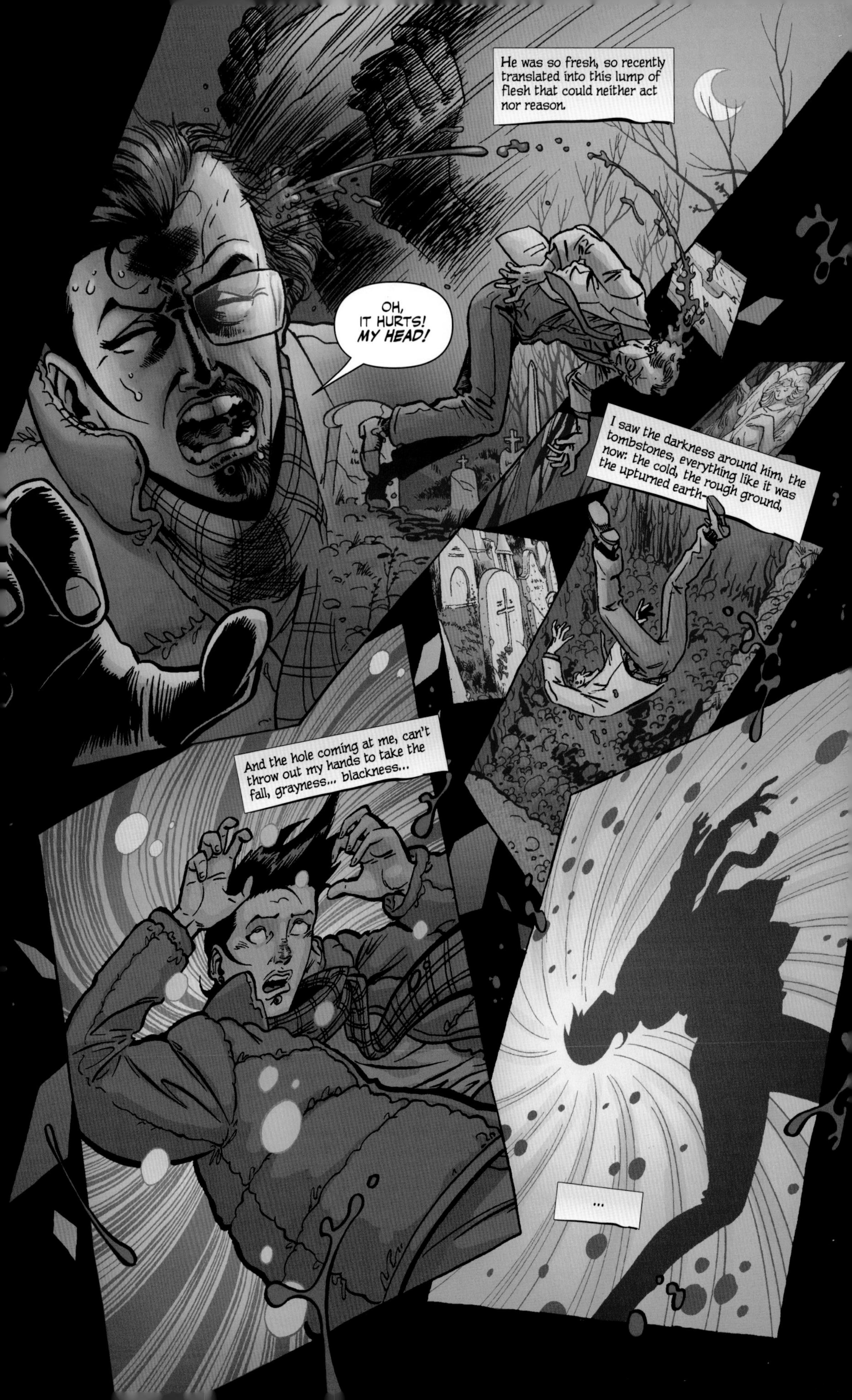
He was so fresh, so recently translated into this lump of flesh that could neither act nor reason.
OH, IT HURTS! MY HEAD!
I saw the darkness around him, the tombstones, everything like it was now: the cold, the rough ground, the upturned earth—
And the hole coming at me, can't throw out my hands to take the fall, grayness... blackness...
...

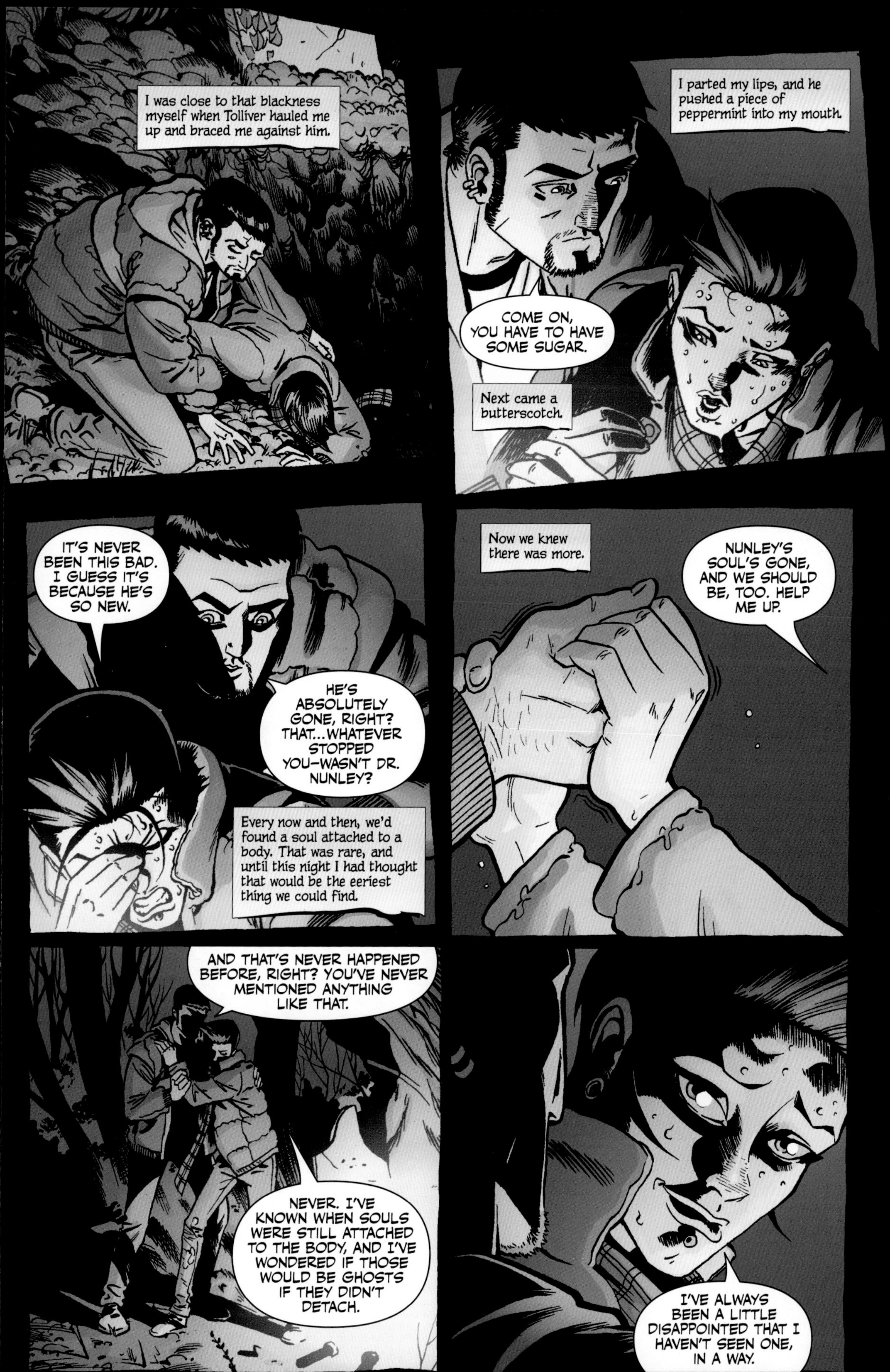
I was close to that blackness myself when Tolliver hauled me up and braced me against him.
I parted my lips, and he pushed a piece of peppermint into my mouth.
COME ON, YOU HAVE TO HAVE SOME SUGAR.
Next came a butterscotch.
IT'S NEVER BEEN THIS BAD. I GUESS IT'S BECAUSE HE'S SO NEW.
HE'S ABSOLUTELY GONE, RIGHT? THAT...WHATEVER STOPPED YOU–WASN'T DR. NUNLEY?
Every now and then, we'd found a soul attached to a body. That was rare, and until this night I had thought that would be the eeriest thing we could find.
Now we knew there was more.
NUNLEY'S SOUL'S GONE, AND WE SHOULD BE, TOO. HELP ME UP.
AND THAT'S NEVER HAPPENED BEFORE, RIGHT? YOU'VE NEVER MENTIONED ANYTHING LIKE THAT.
NEVER. I'VE KNOWN WHEN SOULS WERE STILL ATTACHED TO THE BODY, AND I'VE WONDERED IF THOSE WOULD BE GHOSTS IF THEY DIDN'T DETACH.
I'VE ALWAYS BEEN A LITTLE DISAPPOINTED THAT I HAVEN'T SEEN ONE, IN A WAY.

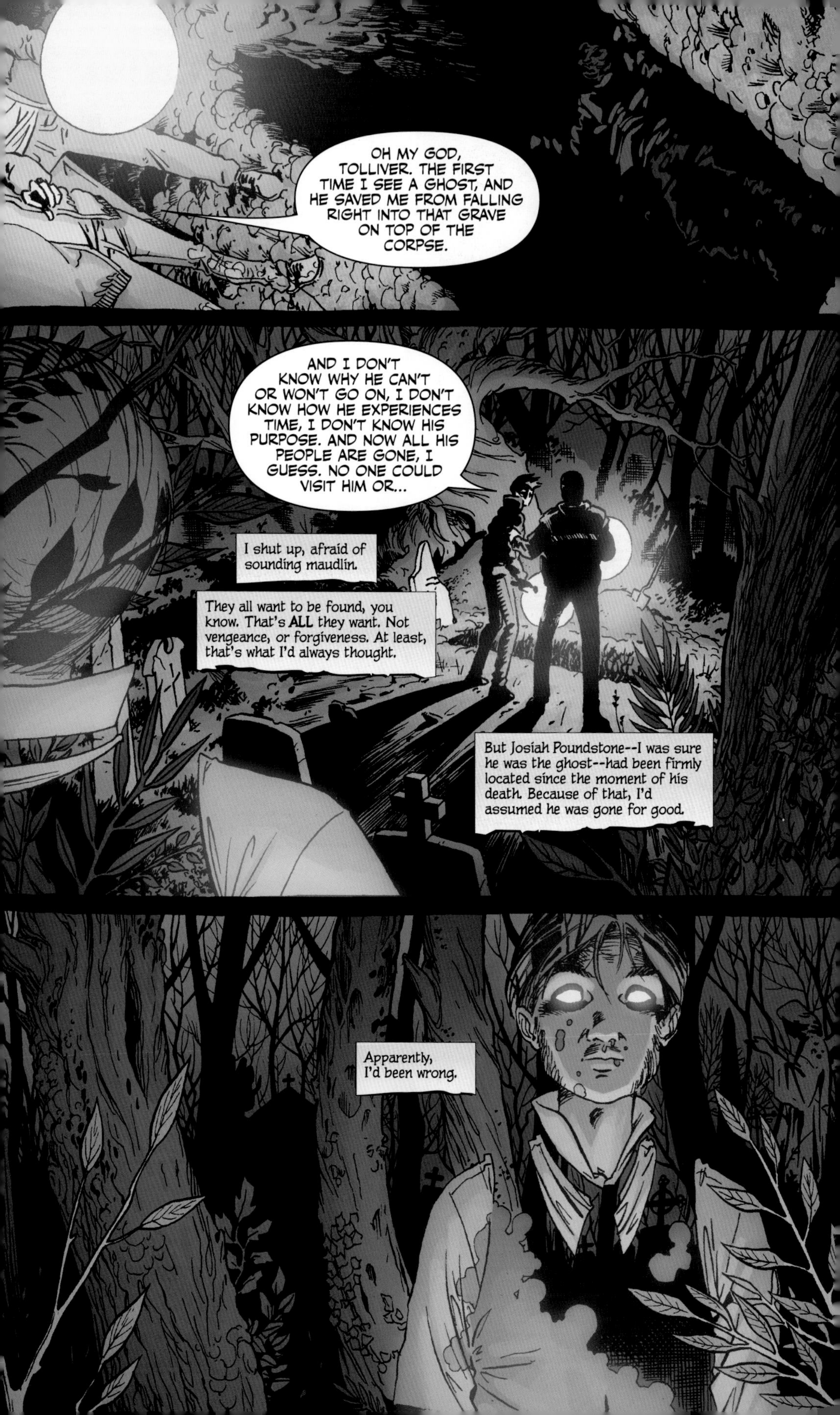
OH MY GOD, TOLLIVER. THE FIRST TIME I SEE A GHOST, AND HE SAVED ME FROM FALLING RIGHT INTO THAT GRAVE ON TOP OF THE CORPSE.
AND I DON'T KNOW WHY HE CAN'T OR WON'T GO ON, I DON'T KNOW HOW HE EXPERIENCES TIME, I DON'T KNOW HIS PURPOSE. AND NOW ALL HIS PEOPLE ARE GONE, I GUESS. NO ONE COULD VISIT HIM OR...
I shut up, afraid of sounding maudlin.
They all want to be found, you know. That's **ALL** they want. Not vengeance, or forgiveness. At least, that's what I'd always thought.
But Josiah Poundstone--I was sure he was the ghost--had been firmly located since the moment of his death. Because of that, I'd assumed he was gone for good.
Apparently, I'd been wrong.

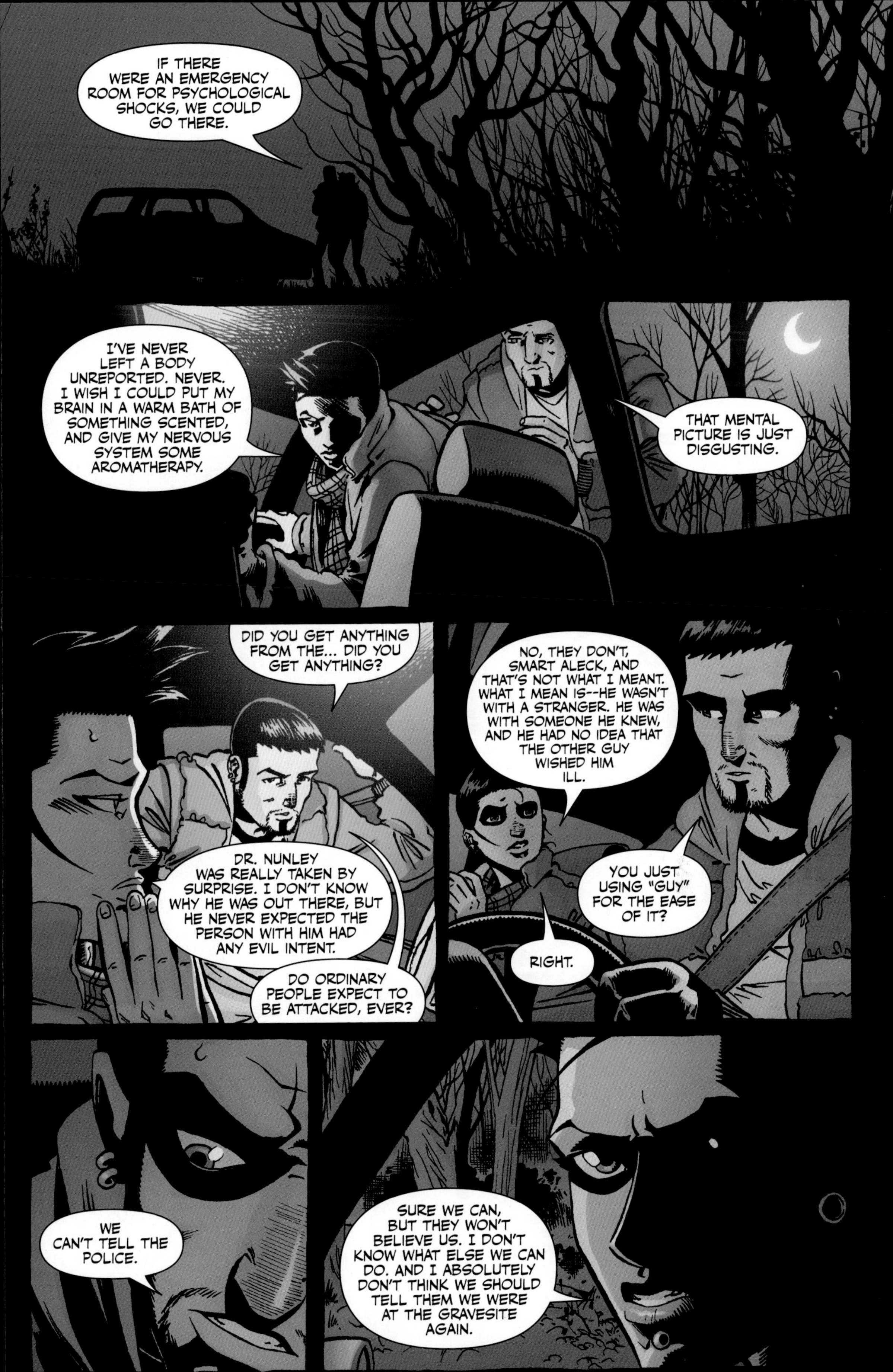
IF THERE WERE AN EMERGENCY ROOM FOR PSYCHOLOGICAL SHOCKS, WE COULD GO THERE.
I'VE NEVER LEFT A BODY UNREPORTED. NEVER. I WISH I COULD PUT MY BRAIN IN A WARM BATH OF SOMETHING SCENTED, AND GIVE MY NERVOUS SYSTEM SOME AROMATHERAPY.
THAT MENTAL PICTURE IS JUST DISGUSTING.
DID YOU GET ANYTHING FROM THE... DID YOU GET ANYTHING?
DR. NUNLEY WAS REALLY TAKEN BY SURPRISE. I DON'T KNOW WHY HE WAS OUT THERE, BUT HE NEVER EXPECTED THE PERSON WITH HIM HAD ANY EVIL INTENT.
DO ORDINARY PEOPLE EXPECT TO BE ATTACKED, EVER?
NO, THEY DON'T, SMART ALECK, AND THAT'S NOT WHAT I MEANT. WHAT I MEAN IS--HE WASN'T WITH A STRANGER. HE WAS WITH SOMEONE HE KNEW, AND HE HAD NO IDEA THAT THE OTHER GUY WISHED HIM ILL.
YOU JUST USING "GUY" FOR THE EASE OF IT?
RIGHT.
WE CAN'T TELL THE POLICE.
SURE WE CAN, BUT THEY WON'T BELIEVE US. I DON'T KNOW WHAT ELSE WE CAN DO. AND I ABSOLUTELY DON'T THINK WE SHOULD TELL THEM WE WERE AT THE GRAVESITE AGAIN.

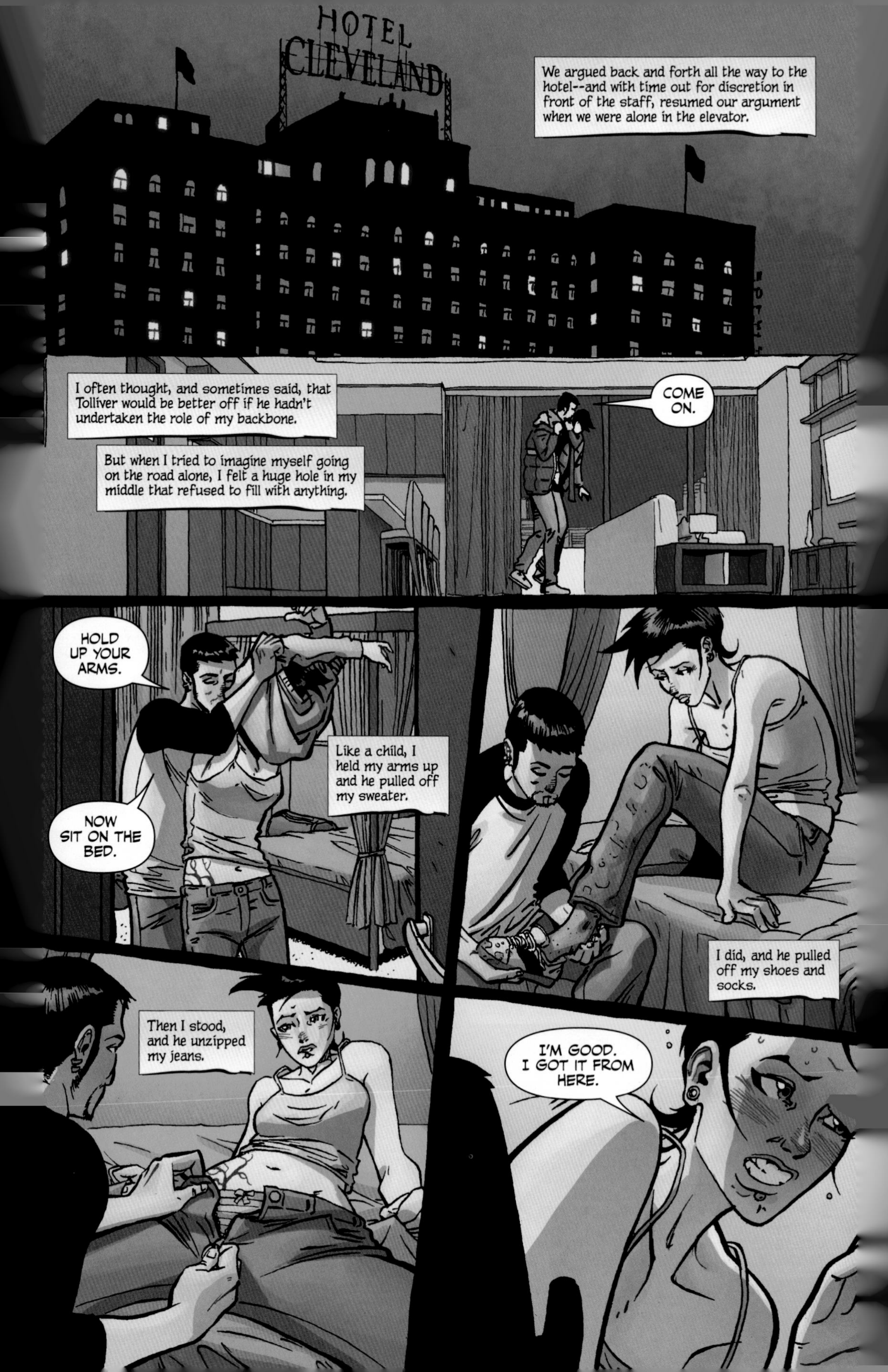
HOTEL CLEVELAND
We argued back and forth all the way to the hotel--and with time out for discretion in front of the staff, resumed our argument when we were alone in the elevator.
I often thought, and sometimes said, that Tolliver would be better off if he hadn't undertaken the role of my backbone.
But when I tried to imagine myself going on the road alone, I felt a huge hole in my middle that refused to fill with anything.
COME ON.
HOLD UP YOUR ARMS.
Like a child, I held my arms up and he pulled off my sweater.
NOW SIT ON THE BED.
I did, and he pulled off my shoes and socks.
Then I stood, and he unzipped my jeans.
I'M GOOD. I GOT IT FROM HERE.

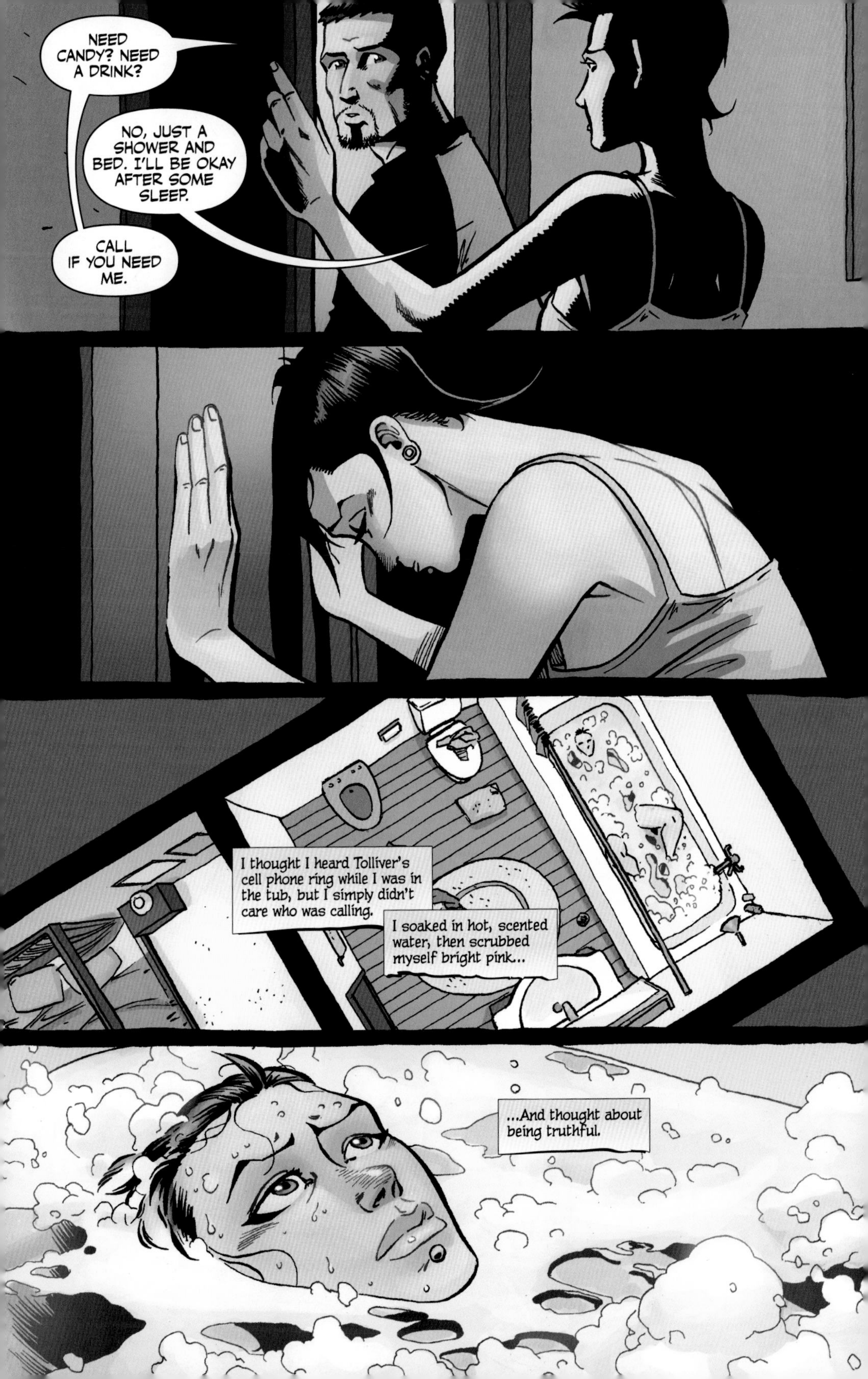
NEED CANDY? NEED A DRINK?
NO, JUST A SHOWER AND BED. I'LL BE OKAY AFTER SOME SLEEP.
CALL IF YOU NEED ME.
I thought I heard Tolliver's cell phone ring while I was in the tub, but I simply didn't care who was calling.
I soaked in hot, scented water, then scrubbed myself bright pink...
...And thought about being truthful.

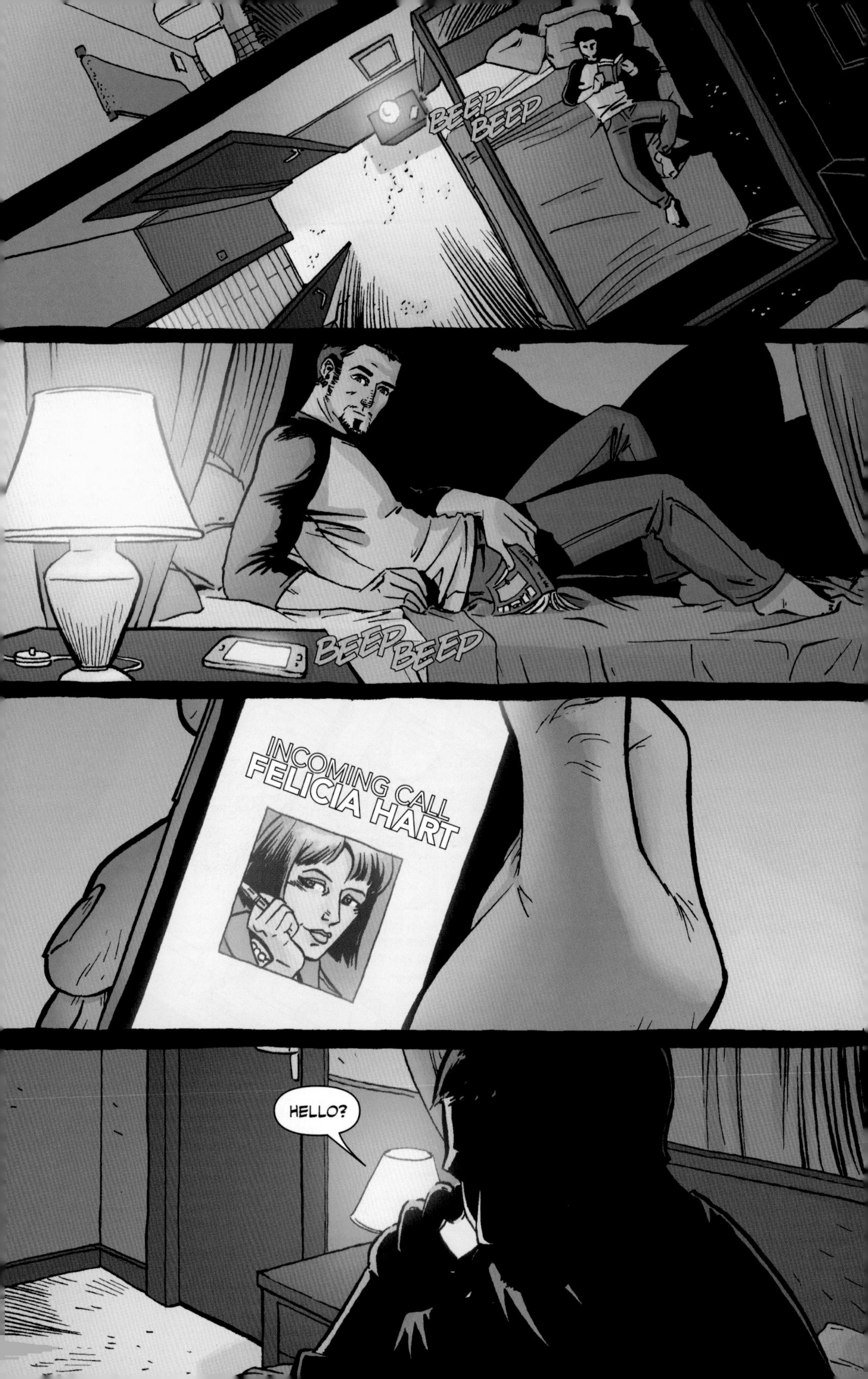
BEEP BEEP
BEEP BEEP
INCOMING CALL
FELICIA HART
HELLO?

CHAPTER FIVE

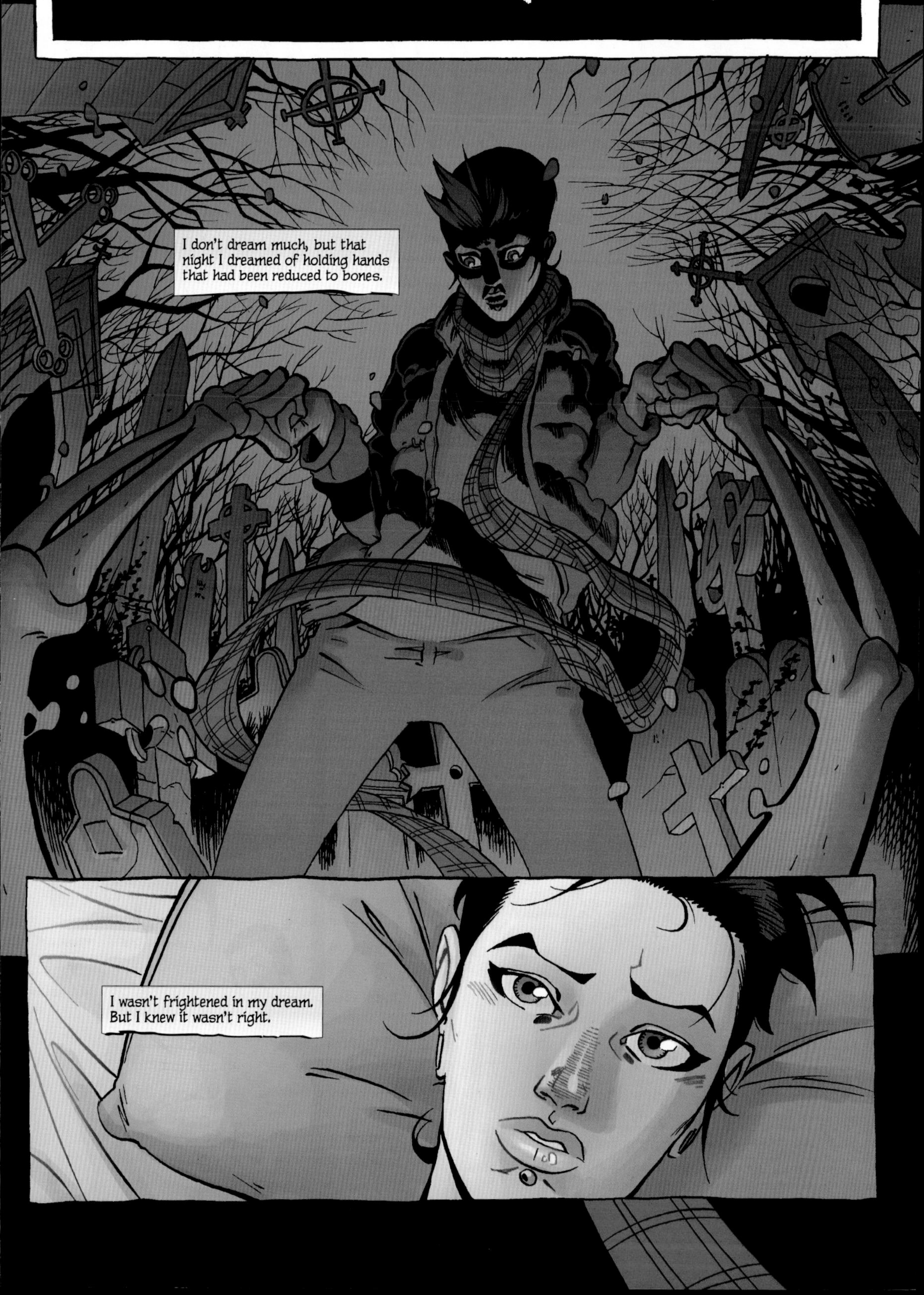
I don't dream much, but that night I dreamed of holding hands that had been reduced to bones.
I wasn't frightened in my dream. But I knew it wasn't right.

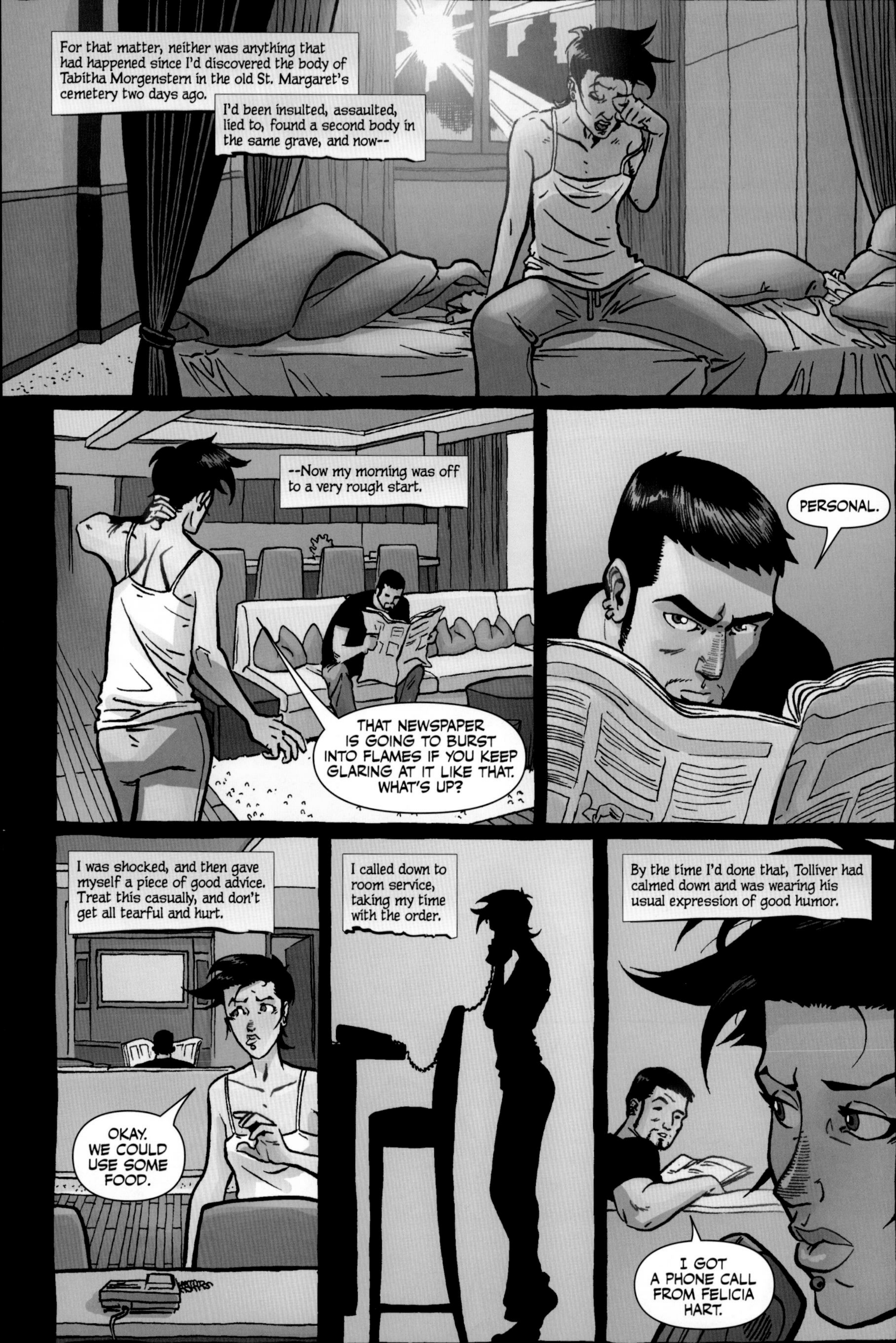
For that matter, neither was anything that had happened since I'd discovered the body of Tabitha Morgenstern in the old St. Margaret's cemetery two days ago.
I'd been insulted, assaulted, lied to, found a second body in the same grave, and now--
--Now my morning was off to a very rough start.
THAT NEWSPAPER IS GOING TO BURST INTO FLAMES IF YOU KEEP GLARING AT IT LIKE THAT. WHAT'S UP?
PERSONAL.
I was shocked, and then gave myself a piece of good advice. Treat this casually, and don't get all tearful and hurt.
OKAY. WE COULD USE SOME FOOD.
I called down to room service, taking my time with the order.
By the time I'd done that, Tolliver had calmed down and was wearing his usual expression of good humor.
I GOT A PHONE CALL FROM FELICIA HART.

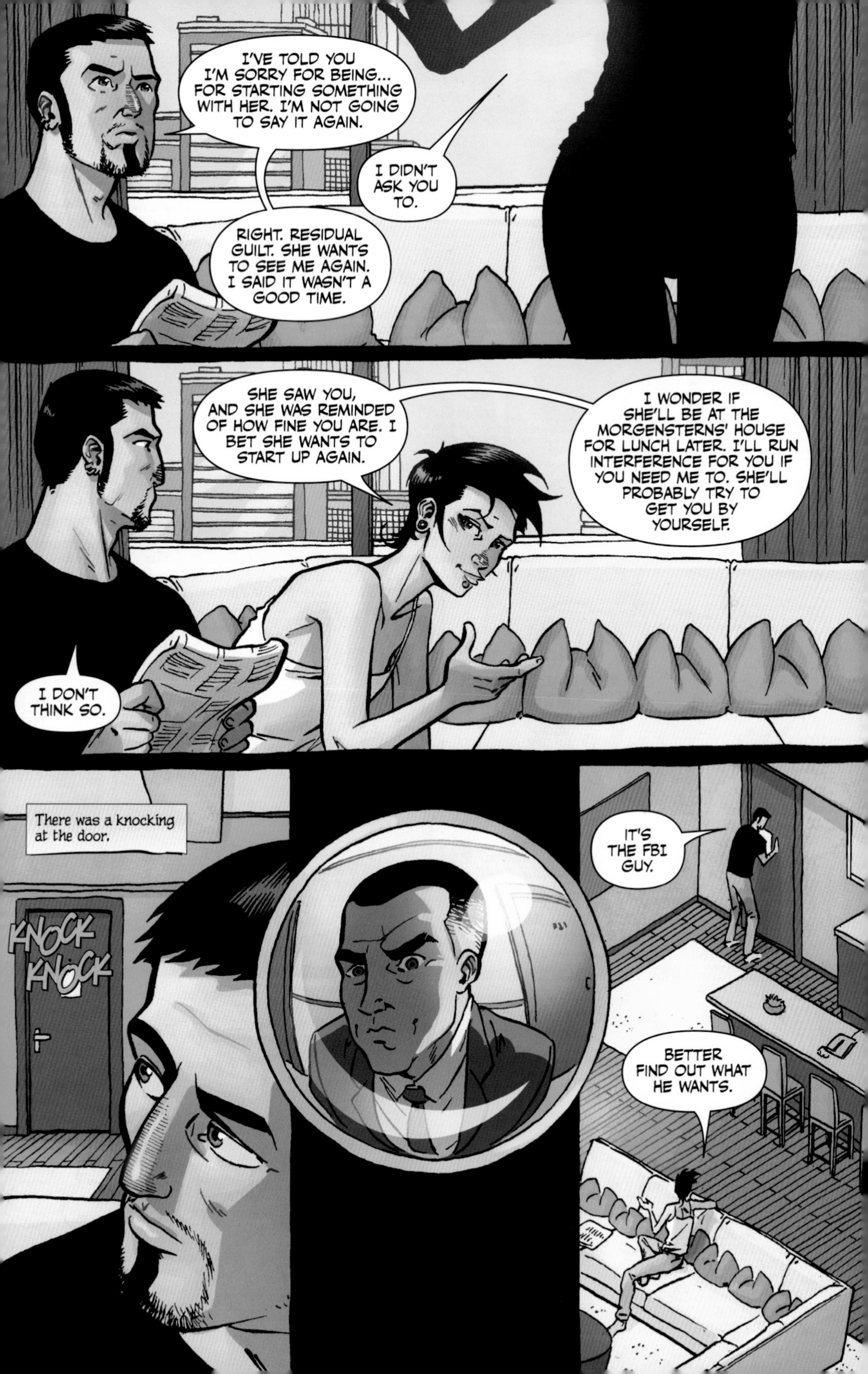
I'VE TOLD YOU I'M SORRY FOR BEING... FOR STARTING SOMETHING WITH HER. I'M NOT GOING TO SAY IT AGAIN.
I DIDN'T ASK YOU TO.
RIGHT. RESIDUAL GUILT. SHE WANTS TO SEE ME AGAIN. I SAID IT WASN'T A GOOD TIME.
SHE SAW YOU, AND SHE WAS REMINDED OF HOW FINE YOU ARE. I BET SHE WANTS TO START UP AGAIN.
I WONDER IF SHE'LL BE AT THE MORGENSTERNS' HOUSE FOR LUNCH LATER. I'LL RUN INTERFERENCE FOR YOU IF YOU NEED ME TO. SHE'LL PROBABLY TRY TO GET YOU BY YOURSELF.
I DON'T THINK SO.
There was a knocking at the door.
KNOCK KNOCK
IT'S THE FBI GUY.
BETTER FIND OUT WHAT HE WANTS.

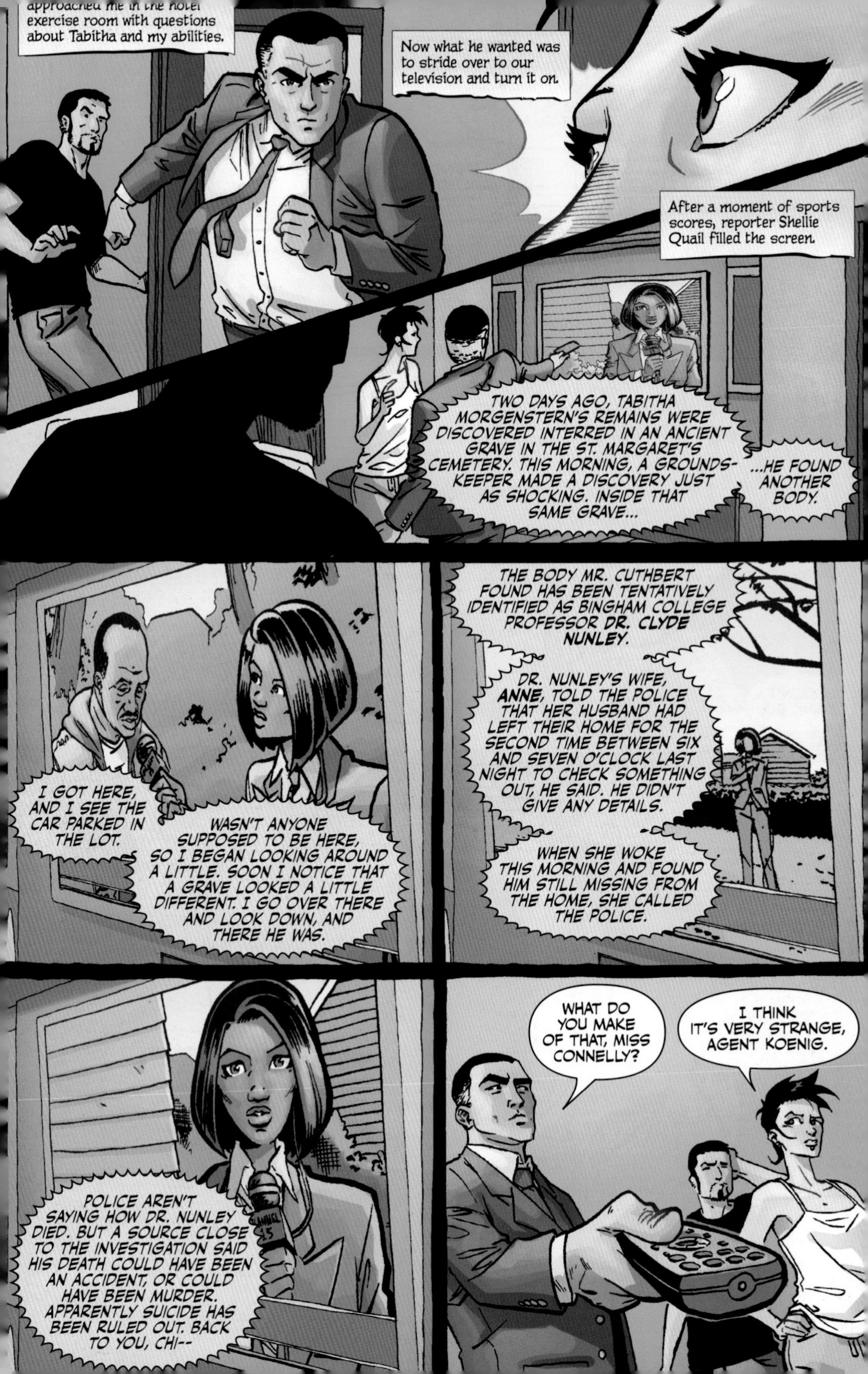
approached me in the hotel exercise room with questions about Tabitha and my abilities.
Now what he wanted was to stride over to our television and turn it on.
After a moment of sports scores, reporter Shellie Quail filled the screen.
TWO DAYS AGO, TABITHA MORGENSTERN'S REMAINS WERE DISCOVERED INTERRED IN AN ANCIENT GRAVE IN THE ST. MARGARET'S CEMETERY. THIS MORNING, A GROUNDS-KEEPER MADE A DISCOVERY JUST AS SHOCKING. INSIDE THAT SAME GRAVE...
...HE FOUND ANOTHER BODY.
I GOT HERE, AND I SEE THE CAR PARKED IN THE LOT.
WASN'T ANYONE SUPPOSED TO BE HERE, SO I BEGAN LOOKING AROUND A LITTLE. SOON I NOTICE THAT A GRAVE LOOKED A LITTLE DIFFERENT. I GO OVER THERE AND LOOK DOWN, AND THERE HE WAS.
THE BODY MR. CUTHBERT FOUND HAS BEEN TENTATIVELY IDENTIFIED AS BINGHAM COLLEGE PROFESSOR DR. CLYDE NUNLEY.
DR. NUNLEY'S WIFE, ANNE, TOLD THE POLICE THAT HER HUSBAND HAD LEFT THEIR HOME FOR THE SECOND TIME BETWEEN SIX AND SEVEN O'CLOCK LAST NIGHT TO CHECK SOMETHING OUT, HE SAID. HE DIDN'T GIVE ANY DETAILS.
WHEN SHE WOKE THIS MORNING AND FOUND HIM STILL MISSING FROM THE HOME, SHE CALLED THE POLICE.
POLICE AREN'T SAYING HOW DR. NUNLEY DIED. BUT A SOURCE CLOSE TO THE INVESTIGATION SAID HIS DEATH COULD HAVE BEEN AN ACCIDENT, OR COULD HAVE BEEN MURDER. APPARENTLY SUICIDE HAS BEEN RULED OUT. BACK TO YOU, CHI--
WHAT DO YOU MAKE OF THAT, MISS CONNELLY?
I THINK IT'S VERY STRANGE, AGENT KOENIG.

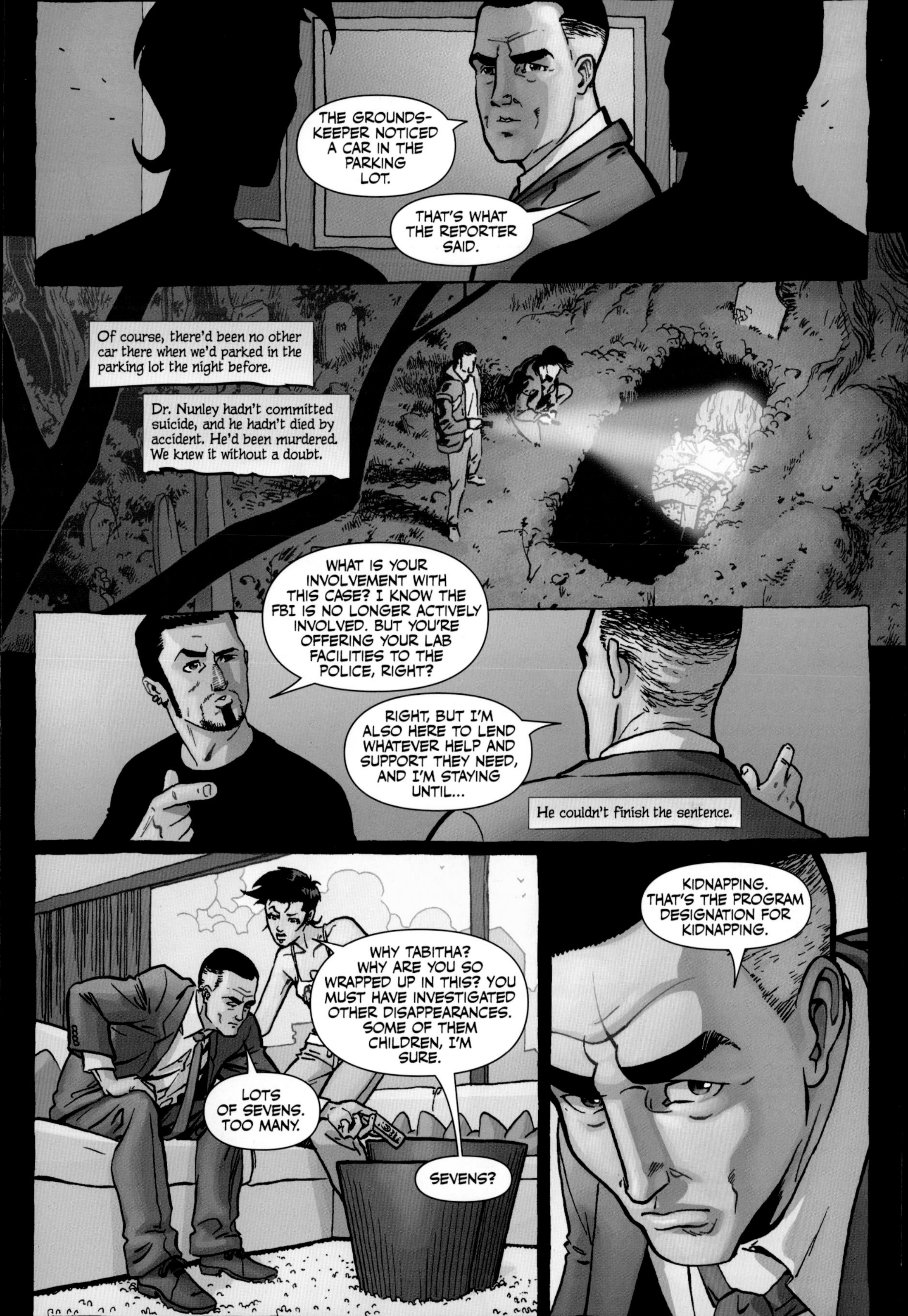
THE GROUNDS-KEEPER NOTICED A CAR IN THE PARKING LOT.
THAT'S WHAT THE REPORTER SAID.
Of course, there'd been no other car there when we'd parked in the parking lot the night before.
Dr. Nunley hadn't committed suicide, and he hadn't died by accident. He'd been murdered. We knew it without a doubt.
WHAT IS YOUR INVOLVEMENT WITH THIS CASE? I KNOW THE FBI IS NO LONGER ACTIVELY INVOLVED. BUT YOU'RE OFFERING YOUR LAB FACILITIES TO THE POLICE, RIGHT?
RIGHT, BUT I'M ALSO HERE TO LEND WHATEVER HELP AND SUPPORT THEY NEED, AND I'M STAYING UNTIL...
He couldn't finish the sentence.
WHY TABITHA? WHY ARE YOU SO WRAPPED UP IN THIS? YOU MUST HAVE INVESTIGATED OTHER DISAPPEARANCES. SOME OF THEM CHILDREN, I'M SURE.
LOTS OF SEVENS. TOO MANY.
SEVENS?
KIDNAPPING. THAT'S THE PROGRAM DESIGNATION FOR KIDNAPPING.

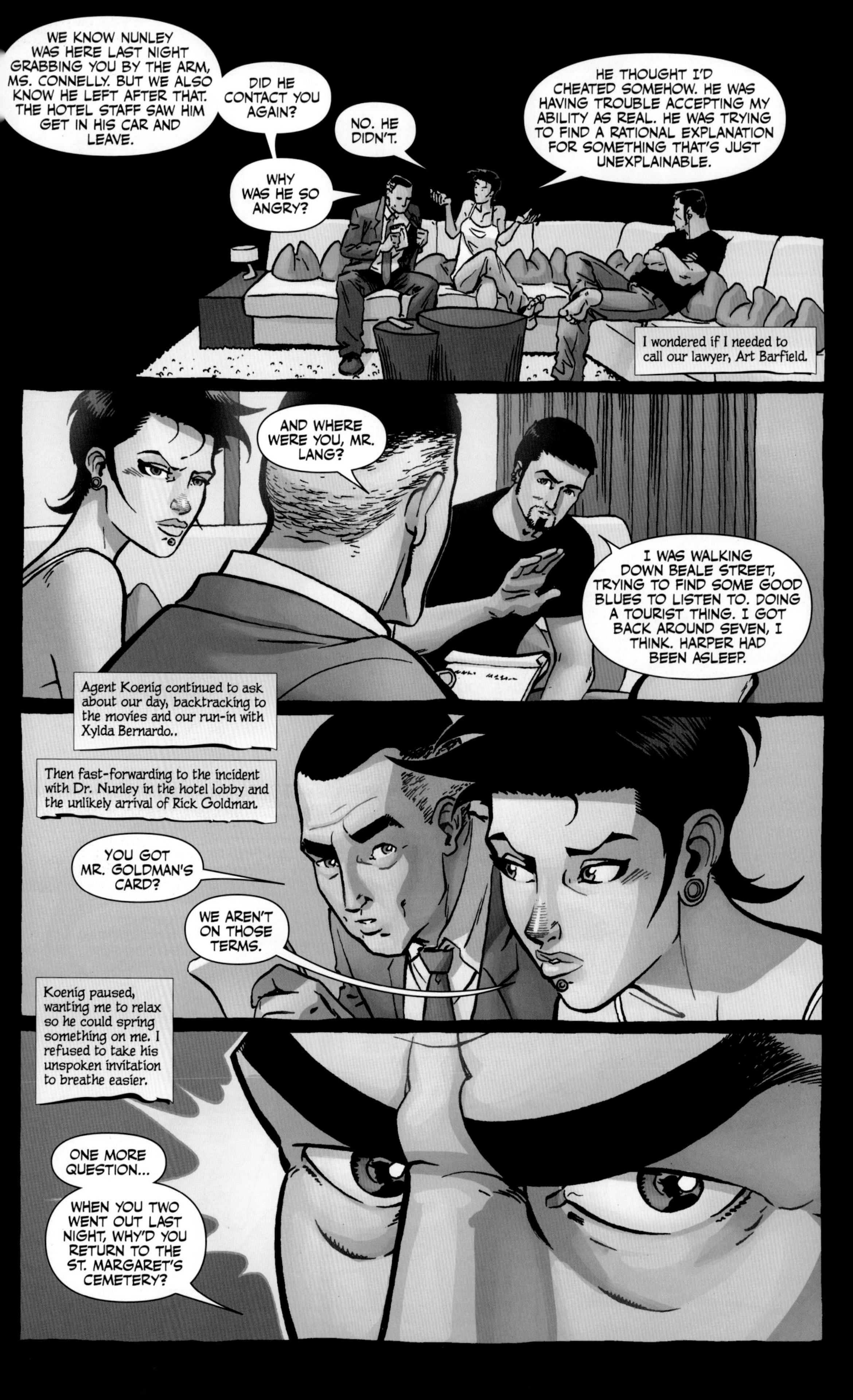
WE KNOW NUNLEY WAS HERE LAST NIGHT GRABBING YOU BY THE ARM, MS. CONNELLY. BUT WE ALSO KNOW HE LEFT AFTER THAT. THE HOTEL STAFF SAW HIM GET IN HIS CAR AND LEAVE.
DID HE CONTACT YOU AGAIN?
NO. HE DIDN'T.
WHY WAS HE SO ANGRY?
HE THOUGHT I'D CHEATED SOMEHOW. HE WAS HAVING TROUBLE ACCEPTING MY ABILITY AS REAL. HE WAS TRYING TO FIND A RATIONAL EXPLANATION FOR SOMETHING THAT'S JUST UNEXPLAINABLE.
I wondered if I needed to call our lawyer, Art Barfield.
AND WHERE WERE YOU, MR. LANG?
I WAS WALKING DOWN BEALE STREET, TRYING TO FIND SOME GOOD BLUES TO LISTEN TO. DOING A TOURIST THING. I GOT BACK AROUND SEVEN, I THINK. HARPER HAD BEEN ASLEEP.
Agent Koenig continued to ask about our day, backtracking to the movies and our run-in with Xylda Bernardo..
Then fast-forwarding to the incident with Dr. Nunley in the hotel lobby and the unlikely arrival of Rick Goldman.
YOU GOT MR. GOLDMAN'S CARD?
WE AREN'T ON THOSE TERMS.
Koenig paused, wanting me to relax so he could spring something on me. I refused to take his unspoken invitation to breathe easier.
ONE MORE QUESTION...
WHEN YOU TWO WENT OUT LAST NIGHT, WHY'D YOU RETURN TO THE ST. MARGARET'S CEMETERY?

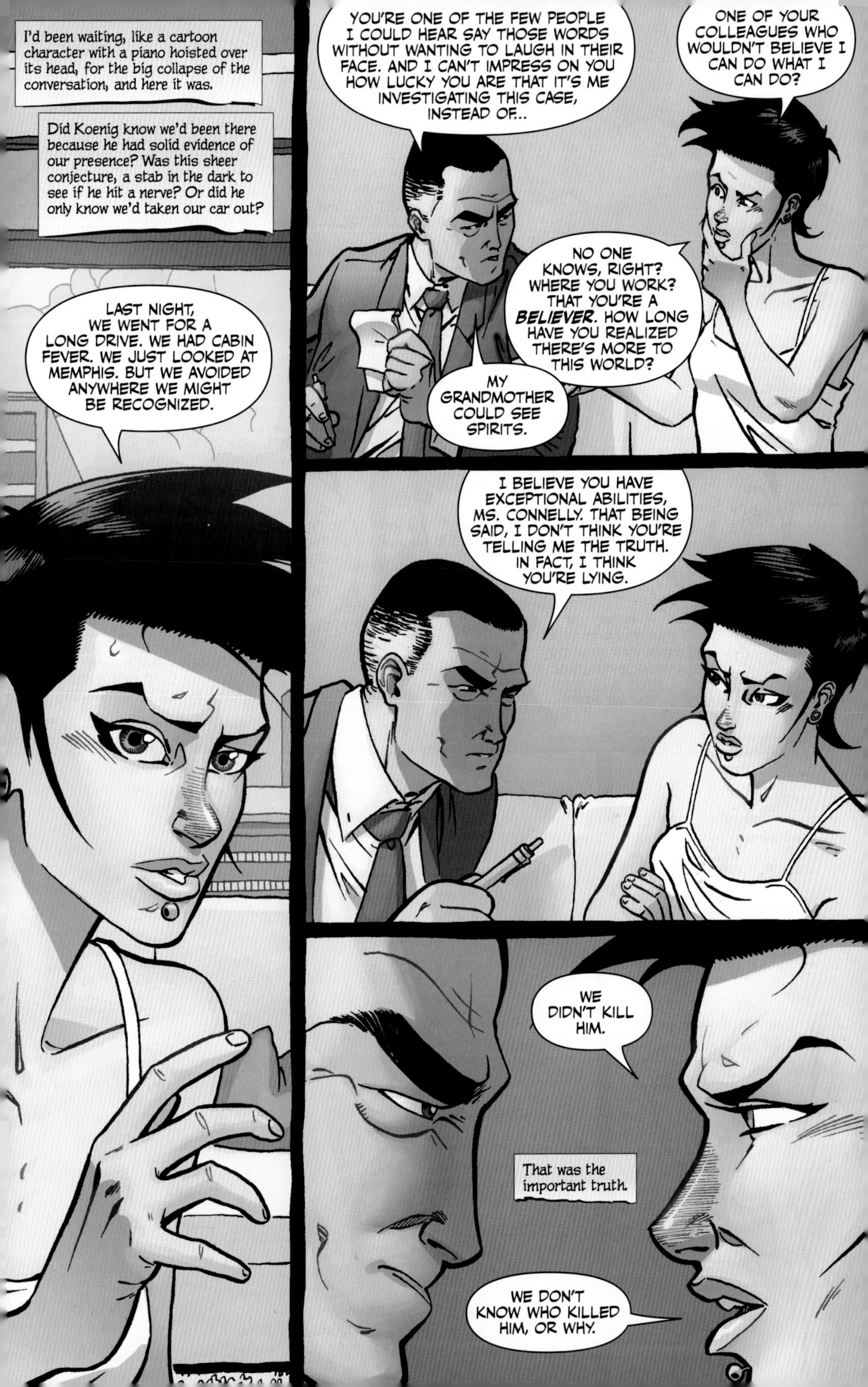
I'd been waiting, like a cartoon character with a piano hoisted over its head, for the big collapse of the conversation, and here it was.
Did Koenig know we'd been there because he had solid evidence of our presence? Was this sheer conjecture, a stab in the dark to see if he hit a nerve? Or did he only know we'd taken our car out?
LAST NIGHT, WE WENT FOR A LONG DRIVE. WE HAD CABIN FEVER. WE JUST LOOKED AT MEMPHIS. BUT WE AVOIDED ANYWHERE WE MIGHT BE RECOGNIZED.
YOU'RE ONE OF THE FEW PEOPLE I COULD HEAR SAY THOSE WORDS WITHOUT WANTING TO LAUGH IN THEIR FACE. AND I CAN'T IMPRESS ON YOU HOW LUCKY YOU ARE THAT IT'S ME INVESTIGATING THIS CASE, INSTEAD OF...
ONE OF YOUR COLLEAGUES WHO WOULDN'T BELIEVE I CAN DO WHAT I CAN DO?
NO ONE KNOWS, RIGHT? WHERE YOU WORK? THAT YOU'RE A ***BELIEVER***. HOW LONG HAVE YOU REALIZED THERE'S MORE TO THIS WORLD?
MY GRANDMOTHER COULD SEE SPIRITS.
I BELIEVE YOU HAVE EXCEPTIONAL ABILITIES, MS. CONNELLY. THAT BEING SAID, I DON'T THINK YOU'RE TELLING ME THE TRUTH. IN FACT, I THINK YOU'RE LYING.
WE DIDN'T KILL HIM.
That was the important truth.
WE DON'T KNOW WHO KILLED HIM, OR WHY.

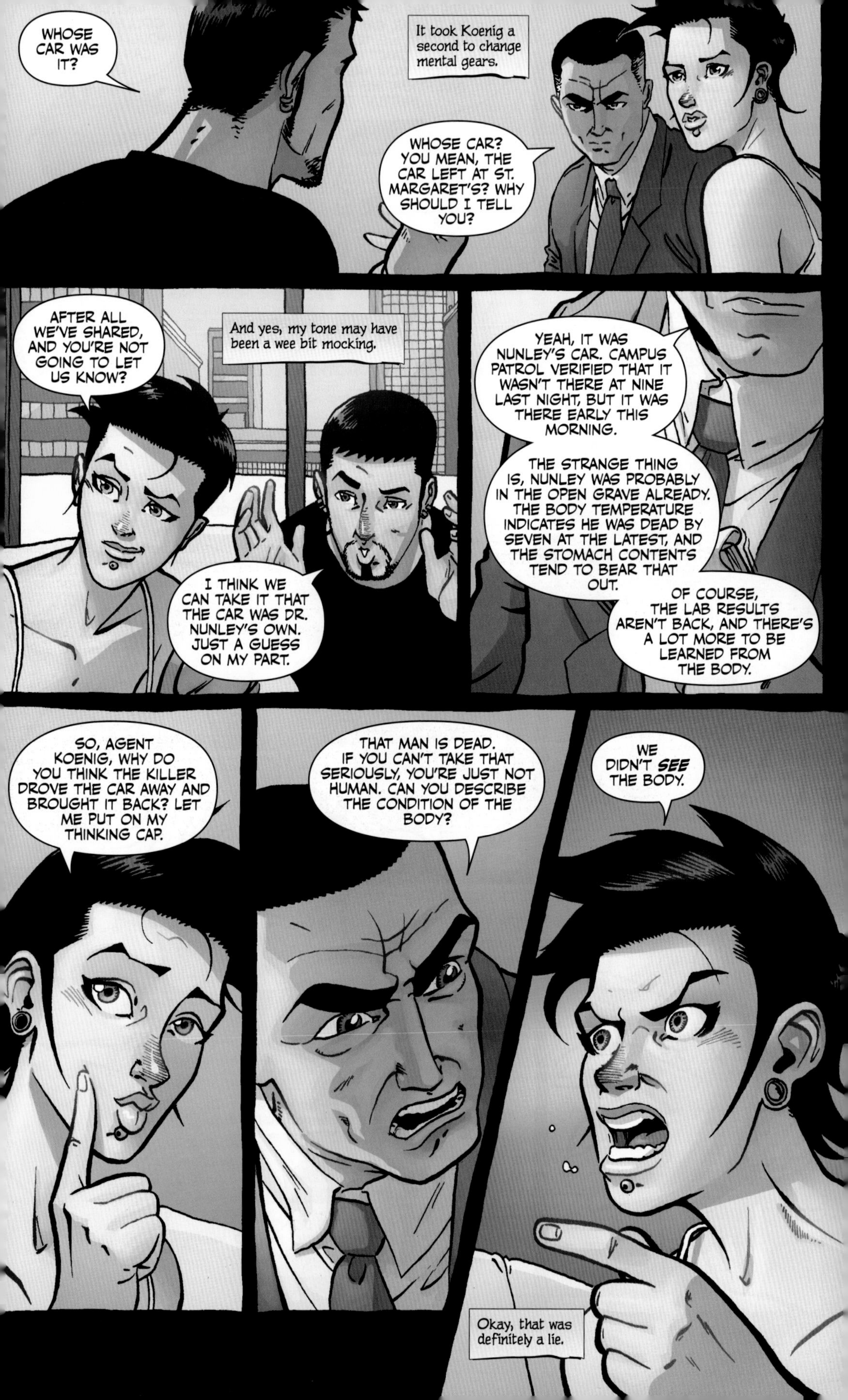
WHOSE CAR WAS IT?
It took Koenig a second to change mental gears.
WHOSE CAR? YOU MEAN, THE CAR LEFT AT ST. MARGARET'S? WHY SHOULD I TELL YOU?
AFTER ALL WE'VE SHARED, AND YOU'RE NOT GOING TO LET US KNOW?
And yes, my tone may have been a wee bit mocking.
I THINK WE CAN TAKE IT THAT THE CAR WAS DR. NUNLEY'S OWN. JUST A GUESS ON MY PART.
YEAH, IT WAS NUNLEY'S CAR. CAMPUS PATROL VERIFIED THAT IT WASN'T THERE AT NINE LAST NIGHT, BUT IT WAS THERE EARLY THIS MORNING.
THE STRANGE THING IS, NUNLEY WAS PROBABLY IN THE OPEN GRAVE ALREADY. THE BODY TEMPERATURE INDICATES HE WAS DEAD BY SEVEN AT THE LATEST, AND THE STOMACH CONTENTS TEND TO BEAR THAT OUT.
OF COURSE, THE LAB RESULTS AREN'T BACK, AND THERE'S A LOT MORE TO BE LEARNED FROM THE BODY.
SO, AGENT KOENIG, WHY DO YOU THINK THE KILLER DROVE THE CAR AWAY AND BROUGHT IT BACK? LET ME PUT ON MY THINKING CAP.
THAT MAN IS DEAD. IF YOU CAN'T TAKE THAT SERIOUSLY, YOU'RE JUST NOT HUMAN. CAN YOU DESCRIBE THE CONDITION OF THE BODY?
WE DIDN'T *SEE* THE BODY.
Okay, that was definitely a lie.

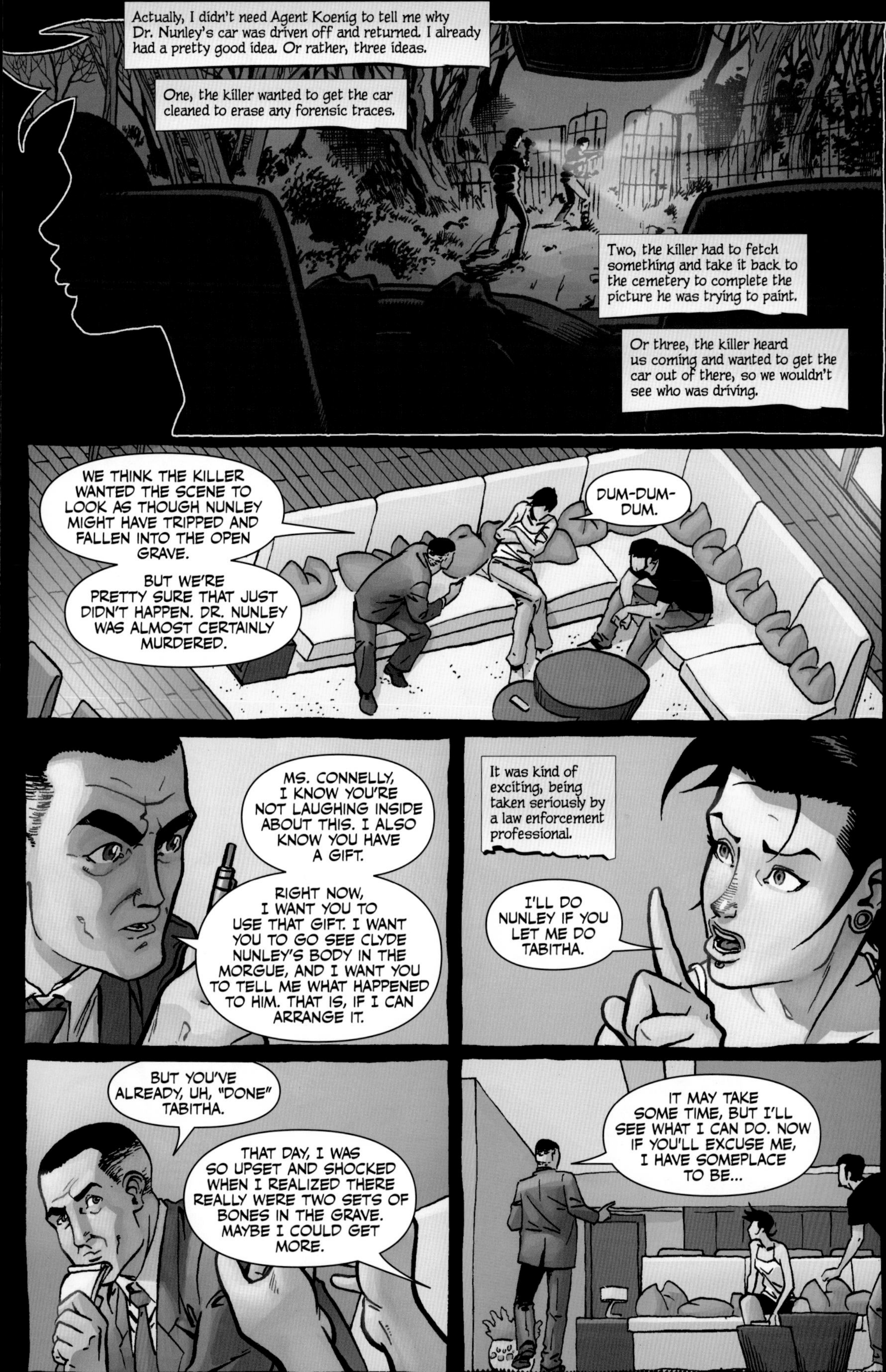
Actually, I didn't need Agent Koenig to tell me why Dr. Nunley's car was driven off and returned. I already had a pretty good idea. Or rather, three ideas.
One, the killer wanted to get the car cleaned to erase any forensic traces.
Two, the killer had to fetch something and take it back to the cemetery to complete the picture he was trying to paint.
Or three, the killer heard us coming and wanted to get the car out of there, so we wouldn't see who was driving.
WE THINK THE KILLER WANTED THE SCENE TO LOOK AS THOUGH NUNLEY MIGHT HAVE TRIPPED AND FALLEN INTO THE OPEN GRAVE.
BUT WE'RE PRETTY SURE THAT JUST DIDN'T HAPPEN. DR. NUNLEY WAS ALMOST CERTAINLY MURDERED.
DUM-DUM-DUM.
MS. CONNELLY, I KNOW YOU'RE NOT LAUGHING INSIDE ABOUT THIS. I ALSO KNOW YOU HAVE A GIFT.
RIGHT NOW, I WANT YOU TO USE THAT GIFT. I WANT YOU TO GO SEE CLYDE NUNLEY'S BODY IN THE MORGUE, AND I WANT YOU TO TELL ME WHAT HAPPENED TO HIM. THAT IS, IF I CAN ARRANGE IT.
It was kind of exciting, being taken seriously by a law enforcement professional.
I'LL DO NUNLEY IF YOU LET ME DO TABITHA.
BUT YOU'VE ALREADY, UH, "DONE" TABITHA.
THAT DAY, I WAS SO UPSET AND SHOCKED WHEN I REALIZED THERE REALLY WERE TWO SETS OF BONES IN THE GRAVE. MAYBE I COULD GET MORE.
IT MAY TAKE SOME TIME, BUT I'LL SEE WHAT I CAN DO. NOW IF YOU'LL EXCUSE ME, I HAVE SOMEPLACE TO BE...

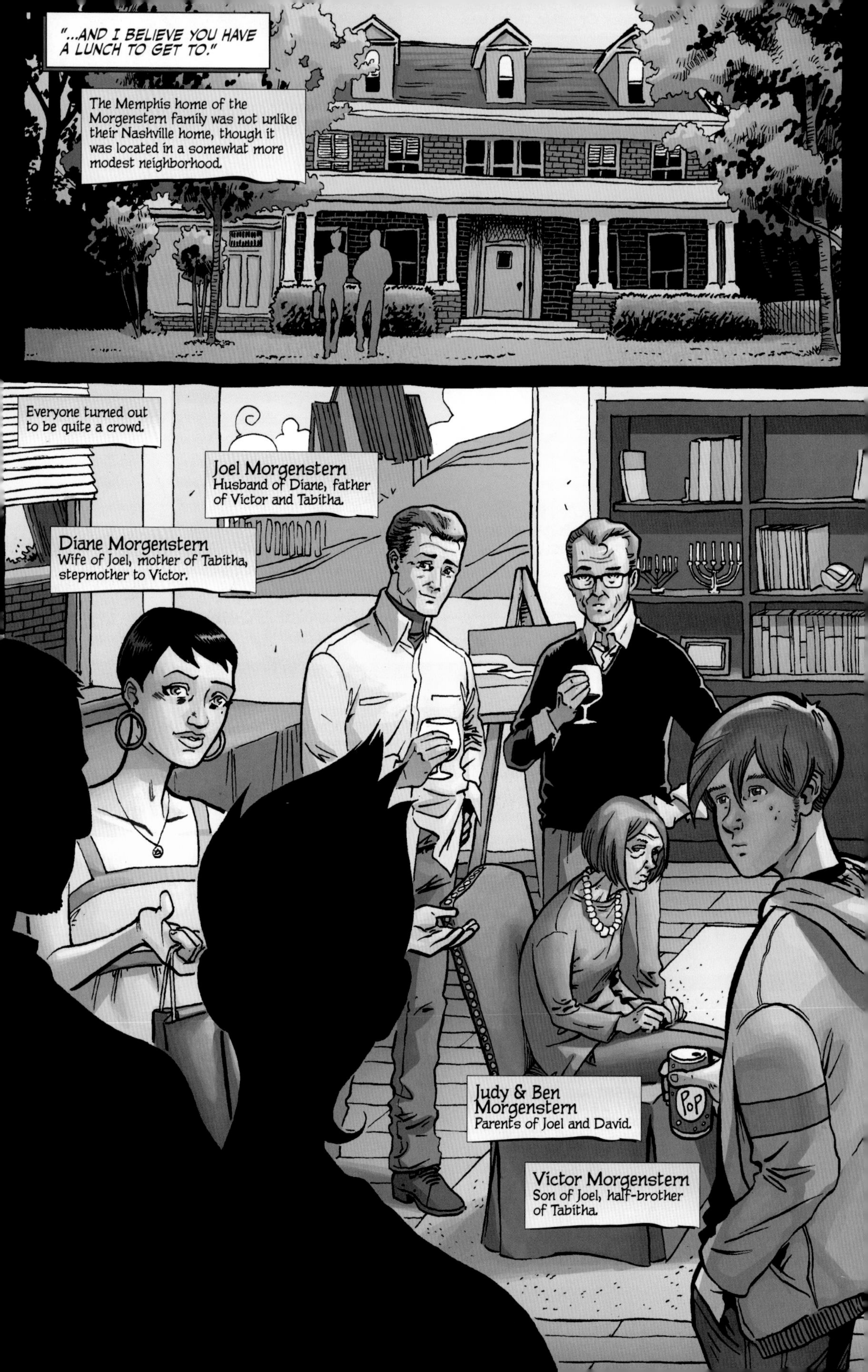
"...AND I BELIEVE YOU HAVE A LUNCH TO GET TO."
The Memphis home of the Morgenstern family was not unlike their Nashville home, though it was located in a somewhat more modest neighborhood.
Everyone turned out to be quite a crowd.
Joel Morgenstern
Husband of Diane, father of Victor and Tabitha.
Diane Morgenstern
Wife of Joel, mother of Tabitha, stepmother to Victor.
Judy & Ben Morgenstern
Parents of Joel and David.
Victor Morgenstern
Son of Joel, half-brother of Tabitha.
POP

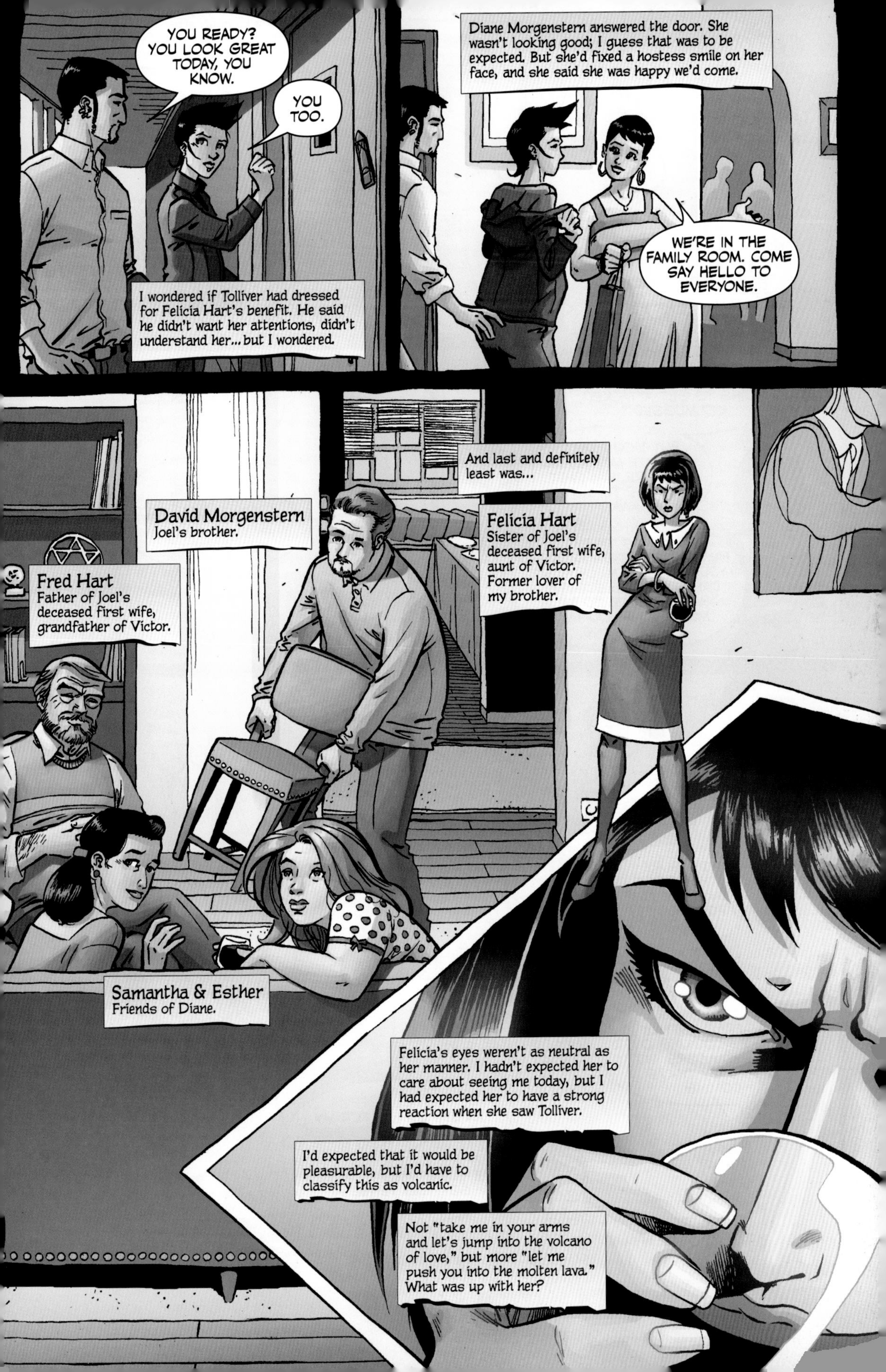
YOU READY? YOU LOOK GREAT TODAY, YOU KNOW.
YOU TOO.
I wondered if Tolliver had dressed for Felicia Hart's benefit. He said he didn't want her attentions, didn't understand her... but I wondered.
Diane Morgenstern answered the door. She wasn't looking good; I guess that was to be expected. But she'd fixed a hostess smile on her face, and she said she was happy we'd come.
WE'RE IN THE FAMILY ROOM. COME SAY HELLO TO EVERYONE.
Fred Hart
Father of Joel's deceased first wife, grandfather of Victor.
David Morgenstern
Joel's brother.
Samantha & Esther
Friends of Diane.
And last and definitely least was...
Felicia Hart
Sister of Joel's deceased first wife, aunt of Victor. Former lover of my brother.
Felicia's eyes weren't as neutral as her manner. I hadn't expected her to care about seeing me today, but I had expected her to have a strong reaction when she saw Tolliver.
I'd expected that it would be pleasurable, but I'd have to classify this as volcanic.
Not "take me in your arms and let's jump into the volcano of love," but more "let me push you into the molten lava." What was up with her?

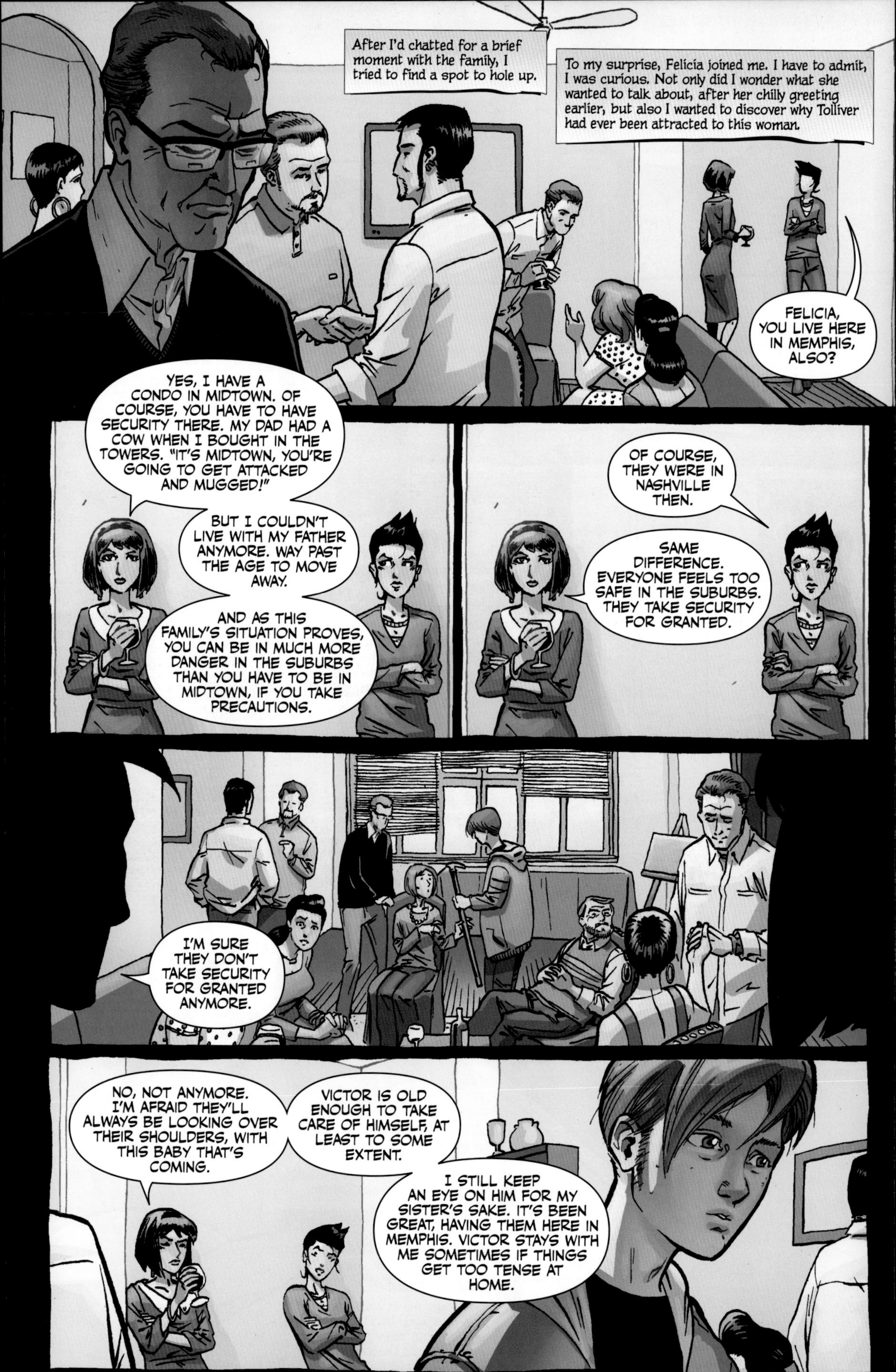
After I'd chatted for a brief moment with the family, I tried to find a spot to hole up.
To my surprise, Felicia joined me. I have to admit, I was curious. Not only did I wonder what she wanted to talk about, after her chilly greeting earlier, but also I wanted to discover why Tolliver had ever been attracted to this woman.
FELICIA, YOU LIVE HERE IN MEMPHIS, ALSO?
YES, I HAVE A CONDO IN MIDTOWN. OF COURSE, YOU HAVE TO HAVE SECURITY THERE. MY DAD HAD A COW WHEN I BOUGHT IN THE TOWERS. "IT'S MIDTOWN, YOU'RE GOING TO GET ATTACKED AND MUGGED!"
BUT I COULDN'T LIVE WITH MY FATHER ANYMORE. WAY PAST THE AGE TO MOVE AWAY.
AND AS THIS FAMILY'S SITUATION PROVES, YOU CAN BE IN MUCH MORE DANGER IN THE SUBURBS THAN YOU HAVE TO BE IN MIDTOWN, IF YOU TAKE PRECAUTIONS.
OF COURSE, THEY WERE IN NASHVILLE THEN.
SAME DIFFERENCE. EVERYONE FEELS TOO SAFE IN THE SUBURBS. THEY TAKE SECURITY FOR GRANTED.
I'M SURE THEY DON'T TAKE SECURITY FOR GRANTED ANYMORE.
NO, NOT ANYMORE. I'M AFRAID THEY'LL ALWAYS BE LOOKING OVER THEIR SHOULDERS, WITH THIS BABY THAT'S COMING.
VICTOR IS OLD ENOUGH TO TAKE CARE OF HIMSELF, AT LEAST TO SOME EXTENT.
I STILL KEEP AN EYE ON HIM FOR MY SISTER'S SAKE. IT'S BEEN GREAT, HAVING THEM HERE IN MEMPHIS. VICTOR STAYS WITH ME SOMETIMES IF THINGS GET TOO TENSE AT HOME.

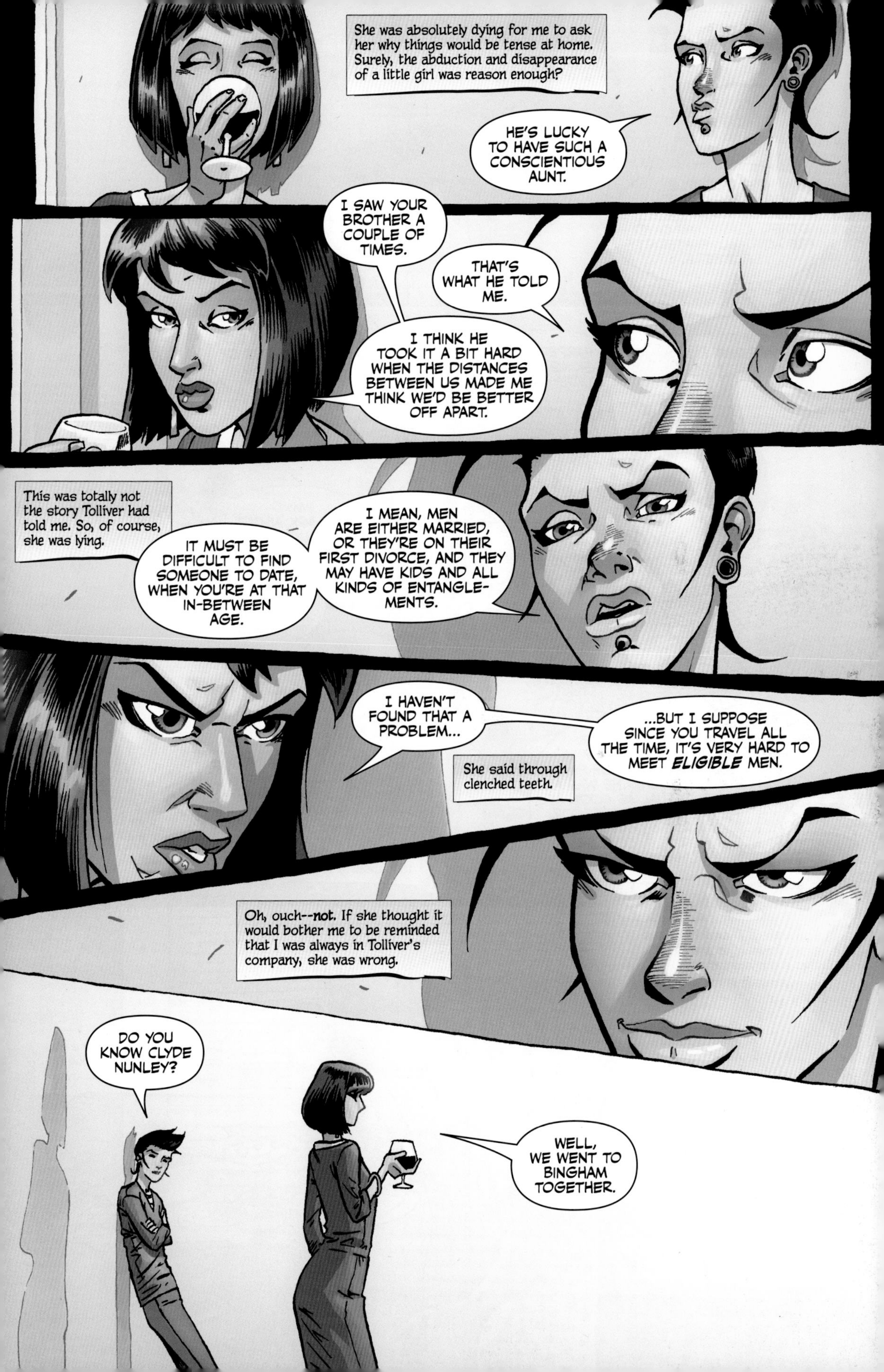
She was absolutely dying for me to ask her why things would be tense at home. Surely, the abduction and disappearance of a little girl was reason enough?
HE'S LUCKY TO HAVE SUCH A CONSCIENTIOUS AUNT.
I SAW YOUR BROTHER A COUPLE OF TIMES.
THAT'S WHAT HE TOLD ME.
I THINK HE TOOK IT A BIT HARD WHEN THE DISTANCES BETWEEN US MADE ME THINK WE'D BE BETTER OFF APART.
This was totally not the story Tolliver had told me. So, of course, she was lying.
IT MUST BE DIFFICULT TO FIND SOMEONE TO DATE, WHEN YOU'RE AT THAT IN-BETWEEN AGE.
I MEAN, MEN ARE EITHER MARRIED, OR THEY'RE ON THEIR FIRST DIVORCE, AND THEY MAY HAVE KIDS AND ALL KINDS OF ENTANGLE-MENTS.
I HAVEN'T FOUND THAT A PROBLEM...
...BUT I SUPPOSE SINCE YOU TRAVEL ALL THE TIME, IT'S VERY HARD TO MEET *ELIGIBLE* MEN.
She said through clenched teeth.
Oh, ouch--**not**. If she thought it would bother me to be reminded that I was always in Tolliver's company, she was wrong.
DO YOU KNOW CLYDE NUNLEY?
WELL, WE WENT TO BINGHAM TOGETHER.

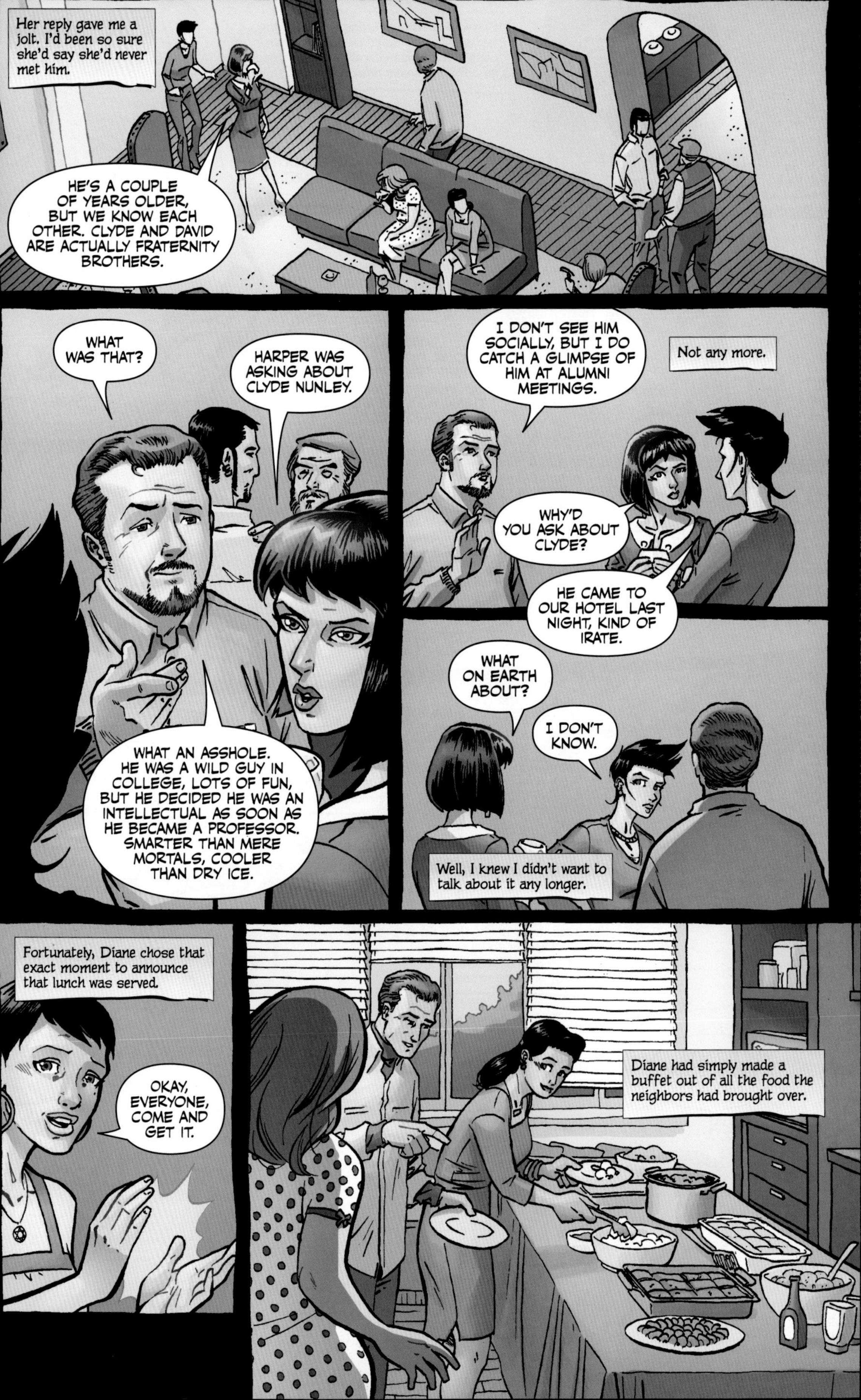
Her reply gave me a jolt. I'd been so sure she'd say she'd never met him.
HE'S A COUPLE OF YEARS OLDER, BUT WE KNOW EACH OTHER. CLYDE AND DAVID ARE ACTUALLY FRATERNITY BROTHERS.
WHAT WAS THAT?
HARPER WAS ASKING ABOUT CLYDE NUNLEY.
WHAT AN ASSHOLE. HE WAS A WILD GUY IN COLLEGE, LOTS OF FUN, BUT HE DECIDED HE WAS AN INTELLECTUAL AS SOON AS HE BECAME A PROFESSOR. SMARTER THAN MERE MORTALS, COOLER THAN DRY ICE.
I DON'T SEE HIM SOCIALLY, BUT I DO CATCH A GLIMPSE OF HIM AT ALUMNI MEETINGS.
Not any more.
WHY'D YOU ASK ABOUT CLYDE?
HE CAME TO OUR HOTEL LAST NIGHT, KIND OF IRATE.
WHAT ON EARTH ABOUT?
I DON'T KNOW.
Well, I knew I didn't want to talk about it any longer.
Fortunately, Diane chose that exact moment to announce that lunch was served.
OKAY, EVERYONE, COME AND GET IT.
Diane had simply made a buffet out of all the food the neighbors had brought over.

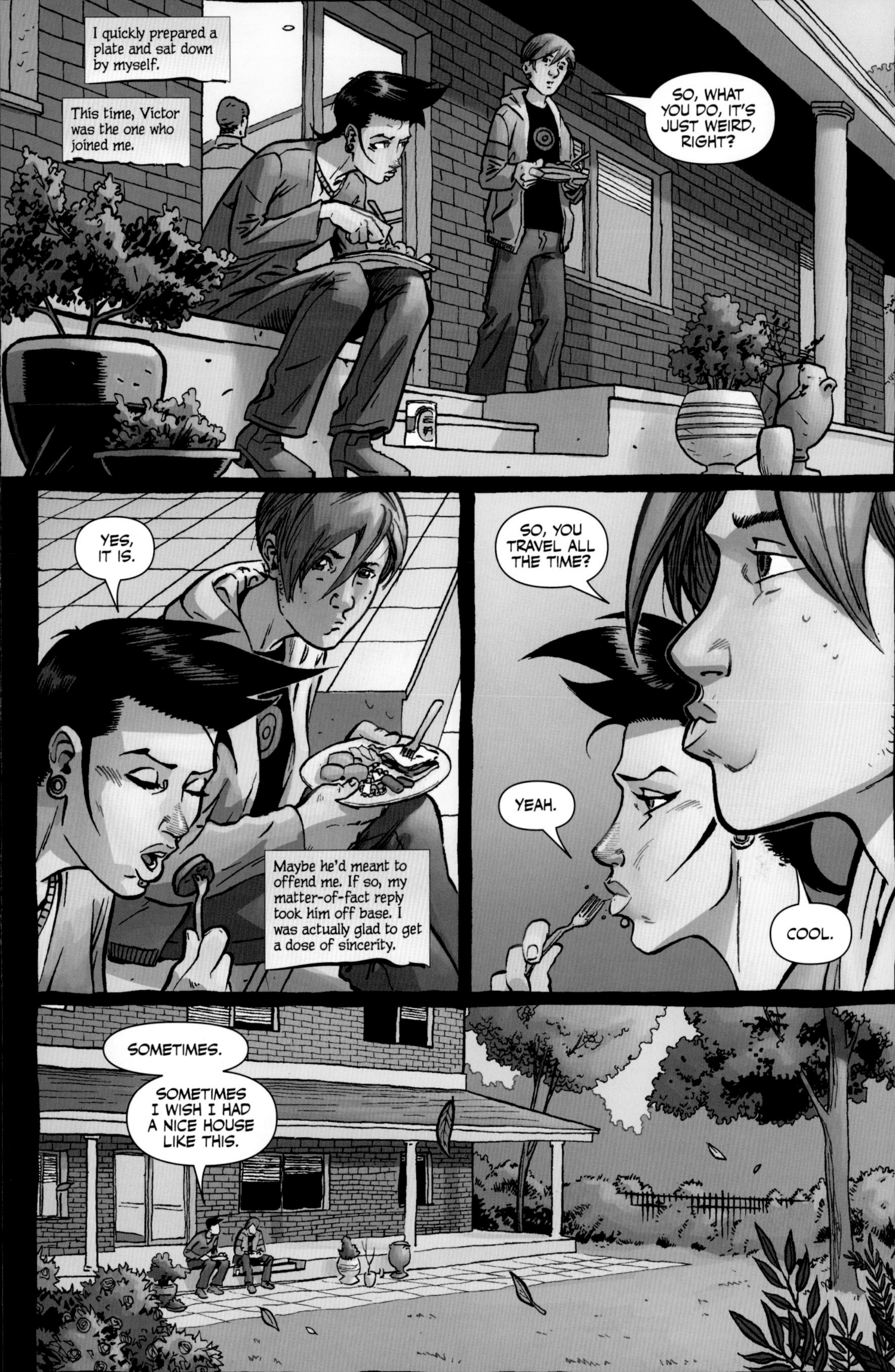
I quickly prepared a plate and sat down by myself.
This time, Victor was the one who joined me.
SO, WHAT YOU DO, IT'S JUST WEIRD, RIGHT?
YES, IT IS.
Maybe he'd meant to offend me. If so, my matter-of-fact reply took him off base. I was actually glad to get a dose of sincerity.
SO, YOU TRAVEL ALL THE TIME?
YEAH.
COOL.
SOMETIMES.
SOMETIMES I WISH I HAD A NICE HOUSE LIKE THIS.

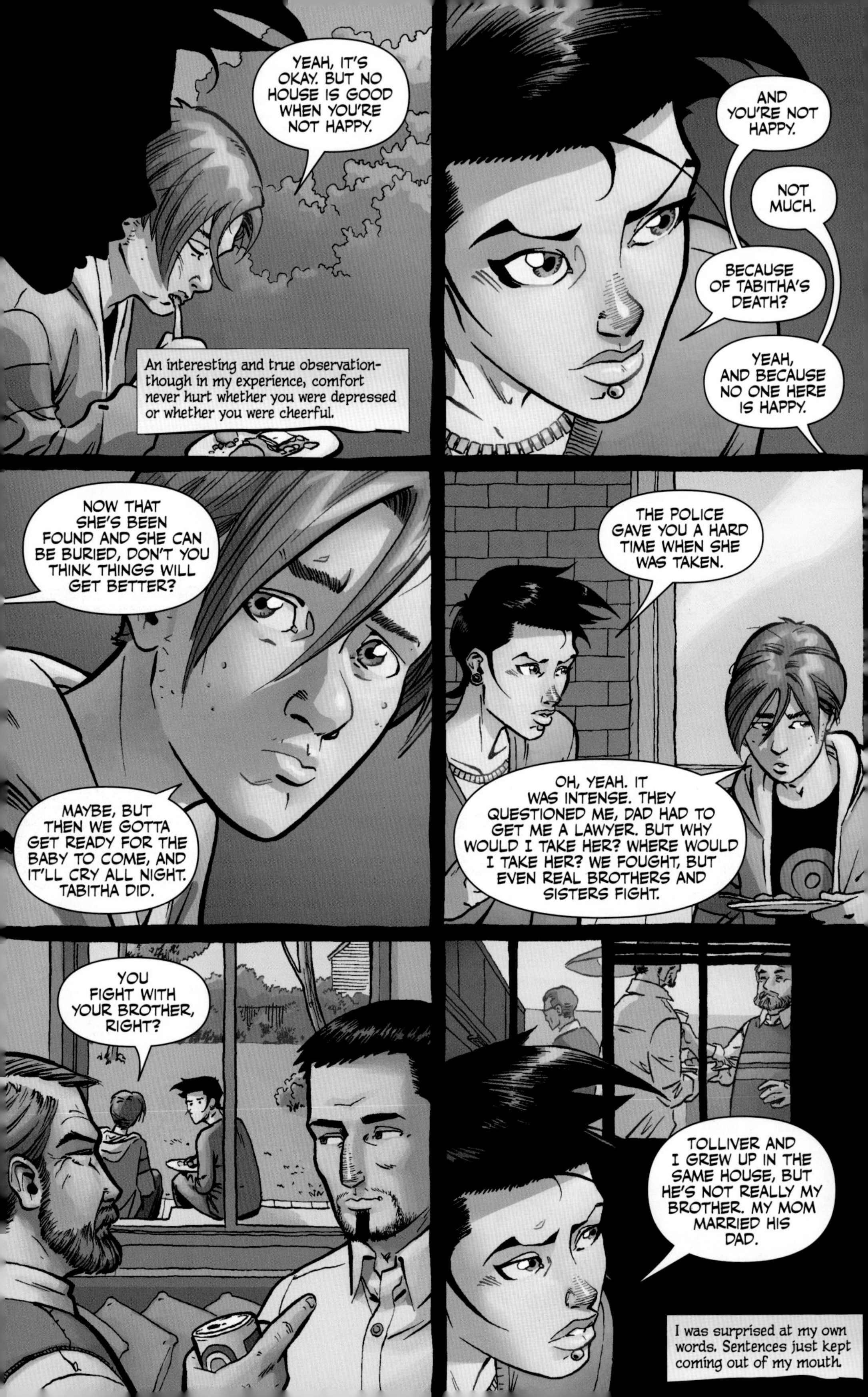
YEAH, IT'S OKAY. BUT NO HOUSE IS GOOD WHEN YOU'RE NOT HAPPY.
An interesting and true observation- though in my experience, comfort never hurt whether you were depressed or whether you were cheerful.
AND YOU'RE NOT HAPPY.
NOT MUCH.
BECAUSE OF TABITHA'S DEATH?
YEAH, AND BECAUSE NO ONE HERE IS HAPPY.
NOW THAT SHE'S BEEN FOUND AND SHE CAN BE BURIED, DON'T YOU THINK THINGS WILL GET BETTER?
MAYBE, BUT THEN WE GOTTA GET READY FOR THE BABY TO COME, AND IT'LL CRY ALL NIGHT. TABITHA DID.
THE POLICE GAVE YOU A HARD TIME WHEN SHE WAS TAKEN.
OH, YEAH. IT WAS INTENSE. THEY QUESTIONED ME, DAD HAD TO GET ME A LAWYER. BUT WHY WOULD I TAKE HER? WHERE WOULD I TAKE HER? WE FOUGHT, BUT EVEN REAL BROTHERS AND SISTERS FIGHT.
YOU FIGHT WITH YOUR BROTHER, RIGHT?
TOLLIVER AND I GREW UP IN THE SAME HOUSE, BUT HE'S NOT REALLY MY BROTHER. MY MOM MARRIED HIS DAD.
I was surprised at my own words. Sentences just kept coming out of my mouth.

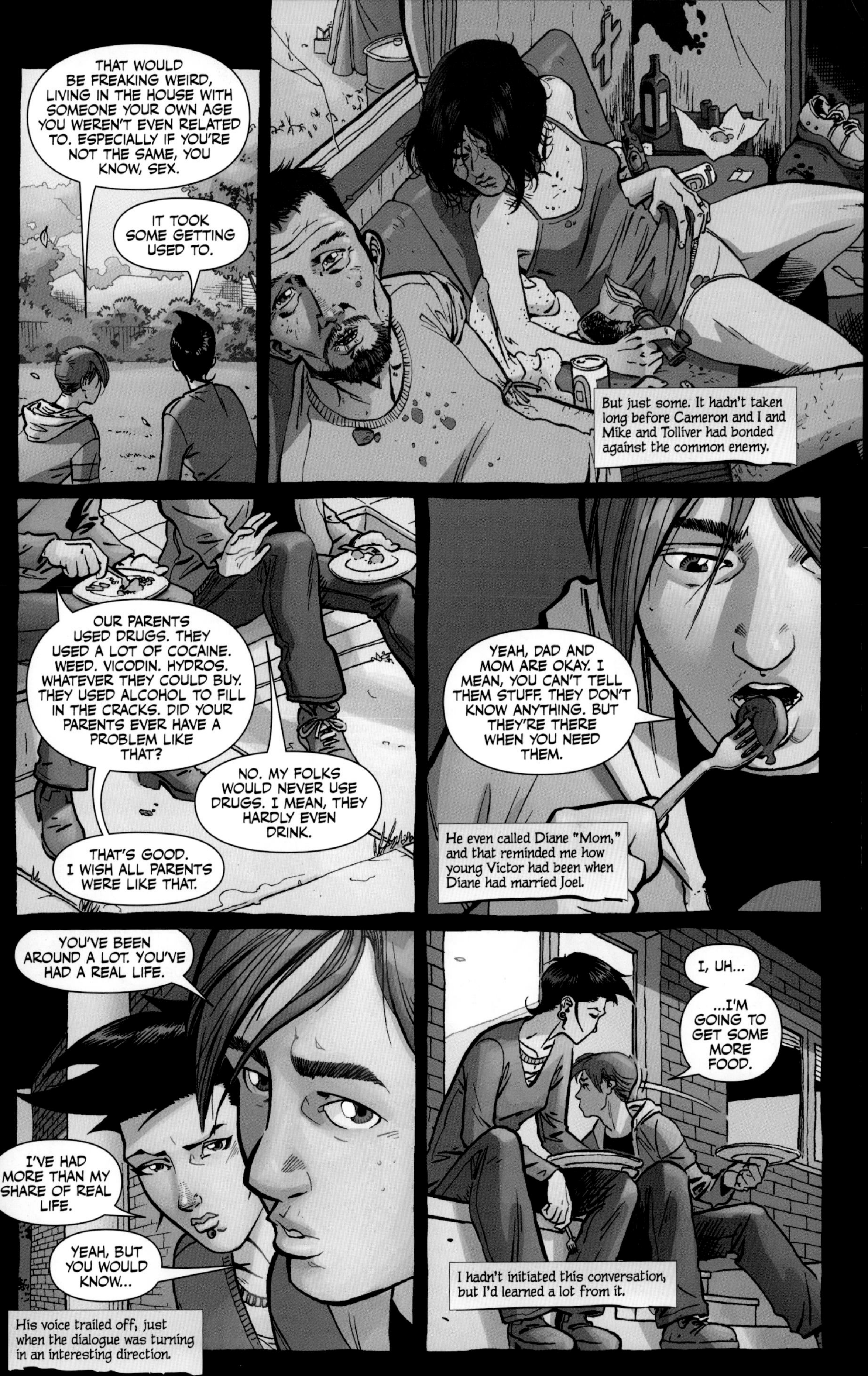

THAT WOULD BE FREAKING WEIRD, LIVING IN THE HOUSE WITH SOMEONE YOUR OWN AGE YOU WEREN'T EVEN RELATED TO. ESPECIALLY IF YOU'RE NOT THE SAME, YOU KNOW, SEX.
IT TOOK SOME GETTING USED TO.
But just some. It hadn't taken long before Cameron and I and Mike and Tolliver had bonded against the common enemy.
OUR PARENTS USED DRUGS. THEY USED A LOT OF COCAINE. WEED. VICODIN. HYDROS. WHATEVER THEY COULD BUY. THEY USED ALCOHOL TO FILL IN THE CRACKS. DID YOUR PARENTS EVER HAVE A PROBLEM LIKE THAT?
NO. MY FOLKS WOULD NEVER USE DRUGS. I MEAN, THEY HARDLY EVEN DRINK.
THAT'S GOOD. I WISH ALL PARENTS WERE LIKE THAT.
YEAH, DAD AND MOM ARE OKAY. I MEAN, YOU CAN'T TELL THEM STUFF. THEY DON'T KNOW ANYTHING. BUT THEY'RE THERE WHEN YOU NEED THEM.
He even called Diane "Mom," and that reminded me how young Victor had been when Diane had married Joel.
YOU'VE BEEN AROUND A LOT. YOU'VE HAD A REAL LIFE.
I'VE HAD MORE THAN MY SHARE OF REAL LIFE.
YEAH, BUT YOU WOULD KNOW...
His voice trailed off, just when the dialogue was turning in an interesting direction.
I, UH...
...I'M GOING TO GET SOME MORE FOOD.
I hadn't initiated this conversation, but I'd learned a lot from it.

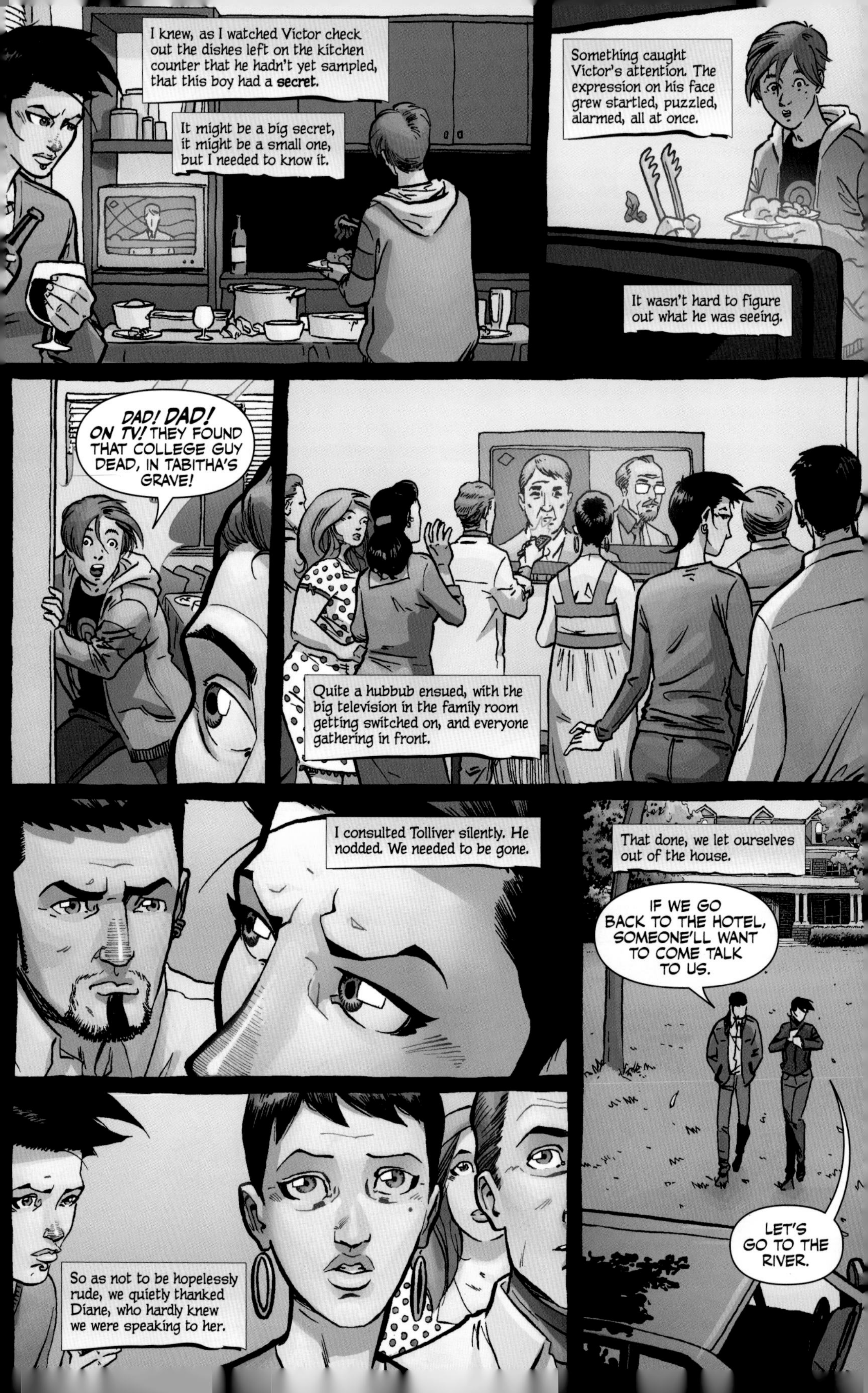

I knew, as I watched Victor check out the dishes left on the kitchen counter that he hadn't yet sampled, that this boy had a **secret**.
It might be a big secret, it might be a small one, but I needed to know it.
Something caught Victor's attention. The expression on his face grew startled, puzzled, alarmed, all at once.
It wasn't hard to figure out what he was seeing.
DAD! DAD! ON TV! THEY FOUND THAT COLLEGE GUY DEAD, IN TABITHA'S GRAVE!
Quite a hubbub ensued, with the big television in the family room getting switched on, and everyone gathering in front.
I consulted Tolliver silently. He nodded. We needed to be gone.
So as not to be hopelessly rude, we quietly thanked Diane, who hardly knew we were speaking to her.
That done, we let ourselves out of the house.
IF WE GO BACK TO THE HOTEL, SOMEONE'LL WANT TO COME TALK TO US.
LET'S GO TO THE RIVER.

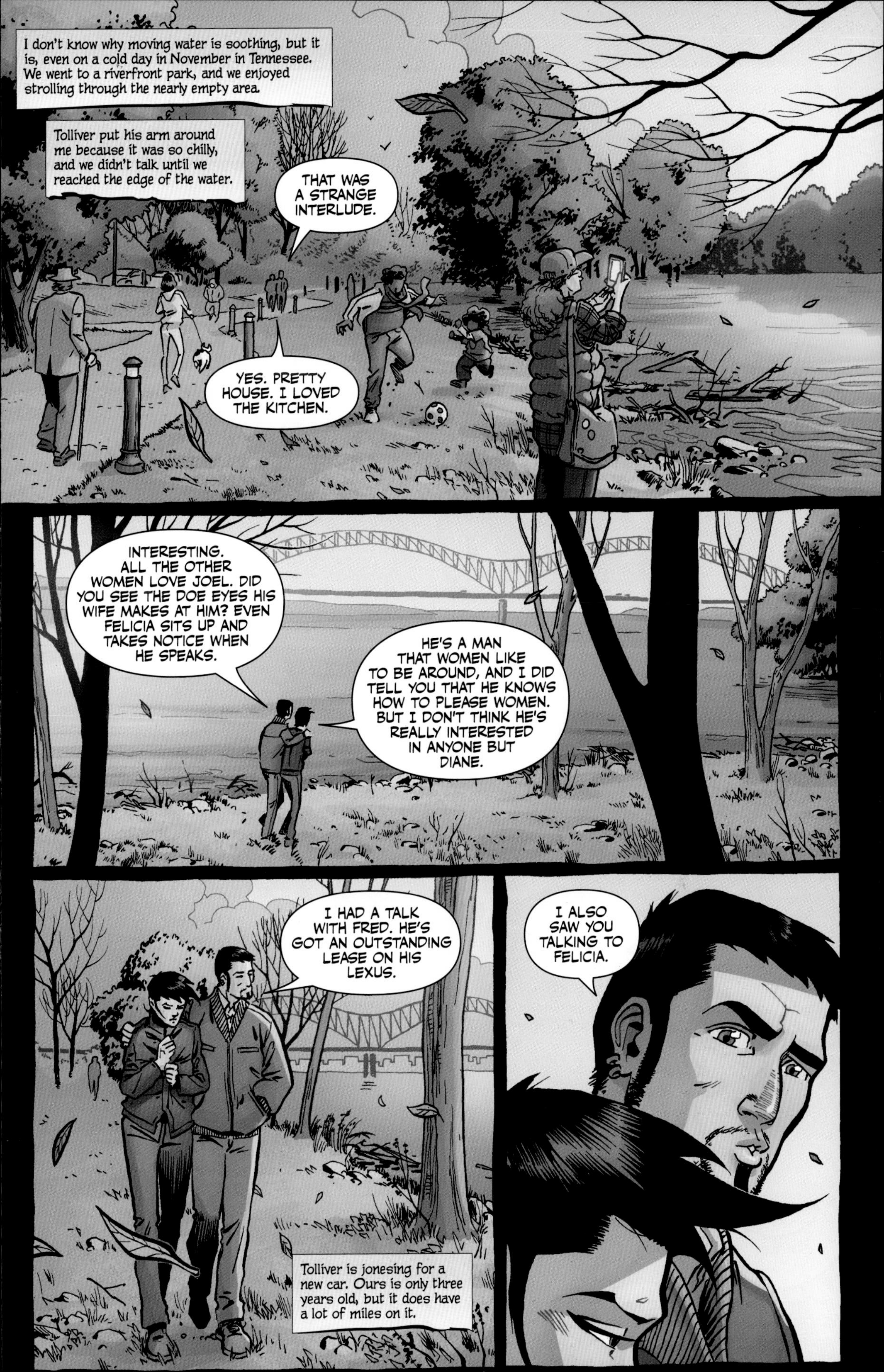
I don't know why moving water is soothing, but it is, even on a cold day in November in Tennessee. We went to a riverfront park, and we enjoyed strolling through the nearly empty area.
Tolliver put his arm around me because it was so chilly, and we didn't talk until we reached the edge of the water.
THAT WAS A STRANGE INTERLUDE.
YES. PRETTY HOUSE. I LOVED THE KITCHEN.
INTERESTING. ALL THE OTHER WOMEN LOVE JOEL. DID YOU SEE THE DOE EYES HIS WIFE MAKES AT HIM? EVEN FELICIA SITS UP AND TAKES NOTICE WHEN HE SPEAKS.
HE'S A MAN THAT WOMEN LIKE TO BE AROUND, AND I DID TELL YOU THAT HE KNOWS HOW TO PLEASE WOMEN. BUT I DON'T THINK HE'S REALLY INTERESTED IN ANYONE BUT DIANE.
I HAD A TALK WITH FRED. HE'S GOT AN OUTSTANDING LEASE ON HIS LEXUS.
Tolliver is jonesing for a new car. Ours is only three years old, but it does have a lot of miles on it.
I ALSO SAW YOU TALKING TO FELICIA.

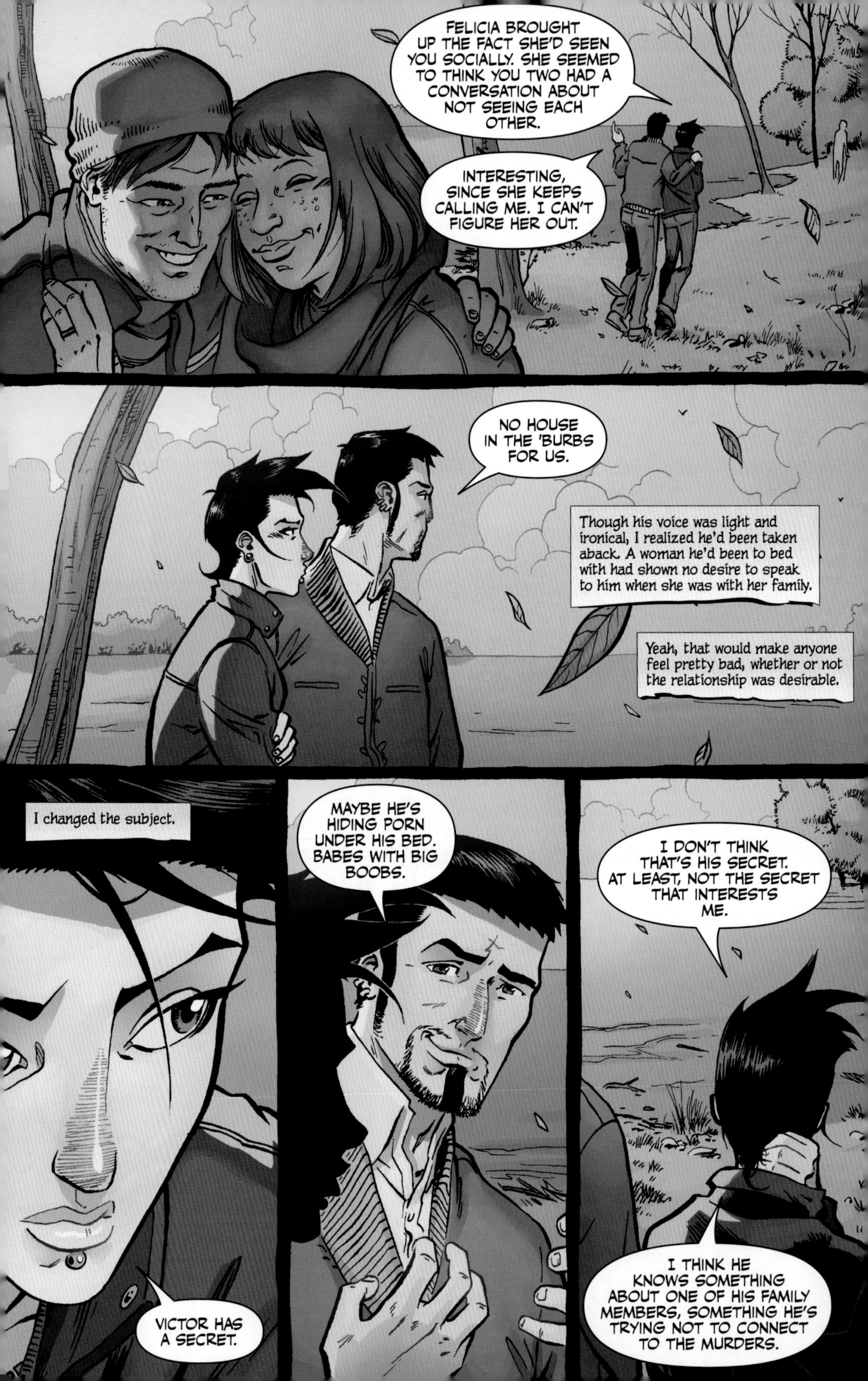
FELICIA BROUGHT UP THE FACT SHE'D SEEN YOU SOCIALLY. SHE SEEMED TO THINK YOU TWO HAD A CONVERSATION ABOUT NOT SEEING EACH OTHER.
INTERESTING, SINCE SHE KEEPS CALLING ME. I CAN'T FIGURE HER OUT.
NO HOUSE IN THE 'BURBS FOR US.
Though his voice was light and ironical, I realized he'd been taken aback. A woman he'd been to bed with had shown no desire to speak to him when she was with her family.
Yeah, that would make anyone feel pretty bad, whether or not the relationship was desirable.
I changed the subject.
VICTOR HAS A SECRET.
MAYBE HE'S HIDING PORN UNDER HIS BED. BABES WITH BIG BOOBS.
I DON'T THINK THAT'S HIS SECRET. AT LEAST, NOT THE SECRET THAT INTERESTS ME.
I THINK HE KNOWS SOMETHING ABOUT ONE OF HIS FAMILY MEMBERS, SOMETHING HE'S TRYING NOT TO CONNECT TO THE MURDERS.

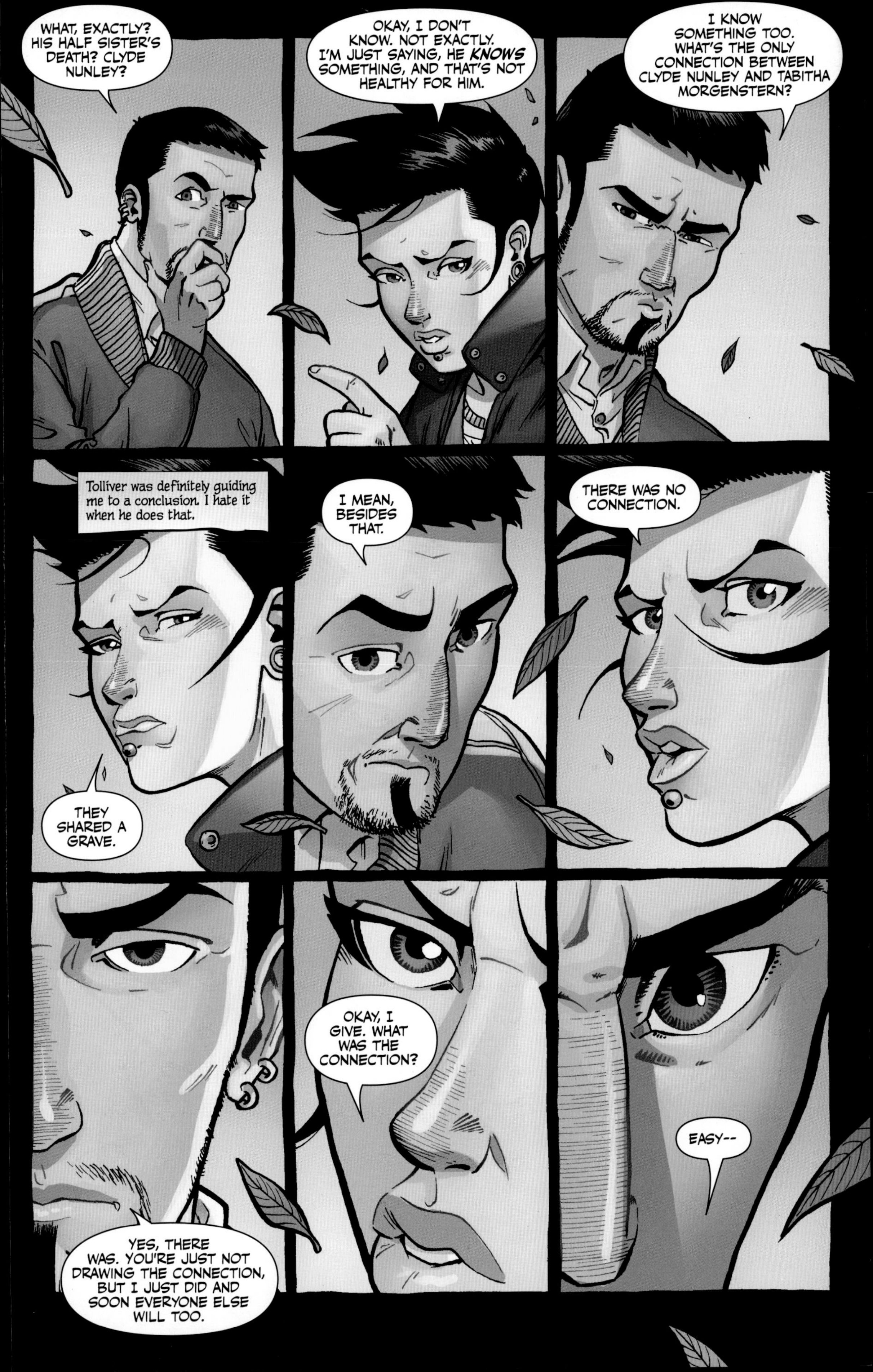
WHAT, EXACTLY? HIS HALF SISTER'S DEATH? CLYDE NUNLEY?
OKAY, I DON'T KNOW. NOT EXACTLY. I'M JUST SAYING, HE KNOWS SOMETHING, AND THAT'S NOT HEALTHY FOR HIM.
I KNOW SOMETHING TOO. WHAT'S THE ONLY CONNECTION BETWEEN CLYDE NUNLEY AND TABITHA MORGENSTERN?
Tolliver was definitely guiding me to a conclusion. I hate it when he does that.
THEY SHARED A GRAVE.
I MEAN, BESIDES THAT.
THERE WAS NO CONNECTION.
YES, THERE WAS. YOU'RE JUST NOT DRAWING THE CONNECTION, BUT I JUST DID AND SOON EVERYONE ELSE WILL TOO.
OKAY, I GIVE. WHAT WAS THE CONNECTION?
EASY--

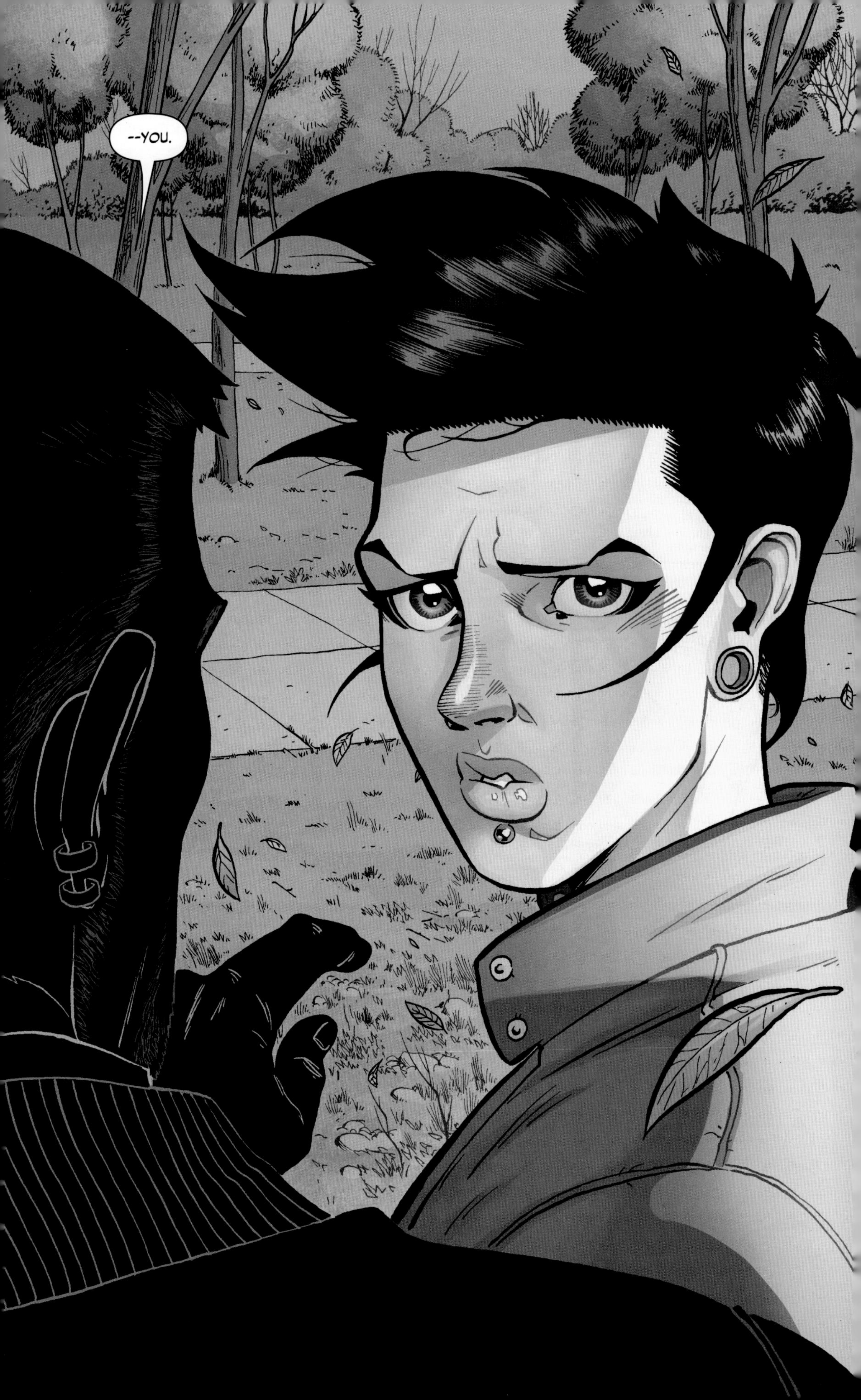
--YOU.

CHAPTER SIX

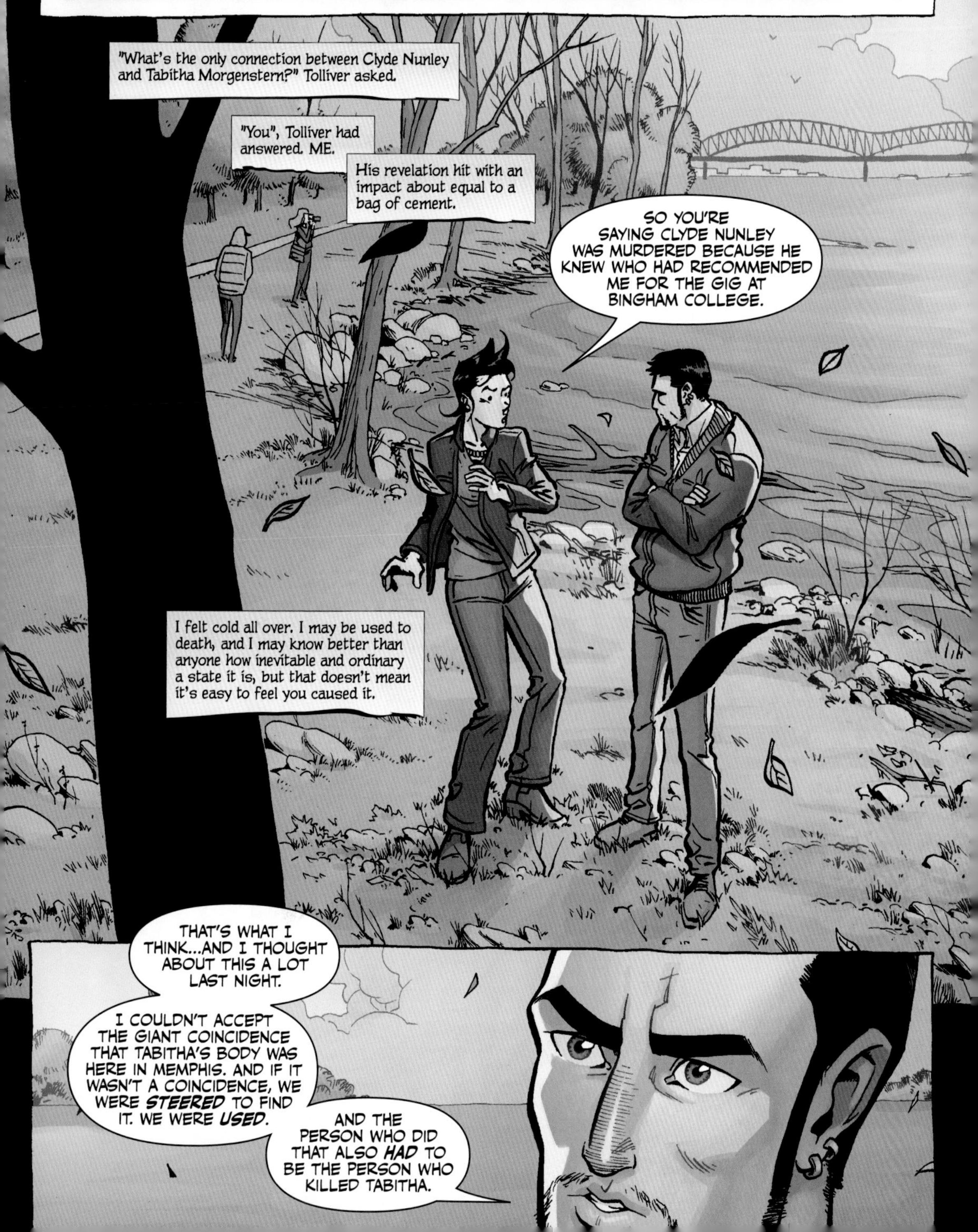
"What's the only connection between Clyde Nunley and Tabitha Morgenstern?" Tolliver asked.
"You", Tolliver had answered. ME.
His revelation hit with an impact about equal to a bag of cement.
SO YOU'RE SAYING CLYDE NUNLEY WAS MURDERED BECAUSE HE KNEW WHO HAD RECOMMENDED ME FOR THE GIG AT BINGHAM COLLEGE.
I felt cold all over. I may be used to death, and I may know better than anyone how inevitable and ordinary a state it is, but that doesn't mean it's easy to feel you caused it.
THAT'S WHAT I THINK...AND I THOUGHT ABOUT THIS A LOT LAST NIGHT.
I COULDN'T ACCEPT THE GIANT COINCIDENCE THAT TABITHA'S BODY WAS HERE IN MEMPHIS. AND IF IT WASN'T A COINCIDENCE, WE WERE *STEERED* TO FIND IT. WE WERE *USED*.
AND THE PERSON WHO DID THAT ALSO *HAD* TO BE THE PERSON WHO KILLED TABITHA.

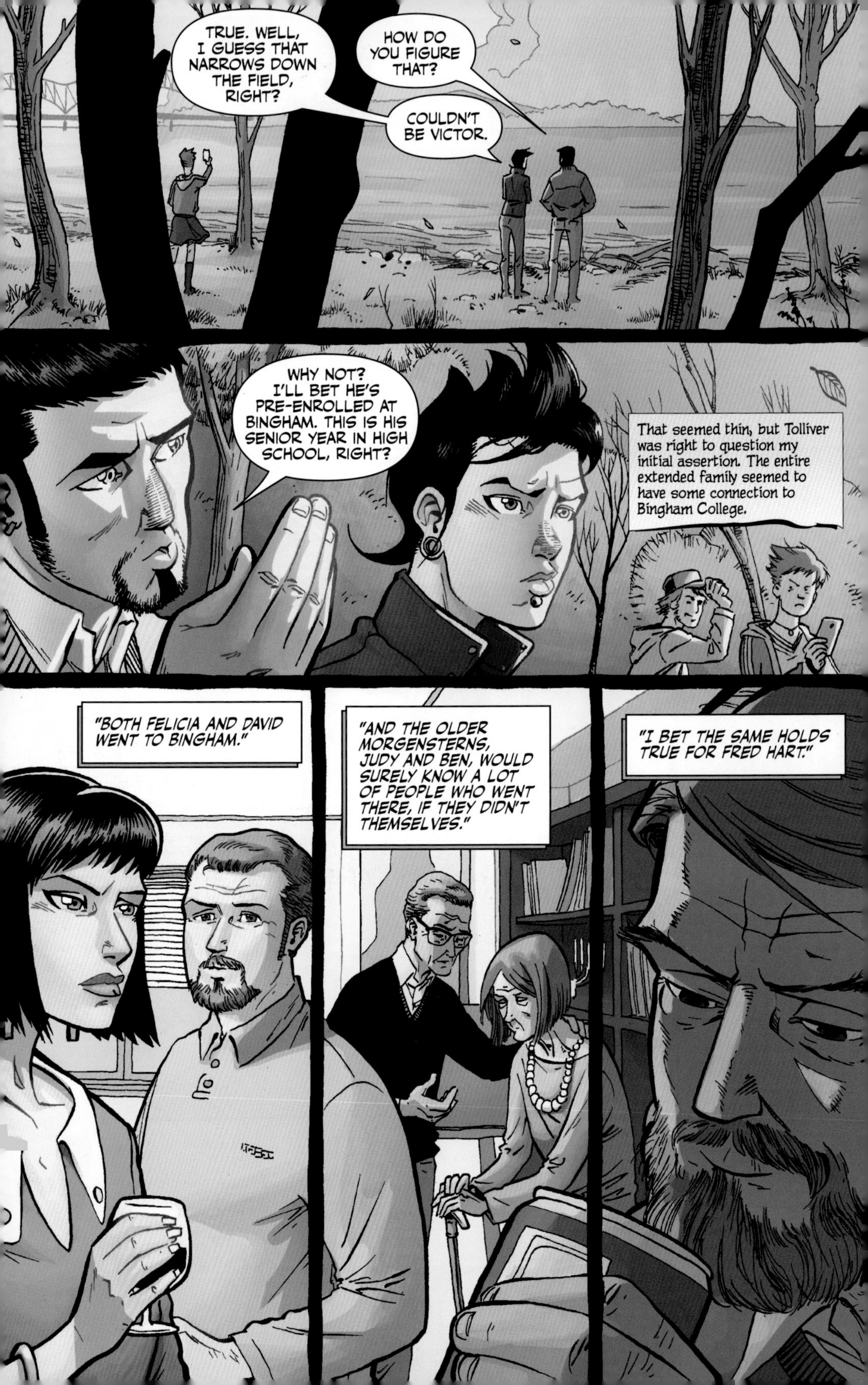
TRUE. WELL, I GUESS THAT NARROWS DOWN THE FIELD, RIGHT?
HOW DO YOU FIGURE THAT?
COULDN'T BE VICTOR.
WHY NOT? I'LL BET HE'S PRE-ENROLLED AT BINGHAM. THIS IS HIS SENIOR YEAR IN HIGH SCHOOL, RIGHT?
That seemed thin, but Tolliver was right to question my initial assertion. The entire extended family seemed to have some connection to Bingham College.
"BOTH FELICIA AND DAVID WENT TO BINGHAM."
"AND THE OLDER MORGENSTERNS, JUDY AND BEN, WOULD SURELY KNOW A LOT OF PEOPLE WHO WENT THERE, IF THEY DIDN'T THEMSELVES."
"I BET THE SAME HOLDS TRUE FOR FRED HART."

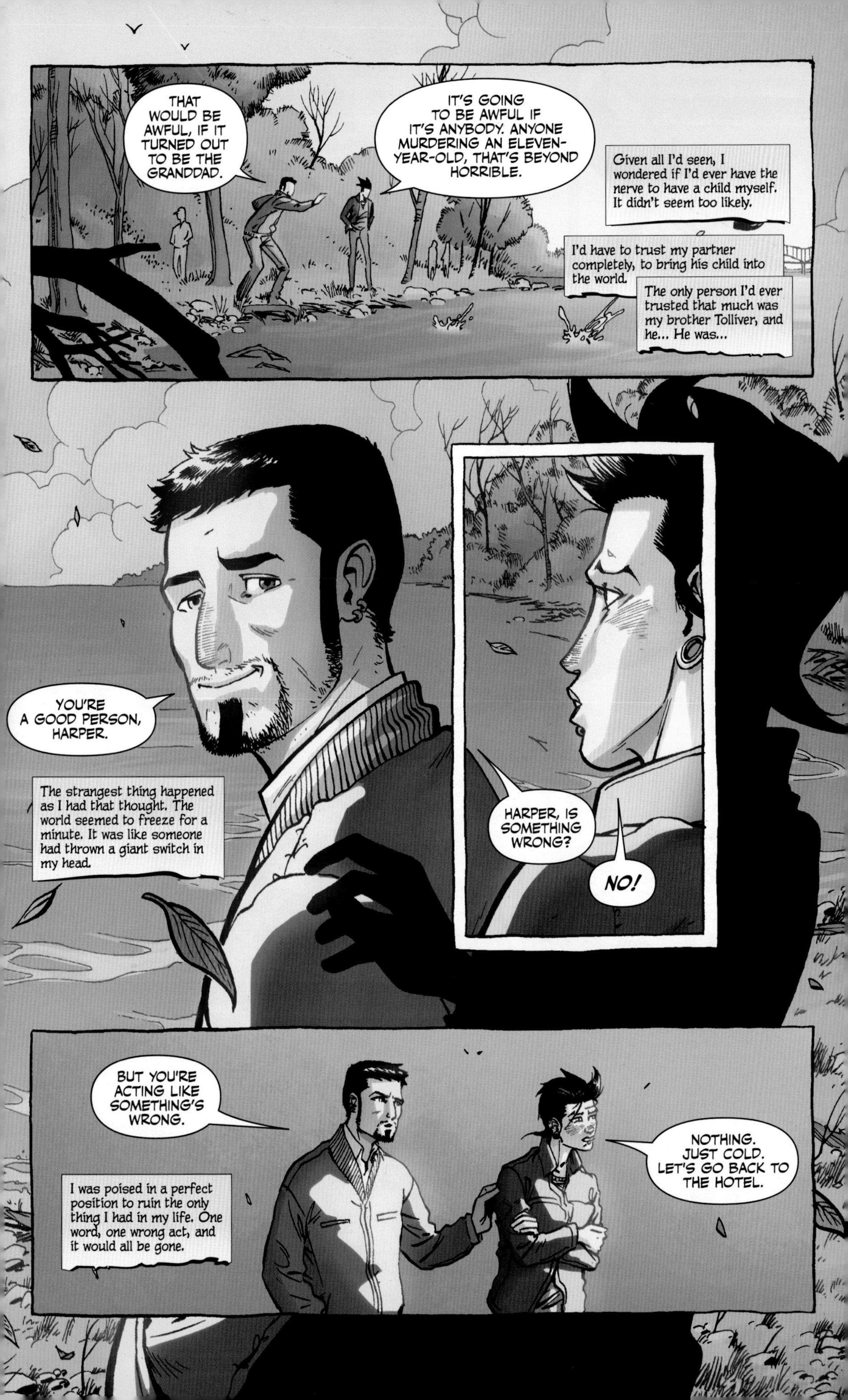
THAT WOULD BE AWFUL, IF IT TURNED OUT TO BE THE GRANDDAD.
IT'S GOING TO BE AWFUL IF IT'S ANYBODY. ANYONE MURDERING AN ELEVEN-YEAR-OLD, THAT'S BEYOND HORRIBLE.
Given all I'd seen, I wondered if I'd ever have the nerve to have a child myself. It didn't seem too likely.
I'd have to trust my partner completely, to bring his child into the world.
The only person I'd ever trusted that much was my brother Tolliver, and he... He was...
YOU'RE A GOOD PERSON, HARPER.
The strangest thing happened as I had that thought. The world seemed to freeze for a minute. It was like someone had thrown a giant switch in my head.
HARPER, IS SOMETHING WRONG?
NO!
BUT YOU'RE ACTING LIKE SOMETHING'S WRONG.
I was poised in a perfect position to ruin the only thing I had in my life. One word, one wrong act, and it would all be gone.
NOTHING. JUST COLD. LET'S GO BACK TO THE HOTEL.

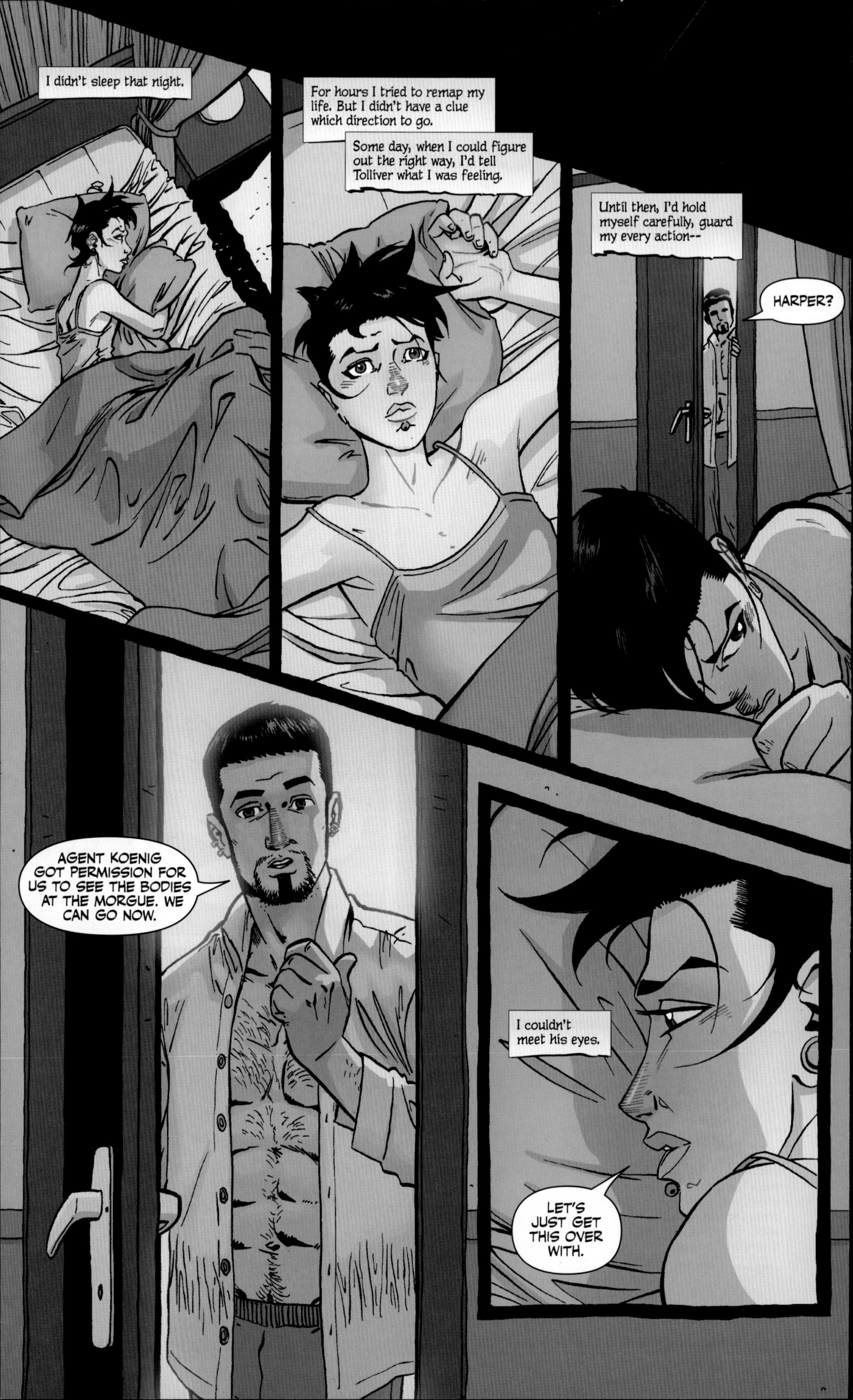
I didn't sleep that night.
For hours I tried to remap my life. But I didn't have a clue which direction to go.
Some day, when I could figure out the right way, I'd tell Tolliver what I was feeling.
Until then, I'd hold myself carefully, guard my every action--
HARPER?
AGENT KOENIG GOT PERMISSION FOR US TO SEE THE BODIES AT THE MORGUE. WE CAN GO NOW.
I couldn't meet his eyes.
LET'S JUST GET THIS OVER WITH.

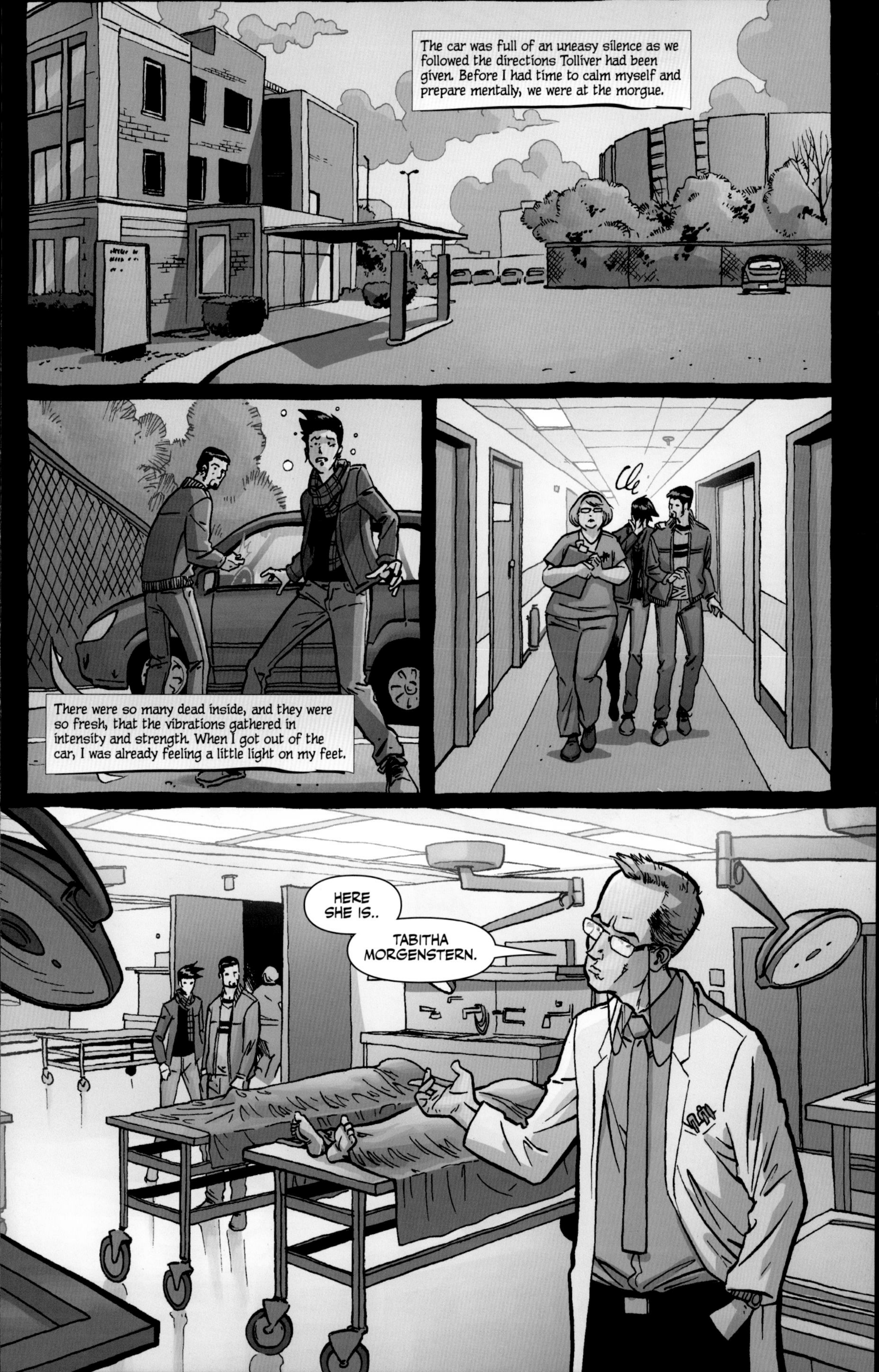
The car was full of an uneasy silence as we followed the directions Tolliver had been given. Before I had time to calm myself and prepare mentally, we were at the morgue.
There were so many dead inside, and they were so fresh, that the vibrations gathered in intensity and strength. When I got out of the car, I was already feeling a little light on my feet.
HERE SHE IS..
TABITHA MORGENSTERN.

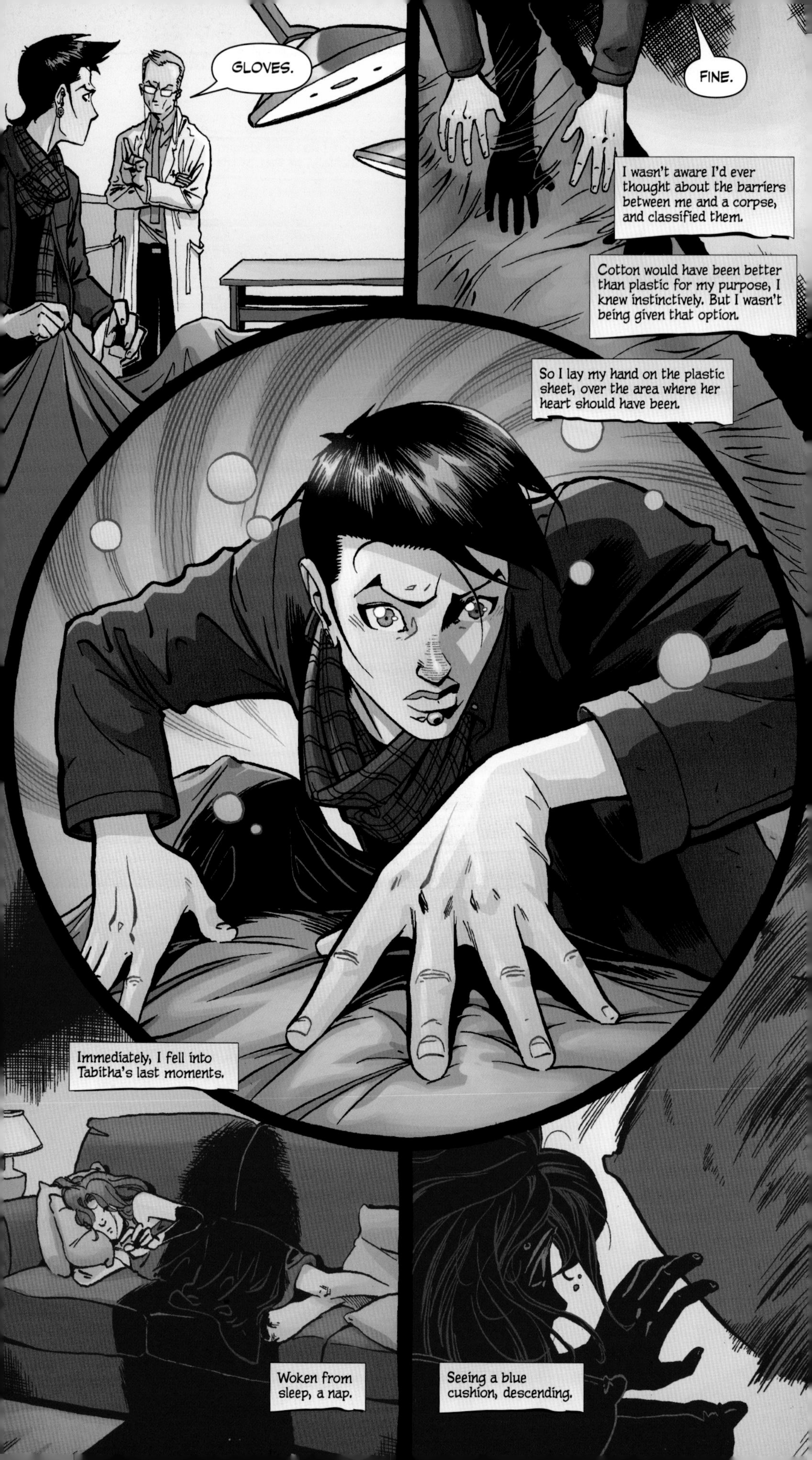
GLOVES.
FINE.
I wasn't aware I'd ever thought about the barriers between me and a corpse, and classified them.
Cotton would have been better than plastic for my purpose, I knew instinctively. But I wasn't being given that option.
So I lay my hand on the plastic sheet, over the area where her heart should have been.
Immediately, I fell into Tabitha's last moments.
Woken from sleep, a nap.
Seeing a blue cushion, descending.

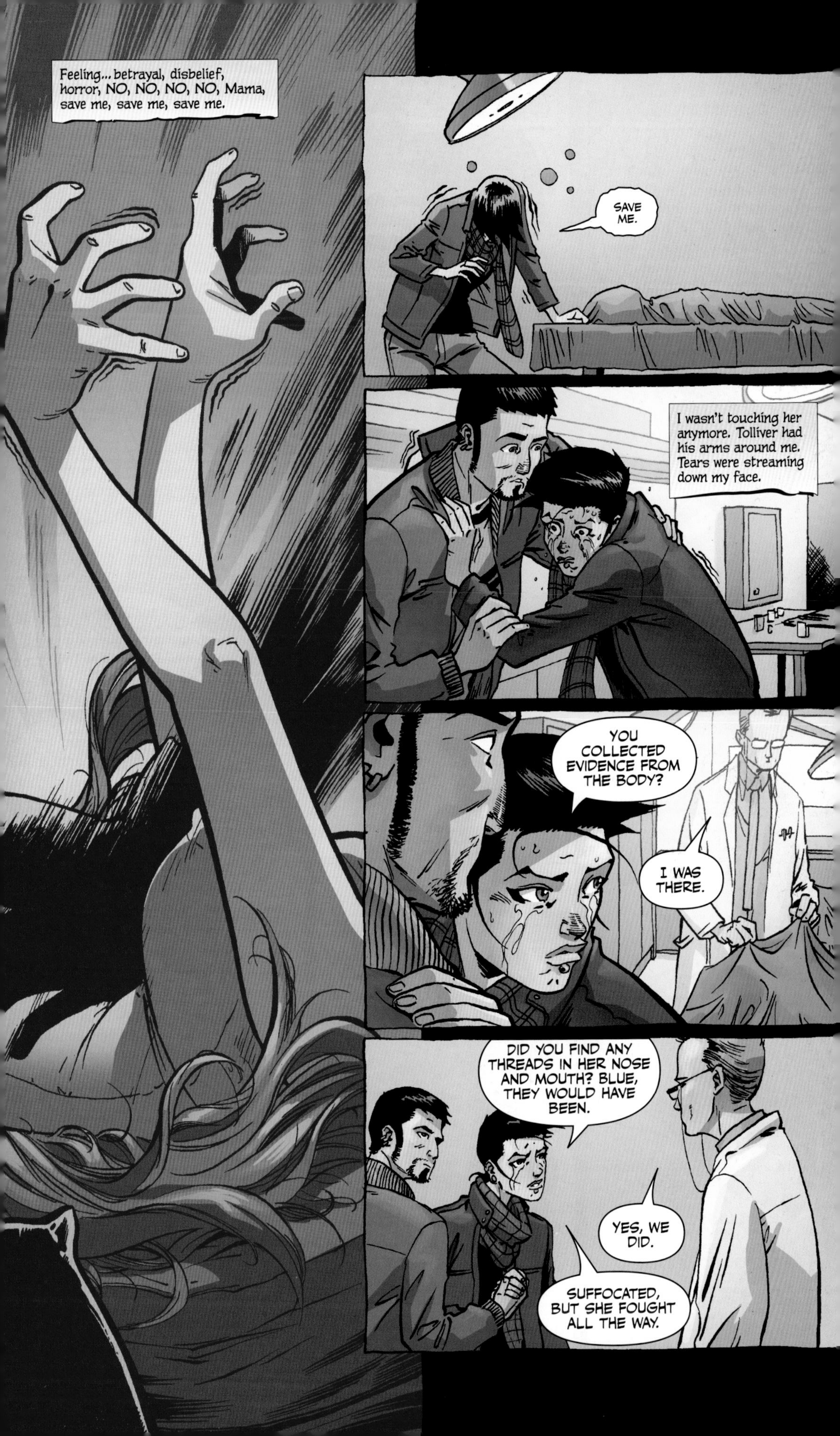

Feeling... betrayal, disbelief, horror, NO, NO, NO, NO, Mama, save me, save me, save me.
SAVE ME.
I wasn't touching her anymore. Tolliver had his arms around me. Tears were streaming down my face.
YOU COLLECTED EVIDENCE FROM THE BODY?
I WAS THERE.
DID YOU FIND ANY THREADS IN HER NOSE AND MOUTH? BLUE, THEY WOULD HAVE BEEN.
YES, WE DID.
SUFFOCATED, BUT SHE FOUGHT ALL THE WAY.

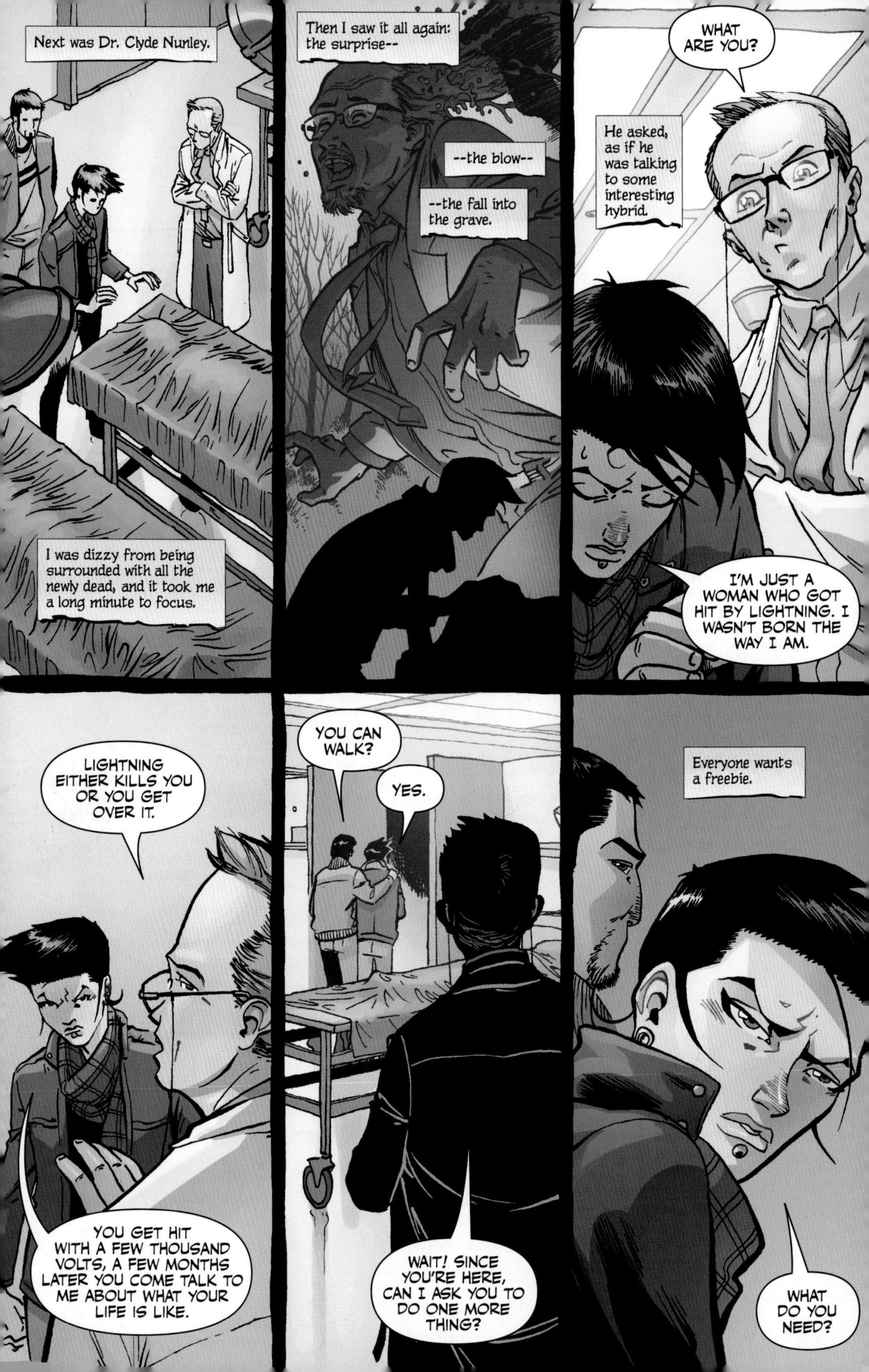

Next was Dr. Clyde Nunley.
I was dizzy from being surrounded with all the newly dead, and it took me a long minute to focus.
Then I saw it all again: the surprise--
--the blow--
--the fall into the grave.
WHAT ARE YOU?
He asked, as if he was talking to some interesting hybrid.
I'M JUST A WOMAN WHO GOT HIT BY LIGHTNING. I WASN'T BORN THE WAY I AM.
LIGHTNING EITHER KILLS YOU OR YOU GET OVER IT.
YOU GET HIT WITH A FEW THOUSAND VOLTS, A FEW MONTHS LATER YOU COME TALK TO ME ABOUT WHAT YOUR LIFE IS LIKE.
YOU CAN WALK?
YES.
WAIT! SINCE YOU'RE HERE, CAN I ASK YOU TO DO ONE MORE THING?
Everyone wants a freebie.
WHAT DO YOU NEED?

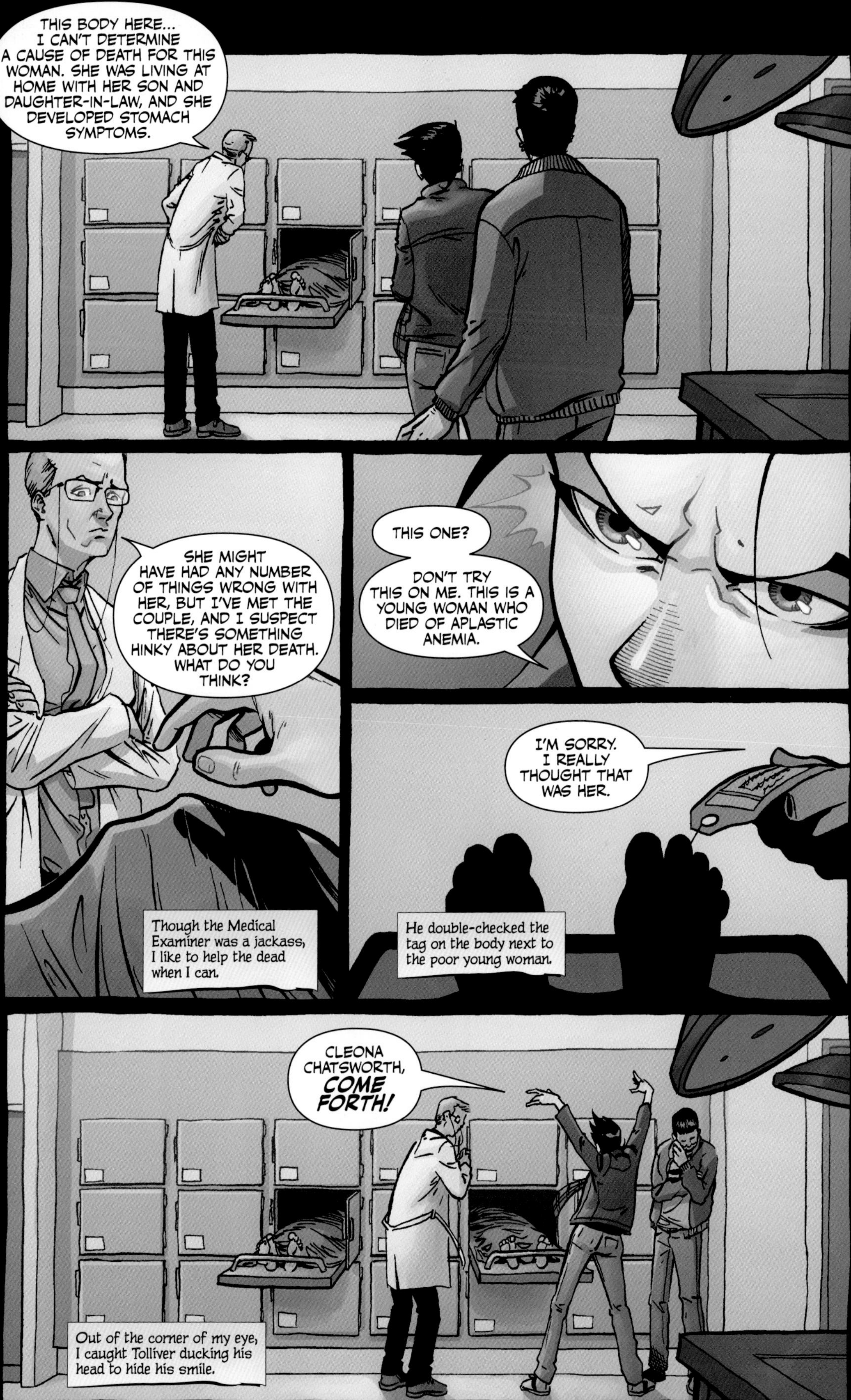
THIS BODY HERE... I CAN'T DETERMINE A CAUSE OF DEATH FOR THIS WOMAN. SHE WAS LIVING AT HOME WITH HER SON AND DAUGHTER-IN-LAW, AND SHE DEVELOPED STOMACH SYMPTOMS.
SHE MIGHT HAVE HAD ANY NUMBER OF THINGS WRONG WITH HER, BUT I'VE MET THE COUPLE, AND I SUSPECT THERE'S SOMETHING HINKY ABOUT HER DEATH. WHAT DO YOU THINK?
Though the Medical Examiner was a jackass, I like to help the dead when I can.
THIS ONE?
DON'T TRY THIS ON ME. THIS IS A YOUNG WOMAN WHO DIED OF APLASTIC ANEMIA.
I'M SORRY. I REALLY THOUGHT THAT WAS HER.
He double-checked the tag on the body next to the poor young woman.
CLEONA CHATSWORTH, COME FORTH!
Out of the corner of my eye, I caught Tolliver ducking his head to hide his smile.

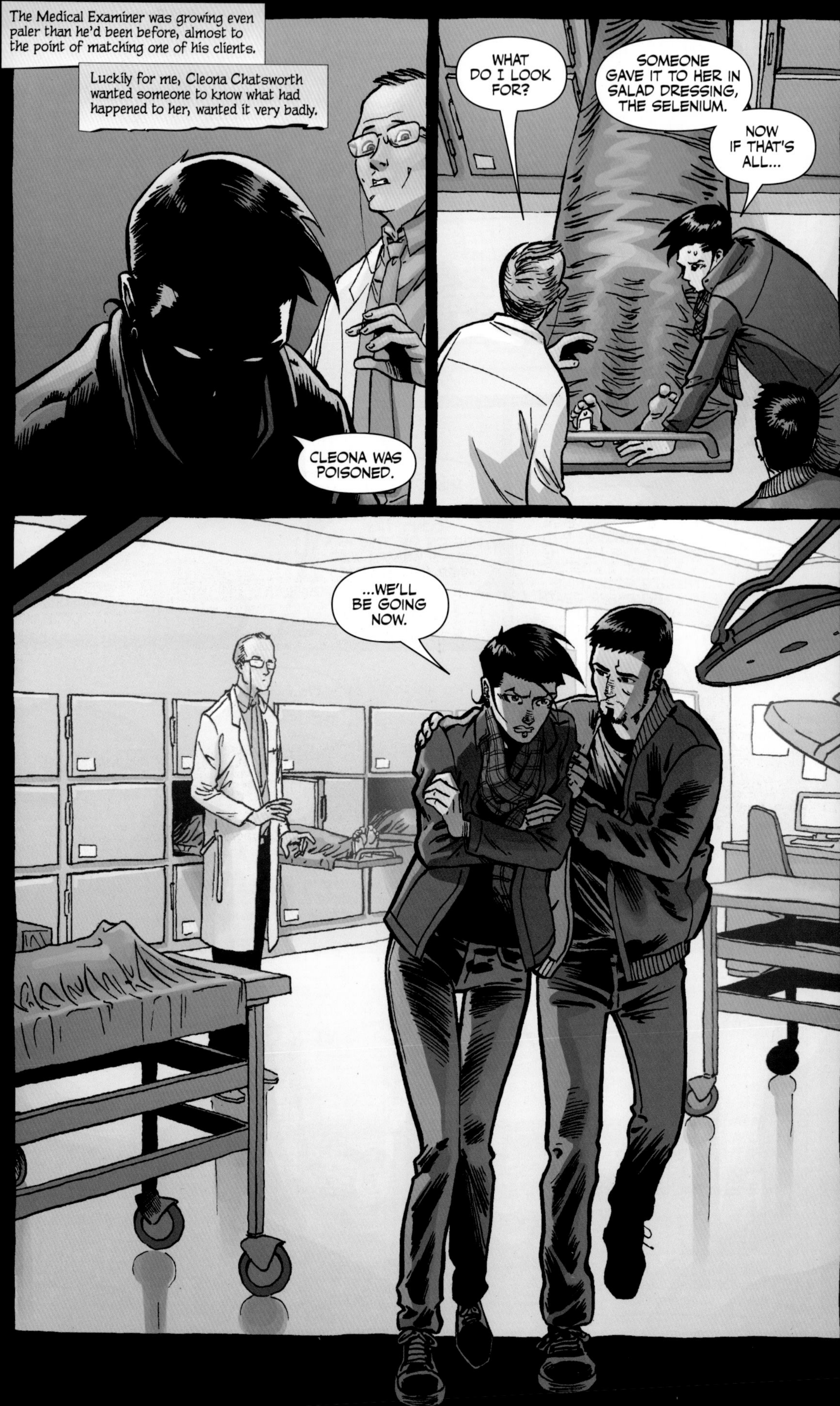

The Medical Examiner was growing even paler than he'd been before, almost to the point of matching one of his clients.
Luckily for me, Cleona Chatsworth wanted someone to know what had happened to her, wanted it very badly.
CLEONA WAS POISONED.
WHAT DO I LOOK FOR?
SOMEONE GAVE IT TO HER IN SALAD DRESSING, THE SELENIUM.
NOW IF THAT'S ALL...
...WE'LL BE GOING NOW.

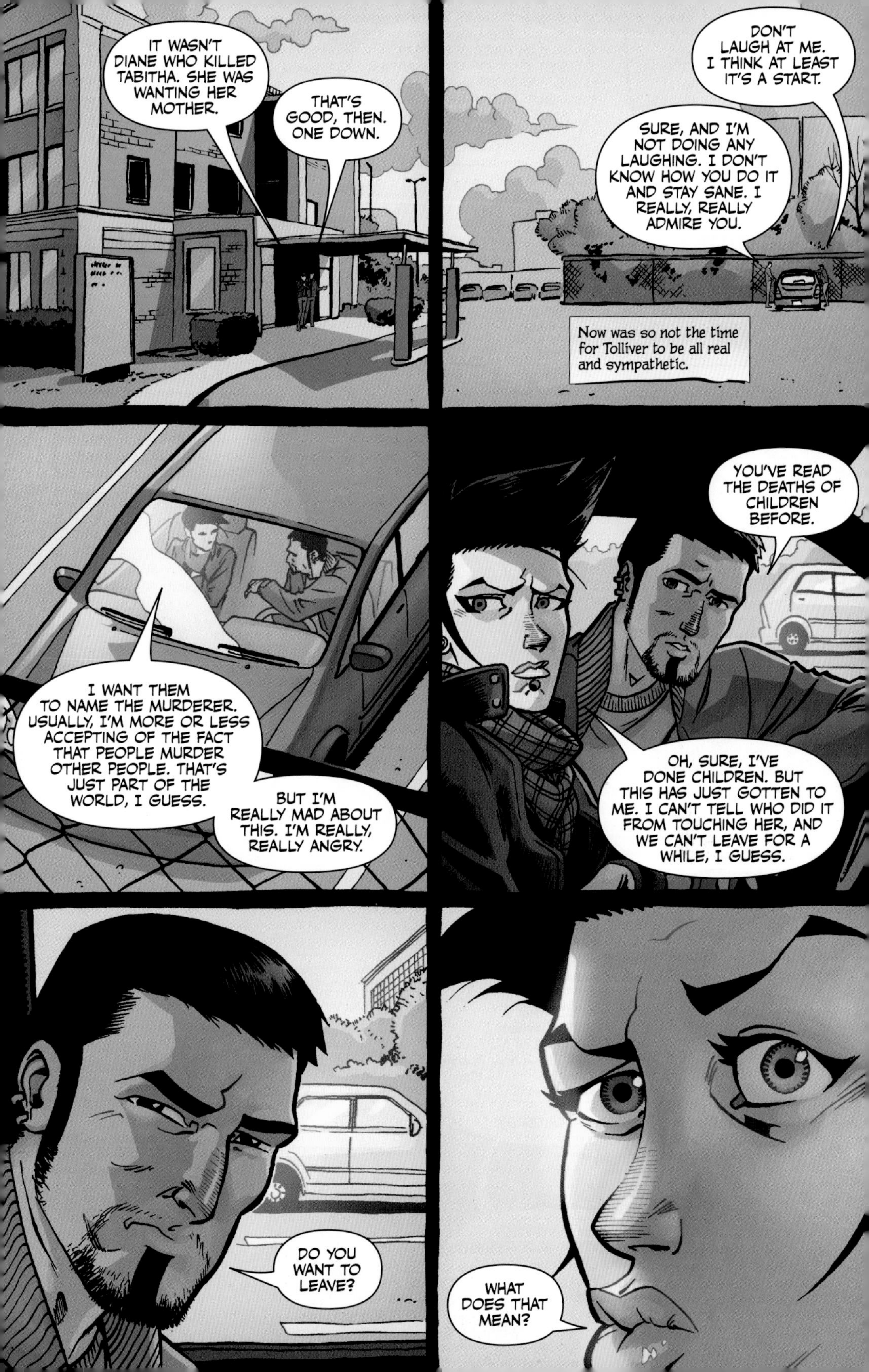
IT WASN'T DIANE WHO KILLED TABITHA. SHE WAS WANTING HER MOTHER.
THAT'S GOOD, THEN. ONE DOWN.
DON'T LAUGH AT ME. I THINK AT LEAST IT'S A START.
SURE, AND I'M NOT DOING ANY LAUGHING. I DON'T KNOW HOW YOU DO IT AND STAY SANE. I REALLY, REALLY ADMIRE YOU.
Now was so not the time for Tolliver to be all real and sympathetic.
I WANT THEM TO NAME THE MURDERER. USUALLY, I'M MORE OR LESS ACCEPTING OF THE FACT THAT PEOPLE MURDER OTHER PEOPLE. THAT'S JUST PART OF THE WORLD, I GUESS.
BUT I'M REALLY MAD ABOUT THIS. I'M REALLY, REALLY ANGRY.
YOU'VE READ THE DEATHS OF CHILDREN BEFORE.
OH, SURE, I'VE DONE CHILDREN. BUT THIS HAS JUST GOTTEN TO ME. I CAN'T TELL WHO DID IT FROM TOUCHING HER, AND WE CAN'T LEAVE FOR A WHILE, I GUESS.
DO YOU WANT TO LEAVE?
WHAT DOES THAT MEAN?

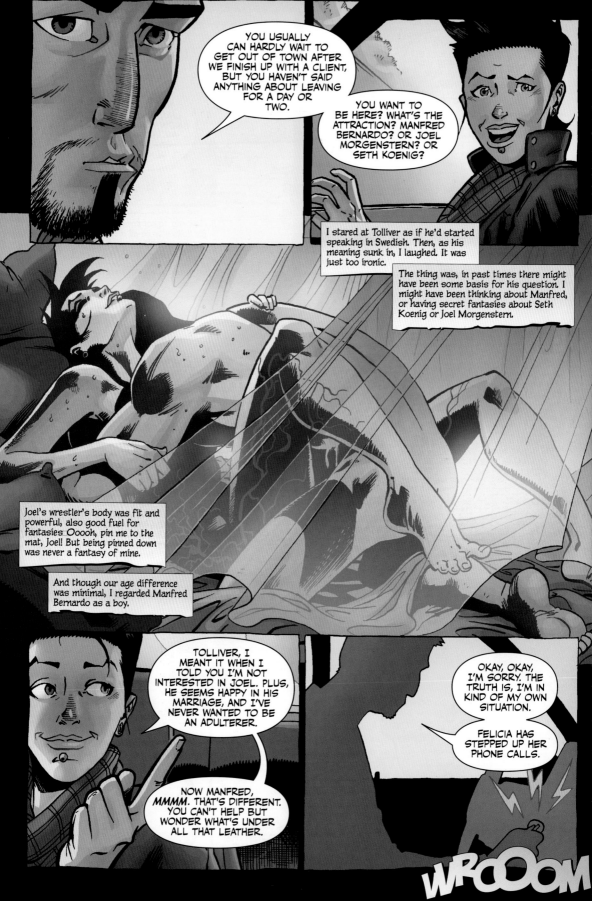

YOU USUALLY CAN HARDLY WAIT TO GET OUT OF TOWN AFTER WE FINISH UP WITH A CLIENT, BUT YOU HAVEN'T SAID ANYTHING ABOUT LEAVING FOR A DAY OR TWO.

YOU WANT TO BE HERE? WHAT'S THE ATTRACTION? MANFRED BERNARDO? OR JOEL MORGENSTERN? OR SETH KOENIG?

I stared at Tolliver as if he'd started speaking in Swedish. Then, as his meaning sunk in, I laughed. It was just too ironic.

The thing was, in past times there might have been some basis for his question. I might have been thinking about Manfred, or having secret fantasies about Seth Koenig or Joel Morgenstern.

Joel's wrestler's body was fit and powerful, also good fuel for fantasies. Ooooh, pin me to the mat, Joel! But being pinned down was never a fantasy of mine.

And though our age difference was minimal, I regarded Manfred Bernardo as a boy.

TOLLIVER, I MEANT IT WHEN I TOLD YOU I'M NOT INTERESTED IN JOEL. PLUS, HE SEEMS HAPPY IN HIS MARRIAGE, AND I'VE NEVER WANTED TO BE AN ADULTERER.

OKAY, OKAY, I'M SORRY. THE TRUTH IS, I'M IN KIND OF MY OWN SITUATION.

FELICIA HAS STEPPED UP HER PHONE CALLS.

NOW MANFRED, *MMMM.* THAT'S DIFFERENT. YOU CAN'T HELP BUT WONDER WHAT'S UNDER ALL THAT LEATHER.

WROOOM

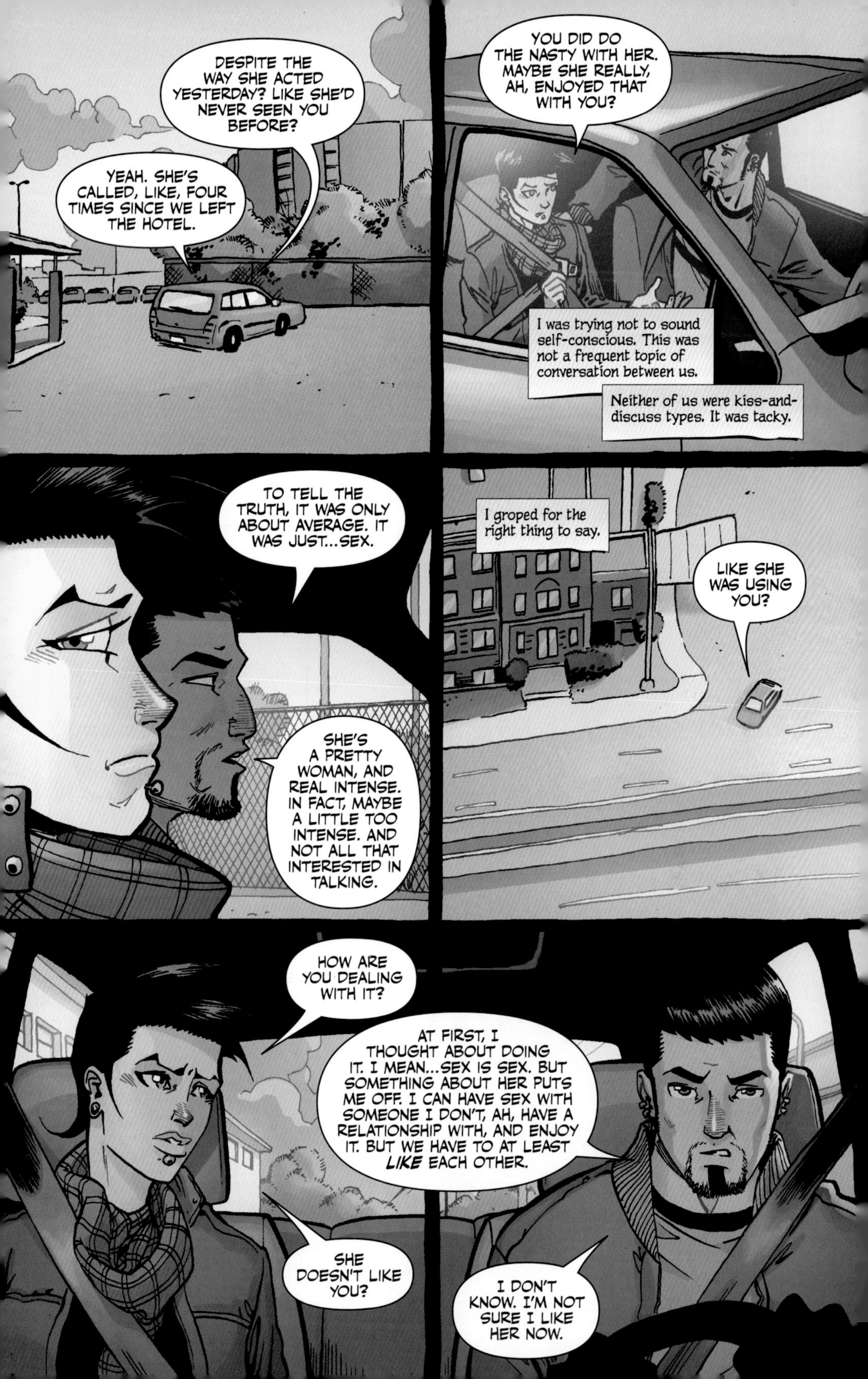
DESPITE THE WAY SHE ACTED YESTERDAY? LIKE SHE'D NEVER SEEN YOU BEFORE?
YEAH. SHE'S CALLED, LIKE, FOUR TIMES SINCE WE LEFT THE HOTEL.
YOU DID DO THE NASTY WITH HER. MAYBE SHE REALLY, AH, ENJOYED THAT WITH YOU?
I was trying not to sound self-conscious. This was not a frequent topic of conversation between us.
Neither of us were kiss-and-discuss types. It was tacky.
TO TELL THE TRUTH, IT WAS ONLY ABOUT AVERAGE. IT WAS JUST...SEX.
SHE'S A PRETTY WOMAN, AND REAL INTENSE. IN FACT, MAYBE A LITTLE TOO INTENSE. AND NOT ALL THAT INTERESTED IN TALKING.
I groped for the right thing to say.
LIKE SHE WAS USING YOU?
HOW ARE YOU DEALING WITH IT?
AT FIRST, I THOUGHT ABOUT DOING IT. I MEAN...SEX IS SEX. BUT SOMETHING ABOUT HER PUTS ME OFF. I CAN HAVE SEX WITH SOMEONE I DON'T, AH, HAVE A RELATIONSHIP WITH, AND ENJOY IT. BUT WE HAVE TO AT LEAST *LIKE* EACH OTHER.
SHE DOESN'T LIKE YOU?
I DON'T KNOW. I'M NOT SURE I LIKE HER NOW.

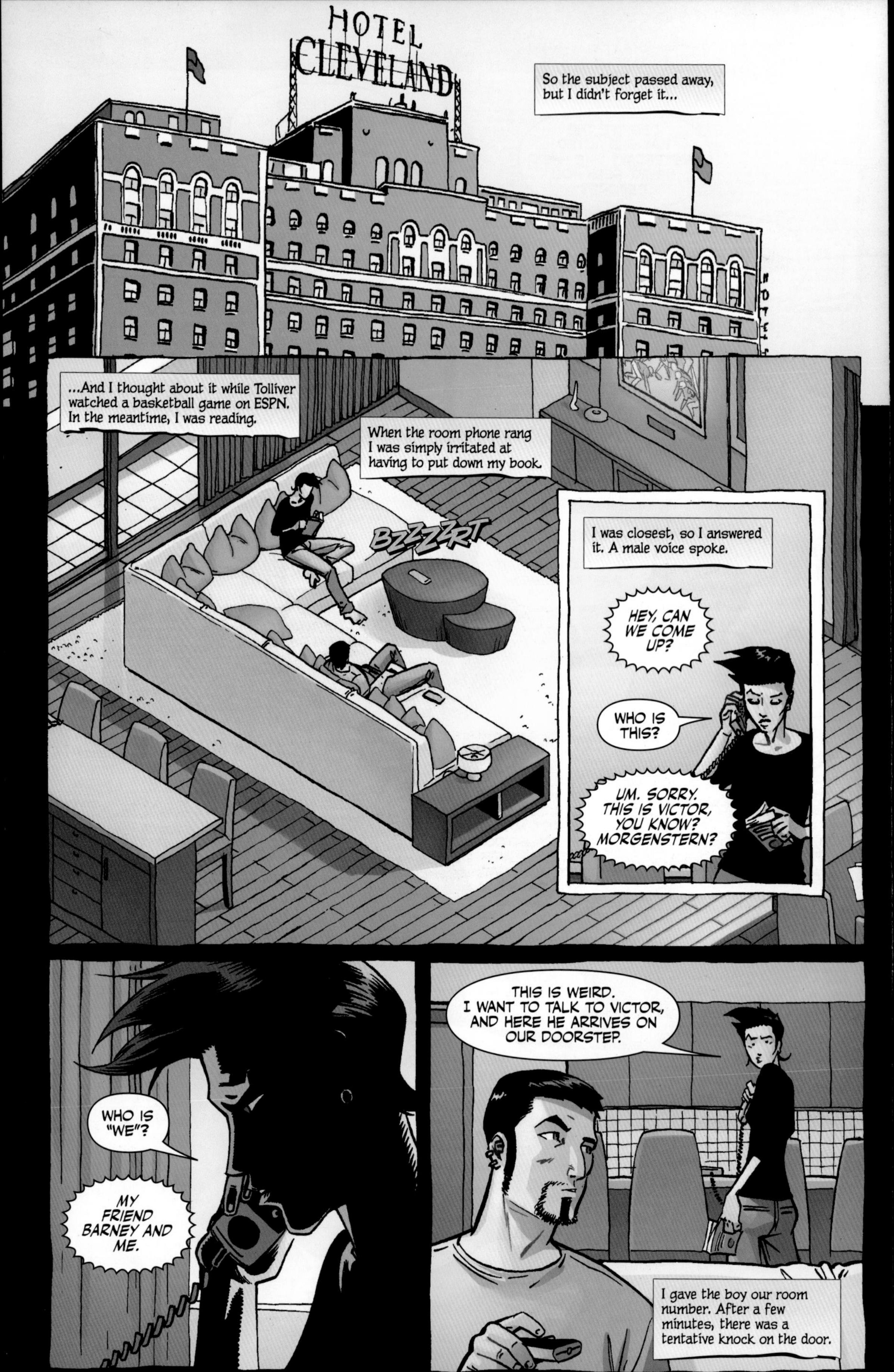
HOTEL CLEVELAND
So the subject passed away, but I didn't forget it...
...And I thought about it while Tolliver watched a basketball game on ESPN. In the meantime, I was reading.
When the room phone rang I was simply irritated at having to put down my book.
BZZZZRT
I was closest, so I answered it. A male voice spoke.
HEY, CAN WE COME UP?
WHO IS THIS?
UM. SORRY. THIS IS VICTOR, YOU KNOW? MORGENSTERN?
WHO IS "WE"?
MY FRIEND BARNEY AND ME.
THIS IS WEIRD. I WANT TO TALK TO VICTOR, AND HERE HE ARRIVES ON OUR DOORSTEP.
I gave the boy our room number. After a few minutes, there was a tentative knock on the door.

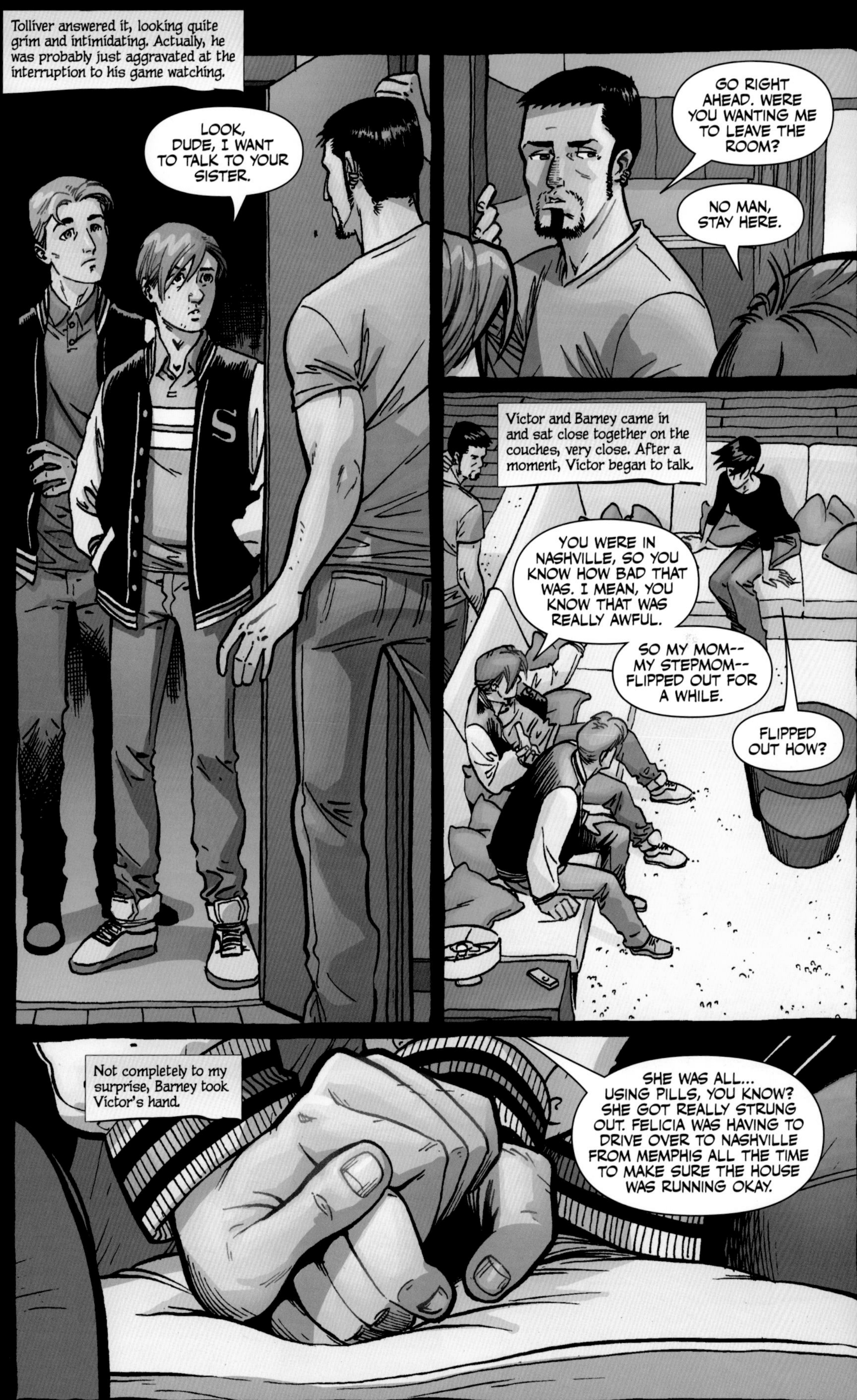
Tolliver answered it, looking quite grim and intimidating. Actually, he was probably just aggravated at the interruption to his game watching.
LOOK, DUDE, I WANT TO TALK TO YOUR SISTER.
GO RIGHT AHEAD. WERE YOU WANTING ME TO LEAVE THE ROOM?
NO MAN, STAY HERE.
Victor and Barney came in and sat close together on the couches, very close. After a moment, Victor began to talk.
YOU WERE IN NASHVILLE, SO YOU KNOW HOW BAD THAT WAS. I MEAN, YOU KNOW THAT WAS REALLY AWFUL.
SO MY MOM-- MY STEPMOM-- FLIPPED OUT FOR A WHILE.
FLIPPED OUT HOW?
Not completely to my surprise, Barney took Victor's hand.
SHE WAS ALL... USING PILLS, YOU KNOW? SHE GOT REALLY STRUNG OUT. FELICIA WAS HAVING TO DRIVE OVER TO NASHVILLE FROM MEMPHIS ALL THE TIME TO MAKE SURE THE HOUSE WAS RUNNING OKAY.

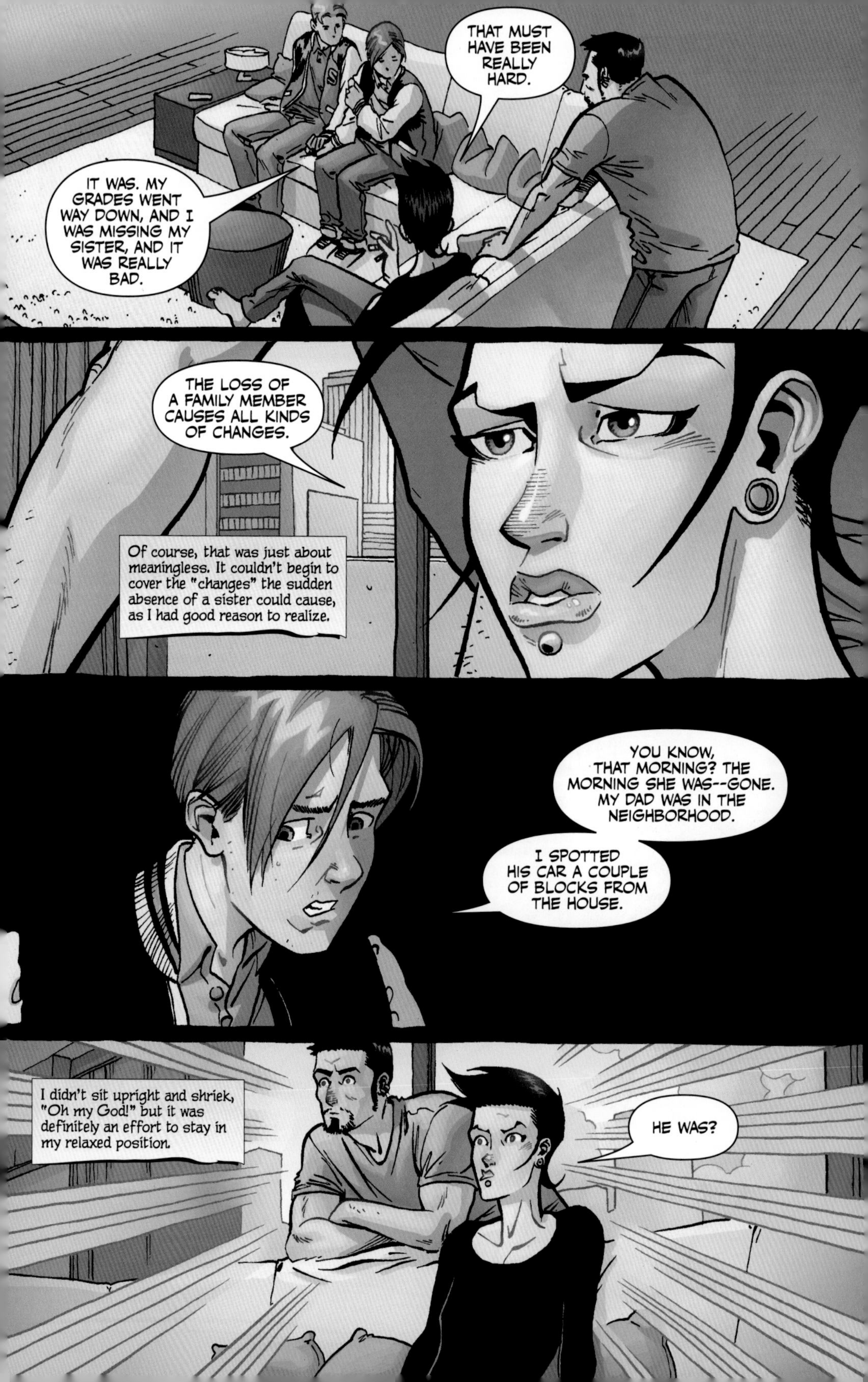
THAT MUST HAVE BEEN REALLY HARD.
IT WAS. MY GRADES WENT WAY DOWN, AND I WAS MISSING MY SISTER, AND IT WAS REALLY BAD.
THE LOSS OF A FAMILY MEMBER CAUSES ALL KINDS OF CHANGES.
Of course, that was just about meaningless. It couldn't begin to cover the "changes" the sudden absence of a sister could cause, as I had good reason to realize.
YOU KNOW, THAT MORNING? THE MORNING SHE WAS--GONE. MY DAD WAS IN THE NEIGHBORHOOD.
I SPOTTED HIS CAR A COUPLE OF BLOCKS FROM THE HOUSE.
I didn't sit upright and shriek, "Oh my God!" but it was definitely an effort to stay in my relaxed position.
HE WAS?

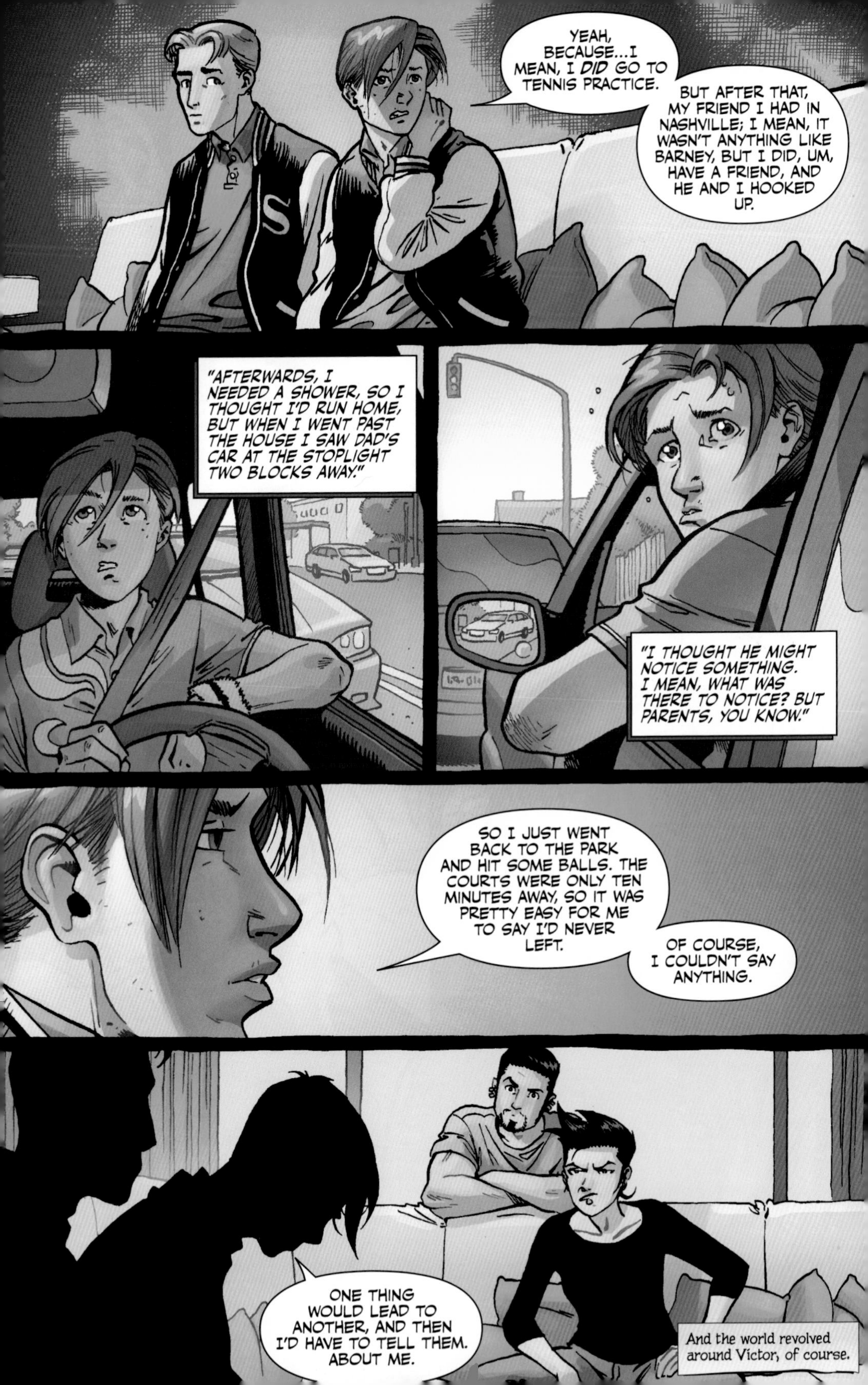
YEAH, BECAUSE...I MEAN, I *DID* GO TO TENNIS PRACTICE.
BUT AFTER THAT, MY FRIEND I HAD IN NASHVILLE; I MEAN, IT WASN'T ANYTHING LIKE BARNEY, BUT I DID, UM, HAVE A FRIEND, AND HE AND I HOOKED UP.
"AFTERWARDS, I NEEDED A SHOWER, SO I THOUGHT I'D RUN HOME, BUT WHEN I WENT PAST THE HOUSE I SAW DAD'S CAR AT THE STOPLIGHT TWO BLOCKS AWAY."
"I THOUGHT HE MIGHT NOTICE SOMETHING. I MEAN, WHAT WAS THERE TO NOTICE? BUT PARENTS, YOU KNOW."
SO I JUST WENT BACK TO THE PARK AND HIT SOME BALLS. THE COURTS WERE ONLY TEN MINUTES AWAY, SO IT WAS PRETTY EASY FOR ME TO SAY I'D NEVER LEFT.
OF COURSE, I COULDN'T SAY ANYTHING.
ONE THING WOULD LEAD TO ANOTHER, AND THEN I'D HAVE TO TELL THEM. ABOUT ME.
And the world revolved around Victor, of course.

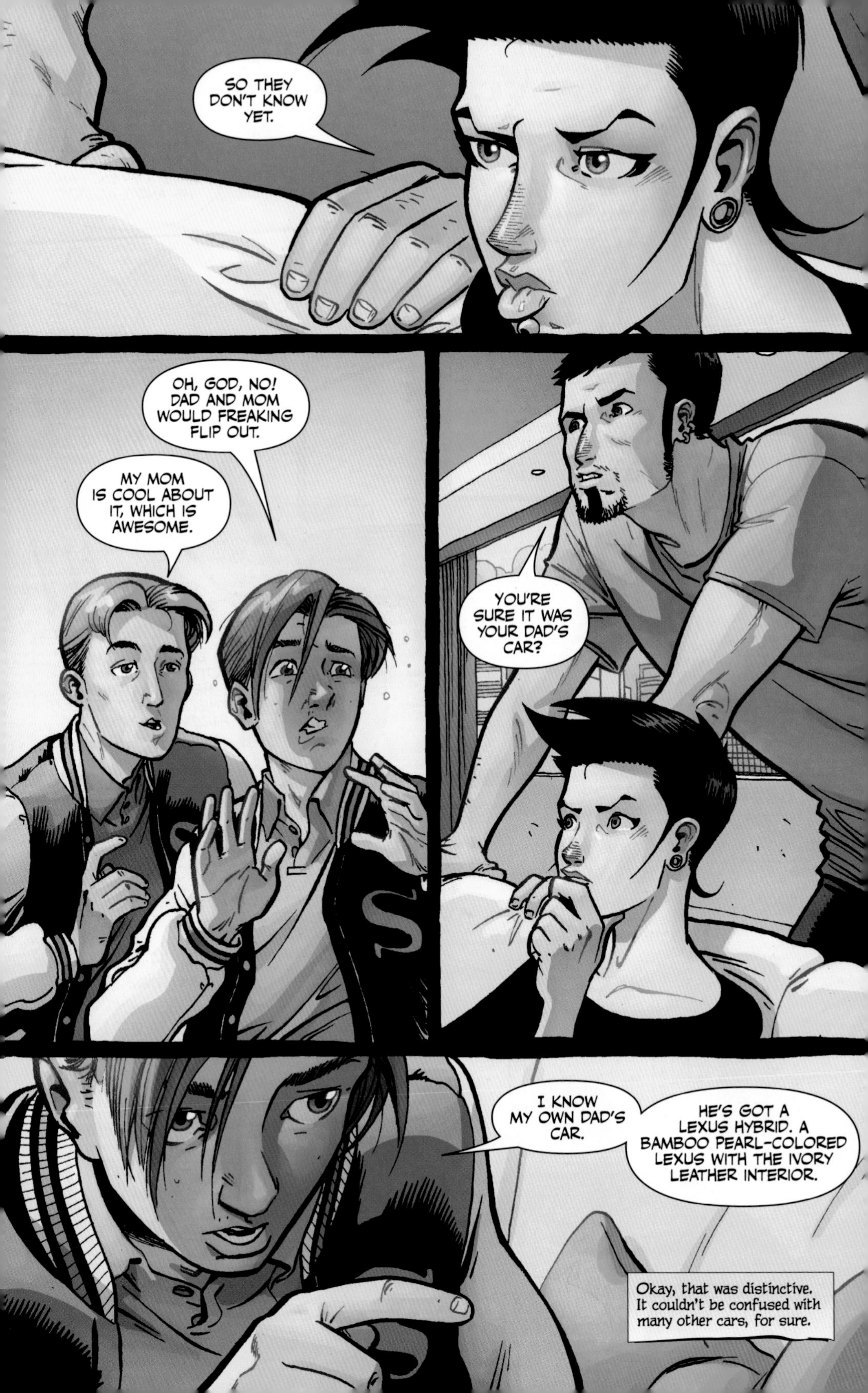
SO THEY DON'T KNOW YET.
OH, GOD, NO! DAD AND MOM WOULD FREAKING FLIP OUT.
MY MOM IS COOL ABOUT IT, WHICH IS AWESOME.
YOU'RE SURE IT WAS YOUR DAD'S CAR?
I KNOW MY OWN DAD'S CAR.
HE'S GOT A LEXUS HYBRID. A BAMBOO PEARL-COLORED LEXUS WITH THE IVORY LEATHER INTERIOR.
Okay, that was distinctive. It couldn't be confused with many other cars, for sure.

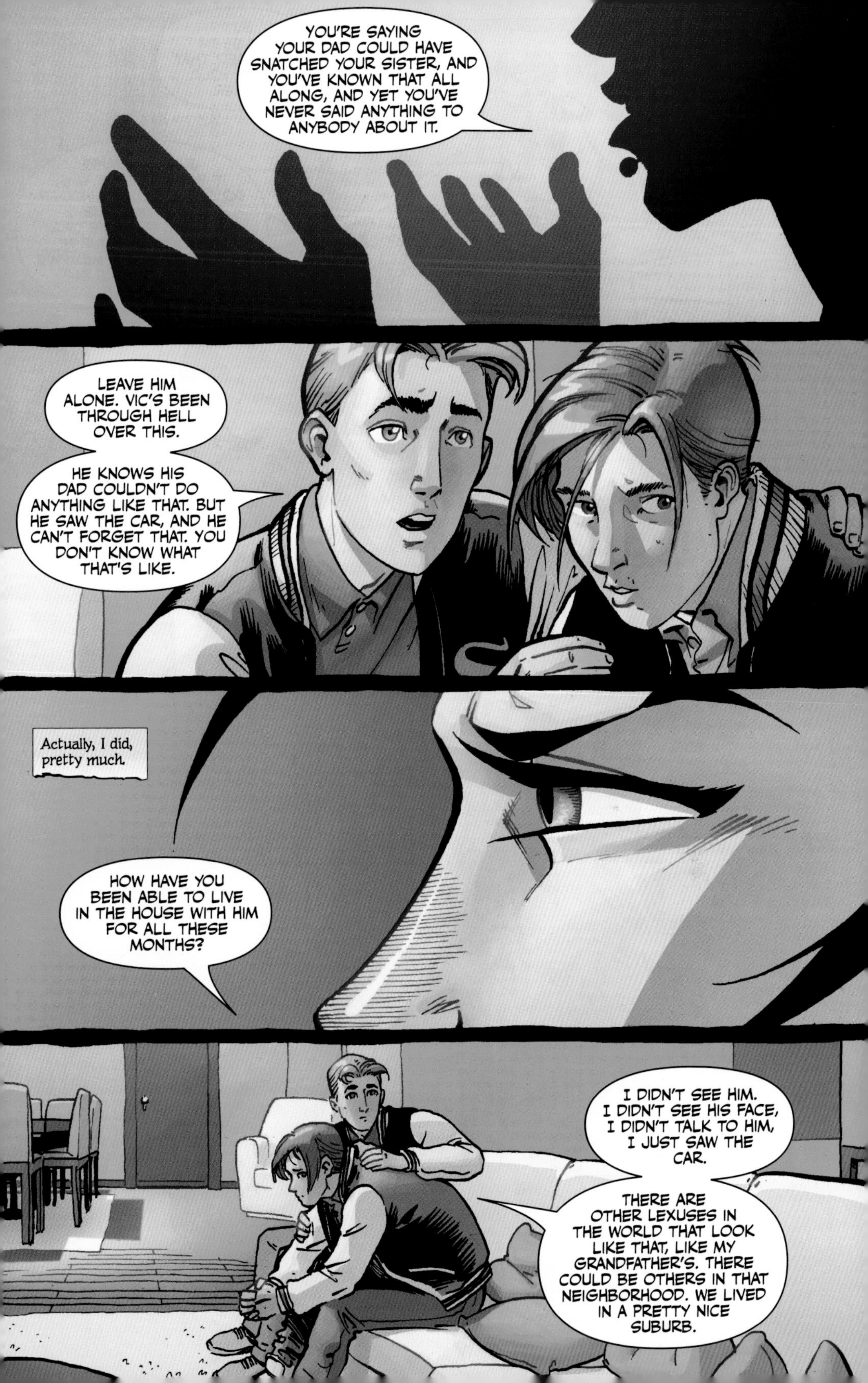
YOU'RE SAYING YOUR DAD COULD HAVE SNATCHED YOUR SISTER, AND YOU'VE KNOWN THAT ALL ALONG, AND YET YOU'VE NEVER SAID ANYTHING TO ANYBODY ABOUT IT.
LEAVE HIM ALONE. VIC'S BEEN THROUGH HELL OVER THIS.
HE KNOWS HIS DAD COULDN'T DO ANYTHING LIKE THAT. BUT HE SAW THE CAR, AND HE CAN'T FORGET THAT. YOU DON'T KNOW WHAT THAT'S LIKE.
Actually, I did, pretty much.
HOW HAVE YOU BEEN ABLE TO LIVE IN THE HOUSE WITH HIM FOR ALL THESE MONTHS?
I DIDN'T SEE HIM. I DIDN'T SEE HIS FACE, I DIDN'T TALK TO HIM, I JUST SAW THE CAR.
THERE ARE OTHER LEXUSES IN THE WORLD THAT LOOK LIKE THAT, LIKE MY GRANDFATHER'S. THERE COULD BE OTHERS IN THAT NEIGHBORHOOD. WE LIVED IN A PRETTY NICE SUBURB.

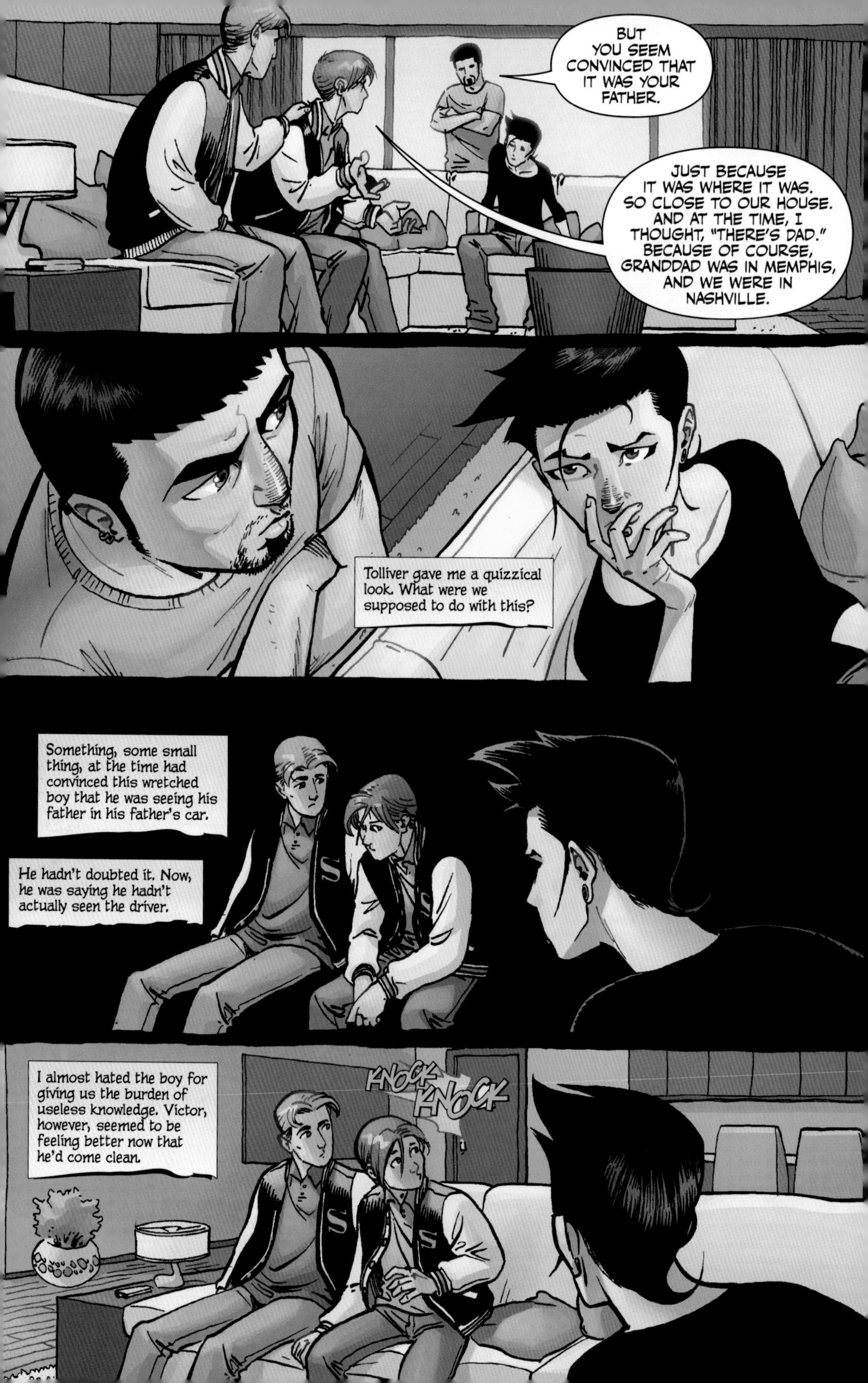
BUT YOU SEEM CONVINCED THAT IT WAS YOUR FATHER.
JUST BECAUSE IT WAS WHERE IT WAS. SO CLOSE TO OUR HOUSE. AND AT THE TIME, I THOUGHT, "THERE'S DAD." BECAUSE OF COURSE, GRANDDAD WAS IN MEMPHIS, AND WE WERE IN NASHVILLE.
Tolliver gave me a quizzical look. What were we supposed to do with this?
Something, some small thing, at the time had convinced this wretched boy that he was seeing his father in his father's car.
He hadn't doubted it. Now, he was saying he hadn't actually seen the driver.
I almost hated the boy for giving us the burden of useless knowledge. Victor, however, seemed to be feeling better now that he'd come clean.
KNOCK KNOCK

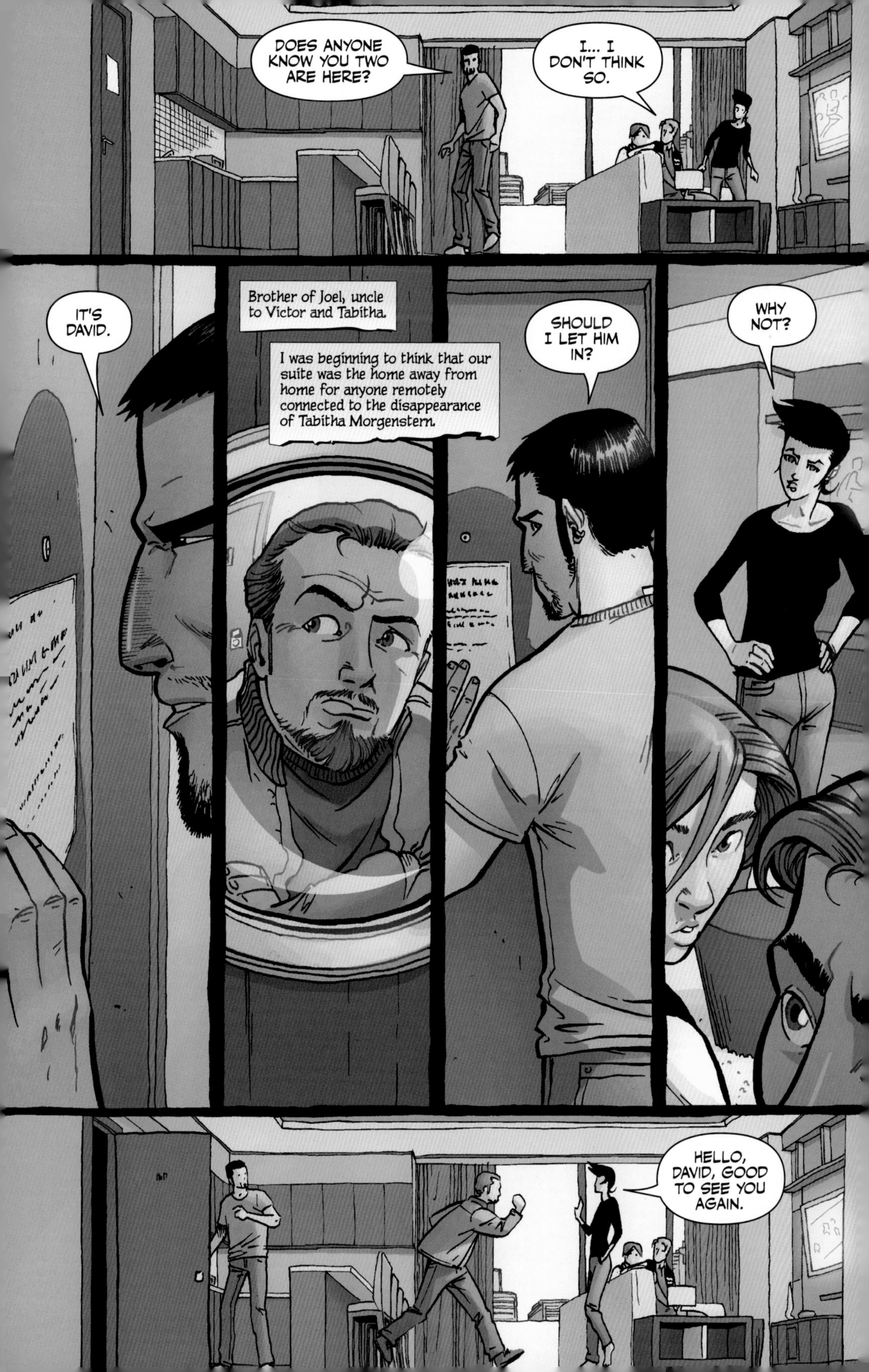
DOES ANYONE KNOW YOU TWO ARE HERE?
I... I DON'T THINK SO.
IT'S DAVID.
Brother of Joel, uncle to Victor and Tabitha.
I was beginning to think that our suite was the home away from home for anyone remotely connected to the disappearance of Tabitha Morgenstern.
SHOULD I LET HIM IN?
WHY NOT?
HELLO, DAVID, GOOD TO SEE YOU AGAIN.

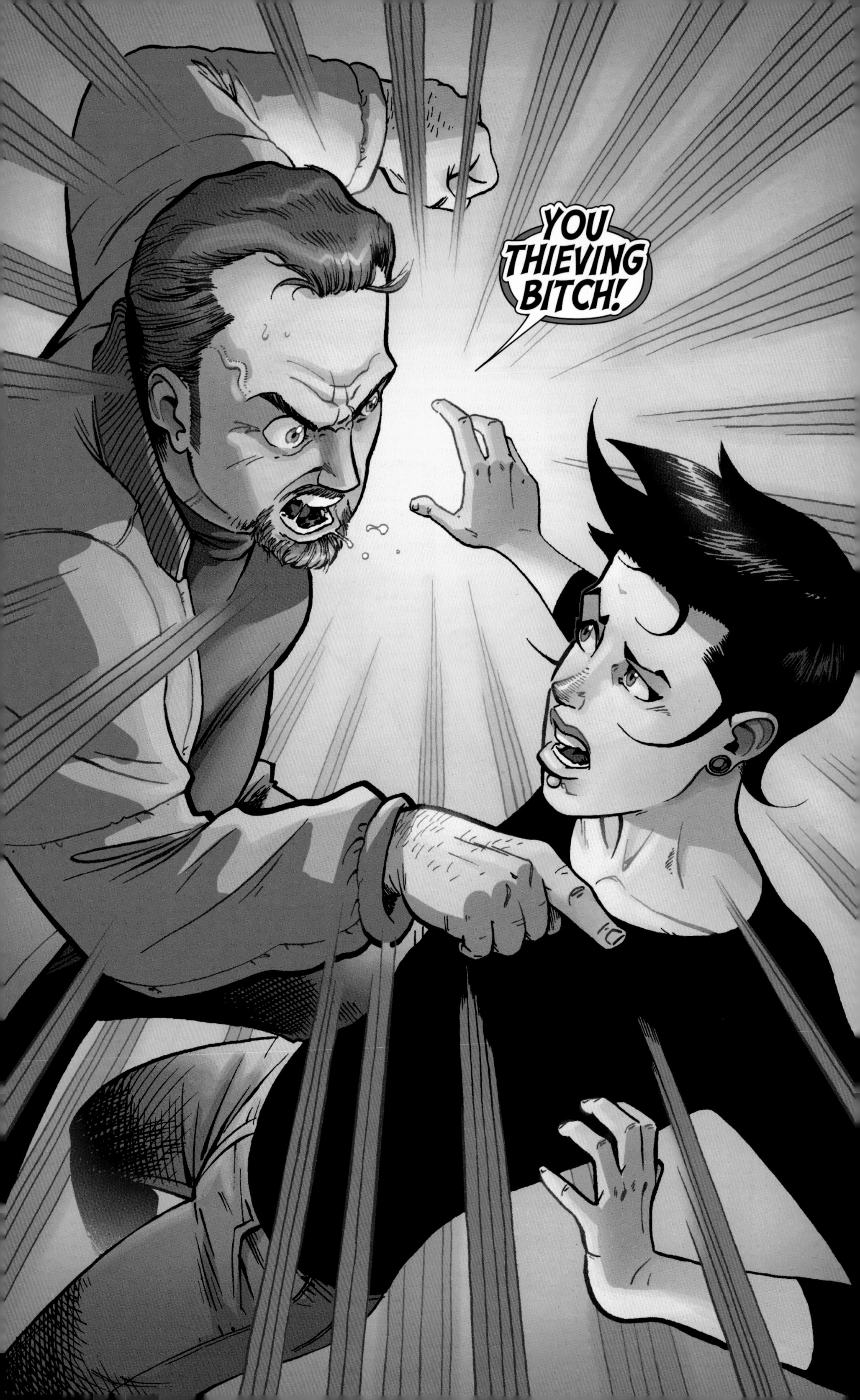
YOU THIEVING BITCH!

CHAPTER SEVEN

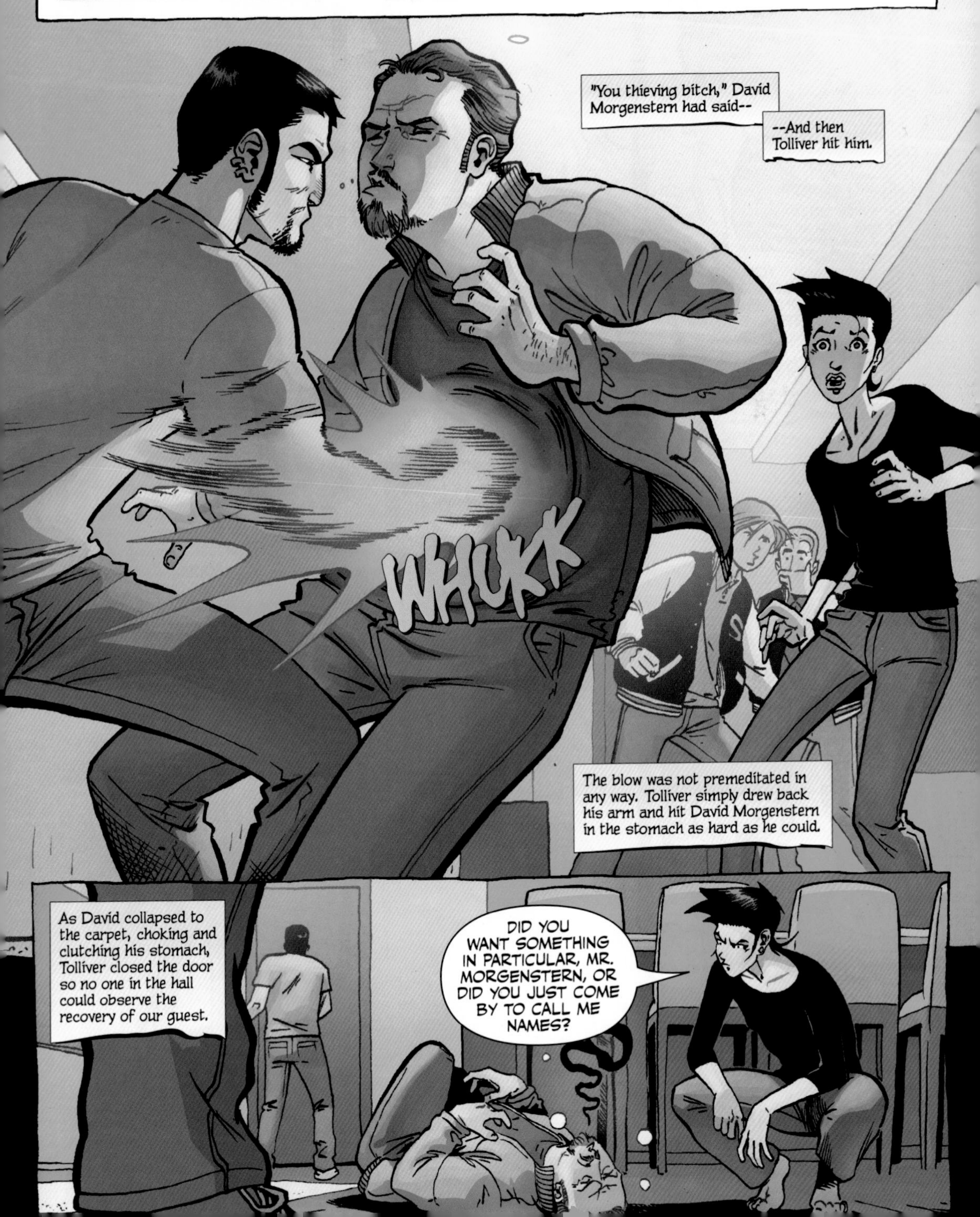
"You thieving bitch," David Morgenstern had said--
--And then Tolliver hit him.
WHUKK
The blow was not premeditated in any way. Tolliver simply drew back his arm and hit David Morgenstern in the stomach as hard as he could.
As David collapsed to the carpet, choking and clutching his stomach, Tolliver closed the door so no one in the hall could observe the recovery of our guest.
DID YOU WANT SOMETHING IN PARTICULAR, MR. MORGENSTERN, OR DID YOU JUST COME BY TO CALL ME NAMES?

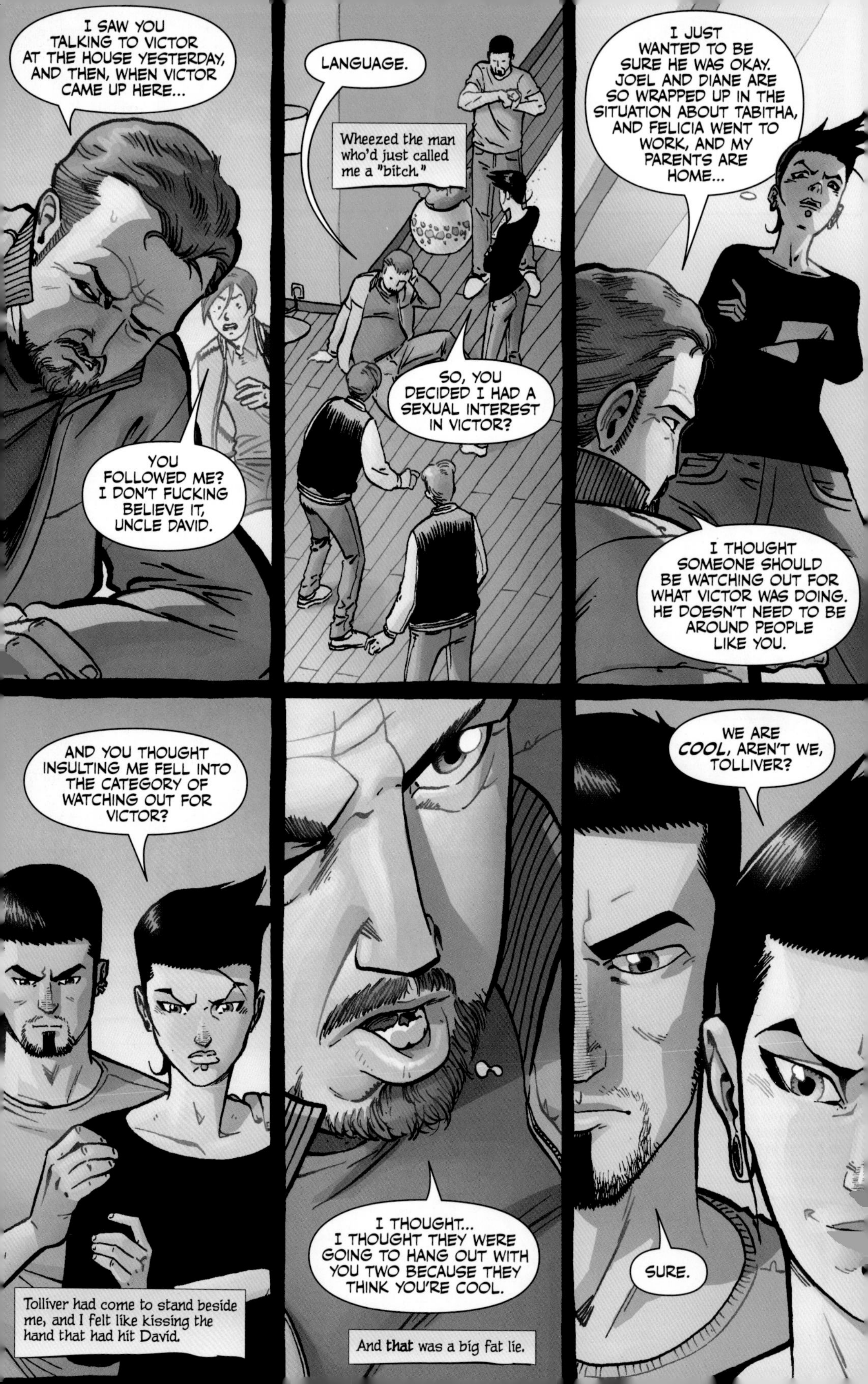
I SAW YOU TALKING TO VICTOR AT THE HOUSE YESTERDAY, AND THEN, WHEN VICTOR CAME UP HERE...
YOU FOLLOWED ME? I DON'T FUCKING BELIEVE IT, UNCLE DAVID.
LANGUAGE.
Wheezed the man who'd just called me a "bitch."
SO, YOU DECIDED I HAD A SEXUAL INTEREST IN VICTOR?
I JUST WANTED TO BE SURE HE WAS OKAY. JOEL AND DIANE ARE SO WRAPPED UP IN THE SITUATION ABOUT TABITHA, AND FELICIA WENT TO WORK, AND MY PARENTS ARE HOME...
I THOUGHT SOMEONE SHOULD BE WATCHING OUT FOR WHAT VICTOR WAS DOING. HE DOESN'T NEED TO BE AROUND PEOPLE LIKE YOU.
AND YOU THOUGHT INSULTING ME FELL INTO THE CATEGORY OF WATCHING OUT FOR VICTOR?
Tolliver had come to stand beside me, and I felt like kissing the hand that had hit David.
I THOUGHT... I THOUGHT THEY WERE GOING TO HANG OUT WITH YOU TWO BECAUSE THEY THINK YOU'RE COOL.
And **that** was a big fat lie.
WE ARE *COOL*, AREN'T WE, TOLLIVER?
SURE.

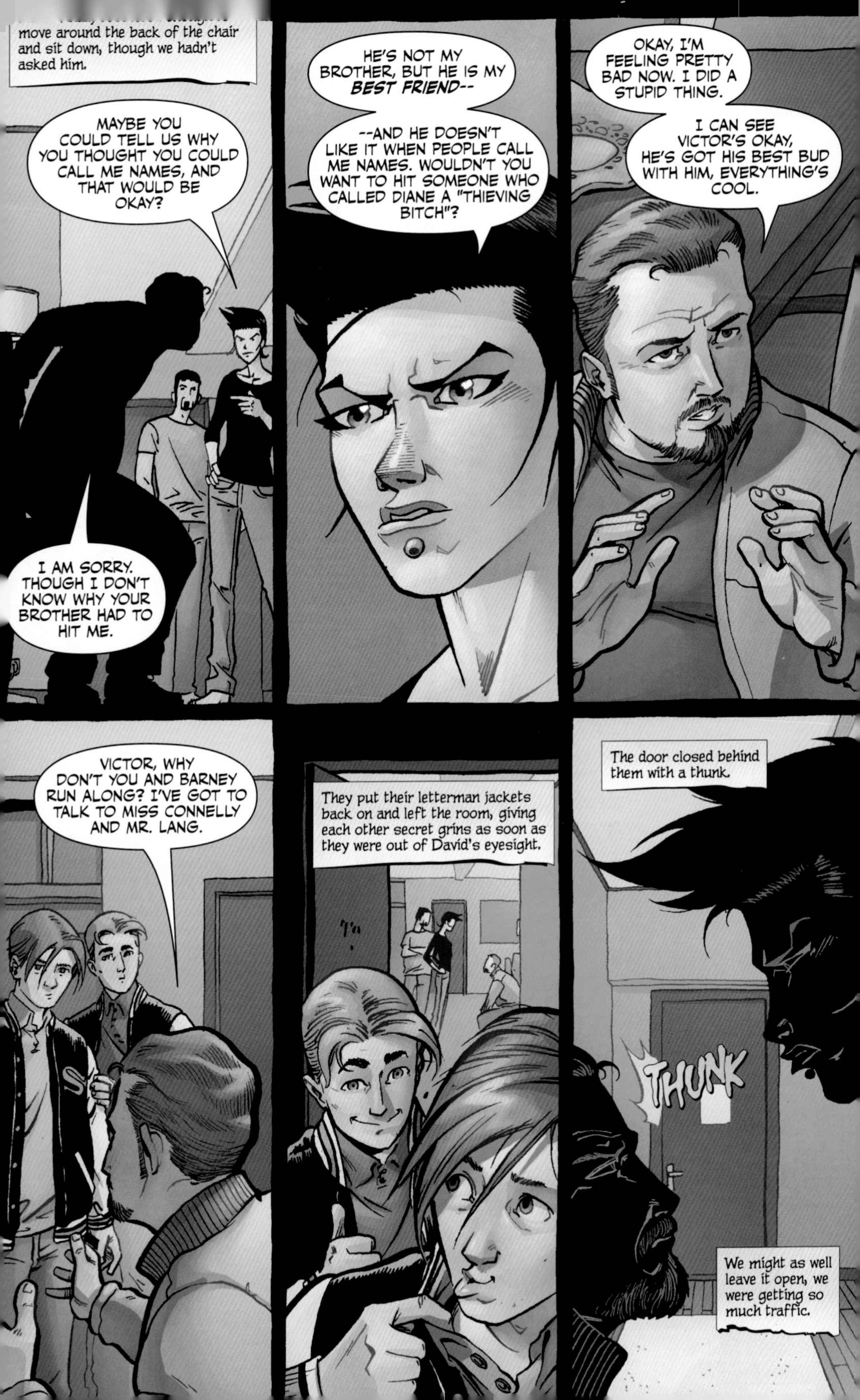
move around the back of the chair and sit down, though we hadn't asked him.
MAYBE YOU COULD TELL US WHY YOU THOUGHT YOU COULD CALL ME NAMES, AND THAT WOULD BE OKAY?
I AM SORRY. THOUGH I DON'T KNOW WHY YOUR BROTHER HAD TO HIT ME.
HE'S NOT MY BROTHER, BUT HE IS MY BEST FRIEND--
--AND HE DOESN'T LIKE IT WHEN PEOPLE CALL ME NAMES. WOULDN'T YOU WANT TO HIT SOMEONE WHO CALLED DIANE A "THIEVING BITCH"?
OKAY, I'M FEELING PRETTY BAD NOW. I DID A STUPID THING.
I CAN SEE VICTOR'S OKAY, HE'S GOT HIS BEST BUD WITH HIM, EVERYTHING'S COOL.
VICTOR, WHY DON'T YOU AND BARNEY RUN ALONG? I'VE GOT TO TALK TO MISS CONNELLY AND MR. LANG.
They put their letterman jackets back on and left the room, giving each other secret grins as soon as they were out of David's eyesight.
The door closed behind them with a thunk.
THUNK
We might as well leave it open, we were getting so much traffic.

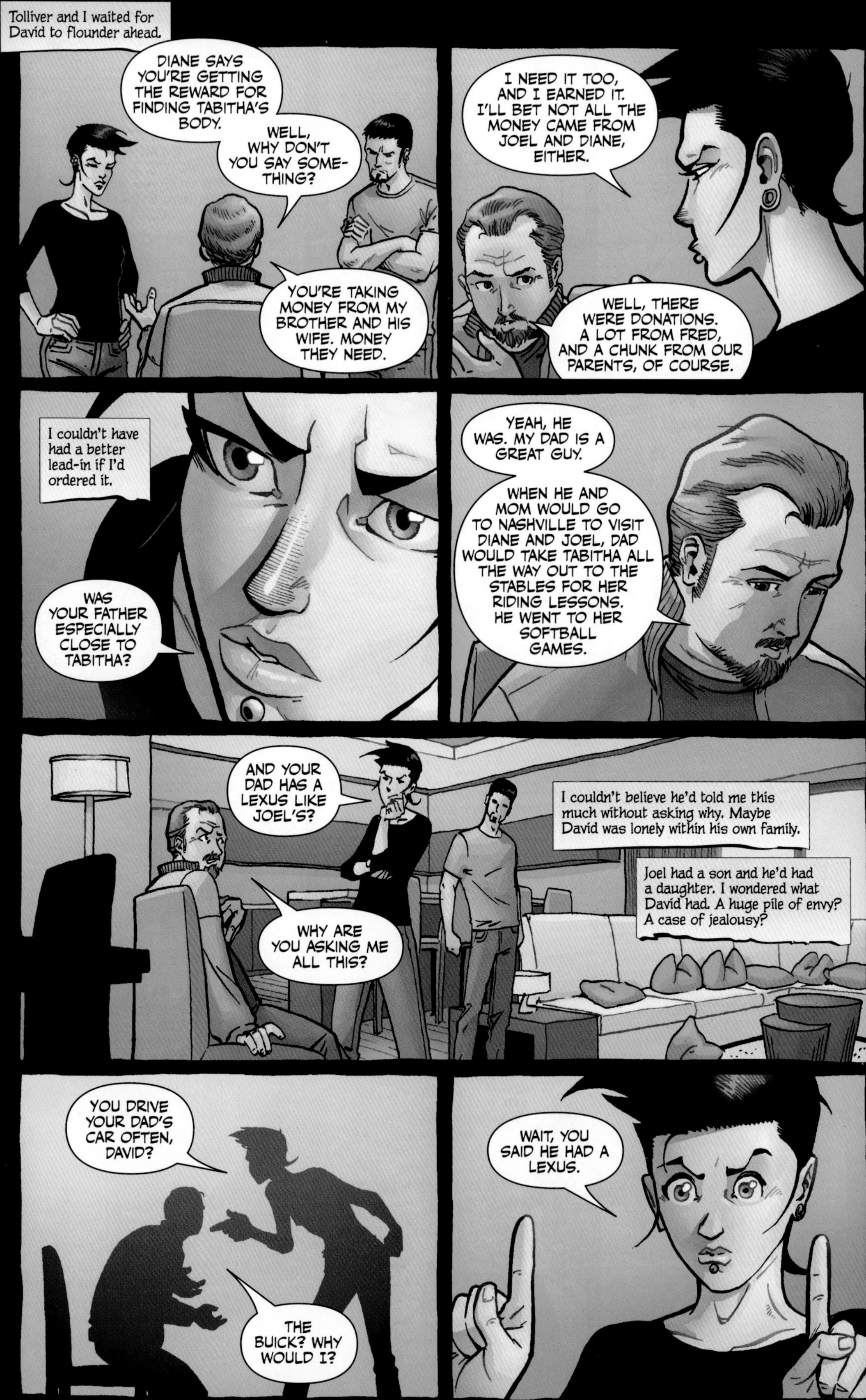
Tolliver and I waited for David to flounder ahead.
DIANE SAYS YOU'RE GETTING THE REWARD FOR FINDING TABITHA'S BODY.
WELL, WHY DON'T YOU SAY SOME-THING?
YOU'RE TAKING MONEY FROM MY BROTHER AND HIS WIFE. MONEY THEY NEED.
I NEED IT TOO, AND I EARNED IT. I'LL BET NOT ALL THE MONEY CAME FROM JOEL AND DIANE, EITHER.
WELL, THERE WERE DONATIONS. A LOT FROM FRED, AND A CHUNK FROM OUR PARENTS, OF COURSE.
I couldn't have had a better lead-in if I'd ordered it.
WAS YOUR FATHER ESPECIALLY CLOSE TO TABITHA?
YEAH, HE WAS. MY DAD IS A GREAT GUY.
WHEN HE AND MOM WOULD GO TO NASHVILLE TO VISIT DIANE AND JOEL, DAD WOULD TAKE TABITHA ALL THE WAY OUT TO THE STABLES FOR HER RIDING LESSONS. HE WENT TO HER SOFTBALL GAMES.
AND YOUR DAD HAS A LEXUS LIKE JOEL'S?
WHY ARE YOU ASKING ME ALL THIS?
I couldn't believe he'd told me this much without asking why. Maybe David was lonely within his own family.
Joel had a son and he'd had a daughter. I wondered what David had. A huge pile of envy? A case of jealousy?
YOU DRIVE YOUR DAD'S CAR OFTEN, DAVID?
THE BUICK? WHY WOULD I?
WAIT, YOU SAID HE HAD A LEXUS.

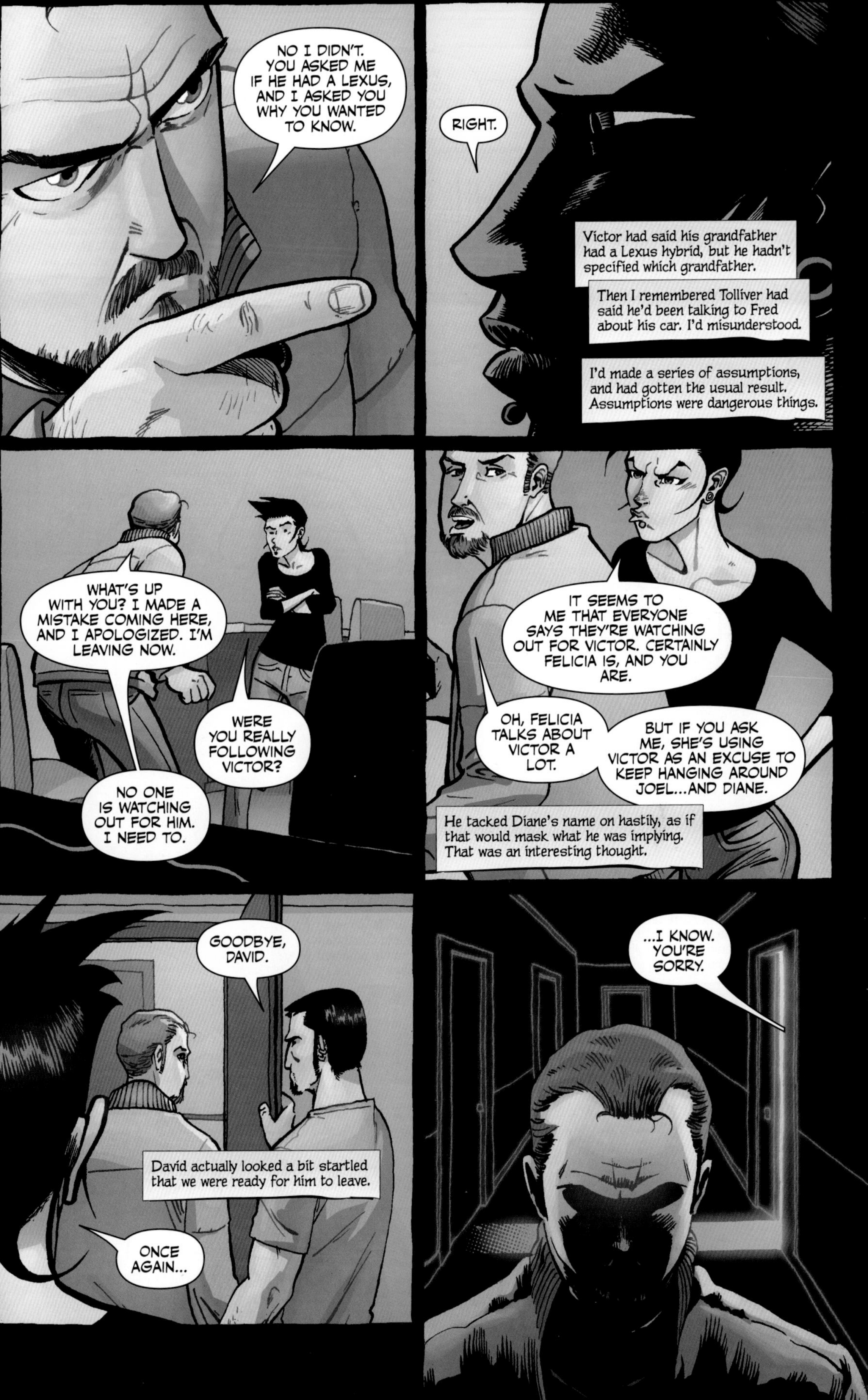
NO I DIDN'T. YOU ASKED ME IF HE HAD A LEXUS, AND I ASKED YOU WHY YOU WANTED TO KNOW.
RIGHT.
Victor had said his grandfather had a Lexus hybrid, but he hadn't specified which grandfather.
Then I remembered Tolliver had said he'd been talking to Fred about his car. I'd misunderstood.
I'd made a series of assumptions, and had gotten the usual result. Assumptions were dangerous things.
WHAT'S UP WITH YOU? I MADE A MISTAKE COMING HERE, AND I APOLOGIZED. I'M LEAVING NOW.
WERE YOU REALLY FOLLOWING VICTOR?
NO ONE IS WATCHING OUT FOR HIM. I NEED TO.
IT SEEMS TO ME THAT EVERYONE SAYS THEY'RE WATCHING OUT FOR VICTOR. CERTAINLY FELICIA IS, AND YOU ARE.
OH, FELICIA TALKS ABOUT VICTOR A LOT.
BUT IF YOU ASK ME, SHE'S USING VICTOR AS AN EXCUSE TO KEEP HANGING AROUND JOEL...AND DIANE.
He tacked Diane's name on hastily, as if that would mask what he was implying. That was an interesting thought.
GOODBYE, DAVID.
David actually looked a bit startled that we were ready for him to leave.
ONCE AGAIN...
...I KNOW. YOU'RE SORRY.

felt so tired I thought my flesh might fall off my bones. It wasn't bedtime yet, and I didn't think I'd eaten since a long-ago light breakfast.

WE'RE GETTING FOOD RIGHT NOW.

He called room service and placed an order, and though we'd called at a strange time, our food arrived quickly.

As we ate silently, I went back over everything I knew.

Tabitha Morgenstern. Eleven. The much-loved child, as far as I could tell, of upper-class professional Jewish parents.

Abducted in Nashville, to end up interred in an old Christian cemetery in Memphis adjacent to Bingham College.

Neither of her parents, the papers had told me, had ever been arrested for anything. Her older half-brother, either.

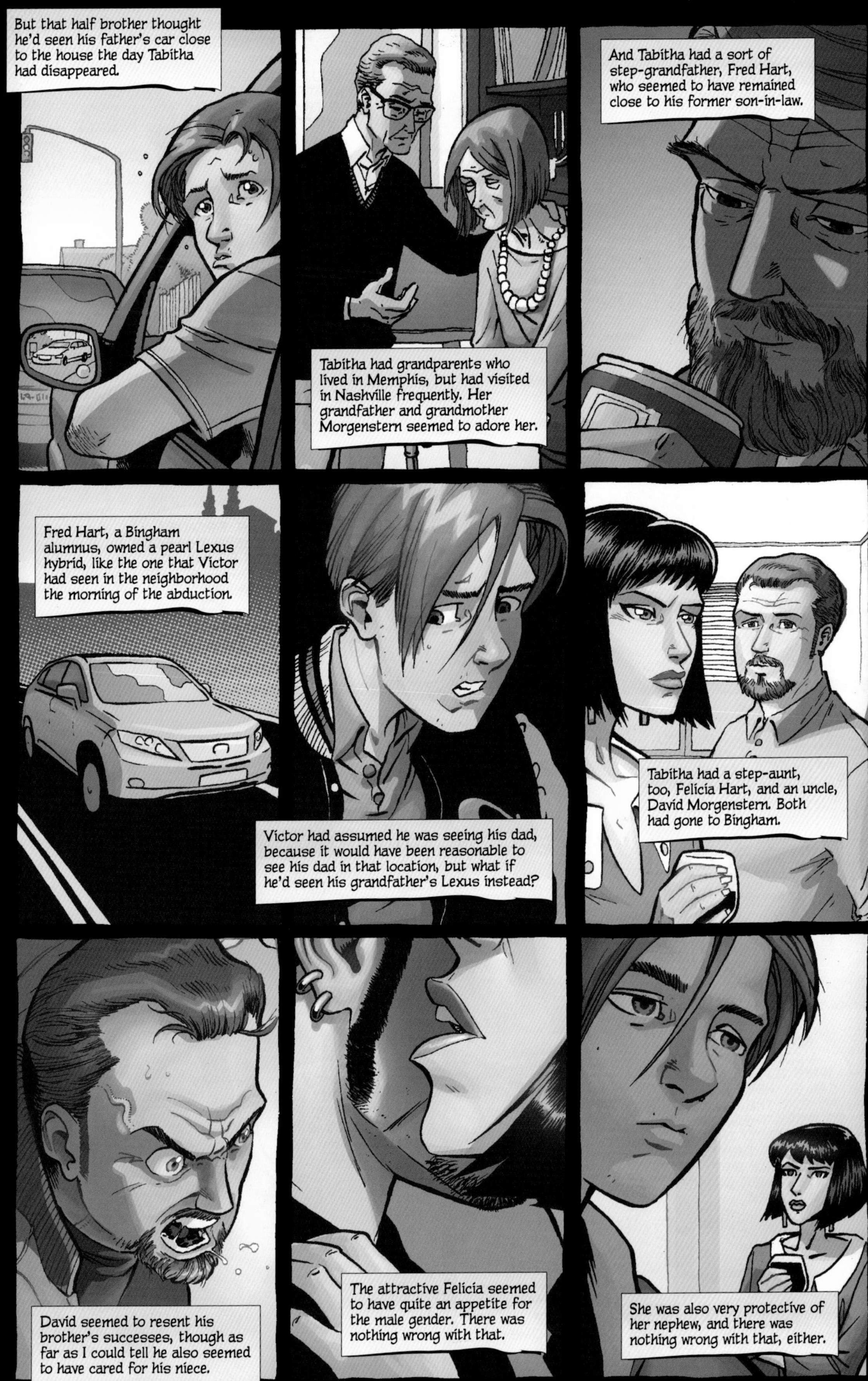
But that half brother thought he'd seen his father's car close to the house the day Tabitha had disappeared.
Tabitha had grandparents who lived in Memphis, but had visited in Nashville frequently. Her grandfather and grandmother Morgenstern seemed to adore her.
And Tabitha had a sort of step-grandfather, Fred Hart, who seemed to have remained close to his former son-in-law.
Fred Hart, a Bingham alumnus, owned a pearl Lexus hybrid, like the one that Victor had seen in the neighborhood the morning of the abduction.
Victor had assumed he was seeing his dad, because it would have been reasonable to see his dad in that location, but what if he'd seen his grandfather's Lexus instead?
Tabitha had a step-aunt, too, Felicia Hart, and an uncle, David Morgenstern. Both had gone to Bingham.
David seemed to resent his brother's successes, though as far as I could tell he also seemed to have cared for his niece.
The attractive Felicia seemed to have quite an appetite for the male gender. There was nothing wrong with that.
She was also very protective of her nephew, and there was nothing wrong with that, either.

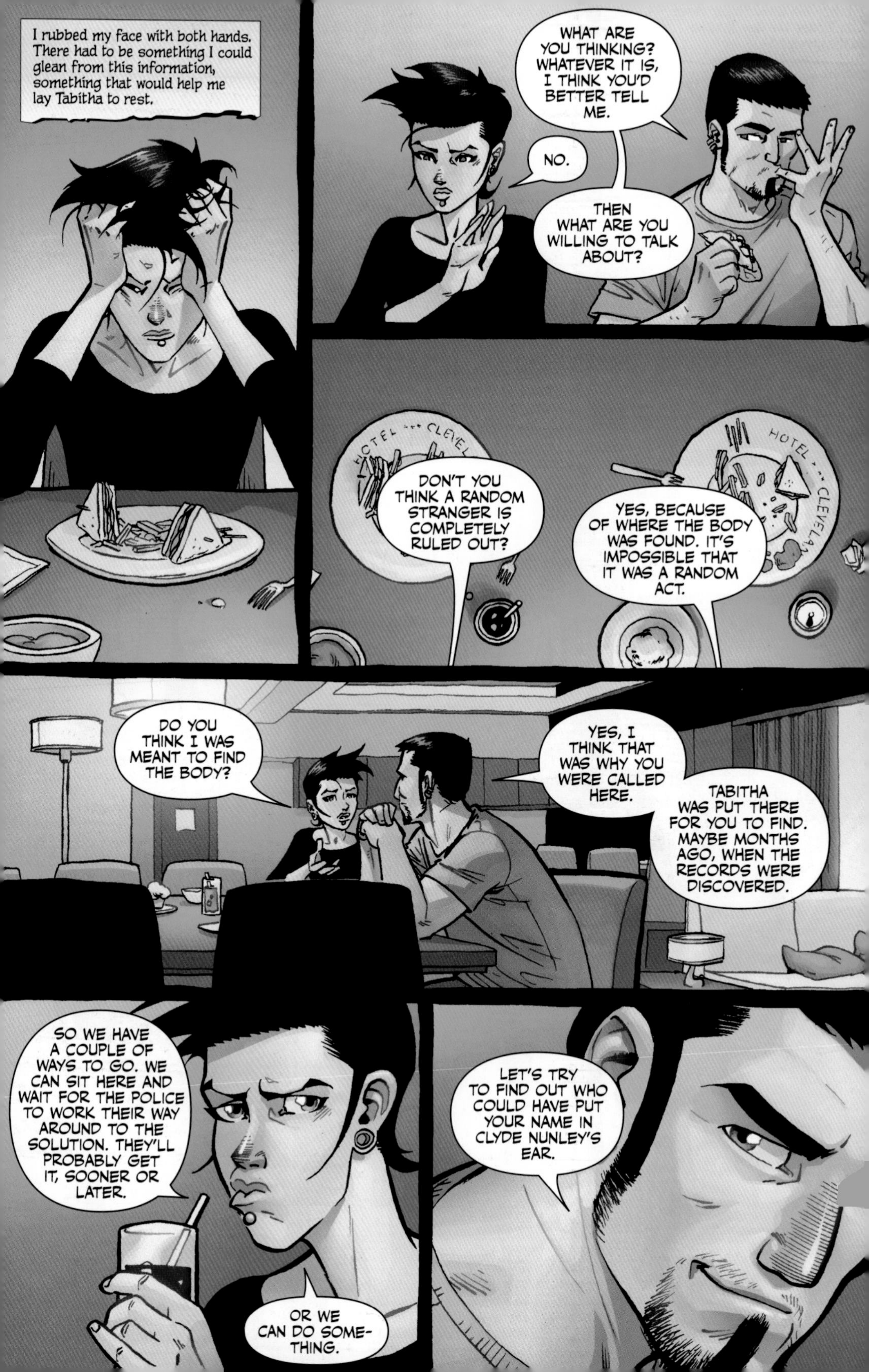
I rubbed my face with both hands. There had to be something I could glean from this information, something that would help me lay Tabitha to rest.
WHAT ARE YOU THINKING? WHATEVER IT IS, I THINK YOU'D BETTER TELL ME.
NO.
THEN WHAT ARE YOU WILLING TO TALK ABOUT?
DON'T YOU THINK A RANDOM STRANGER IS COMPLETELY RULED OUT?
YES, BECAUSE OF WHERE THE BODY WAS FOUND. IT'S IMPOSSIBLE THAT IT WAS A RANDOM ACT.
HOTEL CLEVELAN
DO YOU THINK I WAS MEANT TO FIND THE BODY?
YES, I THINK THAT WAS WHY YOU WERE CALLED HERE.
TABITHA WAS PUT THERE FOR YOU TO FIND. MAYBE MONTHS AGO, WHEN THE RECORDS WERE DISCOVERED.
SO WE HAVE A COUPLE OF WAYS TO GO. WE CAN SIT HERE AND WAIT FOR THE POLICE TO WORK THEIR WAY AROUND TO THE SOLUTION. THEY'LL PROBABLY GET IT, SOONER OR LATER.
OR WE CAN DO SOME-THING.
LET'S TRY TO FIND OUT WHO COULD HAVE PUT YOUR NAME IN CLYDE NUNLEY'S EAR.

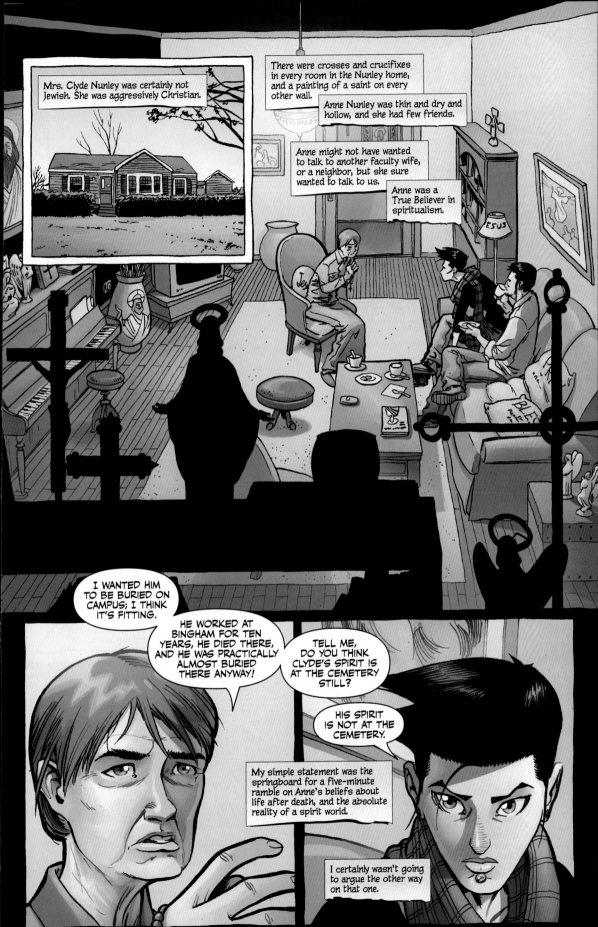

Mrs. Clyde Nunley was certainly not Jewish. She was aggressively Christian.

There were crosses and crucifixes in every room in the Nunley home, and a painting of a saint on every other wall.

Anne Nunley was thin and dry and hollow, and she had few friends.

Anne might not have wanted to talk to another faculty wife, or a neighbor, but she sure wanted to talk to us.

Anne was a True Believer in spiritualism.

I WANTED HIM TO BE BURIED ON CAMPUS; I THINK IT'S FITTING.

HE WORKED AT BINGHAM FOR TEN YEARS, HE DIED THERE, AND HE WAS PRACTICALLY ALMOST BURIED THERE ANYWAY!

TELL ME, DO YOU THINK CLYDE'S SPIRIT IS AT THE CEMETERY STILL?

HIS SPIRIT IS NOT AT THE CEMETERY.

My simple statement was the springboard for a five-minute ramble on Anne's beliefs about life after death, and the absolute reality of a spirit world.

I certainly wasn't going to argue the other way on that one.

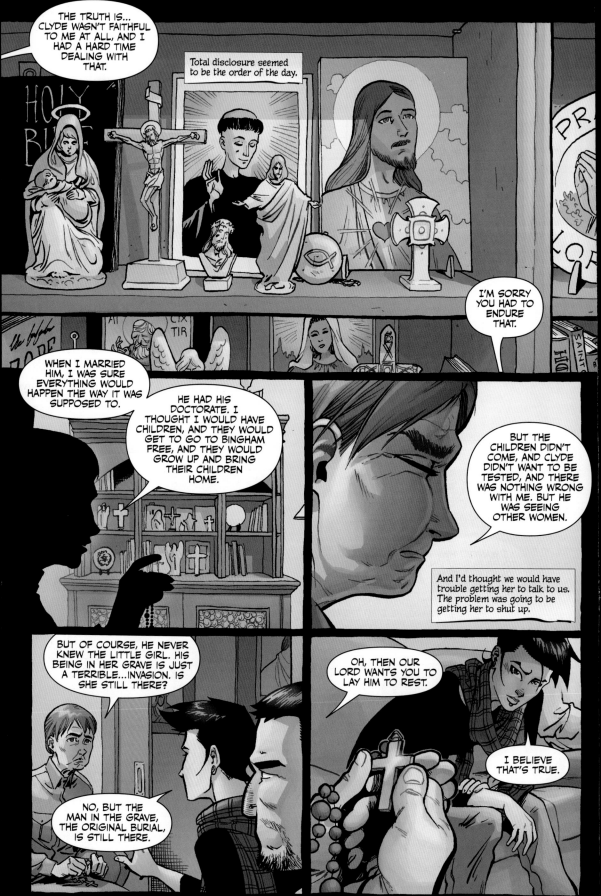

THE TRUTH IS... CLYDE WASN'T FAITHFUL TO ME AT ALL, AND I HAD A HARD TIME DEALING WITH THAT.

Total disclosure seemed to be the order of the day.

I'M SORRY YOU HAD TO ENDURE THAT.

WHEN I MARRIED HIM, I WAS SURE EVERYTHING WOULD HAPPEN THE WAY IT WAS SUPPOSED TO.

HE HAD HIS DOCTORATE. I THOUGHT I WOULD HAVE CHILDREN, AND THEY WOULD GET TO GO TO BINGHAM FREE, AND THEY WOULD GROW UP AND BRING THEIR CHILDREN HOME.

BUT THE CHILDREN DIDN'T COME, AND CLYDE DIDN'T WANT TO BE TESTED, AND THERE WAS NOTHING WRONG WITH ME. BUT HE WAS SEEING OTHER WOMEN.

And I'd thought we would have trouble getting her to talk to us. The problem was going to be getting her to shut up.

BUT OF COURSE, HE NEVER KNEW THE LITTLE GIRL. HIS BEING IN HER GRAVE IS JUST A TERRIBLE...INVASION. IS SHE STILL THERE?

NO, BUT THE MAN IN THE GRAVE, THE ORIGINAL BURIAL, IS STILL THERE.

OH, THEN OUR LORD WANTS YOU TO LAY HIM TO REST.

I BELIEVE THAT'S TRUE.

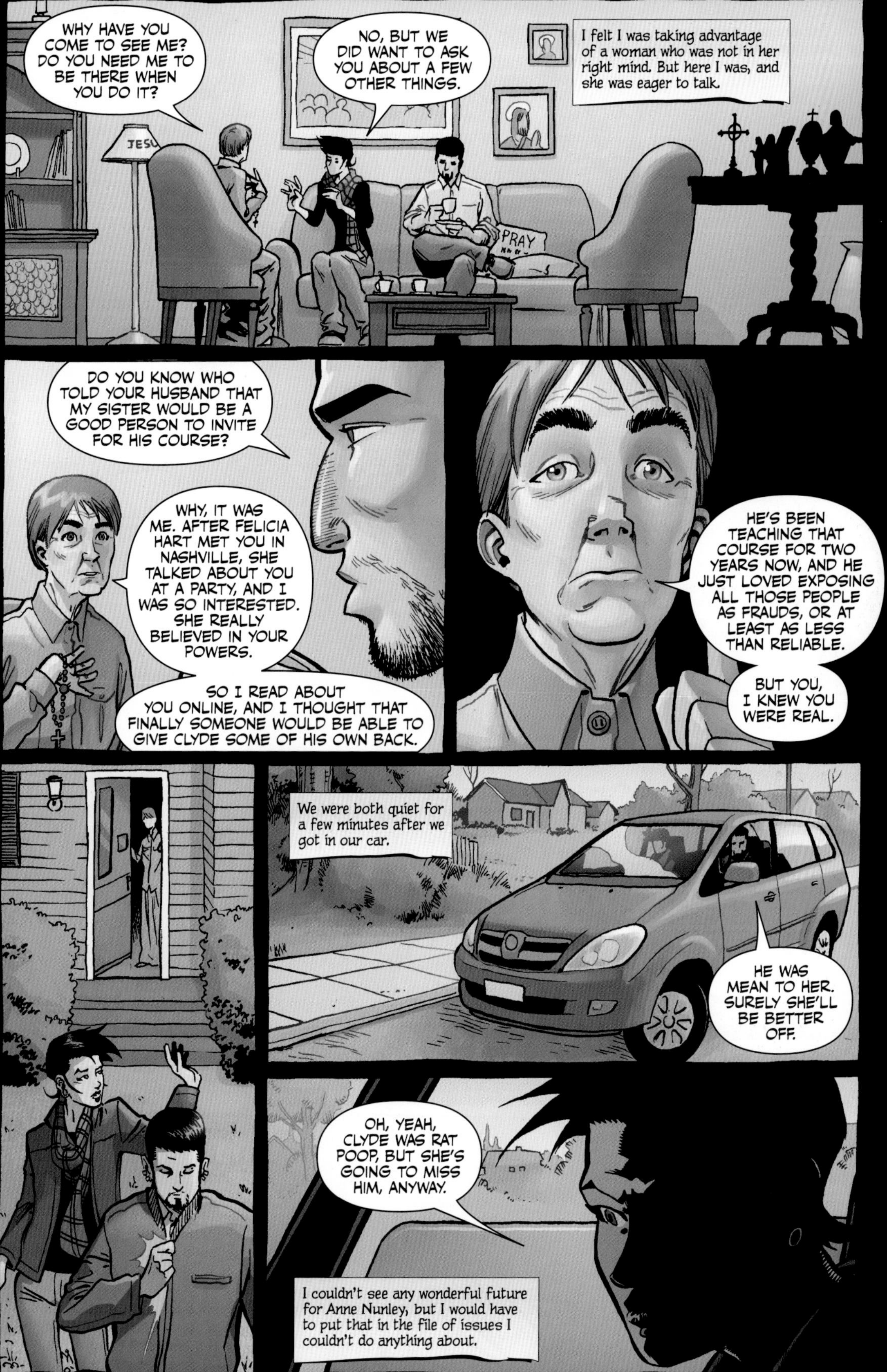
WHY HAVE YOU COME TO SEE ME? DO YOU NEED ME TO BE THERE WHEN YOU DO IT?
NO, BUT WE DID WANT TO ASK YOU ABOUT A FEW OTHER THINGS.
I felt I was taking advantage of a woman who was not in her right mind. But here I was, and she was eager to talk.
JESU
PRAY
DO YOU KNOW WHO TOLD YOUR HUSBAND THAT MY SISTER WOULD BE A GOOD PERSON TO INVITE FOR HIS COURSE?
WHY, IT WAS ME. AFTER FELICIA HART MET YOU IN NASHVILLE, SHE TALKED ABOUT YOU AT A PARTY, AND I WAS SO INTERESTED. SHE REALLY BELIEVED IN YOUR POWERS.
SO I READ ABOUT YOU ONLINE, AND I THOUGHT THAT FINALLY SOMEONE WOULD BE ABLE TO GIVE CLYDE SOME OF HIS OWN BACK.
HE'S BEEN TEACHING THAT COURSE FOR TWO YEARS NOW, AND HE JUST LOVED EXPOSING ALL THOSE PEOPLE AS FRAUDS, OR AT LEAST AS LESS THAN RELIABLE.
BUT YOU, I KNEW YOU WERE REAL.
We were both quiet for a few minutes after we got in our car.
HE WAS MEAN TO HER. SURELY SHE'LL BE BETTER OFF.
OH, YEAH, CLYDE WAS RAT POOP, BUT SHE'S GOING TO MISS HIM, ANYWAY.
I couldn't see any wonderful future for Anne Nunley, but I would have to put that in the file of issues I couldn't do anything about.

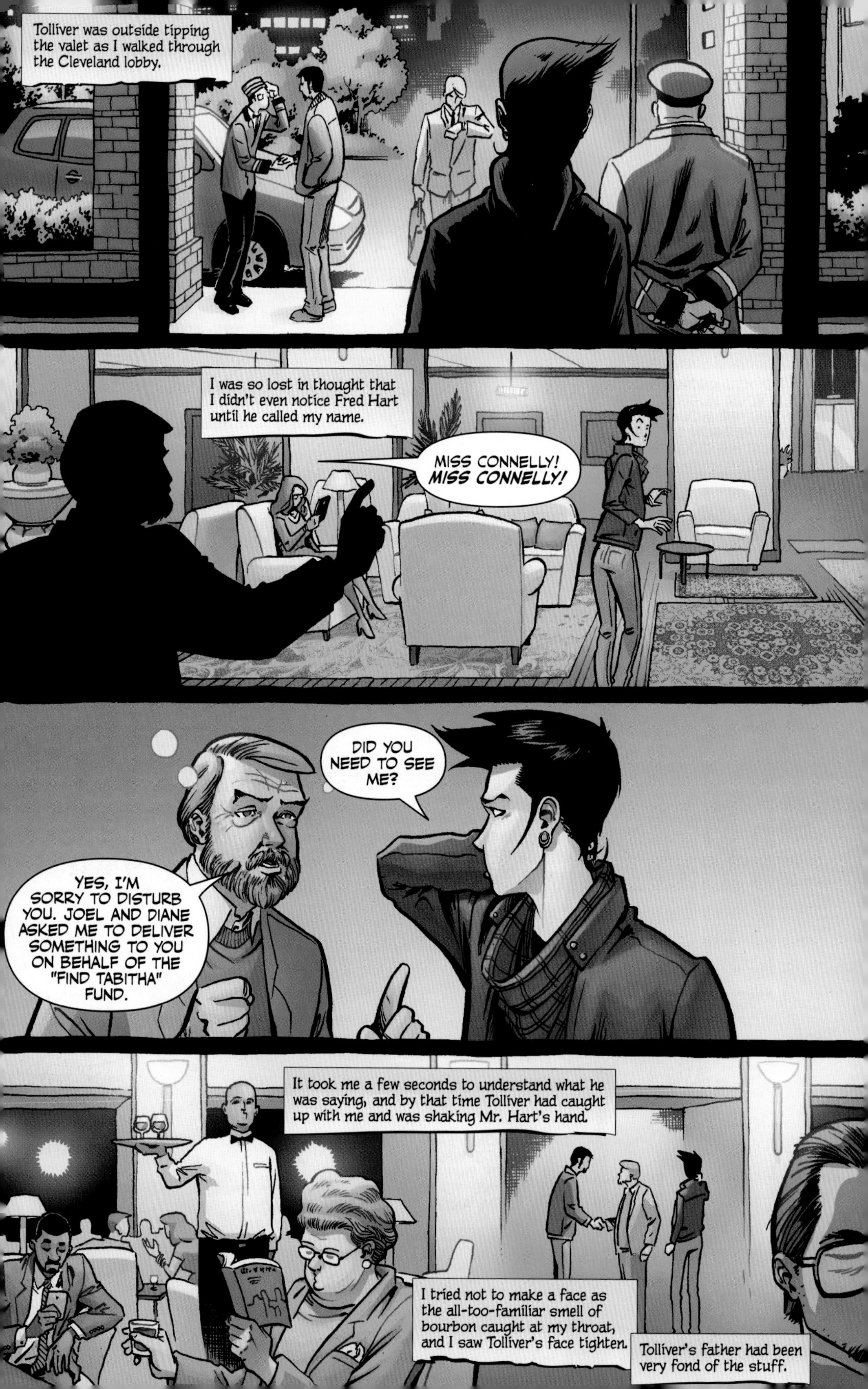
Tolliver was outside tipping the valet as I walked through the Cleveland lobby.
I was so lost in thought that I didn't even notice Fred Hart until he called my name.
MISS CONNELLY! MISS CONNELLY!
DID YOU NEED TO SEE ME?
YES, I'M SORRY TO DISTURB YOU. JOEL AND DIANE ASKED ME TO DELIVER SOMETHING TO YOU ON BEHALF OF THE "FIND TABITHA" FUND.
It took me a few seconds to understand what he was saying, and by that time Tolliver had caught up with me and was shaking Mr. Hart's hand.
I tried not to make a face as the all-too-familiar smell of bourbon caught at my throat, and I saw Tolliver's face tighten.
Tolliver's father had been very fond of the stuff.

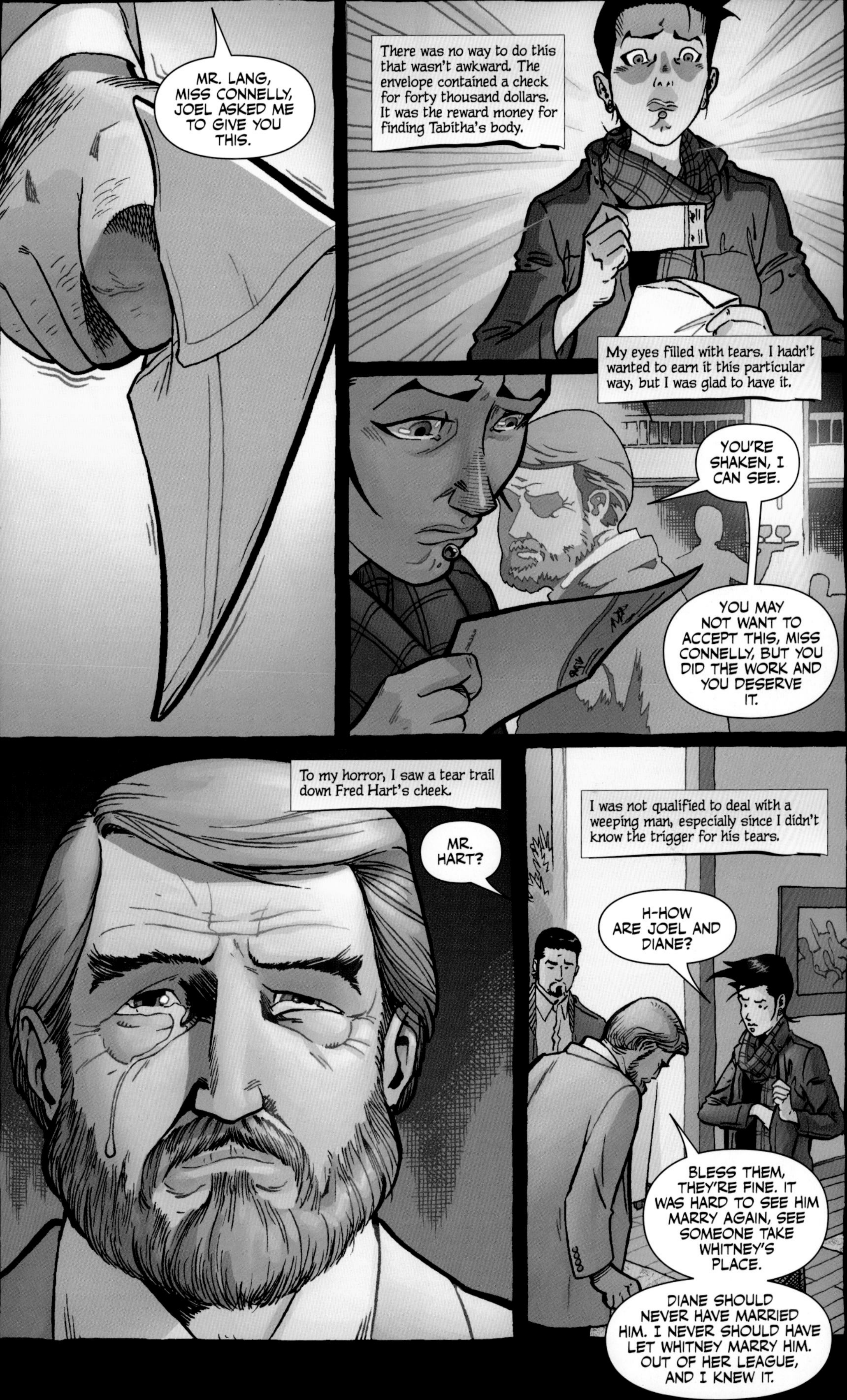
MR. LANG, MISS CONNELLY, JOEL ASKED ME TO GIVE YOU THIS.
There was no way to do this that wasn't awkward. The envelope contained a check for forty thousand dollars. It was the reward money for finding Tabitha's body.
My eyes filled with tears. I hadn't wanted to earn it this particular way, but I was glad to have it.
YOU'RE SHAKEN, I CAN SEE.
YOU MAY NOT WANT TO ACCEPT THIS, MISS CONNELLY, BUT YOU DID THE WORK AND YOU DESERVE IT.
To my horror, I saw a tear trail down Fred Hart's cheek.
MR. HART?
I was not qualified to deal with a weeping man, especially since I didn't know the trigger for his tears.
H-HOW ARE JOEL AND DIANE?
BLESS THEM, THEY'RE FINE. IT WAS HARD TO SEE HIM MARRY AGAIN, SEE SOMEONE TAKE WHITNEY'S PLACE.
DIANE SHOULD NEVER HAVE MARRIED HIM. I NEVER SHOULD HAVE LET WHITNEY MARRY HIM. OUT OF HER LEAGUE, AND I KNEW IT.

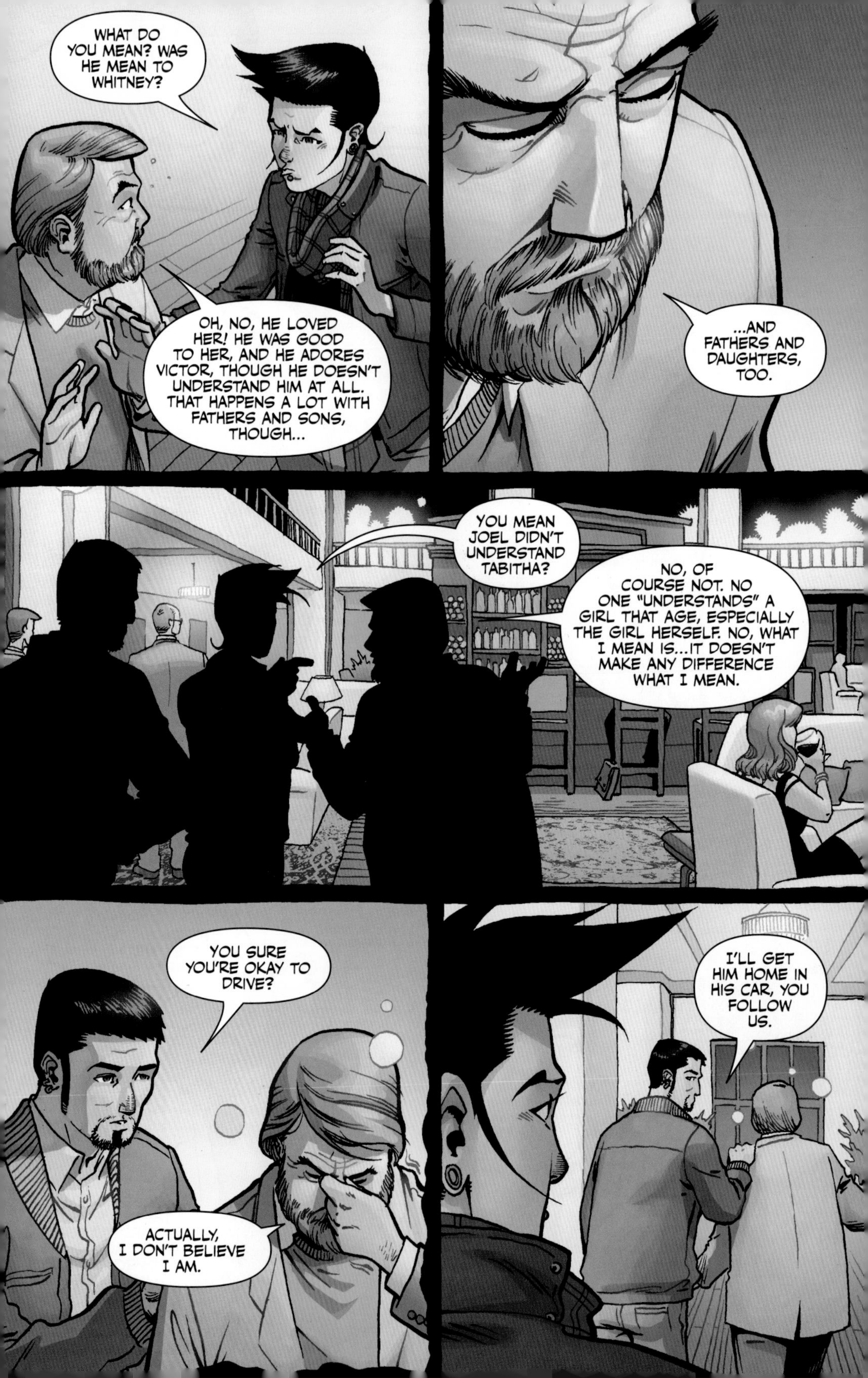
WHAT DO YOU MEAN? WAS HE MEAN TO WHITNEY?
OH, NO, HE LOVED HER! HE WAS GOOD TO HER, AND HE ADORES VICTOR, THOUGH HE DOESN'T UNDERSTAND HIM AT ALL. THAT HAPPENS A LOT WITH FATHERS AND SONS, THOUGH...
...AND FATHERS AND DAUGHTERS, TOO.
YOU MEAN JOEL DIDN'T UNDERSTAND TABITHA?
NO, OF COURSE NOT. NO ONE "UNDERSTANDS" A GIRL THAT AGE, ESPECIALLY THE GIRL HERSELF. NO, WHAT I MEAN IS...IT DOESN'T MAKE ANY DIFFERENCE WHAT I MEAN.
YOU SURE YOU'RE OKAY TO DRIVE?
ACTUALLY, I DON'T BELIEVE I AM.
I'LL GET HIM HOME IN HIS CAR, YOU FOLLOW US.

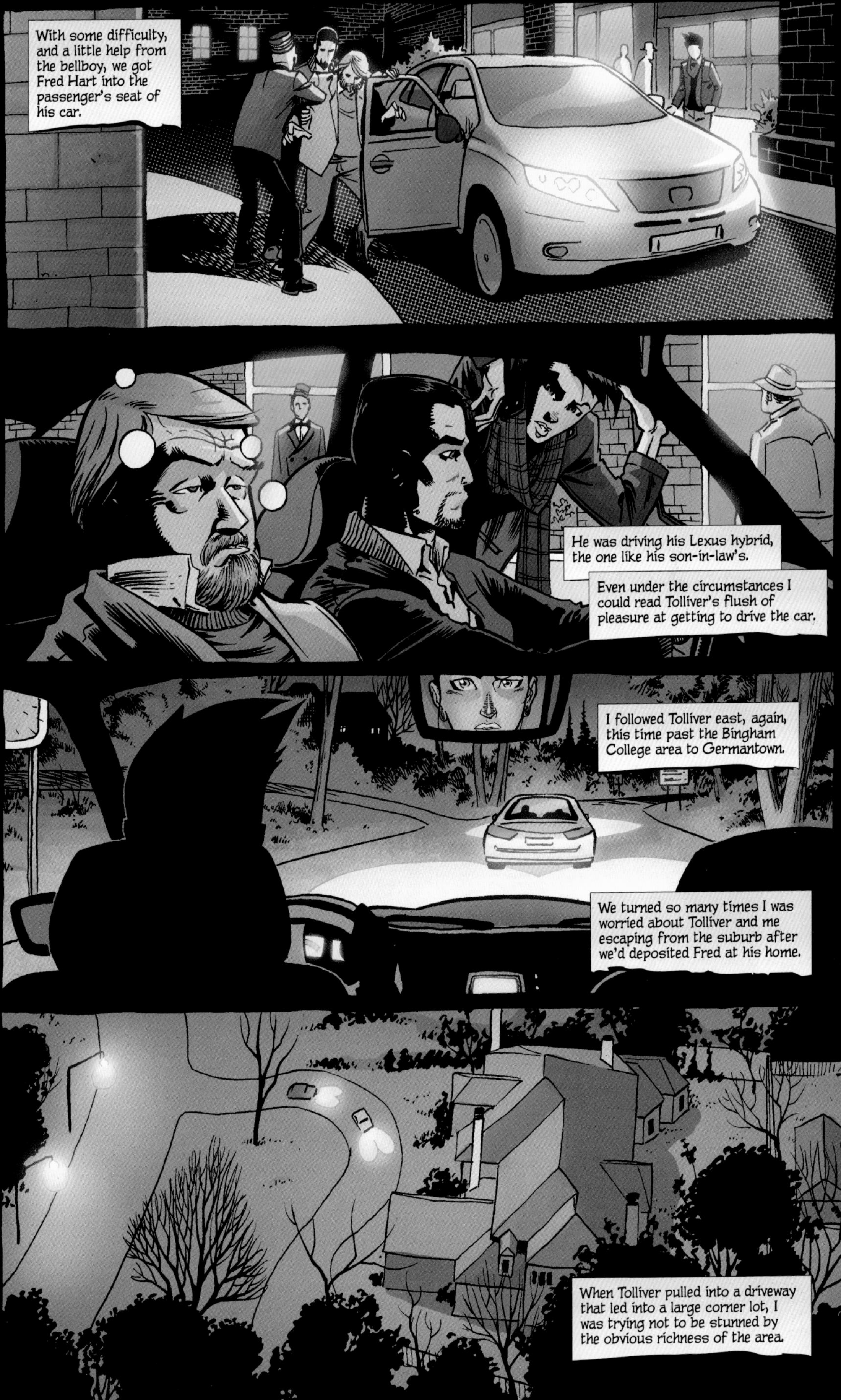

With some difficulty, and a little help from the bellboy, we got Fred Hart into the passenger's seat of his car.
He was driving his Lexus hybrid, the one like his son-in-law's.
Even under the circumstances I could read Tolliver's flush of pleasure at getting to drive the car.
I followed Tolliver east, again, this time past the Bingham College area to Germantown.
We turned so many times I was worried about Tolliver and me escaping from the suburb after we'd deposited Fred at his home.
When Tolliver pulled into a driveway that led into a large corner lot, I was trying not to be stunned by the obvious richness of the area.

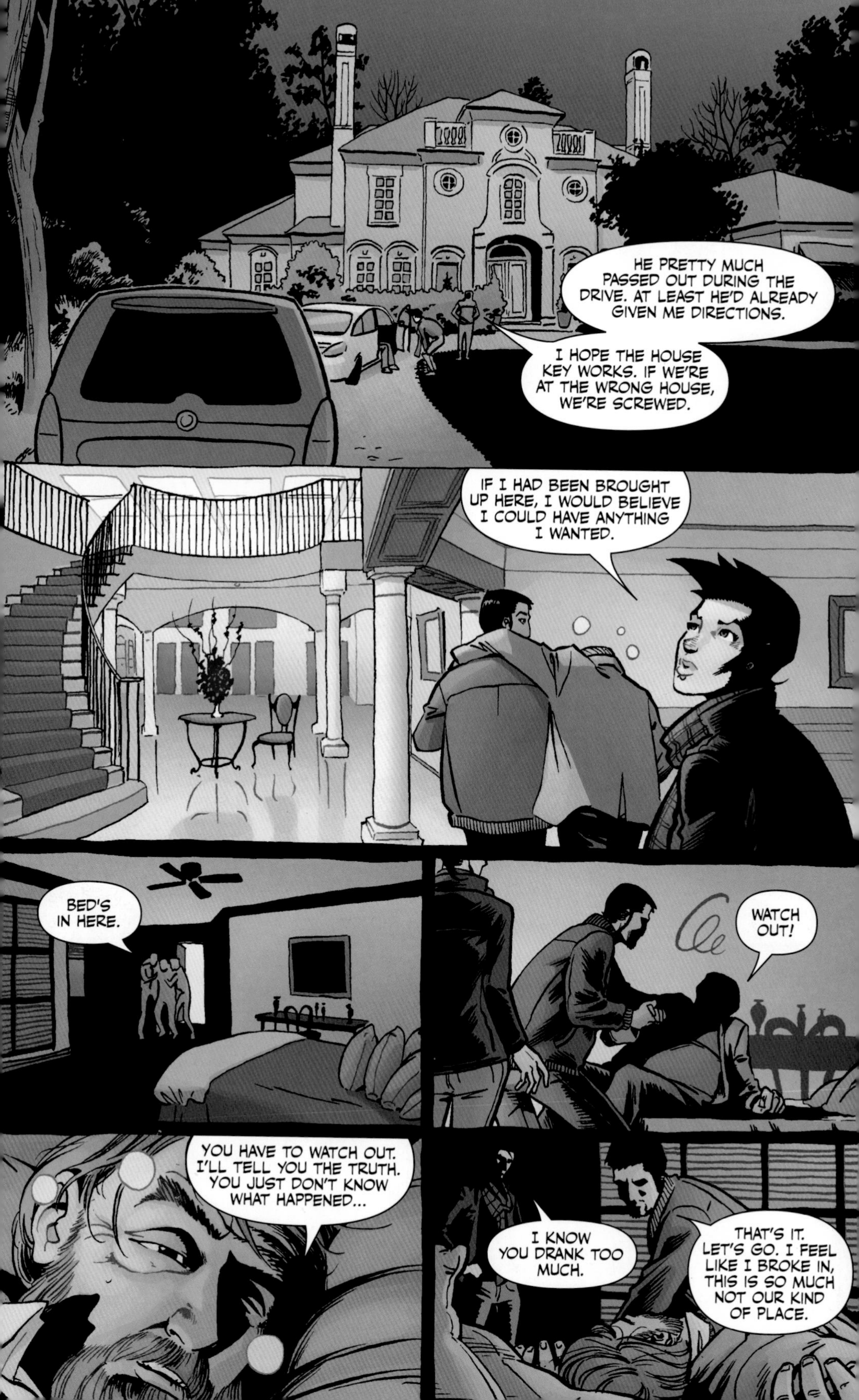
HE PRETTY MUCH PASSED OUT DURING THE DRIVE. AT LEAST HE'D ALREADY GIVEN ME DIRECTIONS.
I HOPE THE HOUSE KEY WORKS. IF WE'RE AT THE WRONG HOUSE, WE'RE SCREWED.
IF I HAD BEEN BROUGHT UP HERE, I WOULD BELIEVE I COULD HAVE ANYTHING I WANTED.
BED'S IN HERE.
WATCH OUT!
YOU HAVE TO WATCH OUT. I'LL TELL YOU THE TRUTH. YOU JUST DON'T KNOW WHAT HAPPENED...
I KNOW YOU DRANK TOO MUCH.
THAT'S IT. LET'S GO. I FEEL LIKE I BROKE IN, THIS IS SO MUCH NOT OUR KIND OF PLACE.

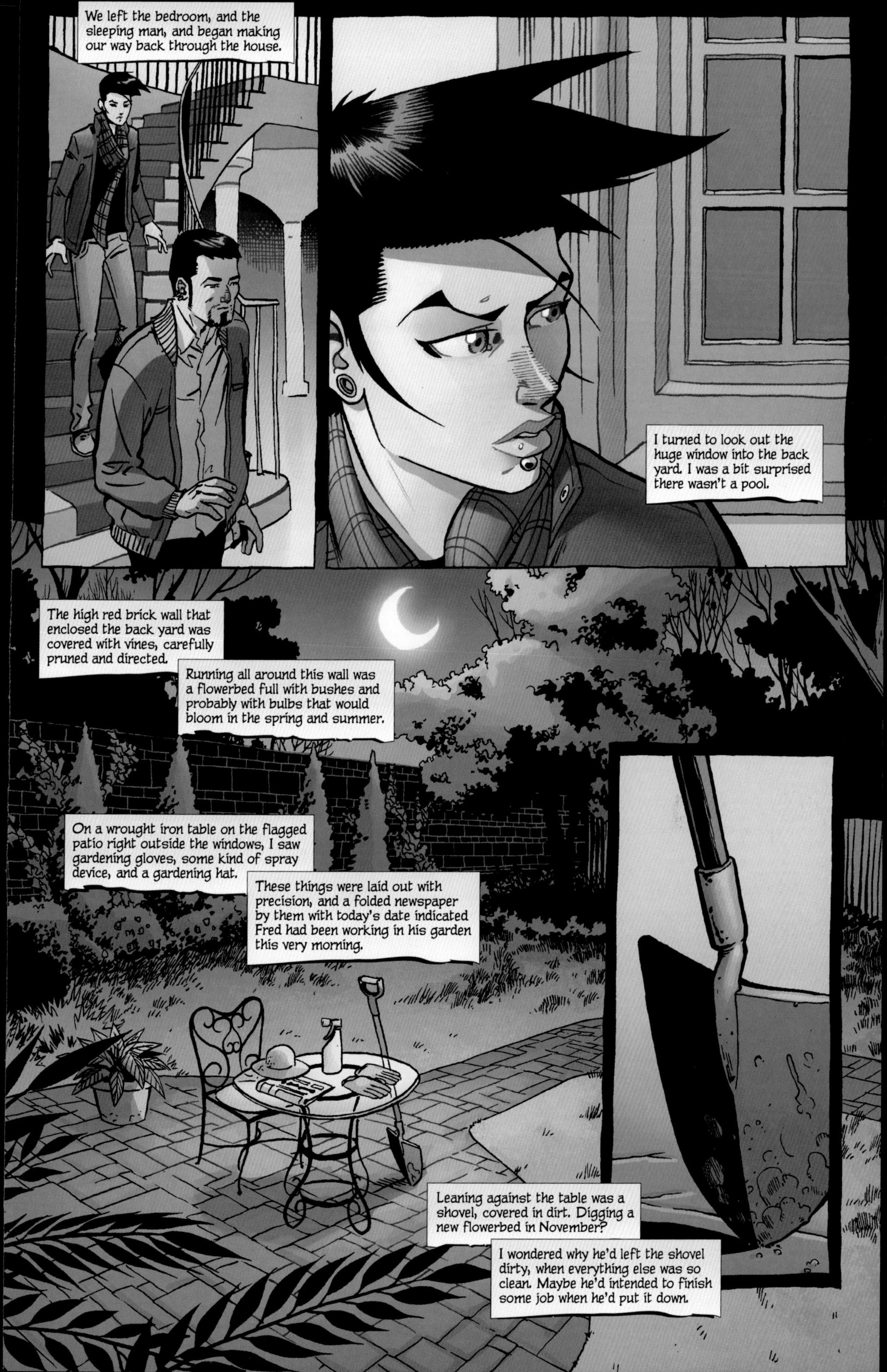
We left the bedroom, and the sleeping man, and began making our way back through the house.
I turned to look out the huge window into the back yard. I was a bit surprised there wasn't a pool.
The high red brick wall that enclosed the back yard was covered with vines, carefully pruned and directed.
Running all around this wall was a flowerbed full with bushes and probably with bulbs that would bloom in the spring and summer.
On a wrought iron table on the flagged patio right outside the windows, I saw gardening gloves, some kind of spray device, and a gardening hat.
These things were laid out with precision, and a folded newspaper by them with today's date indicated Fred had been working in his garden this very morning.
Leaning against the table was a shovel, covered in dirt. Digging a new flowerbed in November?
I wondered why he'd left the shovel dirty, when everything else was so clean. Maybe he'd intended to finish some job when he'd put it down.

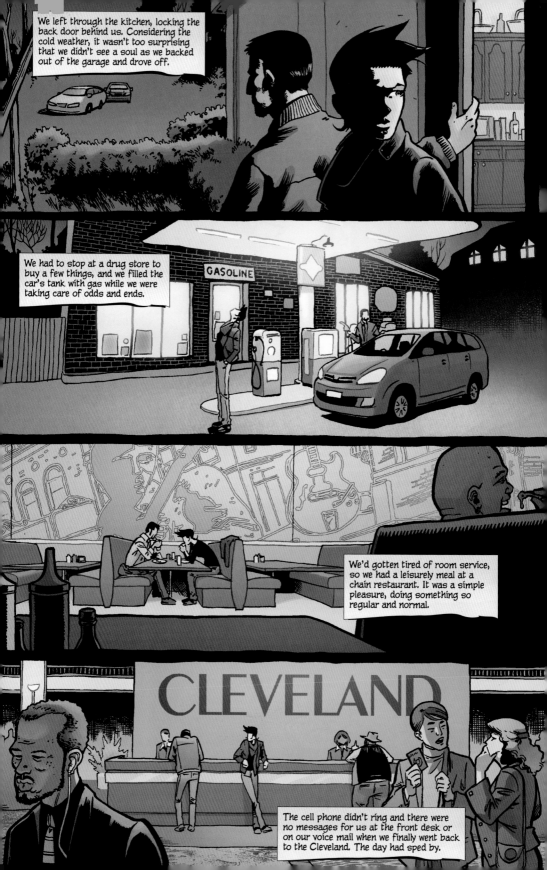

We left through the kitchen, locking the back door behind us. Considering the cold weather, it wasn't too surprising that we didn't see a soul as we backed out of the garage and drove off.

We had to stop at a drug store to buy a few things, and we filled the car's tank with gas while we were taking care of odds and ends.

GASOLINE

We'd gotten tired of room service, so we had a leisurely meal at a chain restaurant. It was a simple pleasure, doing something so regular and normal.

CLEVELAND

The cell phone didn't ring and there were no messages for us at the front desk or on our voice mail when we finally went back to the Cleveland. The day had sped by.

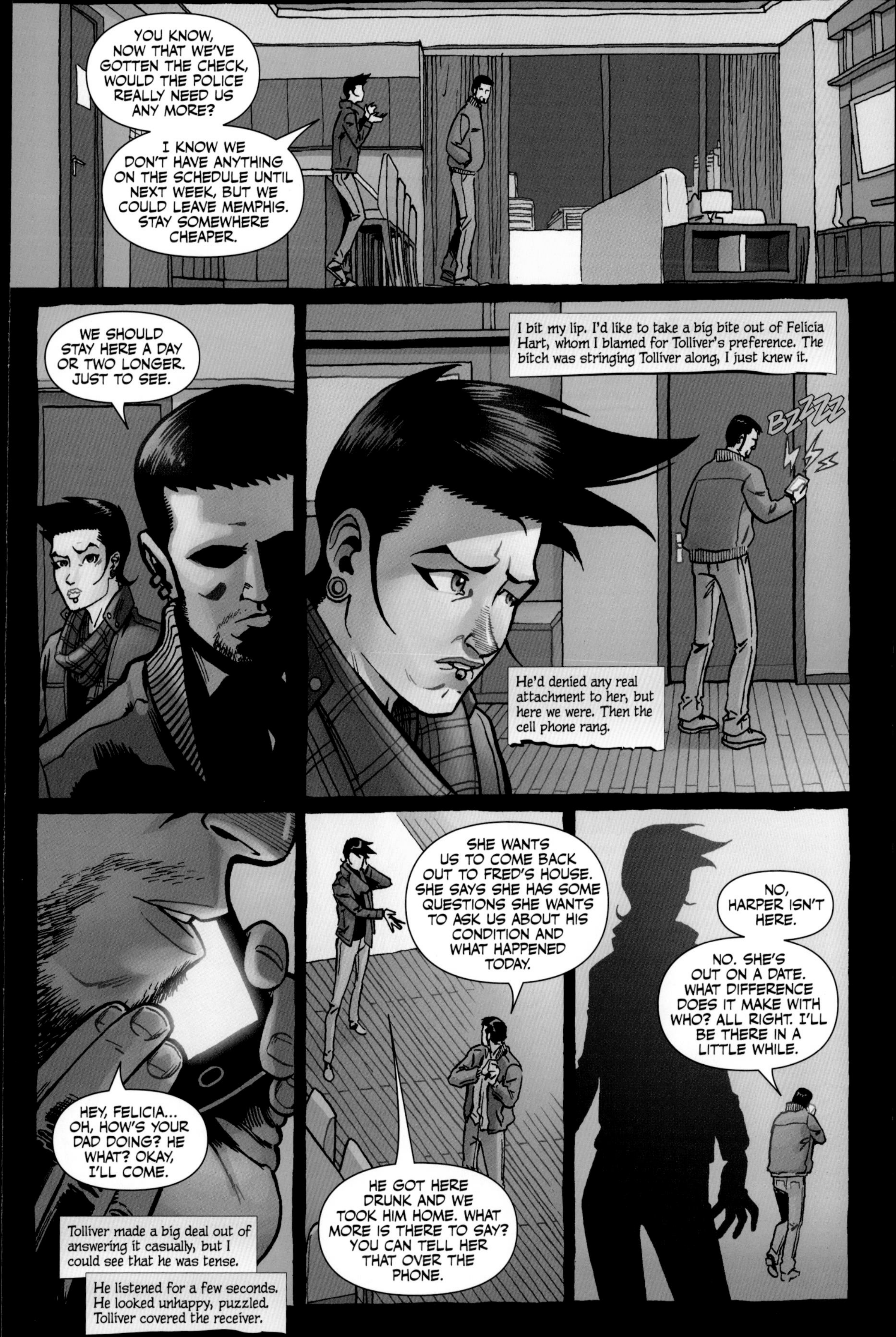
YOU KNOW, NOW THAT WE'VE GOTTEN THE CHECK, WOULD THE POLICE REALLY NEED US ANY MORE?
I KNOW WE DON'T HAVE ANYTHING ON THE SCHEDULE UNTIL NEXT WEEK, BUT WE COULD LEAVE MEMPHIS. STAY SOMEWHERE CHEAPER.
WE SHOULD STAY HERE A DAY OR TWO LONGER. JUST TO SEE.
I bit my lip. I'd like to take a big bite out of Felicia Hart, whom I blamed for Tolliver's preference. The bitch was stringing Tolliver along, I just knew it.
BZZZZ
He'd denied any real attachment to her, but here we were. Then the cell phone rang.
HEY, FELICIA... OH, HOW'S YOUR DAD DOING? HE WHAT? OKAY, I'LL COME.
Tolliver made a big deal out of answering it casually, but I could see that he was tense.
He listened for a few seconds. He looked unhappy, puzzled. Tolliver covered the receiver.
SHE WANTS US TO COME BACK OUT TO FRED'S HOUSE. SHE SAYS SHE HAS SOME QUESTIONS SHE WANTS TO ASK US ABOUT HIS CONDITION AND WHAT HAPPENED TODAY.
HE GOT HERE DRUNK AND WE TOOK HIM HOME. WHAT MORE IS THERE TO SAY? YOU CAN TELL HER THAT OVER THE PHONE.
NO, HARPER ISN'T HERE.
NO. SHE'S OUT ON A DATE. WHAT DIFFERENCE DOES IT MAKE WITH WHO? ALL RIGHT. I'LL BE THERE IN A LITTLE WHILE.

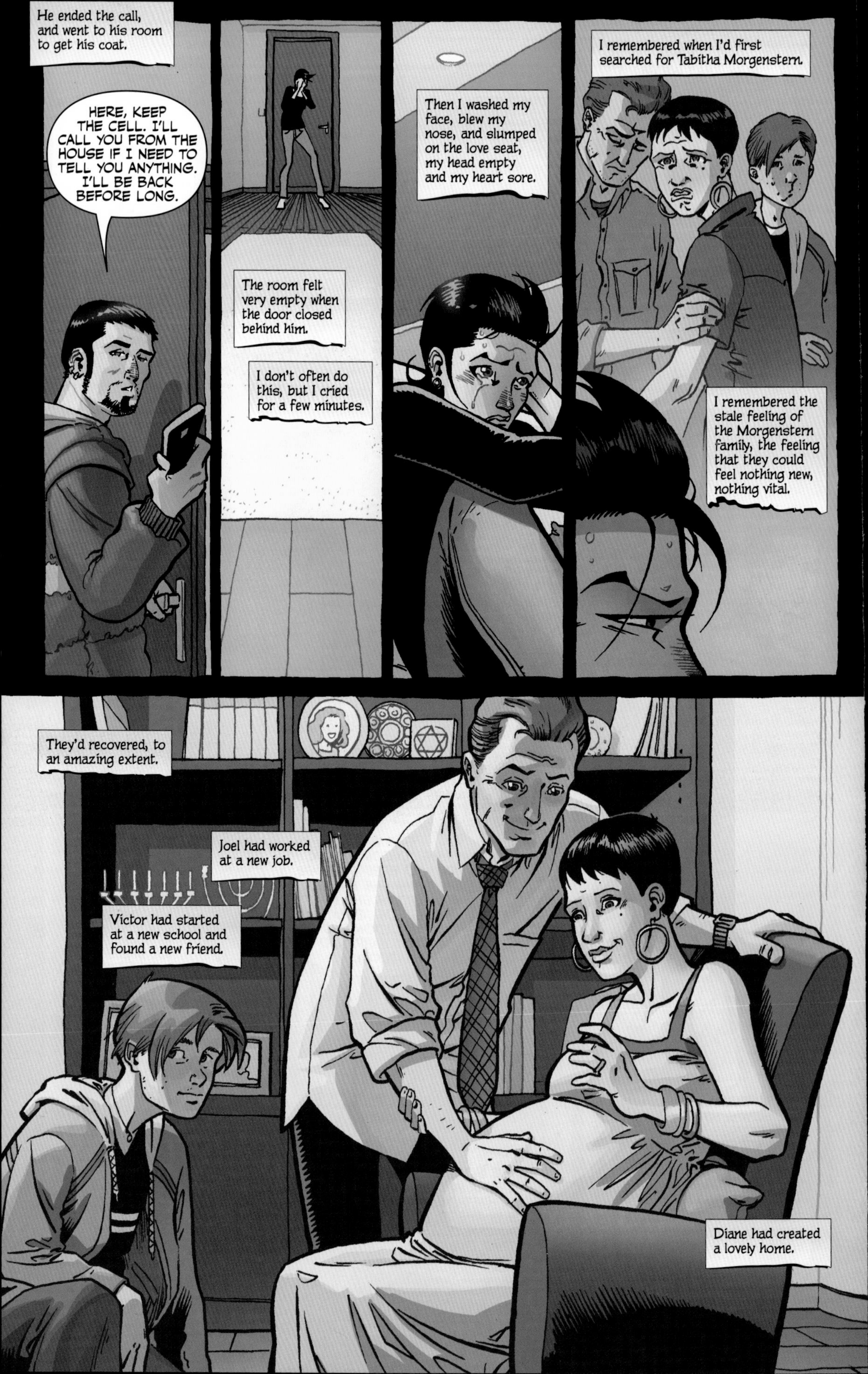

He ended the call, and went to his room to get his coat.
HERE, KEEP THE CELL. I'LL CALL YOU FROM THE HOUSE IF I NEED TO TELL YOU ANYTHING. I'LL BE BACK BEFORE LONG.
The room felt very empty when the door closed behind him.
I don't often do this, but I cried for a few minutes.
Then I washed my face, blew my nose, and slumped on the love seat, my head empty and my heart sore.
I remembered when I'd first searched for Tabitha Morgenstern.
I remembered the stale feeling of the Morgenstern family, the feeling that they could feel nothing new, nothing vital.
They'd recovered, to an amazing extent.
Joel had worked at a new job.
Victor had started at a new school and found a new friend.
Diane had created a lovely home.

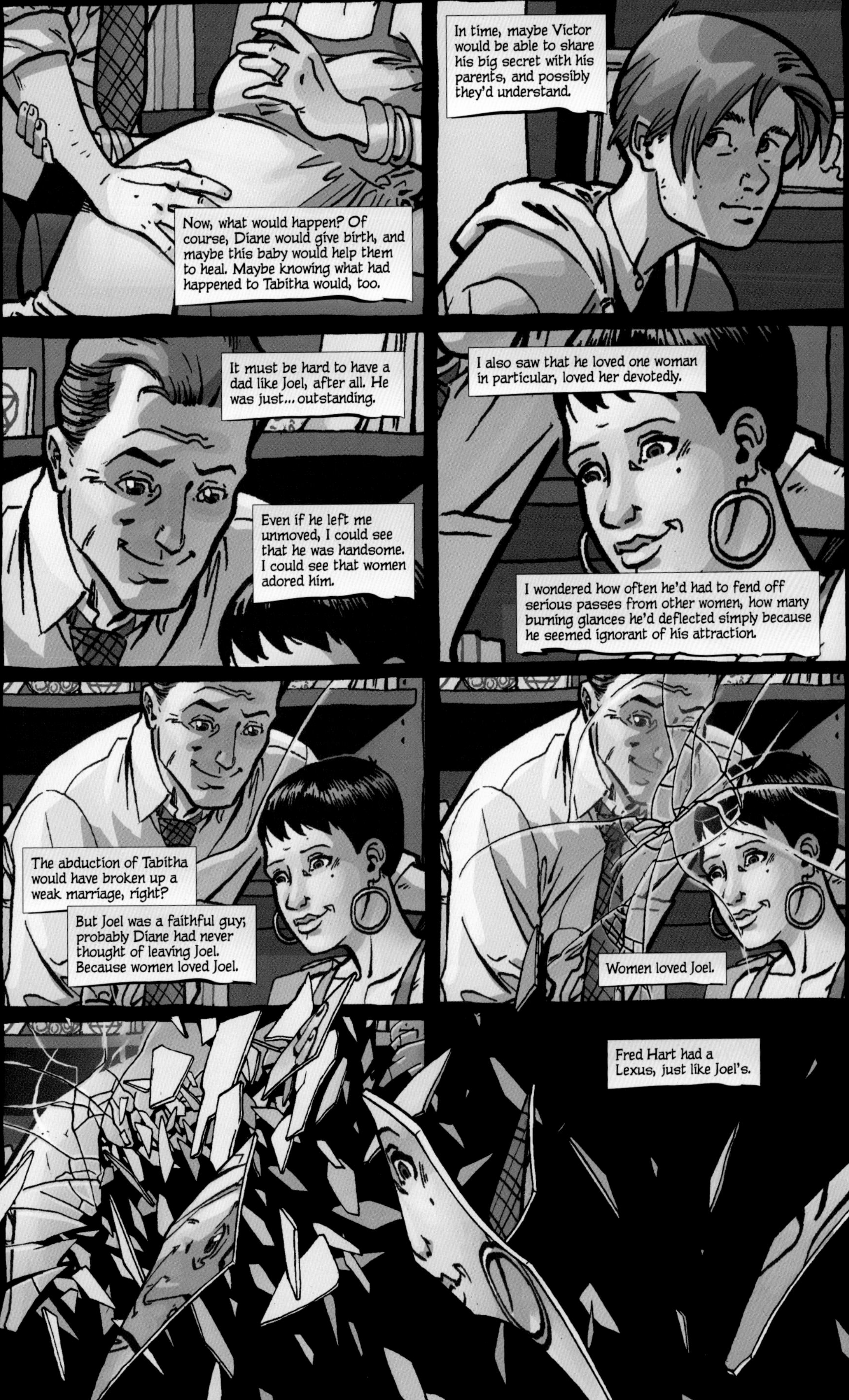
Now, what would happen? Of course, Diane would give birth, and maybe this baby would help them to heal. Maybe knowing what had happened to Tabitha would, too.
In time, maybe Victor would be able to share his big secret with his parents, and possibly they'd understand.
It must be hard to have a dad like Joel, after all. He was just... outstanding.
Even if he left me unmoved, I could see that he was handsome. I could see that women adored him.
I also saw that he loved one woman in particular, loved her devotedly.
I wondered how often he'd had to fend off serious passes from other women, how many burning glances he'd deflected simply because he seemed ignorant of his attraction.
The abduction of Tabitha would have broken up a weak marriage, right?
But Joel was a faithful guy; probably Diane had never thought of leaving Joel. Because women loved Joel.
Women loved Joel.
Fred Hart had a Lexus, just like Joel's.

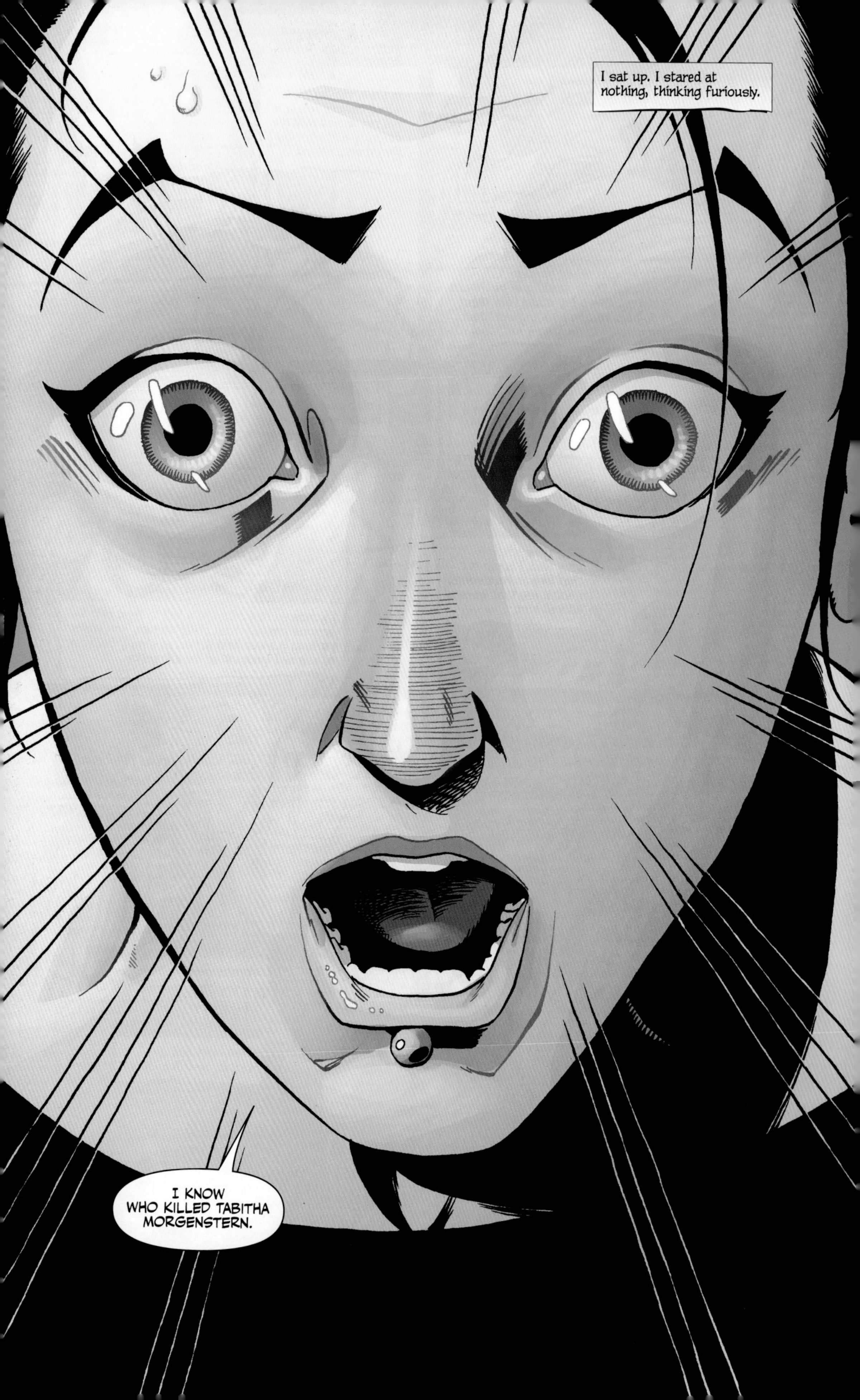
I sat up. I stared at nothing, thinking furiously.
I KNOW WHO KILLED TABITHA MORGENSTERN.

CHAPTER EIGHT

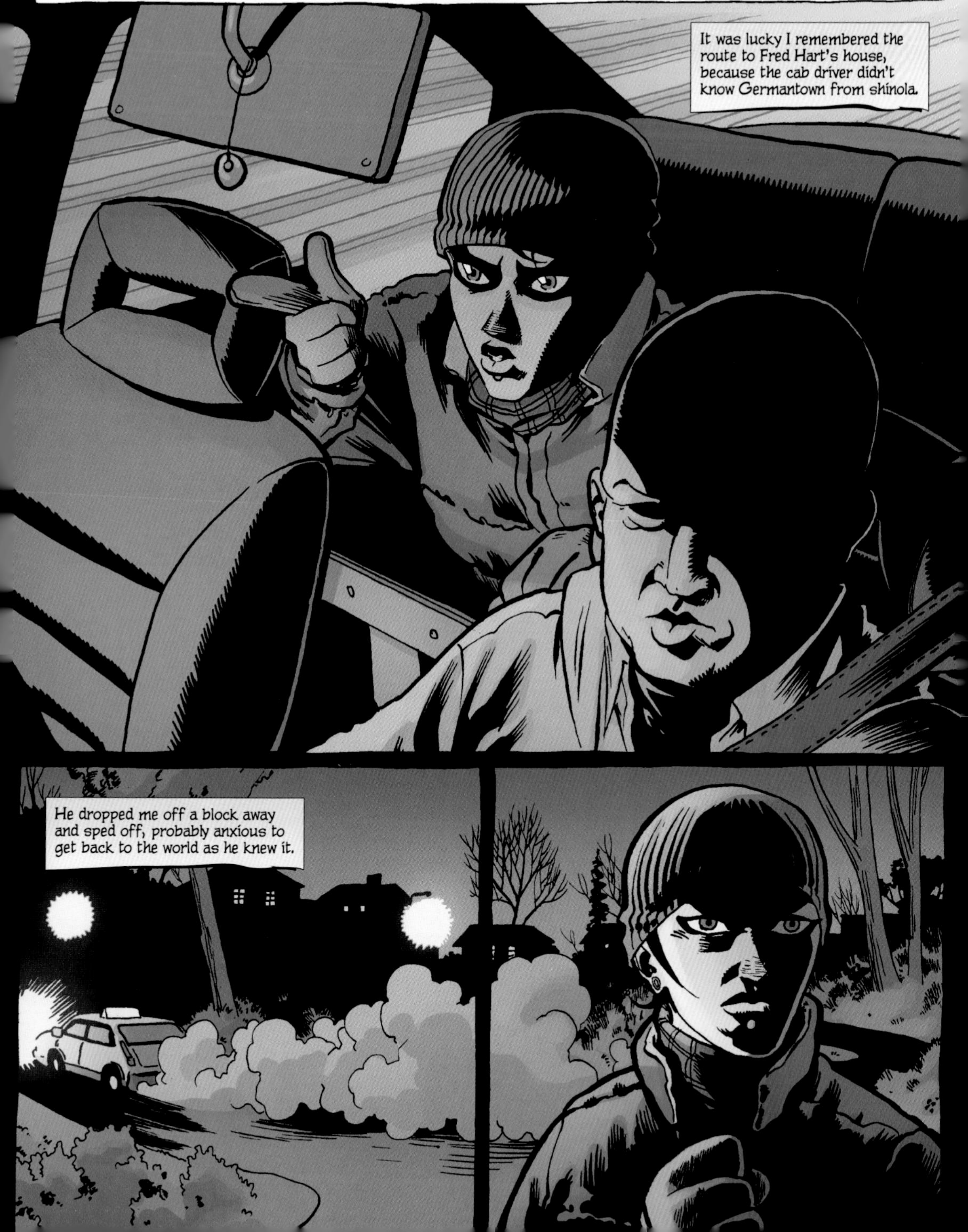
It was lucky I remembered the route to Fred Hart's house, because the cab driver didn't know Germantown from shinola.
He dropped me off a block away and sped off, probably anxious to get back to the world as he knew it.

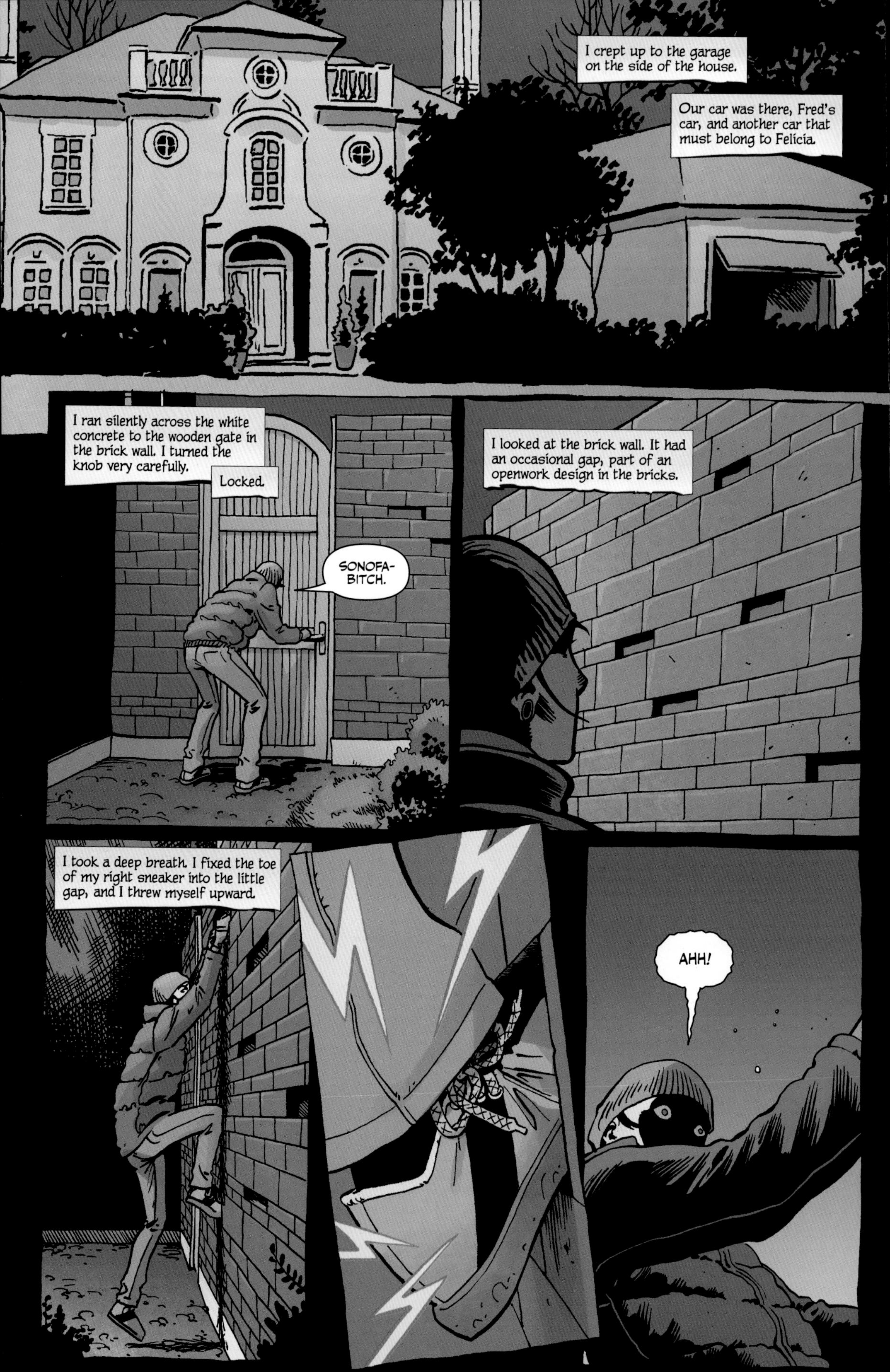
I crept up to the garage on the side of the house.
Our car was there, Fred's car, and another car that must belong to Felícia.
I ran silently across the white concrete to the wooden gate in the brick wall. I turned the knob very carefully.
Locked.
SONOFA-BITCH.
I looked at the brick wall. It had an occasional gap, part of an openwork design in the bricks.
I took a deep breath. I fixed the toe of my right sneaker into the little gap, and I threw myself upward.
AHH!

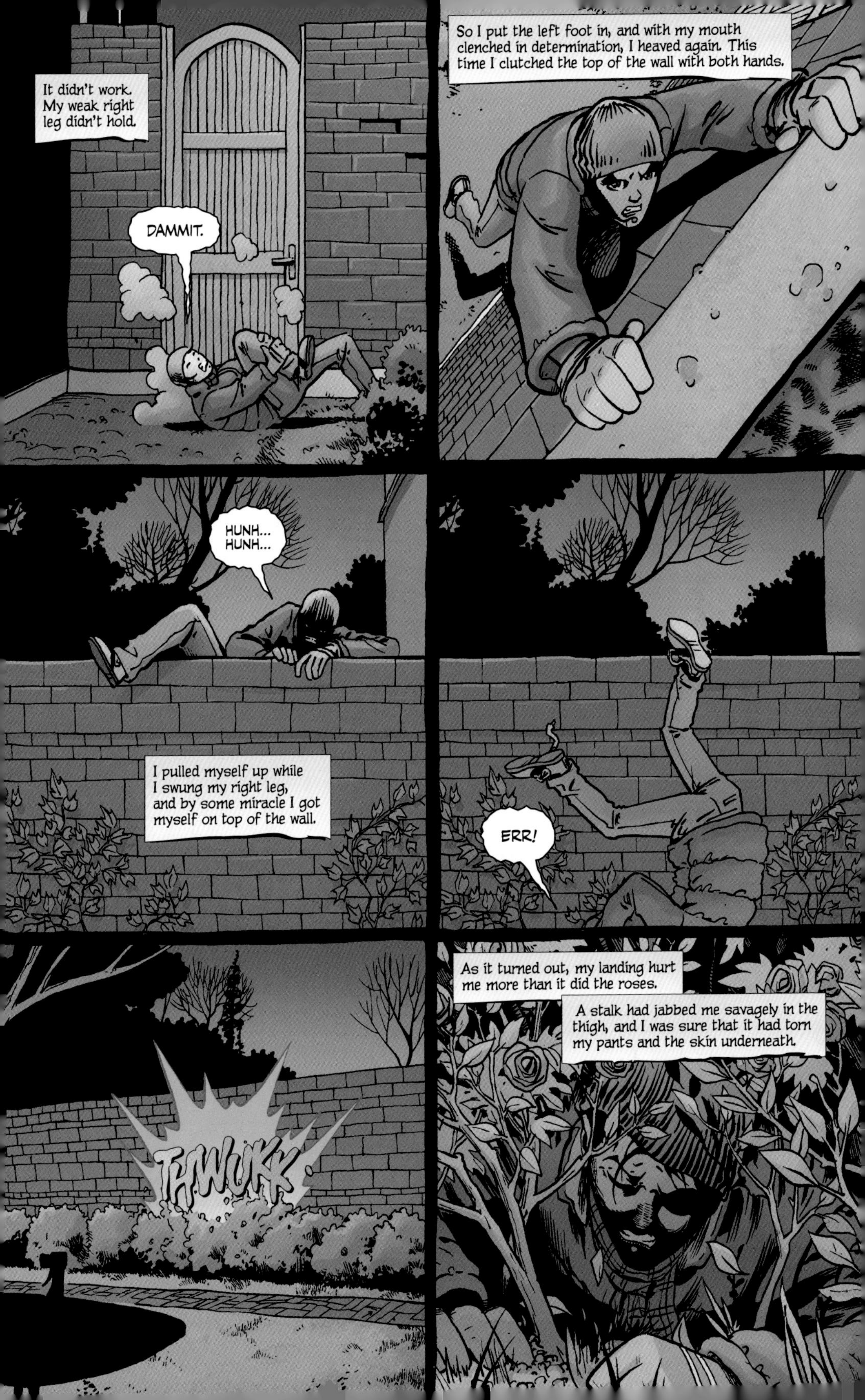
It didn't work. My weak right leg didn't hold.
DAMMIT.
So I put the left foot in, and with my mouth clenched in determination, I heaved again. This time I clutched the top of the wall with both hands.
HUNH... HUNH...
I pulled myself up while I swung my right leg, and by some miracle I got myself on top of the wall.
ERR!
THWUKK!
As it turned out, my landing hurt me more than it did the roses.
A stalk had jabbed me savagely in the thigh, and I was sure that it had torn my pants and the skin underneath.

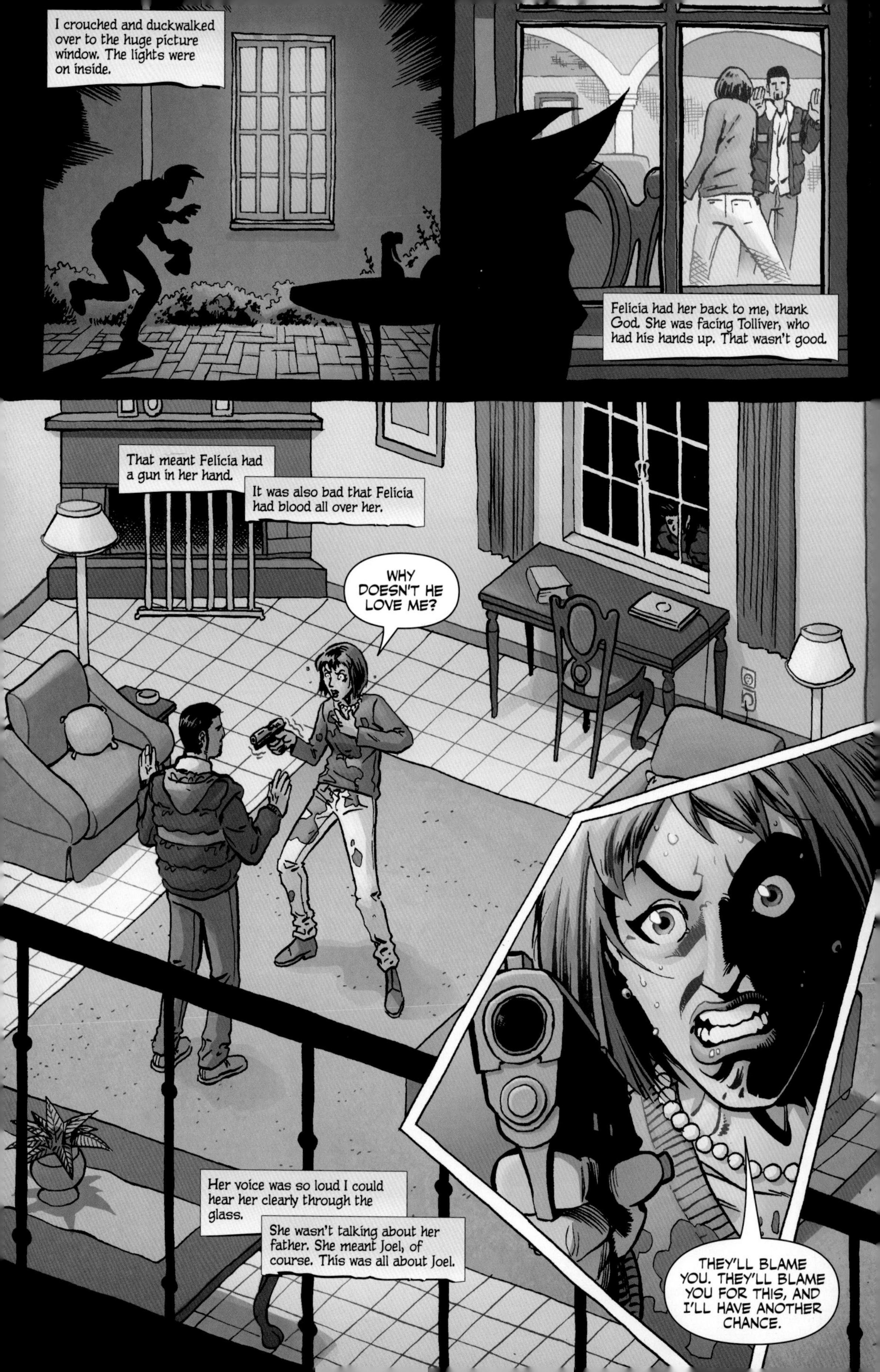
I crouched and duckwalked over to the huge picture window. The lights were on inside.
Felicia had her back to me, thank God. She was facing Tolliver, who had his hands up. That wasn't good.
That meant Felicia had a gun in her hand.
It was also bad that Felicia had blood all over her.
WHY DOESN'T HE LOVE ME?
Her voice was so loud I could hear her clearly through the glass.
She wasn't talking about her father. She meant Joel, of course. This was all about Joel.
THEY'LL BLAME YOU. THEY'LL BLAME YOU FOR THIS, AND I'LL HAVE ANOTHER CHANCE.

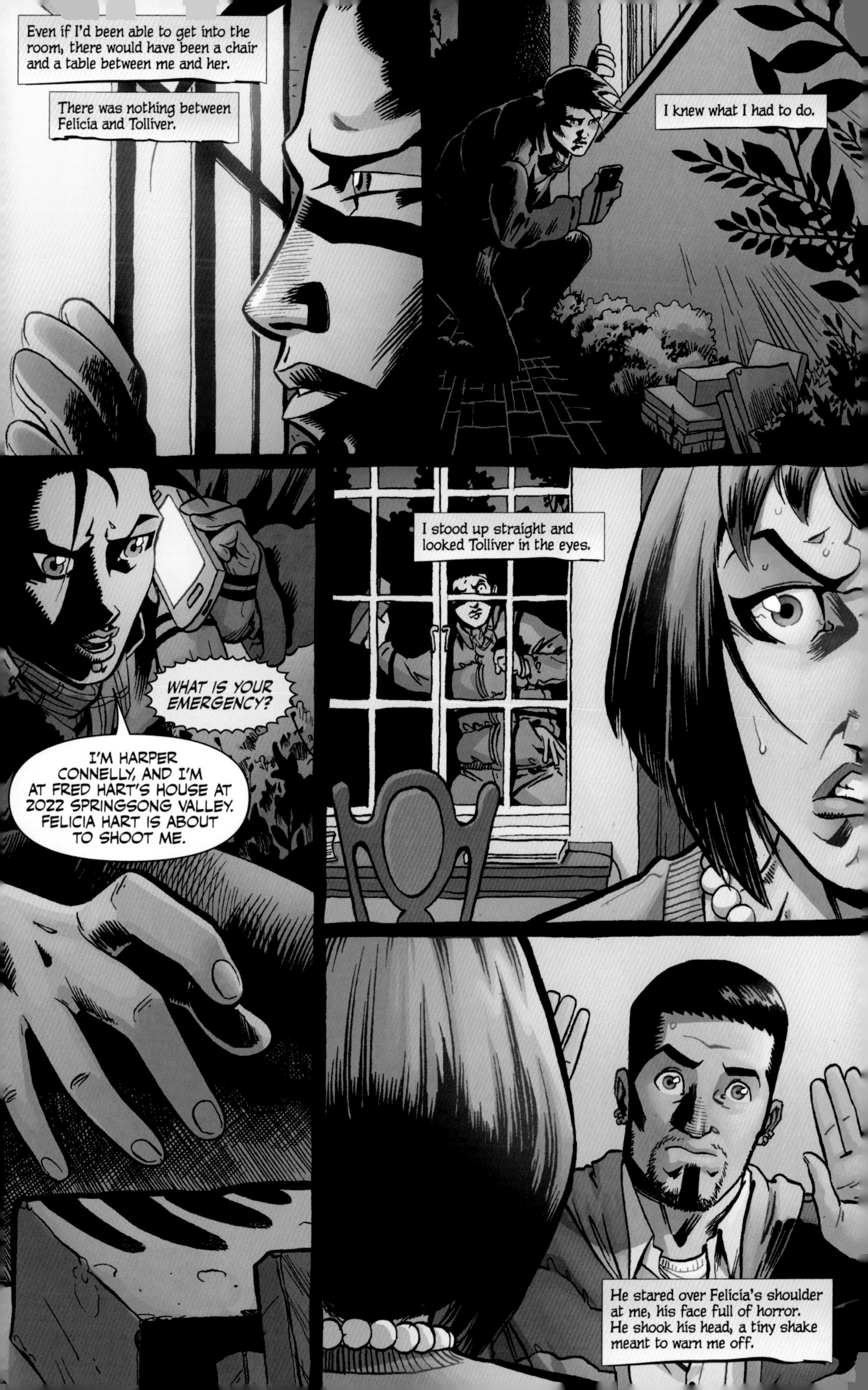
Even if I'd been able to get into the room, there would have been a chair and a table between me and her.
There was nothing between Felicia and Tolliver.
I knew what I had to do.
WHAT IS YOUR EMERGENCY?
I'M HARPER CONNELLY, AND I'M AT FRED HART'S HOUSE AT 2022 SPRINGSONG VALLEY. FELICIA HART IS ABOUT TO SHOOT ME.
I stood up straight and looked Tolliver in the eyes.
He stared over Felicia's shoulder at me, his face full of horror. He shook his head, a tiny shake meant to warn me off.

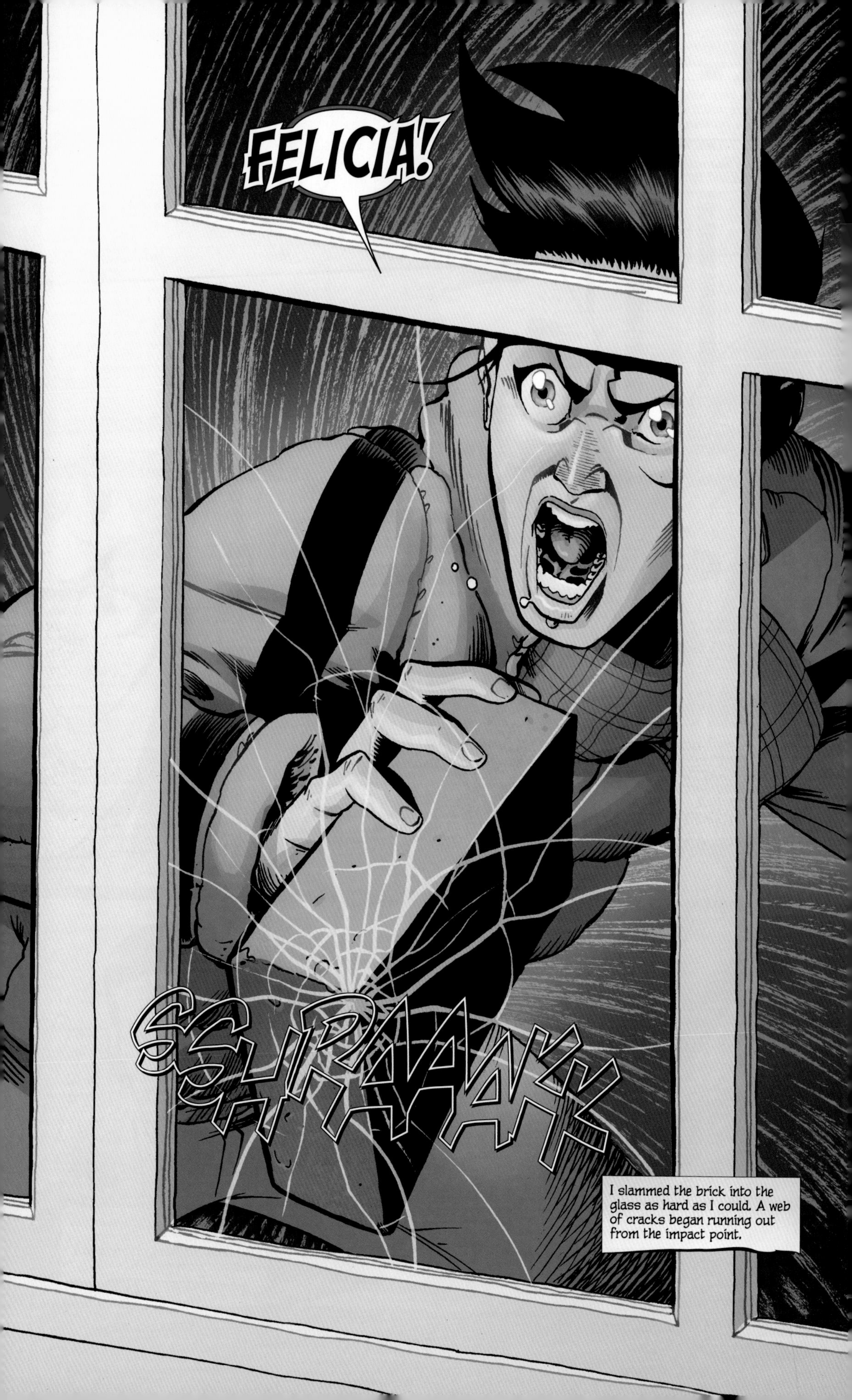
FELICIA!
SSHRAAANKK
I slammed the brick into the glass as hard as I could. A web of cracks began running out from the impact point.

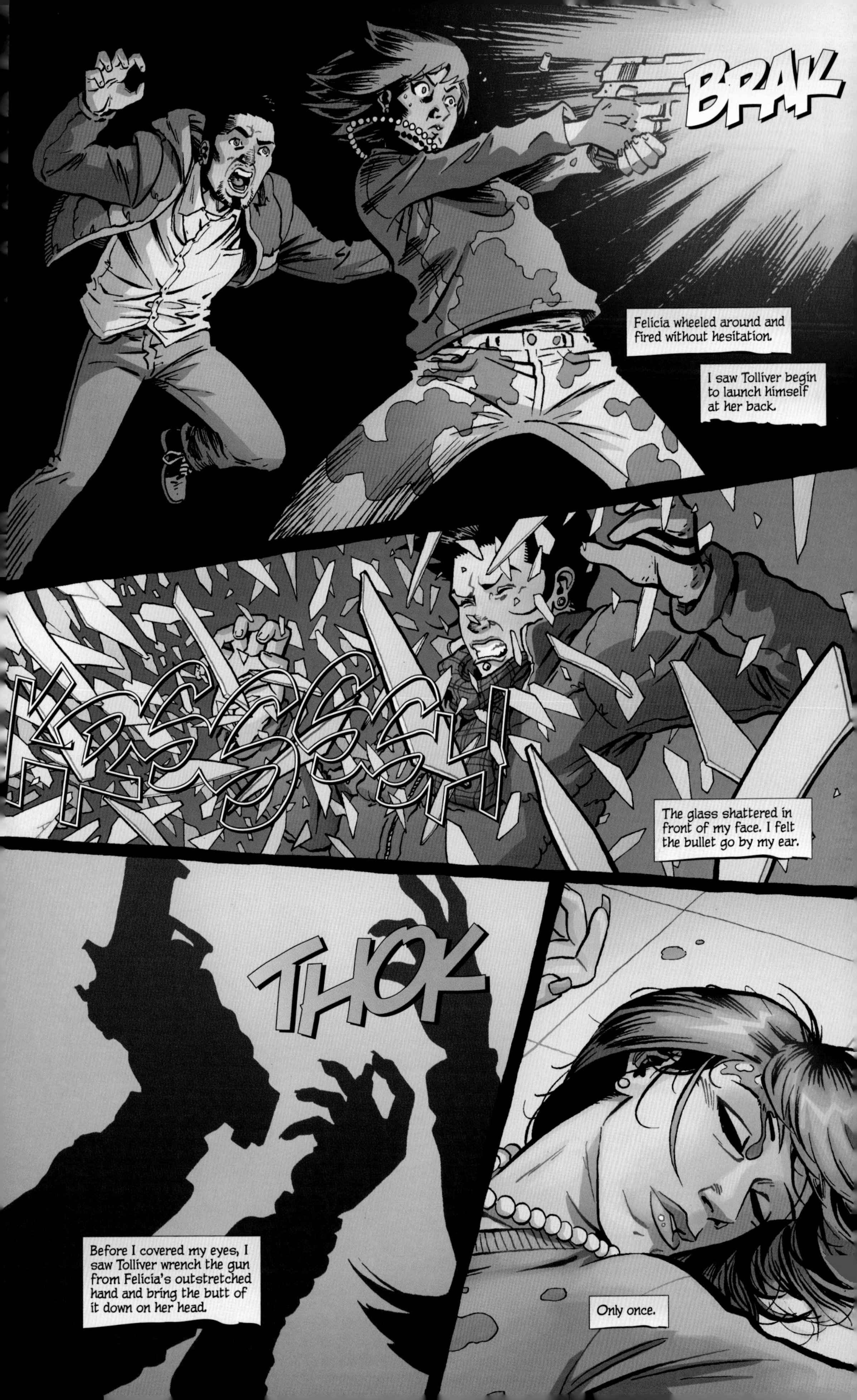
BRAK
Felicia wheeled around and fired without hesitation.
I saw Tolliver begin to launch himself at her back.
KRSSSCH
The glass shattered in front of my face. I felt the bullet go by my ear.
THOK
Before I covered my eyes, I saw Tolliver wrench the gun from Felicia's outstretched hand and bring the butt of it down on her head.
Only once.

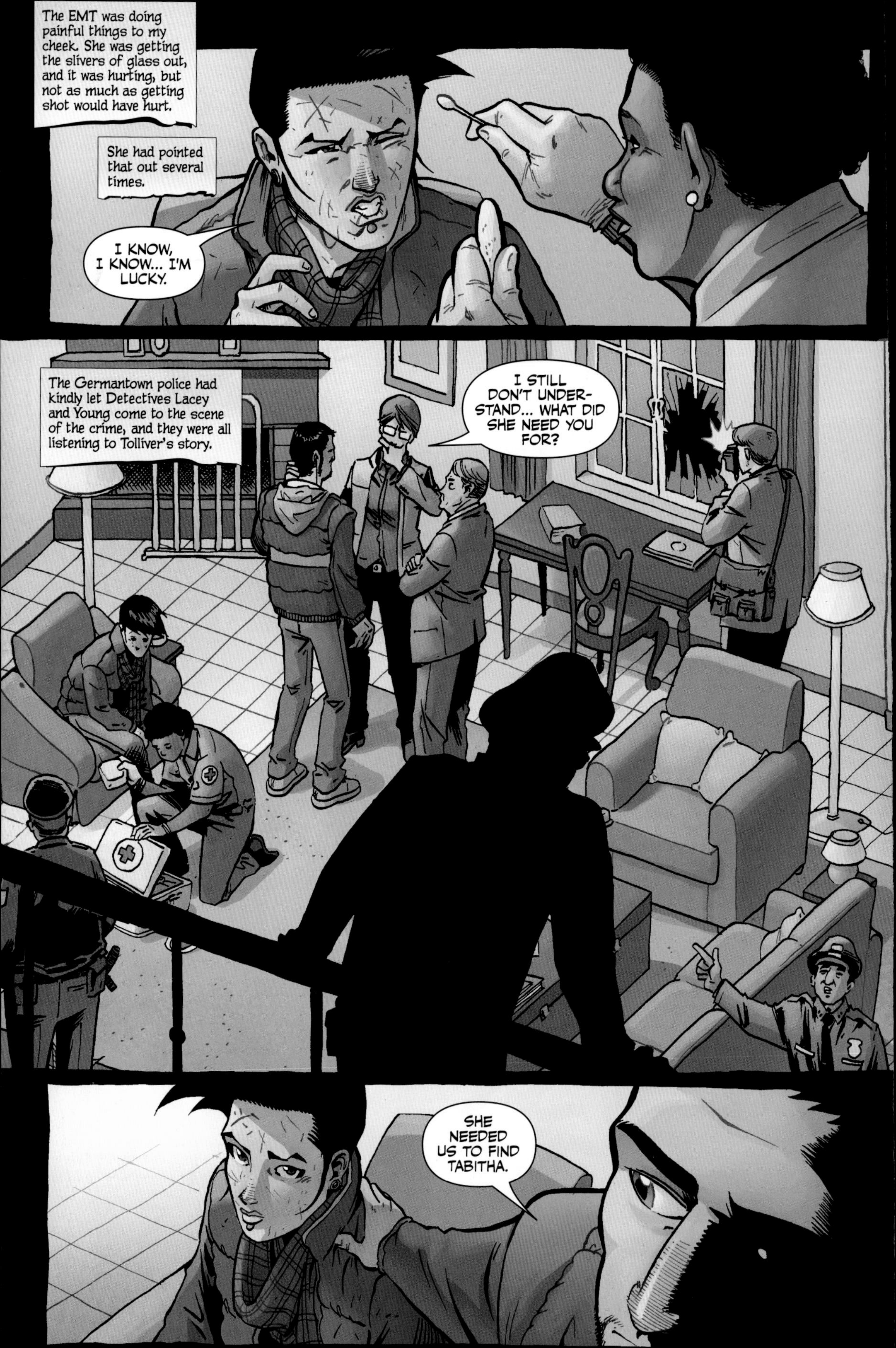
The EMT was doing painful things to my cheek. She was getting the slivers of glass out, and it was hurting, but not as much as getting shot would have hurt.
She had pointed that out several times.
I KNOW, I KNOW... I'M LUCKY.
The Germantown police had kindly let Detectives Lacey and Young come to the scene of the crime, and they were all listening to Tolliver's story.
I STILL DON'T UNDER-STAND... WHAT DID SHE NEED YOU FOR?
SHE NEEDED US TO FIND TABITHA.

YOU'RE SAYING SHE CONFESSED TO TAKING HER?

YES, SHE DID.

"SHE KNEW TABITHA WOULD GET IN THE CAR WITH HER."

"PLUS, SHE DIDN'T LIKE TABITHA. SHE THOUGHT THE GIRL WAS GETTING PREFERENTIAL TREATMENT OVER HER OWN NEPHEW, VICTOR."

"FELICIA THOUGHT MAYBE THE STRESS OF THE WHOLE THING WOULD RIP JOEL AND DIANE'S MARRIAGE APART, EVEN IF MUTUAL SUSPICION DIDN'T."

SO FELICIA WORKED ON THIS PLAN, WORKED ON IT FOR A LONG TIME. SHE TOOK TABITHA BACK TO THIS HOUSE, SMOTHERED HER THERE ON THE COUCH.

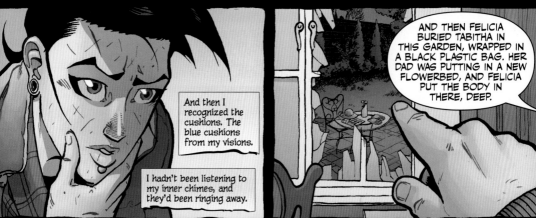

And then I recognized the cushions. The blue cushions from my visions.

I hadn't been listening to my inner chimes, and they'd been ringing away.

AND THEN FELICIA BURIED TABITHA IN THIS GARDEN, WRAPPED IN A BLACK PLASTIC BAG. HER DAD WAS PUTTING IN A NEW FLOWERBED, AND FELICIA PUT THE BODY IN THERE, DEEP.

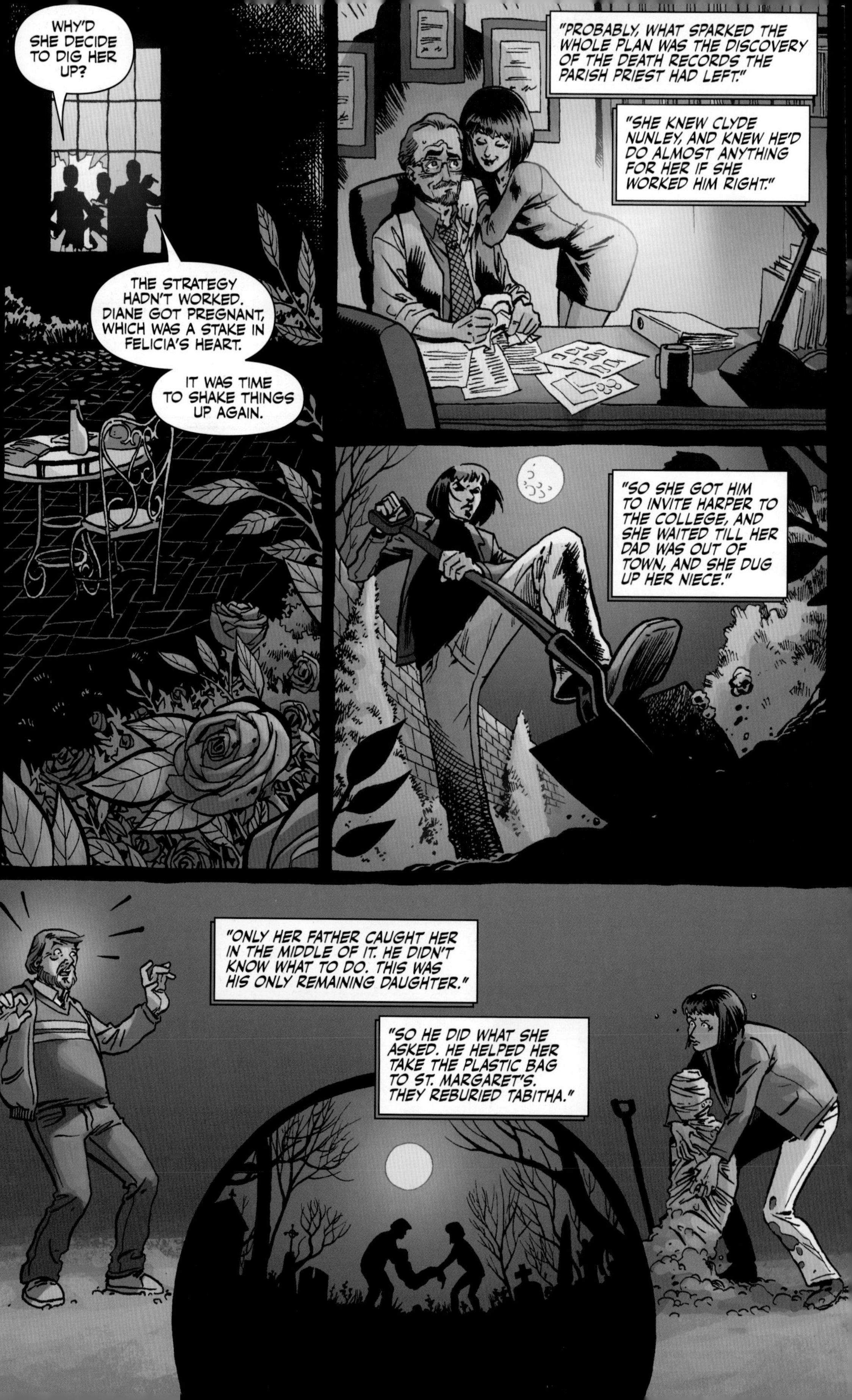
WHY'D SHE DECIDE TO DIG HER UP?
THE STRATEGY HADN'T WORKED. DIANE GOT PREGNANT, WHICH WAS A STAKE IN FELICIA'S HEART.
IT WAS TIME TO SHAKE THINGS UP AGAIN.
"PROBABLY, WHAT SPARKED THE WHOLE PLAN WAS THE DISCOVERY OF THE DEATH RECORDS THE PARISH PRIEST HAD LEFT."
"SHE KNEW CLYDE NUNLEY, AND KNEW HE'D DO ALMOST ANYTHING FOR HER IF SHE WORKED HIM RIGHT."
"SO SHE GOT HIM TO INVITE HARPER TO THE COLLEGE, AND SHE WAITED TILL HER DAD WAS OUT OF TOWN, AND SHE DUG UP HER NIECE."
"ONLY HER FATHER CAUGHT HER IN THE MIDDLE OF IT. HE DIDN'T KNOW WHAT TO DO. THIS WAS HIS ONLY REMAINING DAUGHTER."
"SO HE DID WHAT SHE ASKED. HE HELPED HER TAKE THE PLASTIC BAG TO ST. MARGARET'S. THEY REBURIED TABITHA."

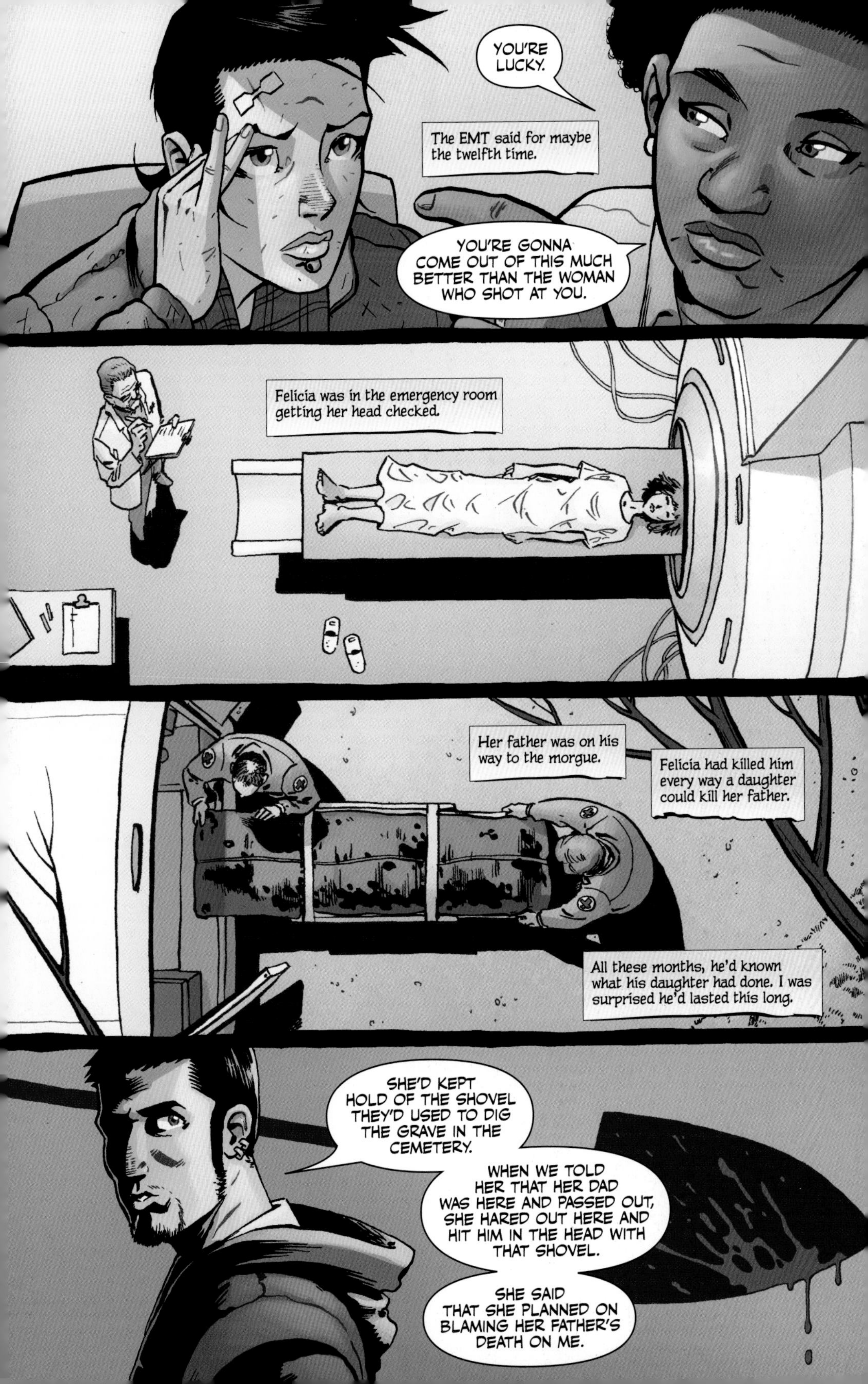
YOU'RE LUCKY.
The EMT said for maybe the twelfth time.
YOU'RE GONNA COME OUT OF THIS MUCH BETTER THAN THE WOMAN WHO SHOT AT YOU.
Felicia was in the emergency room getting her head checked.
Her father was on his way to the morgue.
Felicia had killed him every way a daughter could kill her father.
All these months, he'd known what his daughter had done. I was surprised he'd lasted this long.
SHE'D KEPT HOLD OF THE SHOVEL THEY'D USED TO DIG THE GRAVE IN THE CEMETERY.
WHEN WE TOLD HER THAT HER DAD WAS HERE AND PASSED OUT, SHE HARED OUT HERE AND HIT HIM IN THE HEAD WITH THAT SHOVEL.
SHE SAID THAT SHE PLANNED ON BLAMING HER FATHER'S DEATH ON ME.

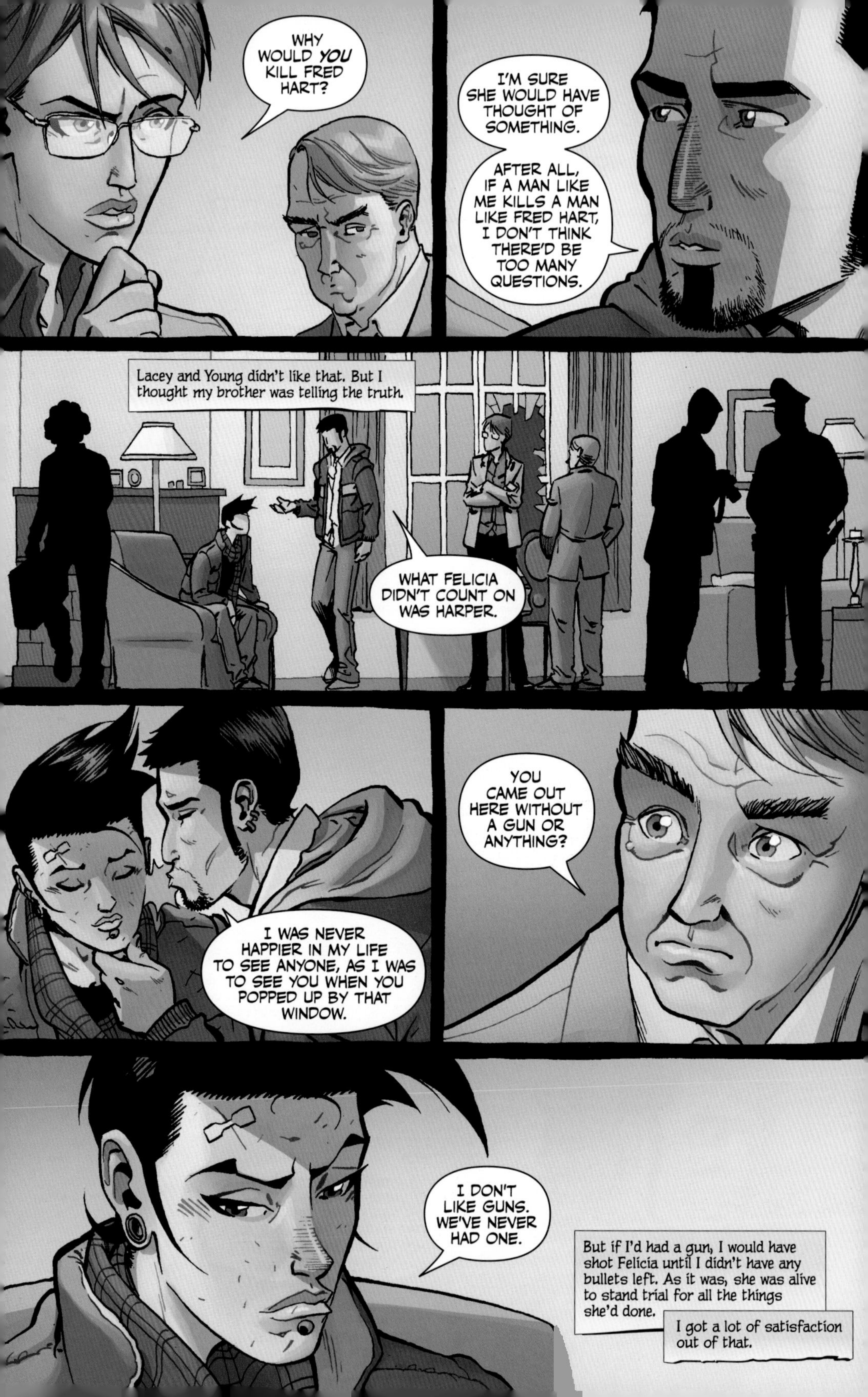
WHY WOULD *YOU* KILL FRED HART?
I'M SURE SHE WOULD HAVE THOUGHT OF SOMETHING.
AFTER ALL, IF A MAN LIKE ME KILLS A MAN LIKE FRED HART, I DON'T THINK THERE'D BE TOO MANY QUESTIONS.
Lacey and Young didn't like that. But I thought my brother was telling the truth.
WHAT FELICIA DIDN'T COUNT ON WAS HARPER.
I WAS NEVER HAPPIER IN MY LIFE TO SEE ANYONE, AS I WAS TO SEE YOU WHEN YOU POPPED UP BY THAT WINDOW.
YOU CAME OUT HERE WITHOUT A GUN OR ANYTHING?
I DON'T LIKE GUNS. WE'VE NEVER HAD ONE.
But if I'd had a gun, I would have shot Felicia until I didn't have any bullets left. As it was, she was alive to stand trial for all the things she'd done.
I got a lot of satisfaction out of that.

YOU LOOK LIKE A CAT ATTACKED YOU.

OKAY, NOT FUNNY. I'M JUST REALLY NERVOUS.

I'd figured it might help Victor take his mind off his family situation and at the same time broaden his horizons a bit, so I'd asked him if he wanted to come to the cemetery to help lay Josiah Poundstone's ghost.

I didn't know anything about the business of laying a ghost. So I'd called Xylda Bernardo, and Manfred had brought her.

JOSIAH POUNDSTON 1879-1908 REST IN PEACE BELOVED BROTHER

Manfred, resplendent in black leather and silver, greeted me with a kiss.

HARPER.

YES, HARPER, TELL ME WHAT YOU KNOW.

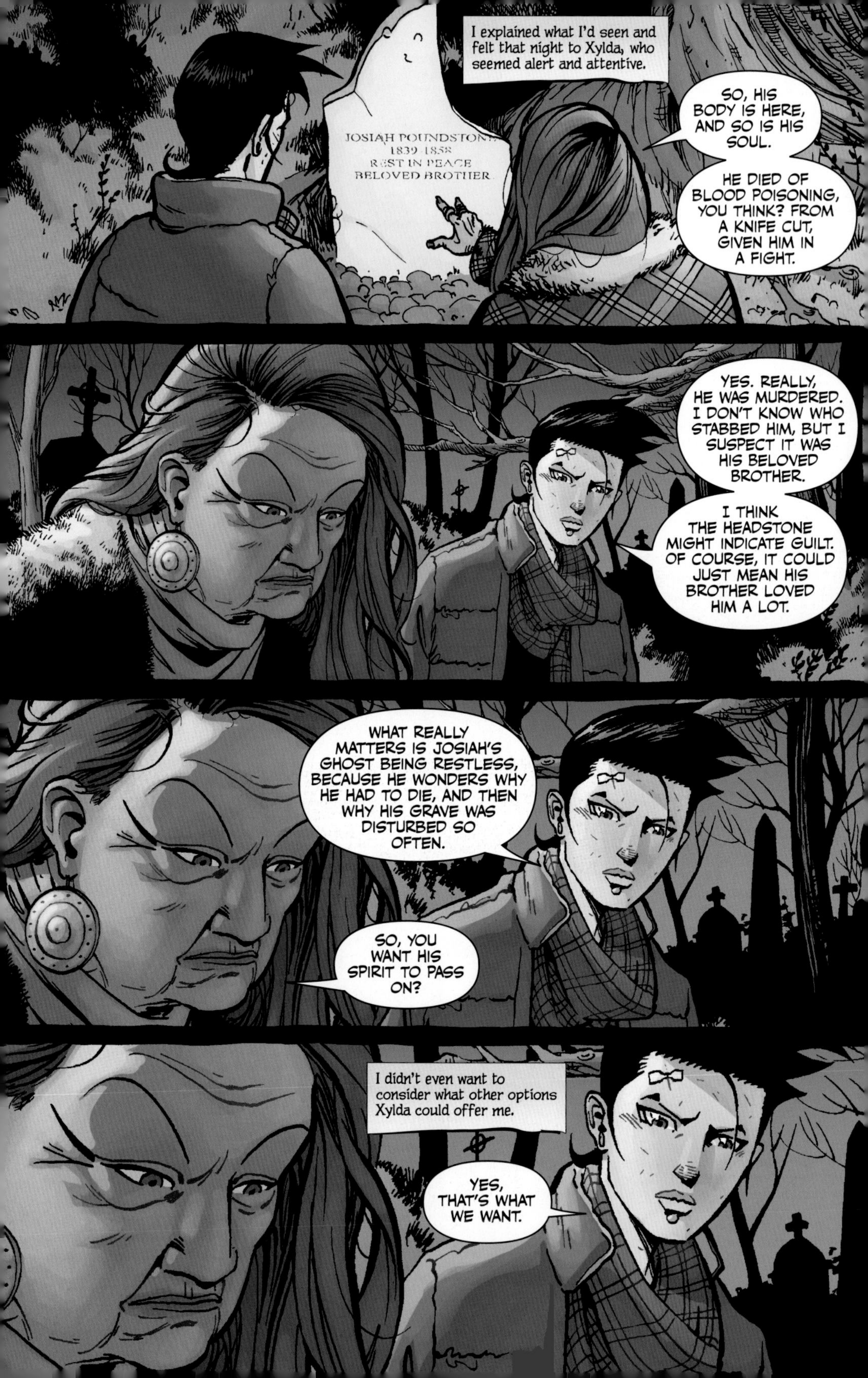
I explained what I'd seen and felt that night to Xylda, who seemed alert and attentive.
JOSIAH POUNDSTONE 1839-1858 REST IN PEACE BELOVED BROTHER
SO, HIS BODY IS HERE, AND SO IS HIS SOUL.
HE DIED OF BLOOD POISONING, YOU THINK? FROM A KNIFE CUT, GIVEN HIM IN A FIGHT.
YES. REALLY, HE WAS MURDERED. I DON'T KNOW WHO STABBED HIM, BUT I SUSPECT IT WAS HIS BELOVED BROTHER.
I THINK THE HEADSTONE MIGHT INDICATE GUILT. OF COURSE, IT COULD JUST MEAN HIS BROTHER LOVED HIM A LOT.
WHAT REALLY MATTERS IS JOSIAH'S GHOST BEING RESTLESS, BECAUSE HE WONDERS WHY HE HAD TO DIE, AND THEN WHY HIS GRAVE WAS DISTURBED SO OFTEN.
SO, YOU WANT HIS SPIRIT TO PASS ON?
I didn't even want to consider what other options Xylda could offer me.
YES, THAT'S WHAT WE WANT.

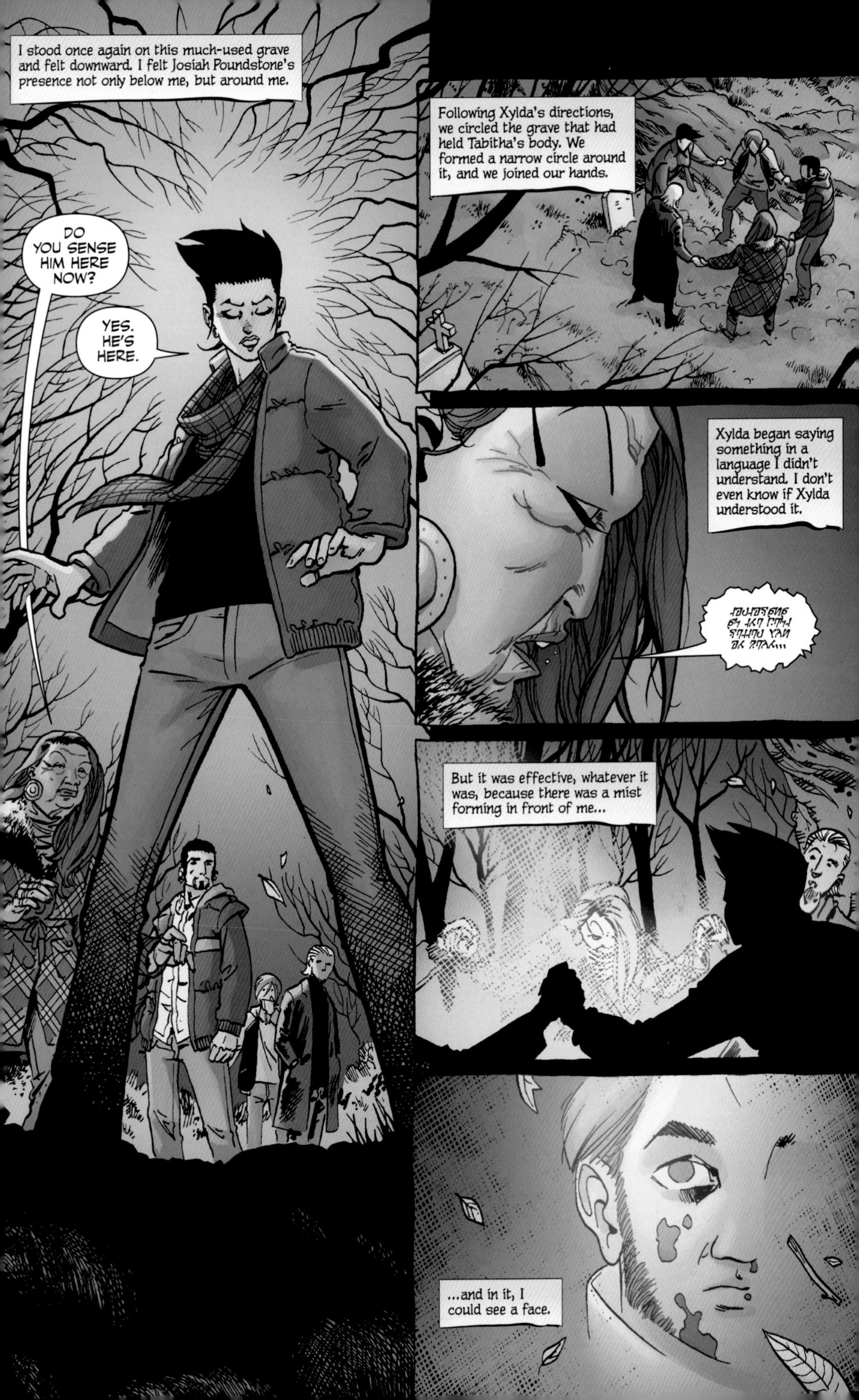
I stood once again on this much-used grave and felt downward. I felt Josiah Poundstone's presence not only below me, but around me.
DO YOU SENSE HIM HERE NOW?
YES. HE'S HERE.
Following Xylda's directions, we circled the grave that had held Tabitha's body. We formed a narrow circle around it, and we joined our hands.
Xylda began saying something in a language I didn't understand. I don't even know if Xylda understood it.
But it was effective, whatever it was, because there was a mist forming in front of me...
...and in it, I could see a face.

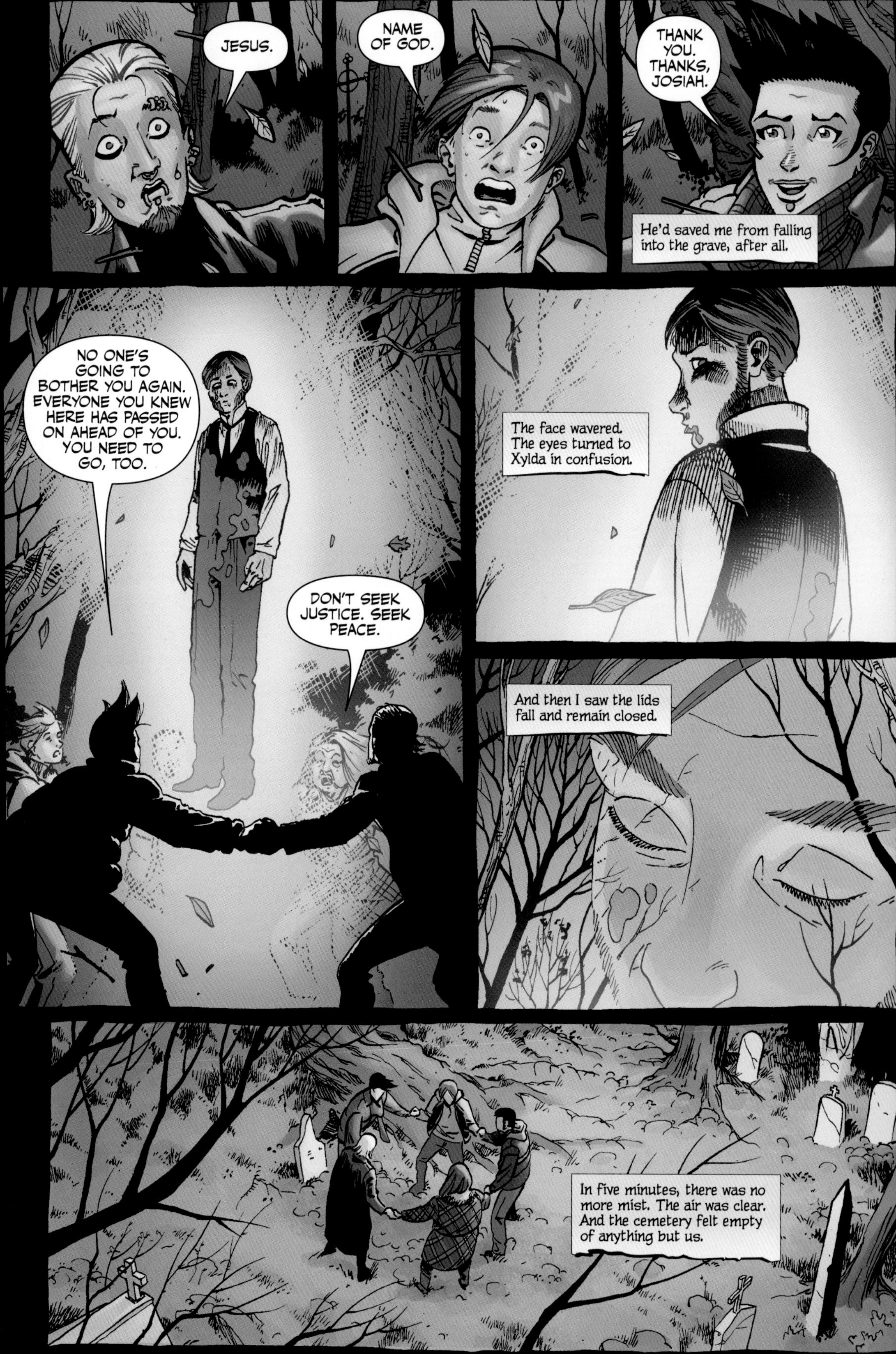
JESUS.
NAME OF GOD.
THANK YOU. THANKS, JOSIAH.
He'd saved me from falling into the grave, after all.
NO ONE'S GOING TO BOTHER YOU AGAIN. EVERYONE YOU KNEW HERE HAS PASSED ON AHEAD OF YOU. YOU NEED TO GO, TOO.
DON'T SEEK JUSTICE. SEEK PEACE.
The face wavered. The eyes turned to Xylda in confusion.
And then I saw the lids fall and remain closed.
In five minutes, there was no more mist. The air was clear. And the cemetery felt empty of anything but us.

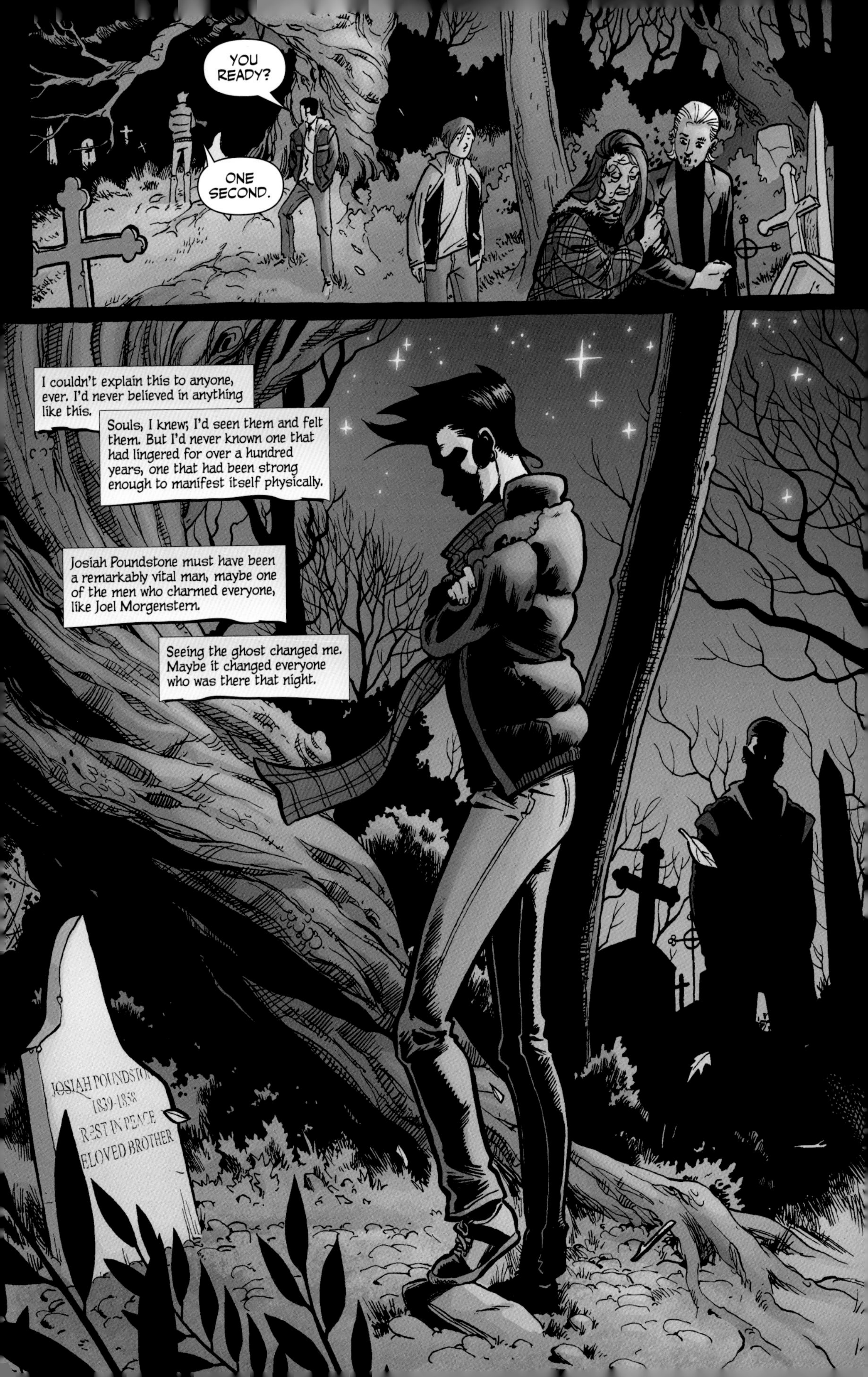
YOU READY?
ONE SECOND.
I couldn't explain this to anyone, ever. I'd never believed in anything like this.
Souls, I knew; I'd seen them and felt them. But I'd never known one that had lingered for over a hundred years, one that had been strong enough to manifest itself physically.
Josiah Poundstone must have been a remarkably vital man, maybe one of the men who charmed everyone, like Joel Morgenstern.
Seeing the ghost changed me. Maybe it changed everyone who was there that night.
JOSIAH POUNDSTO
1839-1858
REST IN PEACE
ELOVED BROTHER

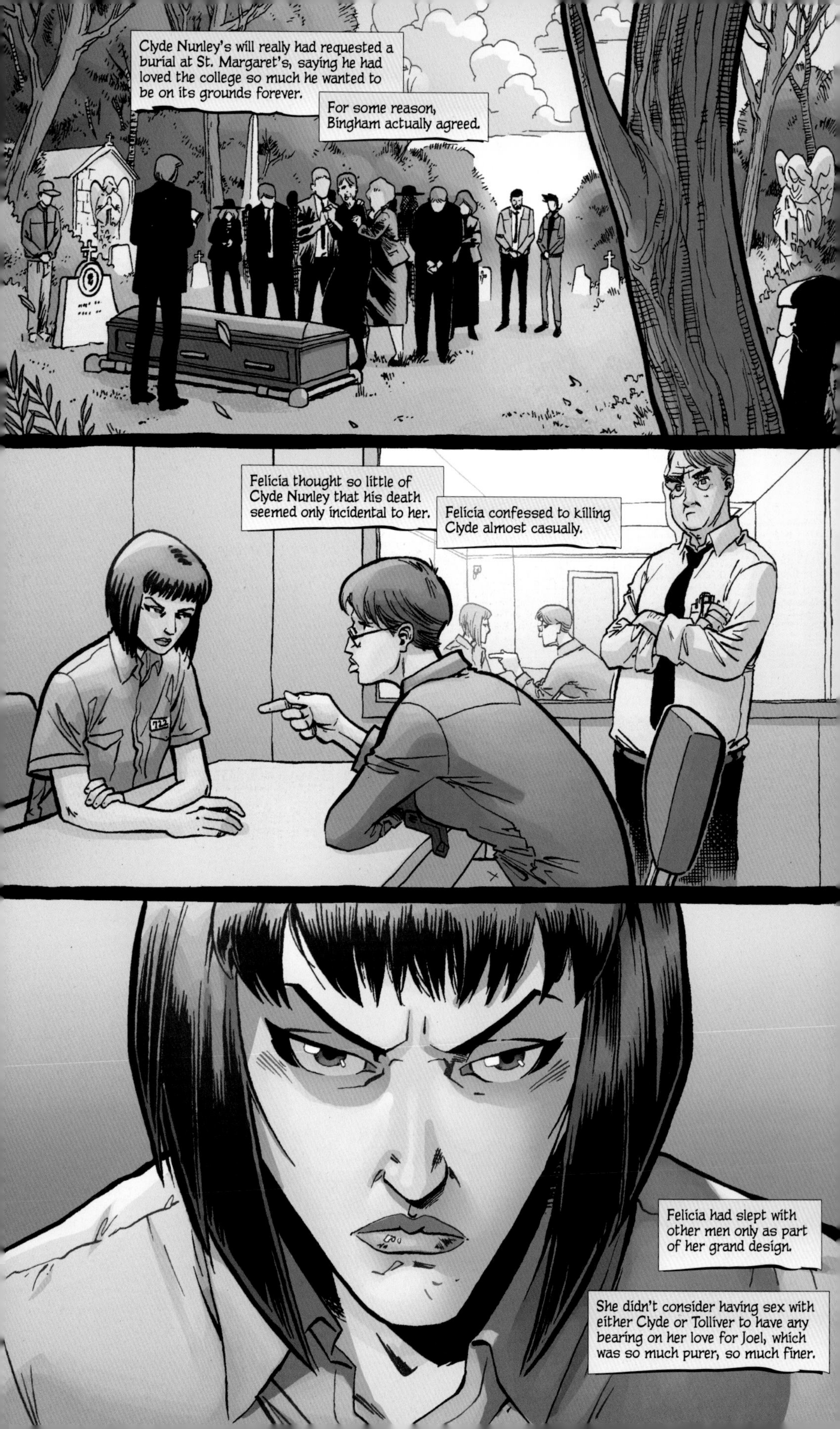
Clyde Nunley's will really had requested a burial at St. Margaret's, saying he had loved the college so much he wanted to be on its grounds forever.
For some reason, Bingham actually agreed.
Felicia thought so little of Clyde Nunley that his death seemed only incidental to her.
Felicia confessed to killing Clyde almost casually.
Felicia had slept with other men only as part of her grand design.
She didn't consider having sex with either Clyde or Tolliver to have any bearing on her love for Joel, which was so much purer, so much finer.

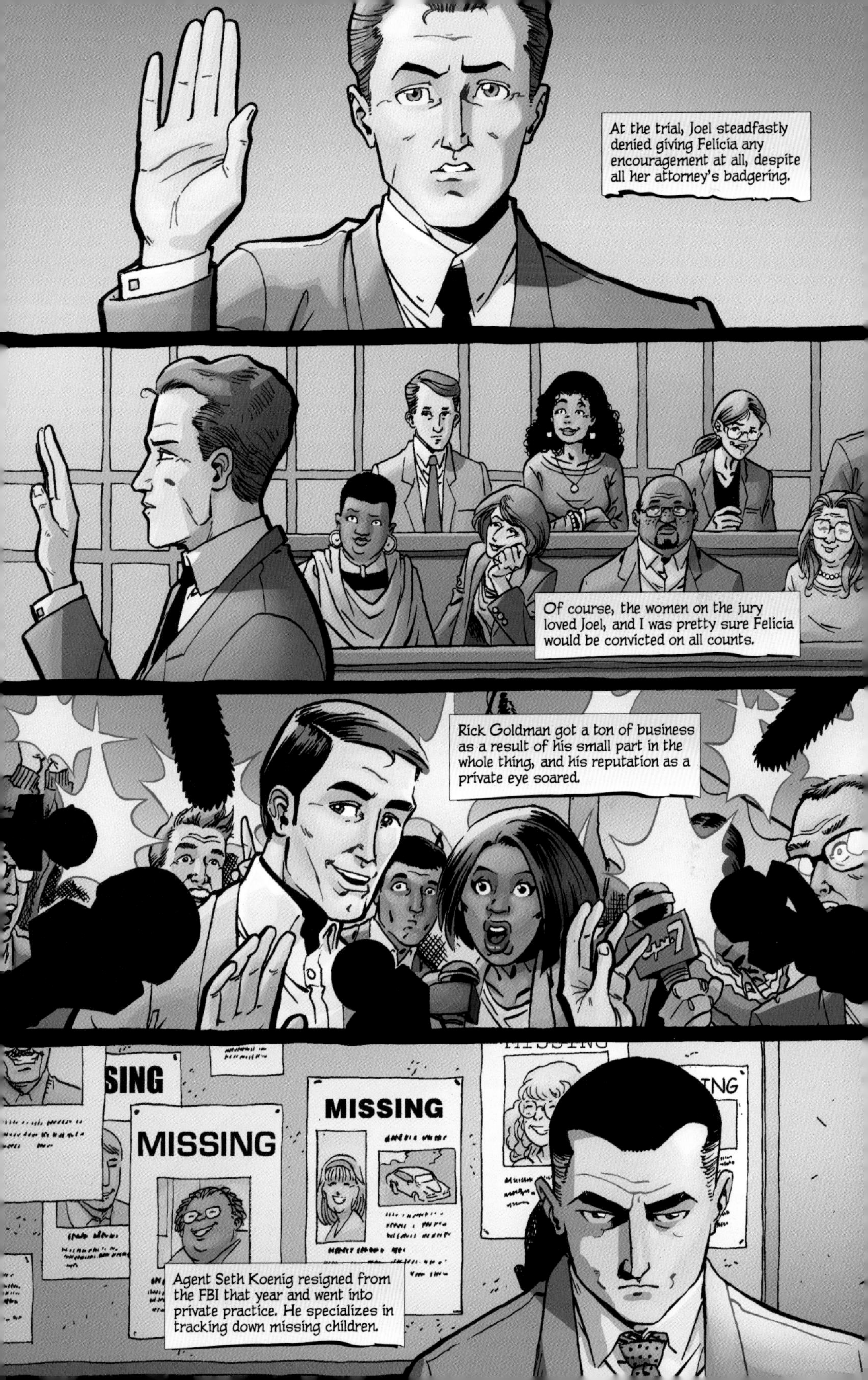
At the trial, Joel steadfastly denied giving Felicia any encouragement at all, despite all her attorney's badgering.
Of course, the women on the jury loved Joel, and I was pretty sure Felicia would be convicted on all counts.
Rick Goldman got a ton of business as a result of his small part in the whole thing, and his reputation as a private eye soared.
MISSING
MISSING
Agent Seth Koenig resigned from the FBI that year and went into private practice. He specializes in tracking down missing children.

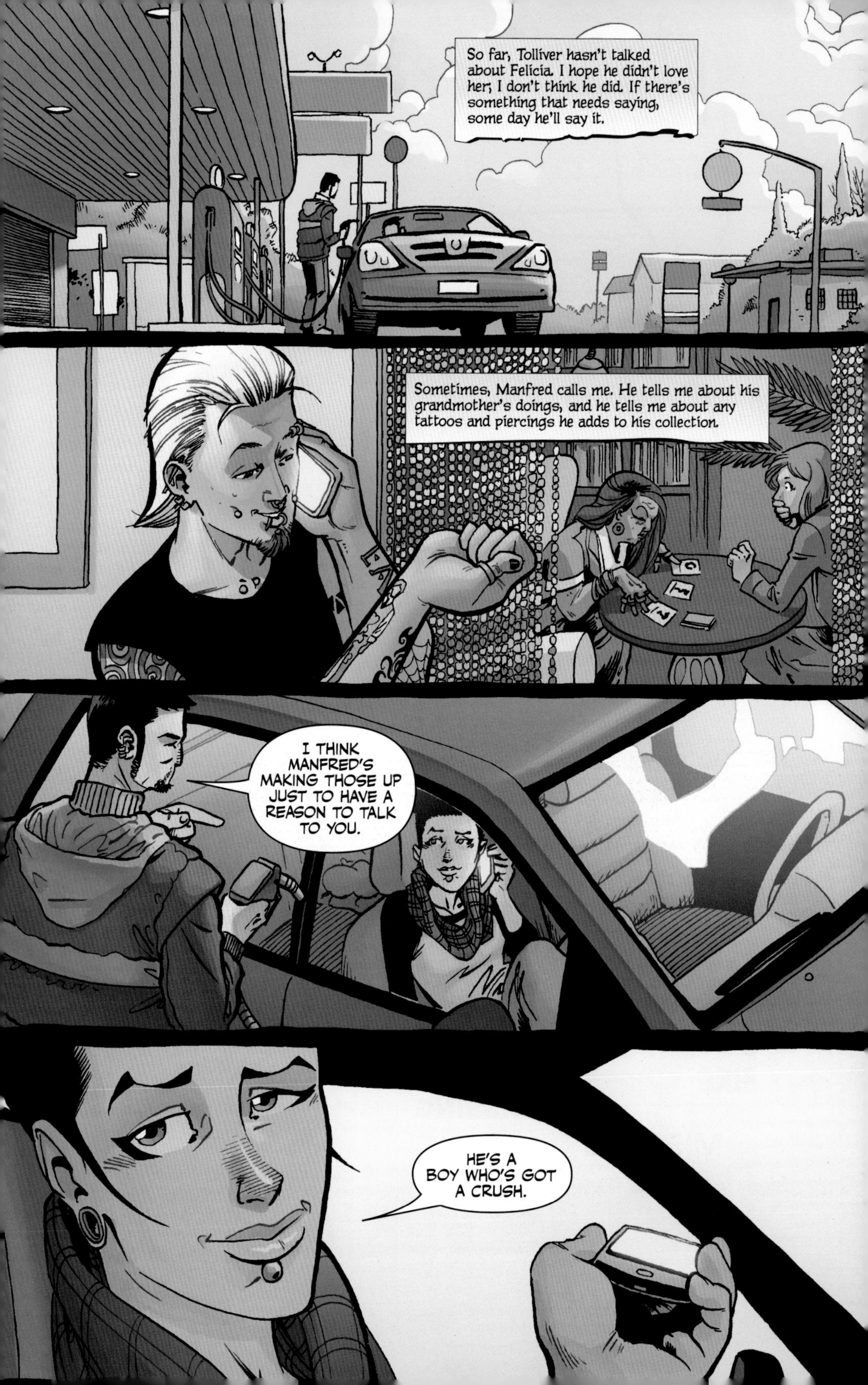
So far, Tolliver hasn't talked about Felicia. I hope he didn't love her; I don't think he did. If there's something that needs saying, some day he'll say it.
Sometimes, Manfred calls me. He tells me about his grandmother's doings, and he tells me about any tattoos and piercings he adds to his collection.
I THINK MANFRED'S MAKING THOSE UP JUST TO HAVE A REASON TO TALK TO YOU.
HE'S A BOY WHO'S GOT A CRUSH.

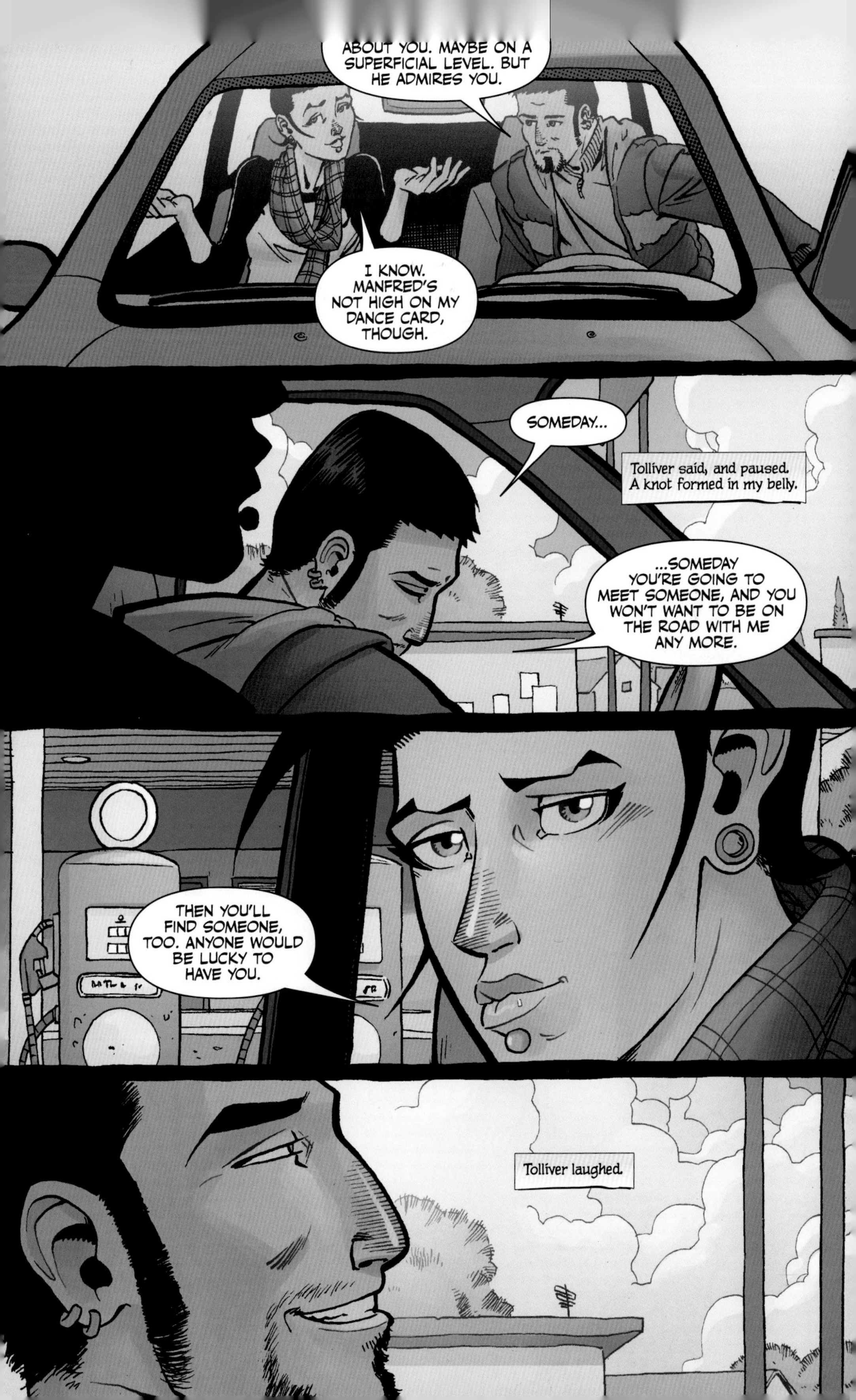
ABOUT YOU. MAYBE ON A SUPERFICIAL LEVEL. BUT HE ADMIRES YOU.
I KNOW. MANFRED'S NOT HIGH ON MY DANCE CARD, THOUGH.
SOMEDAY...
Tolliver said, and paused. A knot formed in my belly.
...SOMEDAY YOU'RE GOING TO MEET SOMEONE, AND YOU WON'T WANT TO BE ON THE ROAD WITH ME ANY MORE.
THEN YOU'LL FIND SOMEONE, TOO. ANYONE WOULD BE LUCKY TO HAVE YOU.
Tolliver laughed.

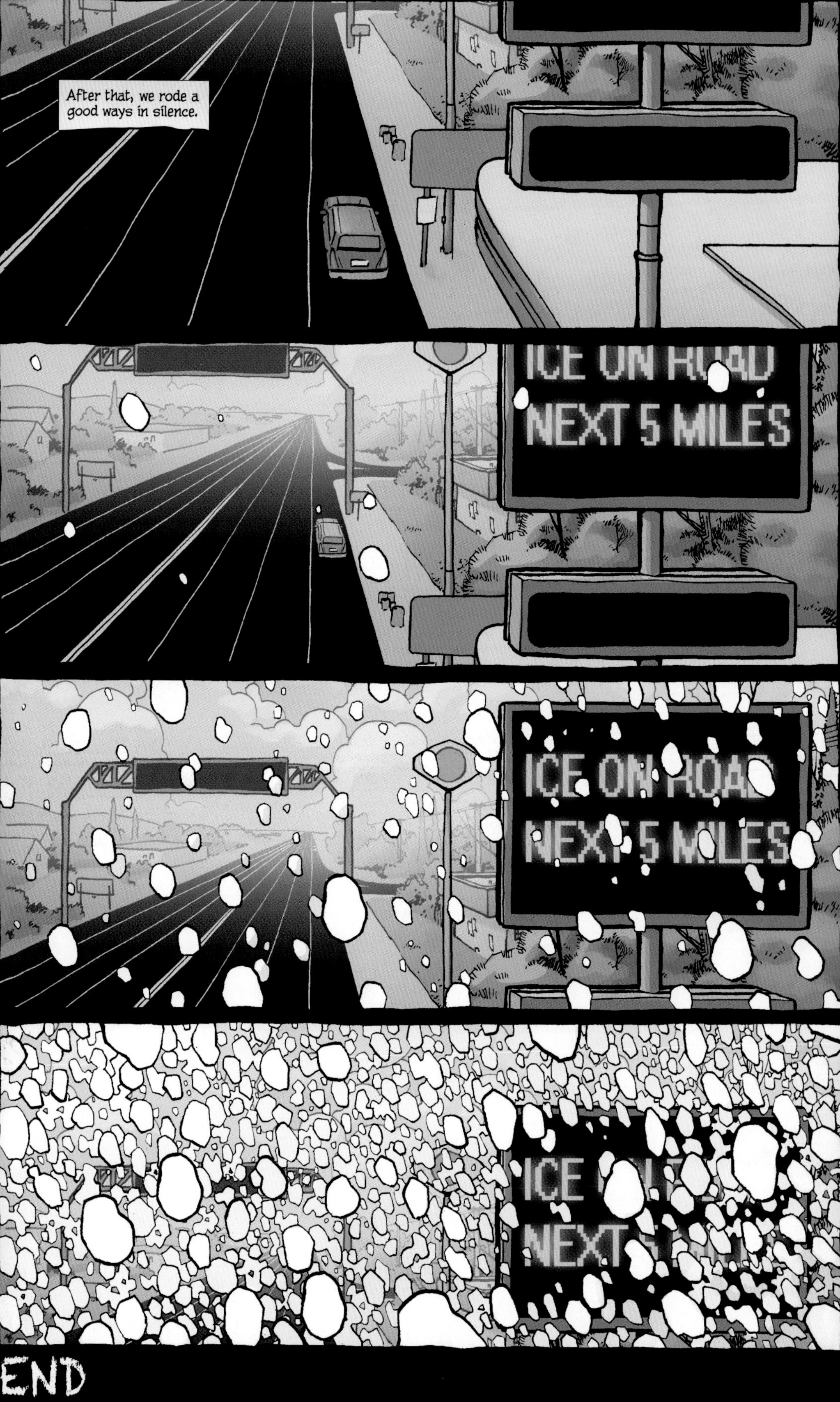
After that, we rode a good ways in silence.
ICE ON ROAD
NEXT 5 MILES
ICE ON ROAD
NEXT 5 MILES
ICE
NEXT
END

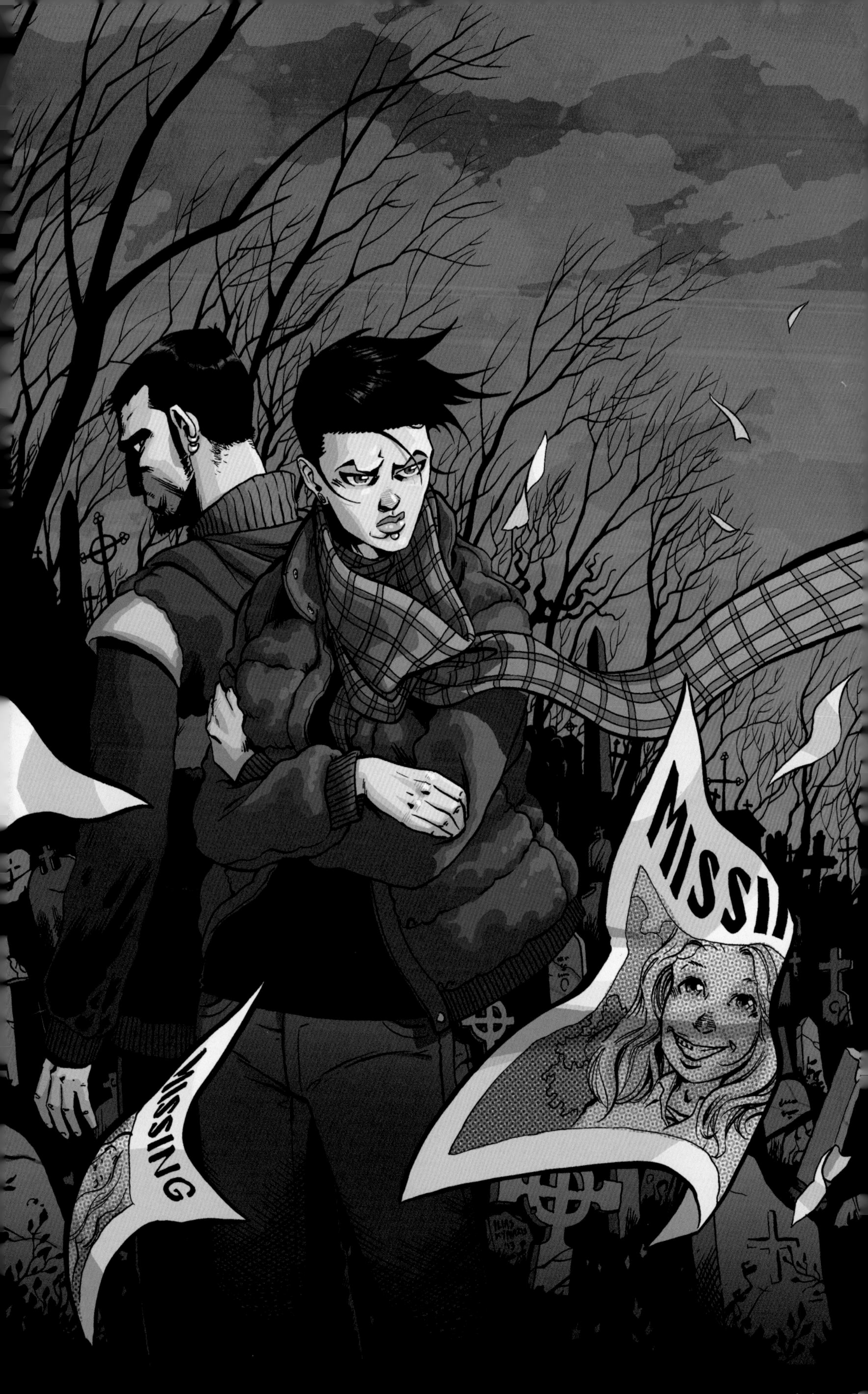
MISSING

undressed collection cover art by ILIAS KYRIAZIS

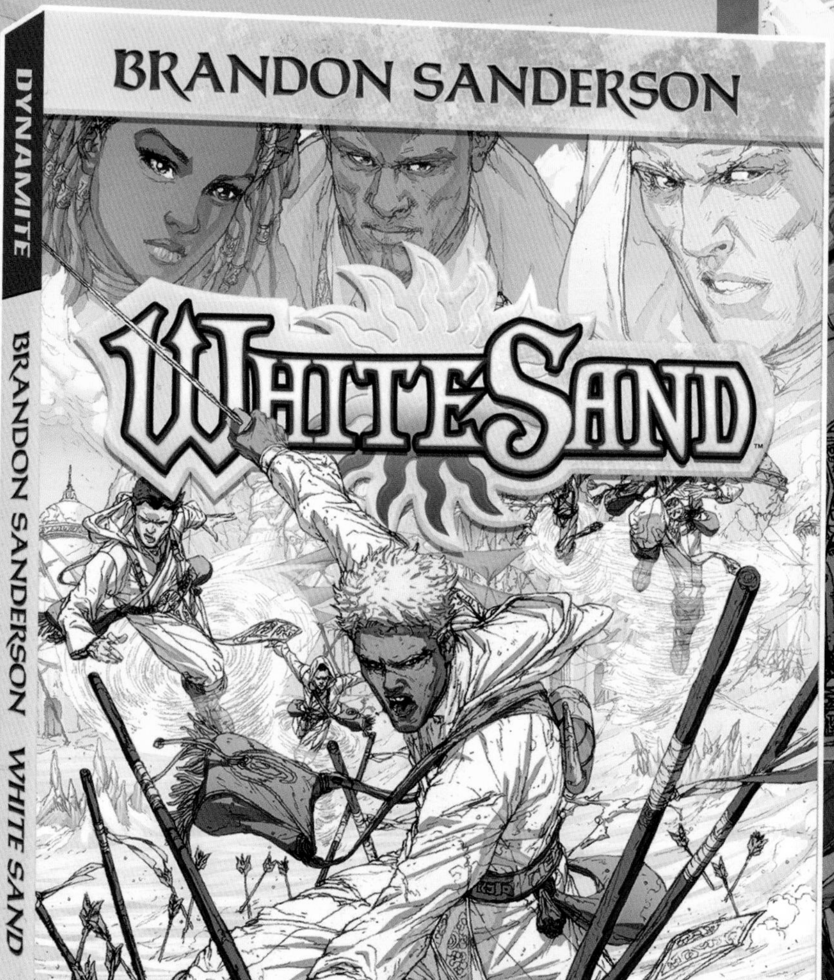

BRANDON SANDERSON
WHITE SAND
RIK HOSKIN · DYNAMITE · JULIUS GOPEZ
DYNAMITE
BRANDON SANDERSON WHITE SAND
RIK HOSKIN JULIUS GOPEZ

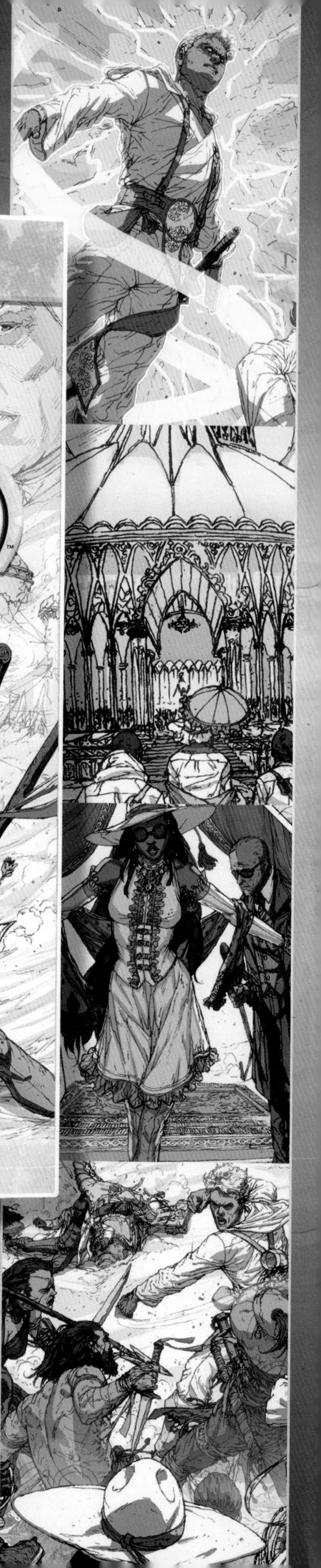

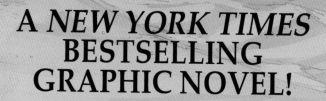

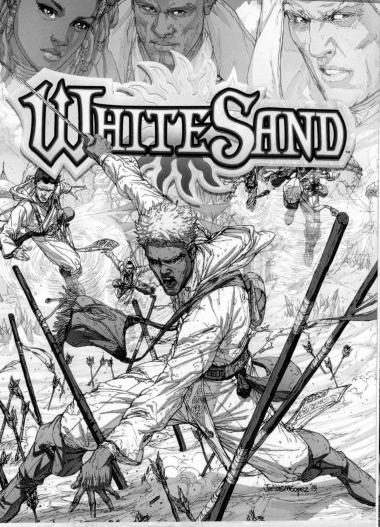

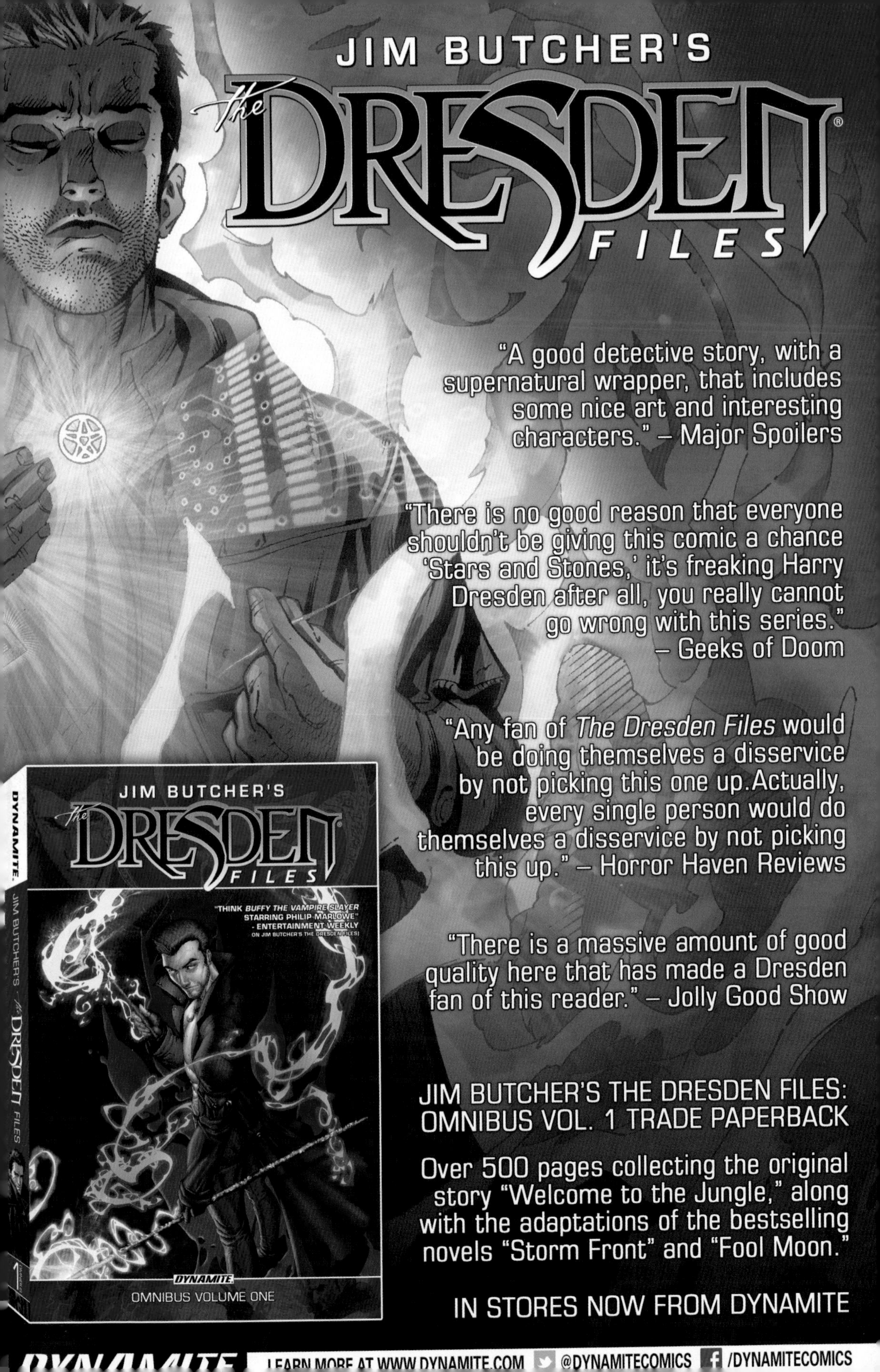

JIM BUTCHER'S
The DRESDEN FILES®
"A good detective story, with a supernatural wrapper, that includes some nice art and interesting characters." – Major Spoilers
"There is no good reason that everyone shouldn't be giving this comic a chance 'Stars and Stones,' it's freaking Harry Dresden after all, you really cannot go wrong with this series." – Geeks of Doom
"Any fan of *The Dresden Files* would be doing themselves a disservice by not picking this one up.Actually, every single person would do themselves a disservice by not picking this up." – Horror Haven Reviews
"There is a massive amount of good quality here that has made a Dresden fan of this reader." – Jolly Good Show
JIM BUTCHER'S
The DRESDEN FILES
"THINK BUFFY THE VAMPIRE SLAYER STARRING PHILIP MARLOWE" - ENTERTAINMENT WEEKLY
ON JIM BUTCHER'S THE DRESDEN FILES
DYNAMITE
OMNIBUS VOLUME ONE
DYNAMITE
JIM BUTCHER'S The DRESDEN FILES
JIM BUTCHER'S THE DRESDEN FILES: OMNIBUS VOL. 1 TRADE PAPERBACK
Over 500 pages collecting the original story "Welcome to the Jungle," along with the adaptations of the bestselling novels "Storm Front" and "Fool Moon."
IN STORES NOW FROM DYNAMITE
DYNAMITE
LEARN MORE AT WWW.DYNAMITE.COM
@DYNAMITECOMICS
/DYNAMITECOMICS